(D)urban Vortex

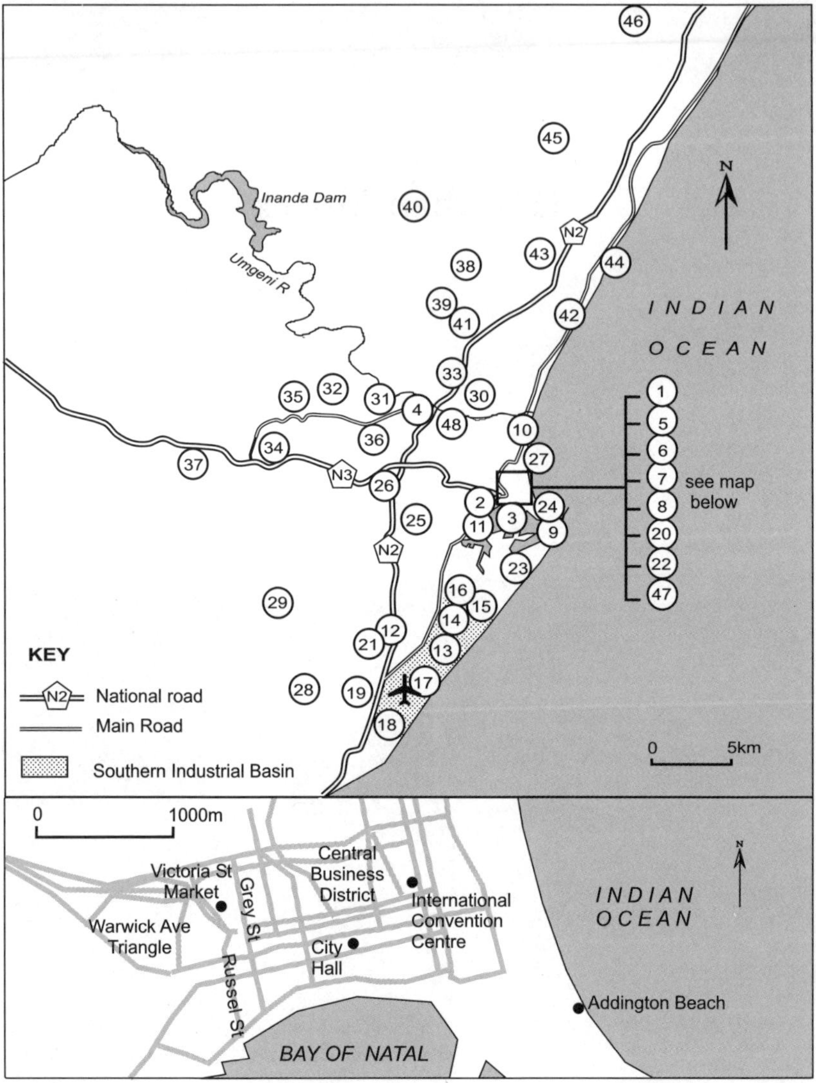

LEGEND

1 Addington Beach
2 Albert Park
3 Bay of Natal
4 Canaan
5 Central Business District
6 City Hall
7 Grey Street
8 Victoria Street Market
9 Island View
10 Kings Park/Kingsmead
11 Maydon Wharf
12 Mobeni
13 Merebank
14 Jacobs
15 Wentworth
16 Clairwood
17 Durban International Airport
18 Prospecton
19 Isipingo
20 International Convention Centre
21 Lamontville
22 Russell Street
23 The Bluff
24 The Point
25 Cato Manor
26 Chesterville
27 Golden Mile/Beachfront
28 Umlazi
29 Chatsworth
30 Springfield Flats
31 Reservoir Hills
32 Clermont
33 Newlands East
34 Pinetown
35 New Germany
36 Westville
37 Mariannridge
38 Phoenix
39 KwaMashu
40 Inanda
41 Effingham Avoca
42 La Lucia
43 Mount Edgecombe
44 Umhlanga Rocks
45 Verulam
46 Tongaat
47 Warwick Avenue Triangle
48 Clare Estate

Metro Durban and Central Business District.

(D)urban Vortex

South African City in Transition

Edited by

BILL FREUND and VISHNU PADAYACHEE

UNIVERSITY OF NATAL PRESS
Pietermaritzburg
2002

Published by
University of Natal Press
Private Bag X01
Scottsville 3209
South Africa
E-mail: books@nu.ac.za

ISBN 1-86914-013-3

Cover photograph: Paul Weinberg

Typeset by Patricia Comrie
Printed and bound by Interpak Books, Pietermaritzburg

Contents

Acknowledgements

Bill Freund would like to thank two geographers, Jeff McCarthy and Mike Sutcliffe, who long ago memorably persuaded him one evening over supper in Hillbrow to consider working in Durban. They are part of a large and stimulating community of individuals from a variety of disciplines who have written about this city over the past 17 years, and encouraged him to contribute to an impressive, if very scattered literature, and to innumerable private and public debates. These include individuals from the University of Natal but also more or less organic intellectuals from the business, labour and government sectors with ideas brimming over. He is grateful to them all. In addition, many individuals agreed to interviews or to contribute out-of-the-way information that helped make this book so informative. Jeff McCarthy made many contributions in the form of ideas, access to individuals and encouragement that require special thanks. Full credit goes to Stein Nesvåg for first thinking of Durban post-modernly as (D)urban.

Vishnu Padayachee would like to thank Bill Freund for encouraging him to carry a long-standing research focus on international and national finance and banking into a contemporary urban context. He also acknowledges with appreciation the support and intellectual stimulation of colleagues at the School of Development Studies, University of Natal. He thanks especially Mike Morris and Imraan Valodia for their support and ideas, and Caroline Skinner whose passion for this city and academic and activist interventions in support of Durban's poorer communities was a continuing source of inspiration and a constant reminder that cities were not just geographical concentrations of financial and industrial power, but were essentially about people, many engaged in constant struggles around work and livelihoods.

We also wish to thank our institutional sponsors. Bill Freund's conceptualisation was greatly assisted by leave time in 1996 in Britain and France. In Oxford he was sponsored by the Oppenheimer Fund and in Paris he was a guest of the Centre Nationale pour Recherche

Nationale/Ecole des Hautes Etudes en Sciences Sociales. The project, and notably our workshop and successful 1998 conference, was generously supported by the Centre for Science Development, the former national research body. The former Deputy Vice-Chancellor for Research at the University of Natal, Professor Eleanor Preston-Whyte, offered encouragement and practical assistance; she was able to see this book as something that rested on the shoulders of a long history of research at the university on local society and economy. Finally the University of Natal awarded us subsidisation, which made publication of this volume possible. Financial support from the Economic History/Development Studies Programme and the School of Development Studies is also acknowledged. Bill Freund particularly thanks Gloria McKay for administrative assistance throughout the City of Durban Project.

The Editors

Contributors

Wendy Annecke is a Programme Leader at the Energy and Development Research Centre, University of Cape Town. She is writing a Ph.D. in the Economic History and Development Studies programme at the University of Natal, Durban.

Bill Freund is Programme Director of Economic History/Development Studies at the University of Natal, Durban.

David Hemson is a Research Director with the Human Sciences Research Council with the responsibility for research into non-farm rural development and he continues an active interest in the labour market and movement.

Trevor Jones is Programme Director of Economics in the School of Economics and Management at the University of Natal, Durban.

Brij Maharaj is a Professor and Discipline Chair (Geography) at the University of Natal, Pietermaritzburg.

Mike Morris is Research Professor in the School of Development Studies at the University of Natal, Durban, where he also heads the Industrial Restructuring Project, a research programme on international competitiveness of South African industry, in which **Justin Barnes** and **Nikki Dunne** are employed.

Stein Inge Nesvåg is currently working for the Norwegian Agency for Development Cooperation (NORAD). He wrote a M.Soc.Sci. in the Economic History and Development Studies programme at the University of Natal, Durban.

Vishnu Padayachee is a Research Professor and Head of the School of Development Studies at the University of Natal, Durban.

Glen Robbins works at the Economic Development Department for the Durban Metropolitan Council. His co-author and former co-worker, **Peter Hall**, is currently completing a Ph.D. in City and Regional Planning at the Univeristy of California, Berkeley.

David Wiley is Professor of Sociology and Director of the African Studies Center at Michigan State University. **Christine Root** holds an M.A. in Economics and is a Faculty Research Specialist in International Studies and Programs at Michigan State University, as well as former Associate Director of the Washington Office on Africa. **Sven (Bobby) Peek**, is the director of Groundwork, a South African environmental NGO in Pietermaritzburg, and was winner of the 1998 Goldman Environmental Prize for Africa.

Harald Witt is a Lecturer in the Economic History/Development Studies programme, at the University of Natal, Durban.

Durban

Structures from the Past, Pressures in the Present, Prospects in the Future

BILL FREUND and VISHNU PADAYACHEE

Cities loom large in contemporary literature on economic development, economic change and economic crisis. Of course as a sociological topic – a site of residence, of material achievement, social interaction and human problems – they have long held sway. Modern life occurs *par excellence* in an urban milieu, although defining and explaining the import of that milieu is not always so easy. This volume does not focus on urban culture or even on urban living in general. It tries to bring to bear insights that are linked to problems in economic and social development, development that can be understood in terms of the progressive self-actualisation of men and women, and what Sen has called 'expanding the real freedoms that people enjoy' (Sen 1998). Can cities by their very being bring about change? What is it about cities that brings most populations together in the course of 'development'? Is there a basic functional pattern which can explain their centrality?

Cities have been around for millennia. Yet they were usually identified as centres of religious and political power that lived off the countryside. The classical economists, even Adam Smith, continued to see agriculture as a fundamental economic activity; manufacture was secondary. Urban economic and social activity was striking but peripheral. The most basic economic activities were those that involved refining the products derived from the natural environment.

Today it is cities that seem the site of fundamental activity; agriculture and aligned primary activities have themselves acquired a peripheral feel to them. They make the activities going on in cities possible. Yet the contemporary city, in most parts of the world, is not witnessing the expansion of manufacturing anymore. One cannot explain urbanisation through the industrial revolution alone. On the contrary, secondary industry today is occupying smaller percentages of the work-force and less physical space. Some of it has become very mobile, with activities divided between different locations, even different countries. Globalisation makes possible a division of labour on a global scale which juxtaposes sharp hierarchical divisions with startling and rapid changes. The economy of the contemporary city, whether one is considering the so-called world cities of New York, London (and perhaps Tokyo and Paris) or the sprawling and gigantic urban agglomerations of the south where growth so often outstrips formal employment opportunities observable in government statistics, is not necessarily based on industry and cannot be understood as a derivation of processes emanating from the smokestack hives of the Industrial Revolution.

At the same time, the once dominant model of the nation-state, whether from the perspective of its business class or the government itself, is under question as the suitable unit for understanding the continuing development of capitalism. Cities have their own impulses leading to growth – and decay – independent to an important extent from the national picture. Again, this may require considering the particular character of business – and labour – in any particular city. It may also require analysing urban government as an agent for stimulating and shaping economic growth, obviously looking at the linkages with civil society and key economic actors. Deeper currents, profound social and cultural trends may in turn be shaping economic and political trajectories; cities are vortices. What really makes particular cities work? Where does the city fit into the broader sweep of development? Cities may need to re-invent themselves, to 'change' – but how? There is no clear pattern, no blueprint to success in the contemporary world.

* * *

This book is inspired by these broad perspectives. Durban is a distinctive and remarkable place in which to test propositions about the significance of the city and the significance of change in the city. For all that one can say about the new urban literature that is advancing internationally, it tends to divide up very sharply between the problems faced by cities in the global centre – cities with major resources although often faced with new and perplexing strategic problems related to economy and society – and the problems faced by cities on the periphery, poor cities thronged by poor people, usually lumbered with an inappropriate heritage from a pre-capitalist or colonial past. Analyses of the latter tend to focus in turn on the emergence of trends unnoticed and uncontrolled by any state; on the initiatives from below that allow different categories of poor people (often with a focus on women) to colonise the city and make it work for them in very basic ways.

In fact, many cities are the site of both kinds of phenomena going on simultaneously. South African cities are places which allow us to observe both phenomena at once. These are cities with strong traditions of forceful planning from above and with considerable capacity to finance change. They witness de-industrialisation and decentring as do so many western cities, but they are also the site of massive squatter settlements and populations that fall outside the functioning of the 'formal' economy. The nature of the post-apartheid state pulls it towards servicing a variety of clientele – the business community that provides growth but on its own terms, the 'emergent' entrepreneurs of colour who count on the African National Congress government now in power to take them forwards, the myriad of poor people who felt completely marginalised under the pre-1994 regime. Perhaps coming to grips with Durban is a way to start bringing two kinds of literature together in order to enrich our picture of what is happening to cities generally in the contemporary world.

Amongst South African cities, Durban is also quite distinctive in a number of ways. Durban developed as a part of the colony of Natal; a South African province after 1910. By contrast with other parts of South Africa however, the reserves or locations to which Africans were confined in Natal were numerous, scattered and broken up. The closest were virtually in walking distance of the port of Natal where Durban (eThekwini in Zulu) was located. Durban owes its rise to economic factors alone; it was never an administrative centre or capital city. It is the second largest industrial city, the most important port by value and the second most important population centre in South Africa. Metropolitan Durban with its estimated population in excess of 2.3 million people (in the 1996 population count) has a substantial proportion of all the South African racial 'groups' recognised under apartheid. It is the home of up to two-thirds of the South African population of Indian origin – a remarkable concentration. The city looks east towards the Indian Ocean that laps the shores of a number of very dynamic countries in south and south-east Asia. The province of KwaZulu-Natal has the thickest population density in South Africa apart from urban Gauteng. Between 50 and 60 per cent of the population are African, largely although not entirely Zulu speaking – a majority but not an overwhelming one. The white population is the only one in the country where the majority are English speakers; Natal was the 'Last

Outpost' of the British Empire and Durban shares the feeling of a provincial and colonial England in some respects.

As in other South African cities, Durban was at once a place where the market brought together, in classic colonial form, a fertile mix of people who created in some respects a common urban culture (Freund 1995). It was also a place where white power gelled to structure a system of racial division and dominance, and in a way which defined 'communities' in racial as well as ethnic terms. The South African racial system was in an important sense an urban system, created in response to the challenges the urban vortex threw up for a society where the dominant discourse was one of racial separation and European cultural hegemony. The rich scholarly literature on race and racial rule in South Africa has long ago pointed out the importance of the 'Durban system' for administering Africans, essentially a migrant male population before the Second World War (Swanson 1976; Crush and Ambler 1992). The starting point for this book is to understand that the 'Durban system' was not only about race but also about economic development and how to shape it; the racial aspect was a part of the way the dominant forces in the city came together to train its growth. This system was in its way very effective and successful as an engine of growth. Certainly it seemed this way to the city 'fathers'.

Success brought about its own problems, however. Alan Paton's introduction to a major social science work of the past, examining the prospects of taking urban racial segregation to major new extremes, proved exactly right: '. . . here in Professor Kuper's book, the reader may study the colossal steps that one city is taking in a journey that will be meaningless tomorrow' (Paton in Kuper et al. 1958: 16). The new democratic urban regime now has to find ways to restructure urban growth without undermining the potential for earning and spending revenue. This was a challenge earlier in the twentieth century as the white working class became stronger as a political factor. Now there is a much larger working class with the right to vote and politics has the potential to upset the plans of the bureaucrats more than ever. Moreover, the context for capitalist development in the city is changing. The means through which the 'Durban system' managers were able to promote the fortunes of the city are no longer so effective or relevant. As in other cities, managers find it necessary to cast about to redefine roles and renew the vitality of the city and explore a variety of nostrums.

The scholarly literature of the 1970s and 1980s that was inspired by the struggle against apartheid is rich in urban studies: political, social and cultural change is highlighted in the work of many authors. The particular strength of this scholarship lay in historical research (for a recent analytical guide on South Africa generally, see Glaser 2001). Thus Swanson's 1965 Harvard University thesis on Durban history was a foundation stone in the emergence of South African urban history. A generation of Durban historical scholarship was captured in the Maylam and Edwards collection, *The People's City: African Life in Twentieth-Century Durban*. This collection by no means exhausts even the major figures who have been involved in writing this history. For example, tied in to economic as well as social themes here were those writings that highlighted labour issues and the politics of labour. Two examples of many would be Hemson (1979) and Padayachee and Vawda (1999).

Scholars of Durban are, moreover, fortunate in that they can also rest on probably the best scholarship concerning the political economy of urban South Africa from the past generation – a strength on which this collection builds. A major published study at the end of the 1950s closely surveyed racial segregation in the city as the group areas removals were in the process of advancing (Kuper et al. 1958). A contemporary work of distinction examined industrialisation in the city and was followed up by a very extensive industrial geography (Katzen 1961; Young 1972). One must also mention the multi-volume studies of society and economy in the province of Natal called the Natal Regional Survey done at this time. Awareness of this literature has been particularly charged in the work of the next generation of activist-scholars, especially geographers such as Davies' student, Jeff McCarthy, and Brij Maharaj. A common feature of all this literature is a sense of restlessness and ceaseless change. This is why it seems not unreasonable to describe Durban, as we choose to do in our title, as a vortex.

There is undoubtedly much to do in the further development of social and cultural studies set in Durban. However, building on these foundations, social and to a lesser extent cultural life are tied into what is essentially a political economy of a changing Durban. The studies that follow are intended neither to prescribe strategies that will readily solve the urban problems of the future nor to fill readers with despair and gloom. Instead, they suggest the contours of change, the ways in which Durban is similar to other cities around the world – industrial cities, port cities, Third World cities, racially divided cities – and the forces that are at play in Durban society whose interaction we would argue in large part will determine its possibilities.

This collection involves writers from numerous disciplines – history, economic history, economics, sociology, geography and more – and many of the pieces written are quite specifically inter-disciplinary. This may superficially create a certain confusion through the multiple theoretical strands that appear. However, whether or not they use the term themselves, most , if not all, authors are concerned with globalisation as already touched on above. Globalisation was critical in the dismantling of apartheid and the old Durban. South African ideas about racial segregation were perfectly acceptable in the international context of the early twentieth century and notably that of the British Empire, the most important reference point. But apartheid did not fit into the dominant international ideas of governance which came to the fore by 1960, if not earlier, although pressure on South Africa only became overwhelming from the 1980s. At the same time, the dominant forces in South African capitalism felt hampered by the relative isolation of the country and the straightjacket of apartheid in terms of participating in the dominant forms of evolution of the multinational firm-dominated world economy of our time. The end of the old system has enabled globalisation, in its close of the twentieth-century guise, to take increasing force in South Africa. Ironically, this may represent a major hurdle in terms of urban social and economic adjustment, about which our participating authors differ in mood and stance while acknowledging its importance. This set of insights should filter through a reading of this book clearly enough.

We have also highlighted areas where research needs to proceed, research that is neither constrained by the narrow dictates of policy agendas and deadlines nor entirely mesmerised into inaction by imaginative observation. We hope this collection will further the study of dynamic South African cities, amongst others, in an era of transition.

REFERENCES

Castells, M. and P. Hall. 1994. *Technopoles of the World: The Making of Twenty First Century Industrial Complexes.* London and New York: Routledge.

Crush, J. and C. Ambler (eds). 1992. *Liquor and Labor in Southern Africa.* Athens: Ohio University Press.

Freund, B. 1995. *Insiders and Outsiders: The Indian Working Class of Durban, 1910–1990.* Pietermaritzburg, London and Portsmouth: University of Natal Press, James Currey and Heinemann.

Friedman, S. 1987. *Building Tomorrow Today: African Workers in Trade Unions, 1970–84.* Johannesburg: Ravan Press.

Glaser, D. 2001. *Politics and Society in South Africa*, London: Sage.

Hemson, D. 1979. 'Class Consciousness and Migrant Workers: Dockworkers of Durban'. Ph.D. thesis, University of Warwick.

Hindson, D. and J. McCarthy (eds). 1994. *Here to Stay: Informal Settlements in KwaZulu-Natal.* Durban: Indicator Press.

Institute of Industrial Education. 1974. *The Durban Strikes*. Durban and Johannesburg: IIE and Ravan Press.

Katzen, M. 1961. *Industry in Greater Durban*. Pietermaritzburg: Natal Town and Regional Planning Commission.

Kuper, L., H. Watts and R. Davies. 1958. *Durban: A Study in Racial Ecology*. London: Jonathan Cape.

Logan, J.R. and H.R. Molotch. 1987. *Urban Fortunes: The Political Economy of Place*. Los Angeles: University of California Press.

Maylam, P. and I. Edwards (eds). 1996. *The People's City: African Life in Twentieth-Century Durban*. Pietermaritzburg and Portsmouth: University of Natal Press and Heinemann.

Morris, M. and D. Hindson. 'Power Relations in Informal Settlements'. In Hindson and McCarthy, *Here to Stay*.

Padayachee, V. and S. Vawda. 1999. 'Indian Workers and Worker Action in Durban, 1935–45'. *South African Historical Journal*, 40.

Sen, A. 1998. *Development as Freedom*. London: Oxford University Press.

Swanson, M.W. 1965. 'The Rise of Multiracial Durban: Urban History and Race Policy in South Africa 1830–1930'. Ph.D. thesis, Harvard University.

——. 1976. '"The Durban System": Roots of Urban Apartheid in Colonial Natal'. *African Studies*, 35.

Young, B. 1972. 'The Industrial Geography of the Durban Region'. Ph.D. thesis, University of Natal, Durban.

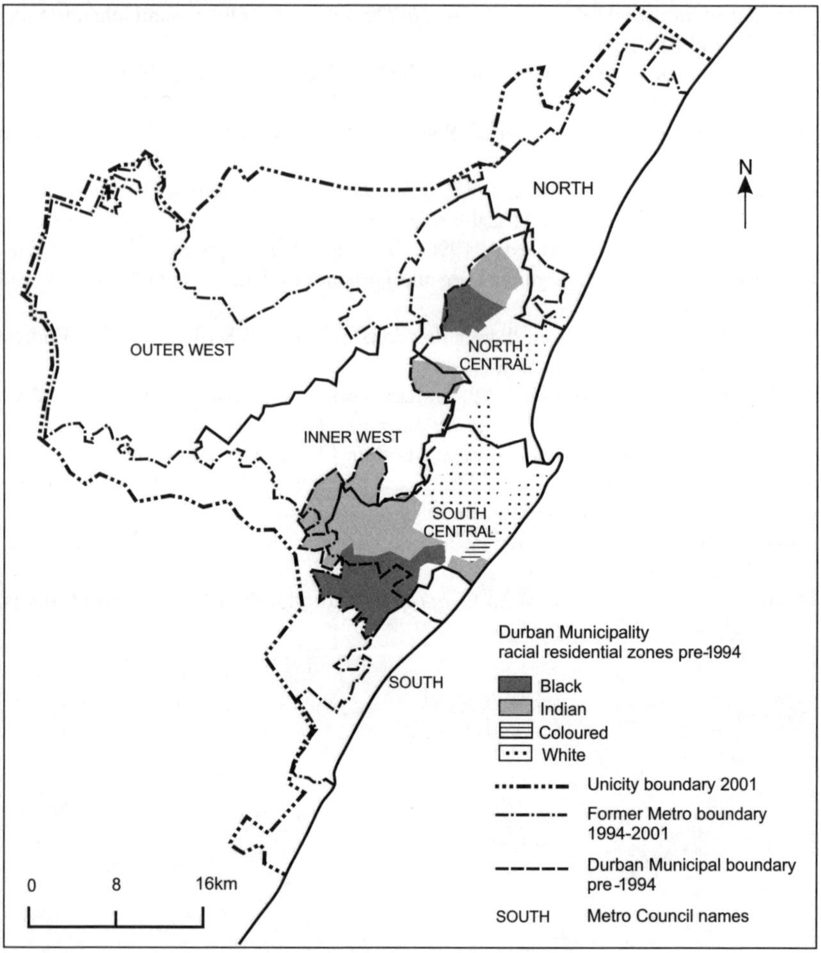

Political boundary changes in Durban, 1994–2001.

Part One

The Local State

Freund's chapter in this part traces how the local state developed in Durban and how, through different phases, it welded together ideas about development, power and race that often seemed to white South Africans a particularly relevant and successful model. The Group Areas legislation of the apartheid era went together with a period of unprecedented growth when Durban benefited from the kind of import-substitution industrialisation and natural products export economy to a greater extent than South Africa on the whole. In key phases, City Hall has definitely had things its way, admittedly within larger political parameters determined by class forces and conflicts. In other phases, for instance during the transition years away from apartheid, politics created an environment of uncertainty in which decisive action became difficult to sustain consistently.

In fact, the local state, with its budget of several billion rands and its staff of thousands of workers, is a complex world with its own rules and organisation, its own means of operating, its own history and its own contradictions. A Metropolitan Council, eager to take the role of planning for a region of well over 1 000 km^2 and a larger budget than the province of KwaZulu-Natal, can seem remote to the actual lived experiences of Durbanites trying to function in a political arena.

Contemporary wisdom tends to focus on adapting the city towards the dictates of business. This means promoting the city as a business centre through various marketing devices and concessions, assuming that the local state serves fundamentally as a *facilitator* in fulfilling the needs of business. However, the ways that this has been done over time are no longer relevant to the spatial and labour requirements of capital at the end of the twentieth century and repositioning to attract investment and renewal is essential. As Hall and Robbins point out in their chapter, 'there is considerable uncertainty over how to achieve local economic development.' They provide us with a view from within the most advanced sector of the city bureaucracy as it tries to come up with a coherent response to these shifts. Hall and Robbins show that while the old system for city management worked best through line function departments with considerable technical expertise and tradition, the creation of a new Economic Development Department, which they feel is 'meta-organisational', attempting to move into new terrain, is critical at the Metro level for uncovering and starting to service new perspectives. In 2000, the creation of the new Metro government with widely extended boundaries, placed a vast terrain under a city government with no substructures (as they existed in 1996–2000). Thus, direct representation is diffused in a very large council system which will make localised voices hard to hear.

American cities are often described as renewing themselves. When they do so successfully, it is through the adaptation of *growth coalitions* – coalitions between locally rooted business interests, government and other role players that have been very effective in places such as Atlanta, Pittsburgh or Boston. However, Durban's big economic players are not so locally rooted or committed. Moreover, there is a sharp historic divide between the old local establishment and the new forces thrown up through democratisation which recalls the problems American cities faced when confronted with massive immigration a century ago, problems that could be faced there under much more dynamic economic conditions. The contemporary growth coalition ethos is tending to become more and more skewed to serving the business 'partner'. Adopting such a model can lead to a suppression of public needs in the interests of servicing business that has been called into question elsewhere (Logan and Molotch 1987).

Currently, public-private partnerships (PPPs) have become a fashionable policy term, but what such partnerships mean and who they benefit needs to be scrutinised as they can easily be taken over by particular private interests. With the arrival of a democratic political dispensation, it is possible for the resources that Durban has built up (human and financial) to be applied to the basic needs of its less privileged citizens. But the related imperative, to create an environment that will complement the changing nature of the economy, is far more uncertain and remains in question.

Nor, of course, can one assume that the state knows best for the public. It is also part of current discourse to doubt the validity of the state, including the local state, and champion the social movement from below – the living embodiment of community needs. This part of the book looks at the city from on high, if questioningly; later on, there will be a corrective as it shifts its perspective to the view from below in terms of basic needs and the citizenry.

CHAPTER ONE

City Hall and the Direction of Development

The Changing Role of the Local State as a Factor in Economic Planning and Development in Durban

BILL FREUND

The central argument of this chapter is that an understanding of economic development requires a knowledge of the way the state has participated and intervened in the economy. This proposition holds not only at the national level, where it is the subject of a massive historical and contemporary literature, but equally at a regional and local level. Economies are in part local; moreover the political and administrative agencies and institutions which intersect with economies are localised. To comprehend the changing political economy of the city of Durban, the second most important economic and demographic urban nexus in South Africa, is to consider the changing nature of state intervention and involvement in the development of this great port city. In the mid-1990s, Metro Durban, with its population of almost 2.5 million, controlled a budget of R2.5 billion, the highest credit rating of any South African city, assets of R3.5 billion and a work-force of 16 000 people (McCarthy n.d.). The relationship between the city administration and its economic environment is not simply ordained from the centre; it can only be understood with relevance to the self-activity of existing, historically shaped local actors. While the national and regional context certainly constrains local government, they do not entirely determine its means of operating or eliminate the need for studying its internal administrative culture.

What follows consists of three parts. First, I consider the relation of the local state to the economy as it evolved historically from the incorporation of the city in the 1850s into the modern era. A periodisation developed elsewhere is the foundation for the logic of this advancing progression (Freund 2000). Then, I will consider a transitional period during the 1970s and 1980s: a key feature of this period was the importance of the main legal opposition party to the left of the national government, the Progressive Party (and its later adaptations) to city politics. Another feature was the growing economic stress which reflected both South Africa's particular problems and the intensifying change in international capitalism at that time. Finally, the third section aims to consider the emerging new construction of economic policies by the Metro government that was created in 1994. This construction reflects a new political configuration, but also a new range of economic constraints and pressures apart from those that emanate directly from the inheritance of the past.

Durban Corporation as an Engine of Economic Development and Social Control

Colonial nineteenth-century Durban arose as an urban centre with a logic determined largely by its location on the Bay of Natal. Easily secured strategically by a naval power, it was the obvious point at which imports and exports would be transshipped from the ocean overland and from the interior of the sub-continent overseas. The rise of Durban as a city was closely related to the systematic mining of gold on the Witwatersrand after 1886; the rail and ship links that connected the Rand to the world made a critical juncture there. This places Durban squarely amongst one major category of modern urban agglomerations: the relationship of transport linkages to the exploitation of natural resources has been fundamental to the rise of some of the greatest cities to emerge since the Industrial Revolution (Cronon 1991).

The dominant impulse in nineteenth-century Durban was commercial. It has been convincingly argued that merchants were very much the principal element in the urban bourgeoisie. Investment, beyond mercantile activities, focused on the expansion of transport and the transport link between port, rail and town. The first Council after incorporation in 1854 consisted of three merchants, two shopkeepers, one physician and George Cato, gentleman, who was perhaps the most important of all the early merchant-cum-property speculators of Durban and the force behind the first railway construction in southern Africa as well as the first bank in Durban (Bjorvig 1994: 12ff.; Green 1957: 36). Merchants played a key role throughout the colony period and beyond in local government and were instrumental in the creation of an urban infrastructure that suited their needs. Before the turn of the century, the city had created a police force, instituted electrification and telephone services and promoted economic interests that benefited the growth of the city (Freund 2000; Interview, Gordon Haygarth, 09.09.96). A recent thesis has even examined the frequency of inter-marriage and familial, as well as business, ties within an inter-locked community (Bjorvig 1994). This community was not only white but overwhelmingly consisted of Protestants of British immigrant stock who networked through a limited range of social institutions – charitable, educational, recreational, etc.

By the early twentieth century, however, this elite was faced with a rapidly growing population of increasing complexity. The white population itself contained a restive and expanding working class of different skill levels. The city, or more accurately, the urban periphery, attracted many Indian labourers who chose not to renew their indenture terms but to stay in Natal. Although largely transient and male, an African population, employed on the docks, in the railways, as rickshaw porters and as domestic workers, was also very considerable. If the economic essence of the city remained commerce and transport, this in turn generated a range of manufacturing activities. These were of a sufficient complexity, interactive relationship and called on a sophisticated enough range of skills as to suggest to May Katzen, the best observer of Durban's economy in mid-century, that Durban exemplified Alfred Marshall's concept of an 'industrial district' (Katzen 1961: 123). The reference to Marshall is especially interesting because of the fashionable present-day revival of his concept within the rubric of today's ideas about integrated, regional industrial development.

The nineteenth century British city combined – sometimes very uncomfortably – laissez-faire ideology with a growing interventionism not only in the provision of infrastructure, and not only in a range of social amenities that served the different classes that had emerged with the industrial revolution but, to some extent, in developmental functions that directly affected the economic prospects of particular cities. This was inherent in the civic gospel of the mid-Victorians (Jay 1981). On the one hand, classic liberals denounced what was known as 'municipal trading'; on the other, reformers not only tried to improve schooling and health care, they also began to speculate in land purchase in order to expand municipal economic power. The rate payment system gave the city a revenue basis while the creation of energy and transport related infrastructure – water provision, gasworks, electrification, trams – gave room for the shaping of economic development. Birmingham, under the political leadership of Joseph Chamberlain, and so-called 'municipal socialism' were paradigmatic here (Jay 1981; Roberts 1984). Whilst the formal political power of the city was limited in the context of British centralism, the city was in fact an important and distinctive site of class struggles over social and economic affairs. This would become truer in the twentieth century when public housing estates began to fill growing amounts of urban land and the state became committed to improving the living standard of the working urban masses. The municipality could play a central role in channelling and negotiating the outcome of such struggles.

Durban largely borrowed the municipal discourse and regulatory structure typical of British cities but it was the site of a different and growingly distinctive history despite the important imperial parallels. From the perspective of direct economic intervention, some matters were out of Durban's direct remit. The central state, through the agency of the South African Railways & Harbours authority, controlled the port itself as well as the railway system (and after the 1960s, the national highways that connected Durban to the grid). It was the city which offered to business cheap water and a good electric supply, however. Durban water was not even metered until 1970 (Interview, Peter Johnston, 21.08.96).[1] The brief of the Barns Commission of 1943 sums up the categories that were considered the normal concern of the Council at the time – housing, roads, tourism, industry, recreation, public health.[2]

Where the Corporation played an active role of particular importance lay in the provision of land. This was especially important to industry, particularly for the construction of large plants on low-lying even ground with access to the line of rail. In Durban, flat land was at a premium. As early as the beginning of the century, the provision of very cheap land was critical in the choice of Durban as a site for Lever Brothers, (later Unilever) on the originally railway owned 'timber wharf', Maydon Wharf, the first major site of concentrated industry in Durban (Interview, Gordon Haygarth, 09.09.96).[3]

The city authorities became increasingly expert at purchasing, selling and leasing land in order to provide attractive conditions for industry and thus bring employment to the city. In effect, Durban itself became a large-scale, effective speculator in property, organising the lease and sale of property in such a way as to profit while creating jobs and building up the economic weight of the city. Intervention revolved around 'planning and planning concessions' (Interview, Gordon Haygarth, 09.09.96).[4] The most dramatic pre-war example lay in the expansion of the city's boundaries, the incorporation of the Outer Boroughs, which took place in 1931. The Outer Boroughs allowed the city to expand for residential activities but taking over a scattered and weak range of small municipalities and outlying farms. This also facilitated access to considerable amounts of desirable flat land which would be available for industrial growth. The Woods Estate sugar estate, purchased in 1928, would become the foundation of the Mobeni and Jacobs industrial estates – the basis of industrial growth in the city after annexation for a generation to follow (Interview, Gordon Haygarth, 09.09.96). By the time of annexation, the Corporation owned no less than 2 724 of the 43 000 acres in the new Durban.[5]

The city, moreover, could and did control the way that land was used. Thus firms that did not have clear plans to involve significant use of Durban labour were waved aside, especially in prosperous years, while others that were geared to sections of the industrial work-force were welcomed on favourable terms. In an interview, former Town Clerk Gordon Haygarth gave the example of the giant paper firm, Mondi. The city arranged for the drainage and treatment of land so that pulp waste would not simply be packed off to sea; in turn Mondi effectively guaranteed at least 600 jobs, essentially geared towards an Indian work-force, in easy commuting distance from the large new Indian township of Chatsworth which was developing at the same time (Interview, Gordon Haygarth, 09.09.96). Often land given in lease by the city automatically reverted back when the lease was surrendered for one reason or another (Interview, Gordon Haygarth, 09.09.96).

The successful manipulation of the land market involved the growth of expertise within the confines of City Hall where increasing professional knowledge of the economy was nurtured by the city bureaucracy. In the immediate post-First World War years, hard times brought out an unprecedented radicalism on the part of the large mass of lower middle class and working class whites in Durban who elected councillors to represent their interests. The city had to cater to them as the most potent political force, on the whole paralleling the situation at national level without the complicating element of Afrikaner nationalism (Afrikaners still being a small portion of the population before the 1940s in Durban). However, the city was also breeding an expert community that saw itself as acting in the broader interests of capital – and the city – as a whole. Town Treasurer, then Clerk, E.B. Scott, a British immigrant, played a key part. In 1929 he created a local branch of the (British) Institute of Municipal Treasurers and Accountants and worked towards professionalisation of the urban public service in a way that made Durban a kind of model and nursery for the whole of South Africa. This included instituting an assisted education scheme that from 1989 involved commercial training at the part-time courses run by the University of Natal on a fixed curriculum.

A central figure here was Ossie Gorven, who served as City Treasurer from 1962 to 1985. Gorven would preside at his peak over the work of some hundred or so university graduates. Departments such as those of the Engineers and Treasury were increasingly based on a wealth of internal expertise and often filled with men who had known each other at school (Interview, Gordon Haygarth, 09.09.96),[6] at university and in other social settings (Interview, Ossie Gorven, 08.12.97).[7]

Gorven is associated by those who remember him as bringing the developmental work of the local state to the highest pitch by his invention and development of what he termed the Capital Fund (Interviews, Ossie Gorven, 08.12.97; Crispin Hemson, 01.09.96; Peter Mansfield, 11.09.96).[8] This fund originated with small windfall sums garnered from the accounts and came to depend on a moderate rates increase. It was used simultaneously to bring down the city's debts and for investment purposes. So successful was the fund that from around 1978, Durban's investments were worth more than its debts and the city could avoid new borrowings through use of its own accumulated capital. Essentially investments were made in property both in Durban but also in other South African cities. Only after Gorven's day was there any possibility of investment in equity. Once the Capital Fund was large enough, rates increases could be held to very moderate levels.[9] This remarkable financial device turned Durban into a kind of engine of development potentially. All that was missing was a consistent economic development policy (Interview, Crispin Hemson, 01.09.96). In effect, Gorven's scheme was half-way between a financial device, aimed at evading the classic problems of sinking funds and indebtedness and a genuine development scheme with non-financial purposes. Its success was predicated, of course, on the political silence of the majority of the working class deprived of the city franchise, in the way in which racial structuration allowed municipal power to operate with a particular autonomy (Interview, Pravin Gordhan, 23.01.98).

Early in Gorven's tenure as Treasurer, the city of Durban's affairs were the subject of investigation of the James Commission of 1965/66. It originated in the doubtful bid of a foreign firm for the erection of expensive sewage equipment intended to distribute Durban's sewage outflow well out to sea, and it became a means through which councillors, often precisely those who were still the inheritors of the populist white political tradition of earlier in the century, were discredited for bribe-taking and other corrupt practices. The triumph of the Commission placed those bureaucrats, who thought of themselves as planning for the city in an honest direction beyond the impulses of the corrupt politicians, in a strong position.[10] It also led to the virtual extinction of the power of the white municipal trade union (Durban Municipal Employees' Society) that had been a strong factor in the city for 40 years (Purcell 1974).[11]

It may be argued as well that from the 1960s, the typical small Durban based business, still often associated with the local Chambers of Commerce and Industry, was declining in importance compared to the big corporations which found the city location attractive but were only interested in the urban environment to a limited extent. Few had their headquarters in Durban. Even firms associated with Durban and employing large numbers of city residents such as Toyota (which in the 1980s became South Africa's most successful motor assembly company) and Unilever, had much of their marketing and managing operations on the Reef (Interview, John Bryce, 06.09.96). Durban never really acquired a distinctive financial base of its own. This context, where specific business lobbying was less potent than might be imagined, may also have empowered the city mandarins.[12] The Marshallian industrial district, conjured up by May Katzen, was giving way to a different kind of structuration in a period of unprecedentedly rapid economic growth.

A particular characteristic of Durban was the important tourist trade. As the seaside terminus of the most important rail link between Johannesburg and the South African shore, the warm climate of Durban naturally inspired the development of a classic sea-orientated tourist trade typical of older resorts in Europe and America, comparable to Brighton or Blackpool in Britain for instance. Over time, the tourist business widened its appeal for the white working class of the Rand, which was increasingly Afrikaner rather than British, and impacted increasingly on the property market. By the middle 1970s, it was claimed that Durban attracted 500 000 visitors per annum spending R250 million (Interview, Felicity Attwell, 01.09.96).[13] The Corporation not only made properties on and near the beachfront (the 'Golden Mile') available to businesses that catered to the tourist industry, it also made a continuous effort to make the beachfront attractive, constructing groynes, systematically shipping sand from the harbour to widen and preserve the ocean beach, erecting shark nets, clearing undesirables.[14] Town officials are unequivocal about the historic weight the local state placed on making sure an attractive environment was available for visitors (Interviews, Felicity Attwell, 01.09.96; Ossie Gorven, 08.12.97; Gordon Haygarth, 09.09.96).[15]

Apart from the seaside, the city provided inexpensive leases for the rugby and cricket stadia erected north of the city centre (Interview, Gordon Haygarth, 09.09.96). This land had once been the swampy Eastern Vlei which had blocked the northern expansion of the city in the nineteenth century. It had been cleared and drained by city organised white labour during the Depression as an employment project (Interview, Gordon Haygarth, 09.09.96).

The most burning question about capitalism in South Africa has concerned its relation to the racially constructed social and political order. This relation was in fact as complex on the local level as on the national level. For much of the century, assumptions about South Africa as a 'white man's country' in which whites were to exert pre-eminence in the cities, were embedded in the strategies of businessmen and local government managers. Durban, like other towns in South Africa, was relatively free to establish its own racial system in the days before Union, with regard to licensing, housing, etc. The city was famous throughout the sub-continent for its invention of the so-called 'Durban system' of municipal beerhalls for Africans. Municipally controlled brewing of 'native' beer was set to be the source of welfare spending on African needs in the city such as it was. This system was especially effective before a major resistance campaign, primarily led by women involved in beer brewing, attacked it in 1929.[16] Similarly, the city colluded to limit Indian shop licensing and effectively confine Indian trading to certain parts of the city in the interests of favouring white competition. Some aspects of the racial structuration of the city were imposed from Pretoria (for instance, the proclamation of the central inland area of Cato Manor as a Group Area for whites, largely for security reasons – thus creating a white inland corridor from Durban centre inland; or the reversion of land proclaimed for African usage to control by the KwaZulu bantustan, notably Umlazi and KwaMashu). However, the most recent historian of the Group Areas Act of 1950 and its application to Durban, Brij Maharaj, has affirmed and detailed the role of the municipality in planning removals and in the construction of a systematically segregated city in the 1960s and 1970s (Maharaj 1992 and in this volume).

Documentation on the post-war planning of Durban from the 1940s takes for granted the need to separate races 'in conflict'. The assumption of the need for empty spaces between races in conflict uses the metaphor of a battleground. The Barns Commission of 1943 talked about the partition, for instance, of the Bluff between white and Indian with a 'neutral zone' in between as though the reference was to a contemporary European war front.[17] The major study of segregation in Durban by

Leo Kuper et al. reveals that this approach remained salient for a long time after. The 1949 race riots were taken as a token of the need to separate the races in the interests of the harmonious development of the city; for most whites there was at the least an inevitability about racial conflict between white, brown and black.

Having said this, it is also important to emphasize that the municipality was sensitive to the economic needs of Durban. In serving as effective ring-keepers for capital in Durban, city officials fell between two imperatives – the powerful political imperative to work for a white city that wanted non-whites classified, marginalised and reduced to impotence, and the economic imperative to provide the basic necessities for a large working class that included Indians and Africans. It became increasingly obvious with the industrial growth that took off from the middle 1930s that an Indian and African work-force was critical to that growth. Even by the 1940s, there was an acceptance of the need to accommodate Durban residents of the major 'racial' groups. The annexation of 1931 had already dramatically increased the size of the 'non-white', especially Indian, population but the economic necessity for this amalgamation was crucial. Indeed, the official literature reveals the importance of control over a population of colour. References to Africans 'for the most part detribalised and under no particular control or supervision' who form a '. . . menace to the respectable inhabitants' were in fact particularly significant.[18] Leaving people of colour 'out' of the city was already adjudged impractical. One small part of the new Durban was planned as the first controlled sector for African urban family life, Lamontville – a 'Native Village'.[19]

Segregation was in general planned to permit the access of workers to the workplace. The new industrial sites developed from the 1940s south of Durban and then in Pinetown to the west were close to some of the new planned townships for Indians and Africans. Late in the Second World War, a remarkable document by a town planning consultant reveals the extent to which housing policy was being shaped in a way that would marry well with employment policy. P.J. Bowring emphasized that planning houses for the unemployed and extending job opportunities for those with no housing access were futile activities. He wrote that '. . . the quality of housing, particularly for the Native population, should be such that it will tend to improve their standard of living and moral and spiritual outlook as well as physical well-being. It should not go so far as to make the cost to the tenant of this desirable standard such that he is perforce reduced to a lower standard through the strain on his pocket.'[20]

Bowring's views were probably considerably more liberal in this regard than some of his successors. However, broadly speaking, Durban expanded through providing housing, schools, health services and other amenities on a segregated and unequal basis. City records in the apartheid era show a paternalistic interest in the maintenance of hostel facilities, tuberculosis inspection, child health provision and slum clearance[21] that represent a classic municipal concern for the sustenance of a minimally skilled and healthy working class with the element of South African racism factored in. This kind of urban structuration, coupled with the extent to which access was defined by colour, can with some modification be classified as 'racial Fordism', given that few workers were employed on assembly lines and that the amenities for African workers in particular were quite rudimentary. It did involve a totalising idea of the conurbation and its development in which municipal government played a key regulatory function in the provision of jobs, welfare, housing and other infrastructure. The city itself became an employer of thousands of workers and had substantial expertise and capacity in the construction of housing and other infrastructure.

In their heyday, I have argued elsewhere that the Durban city fathers and the planners that served them saw themselves as modernisers who adapted South African racial rules to the needs of the most advanced socio-economic thinking.[22] The American political scientist John Purcell commented in the early 1970s that 'in spite of the hostility between the Afrikaans-speaking national political elite and the English-speaking national economic elite, both groups have recognised that the maintenance of white domination and political stability requires careful coordination of political and economic activities to a degree unacceptable to a businessman in the United States.'[23] South African capitalism was able to benefit from some aspects of apartheid, especially in an era when natural resource exports could form an effective basis for rapid economic growth. The widely dispersed, carefully zoned urban model propounded was especially compatible with the post-Marshallian establishment of large firms that occupied an oligopolistic position in most economic activities. The losers in the system were the small entrepreneurs of colour and the possibility of intense networking between service provisioners, workers and employers typical of dense and more loosely regulated urban environments.[24] Whites retained limited scope to benefit from the growth trajectory as proprietors of small business, Indians less so and Africans not at all. However, veteran officials and businessmen active in the 1950s and 1960s tend to pride themselves on turning the utopian *apartheid* of the state into a more practical set of arrangements that did not block key development needs.

Contemporary literature has been increasingly harsh on 'development' in general and modernisation.[25] Studies such as Elizabeth Wilson's *tour de force, The Sphinx in the Garden*, have rightly highlighted that even the most benevolent of planning traditions emphasized control and confinement and sought to contain the loose but dense mix of people that characterises the modern city (Wilson 1991). Although she is not willing to abandon planning entirely, Wilson perceptively notes from her central concern with women, that 'there is a sense in which all town planning contains both a utopian and a heroic, yet authoritarian, element. Although its purposes may seem purely practical, it does claim to offer, like the utopian work, a permanent solution to the flux and flow of the ever-changing city. The plan is always intended to fix the usage of space; the aim the state regulation of urban populations' (Wilson 1991: 20). Even benevolent plans intended to provide for the working class tend to exclude sectors that do not fit the mould.[26] South African cities offer a somewhat extreme example of this point.

The kind of industrial growth that this form of modernised planning favoured was not necessarily very competitive. However, as long as it provided for the domestic market, this was not consequently important. The competitive part of the national economy lay in the provision and export of natural resources, gold, diamonds and other minerals. Secondary industry catered overwhelmingly for the national market and was highly protected in the post-Second World War era. The racial structuring of the labour market and provision of services certainly did not stand in the way of industrial profitability.

The black strike wave of 1972 broke a decade of rapid growth and repressive labour calm which was dominated by the racial Fordist schema. It revealed just how much the squeeze from the national government was operating to make the growing African working class of the city less and less able to cope. Low wages, the imposition of the *induna* system as a means of managing African workers, the lack of housing, were part of the squeeze which, counter to the dominant view of the city fathers, actually wanted to push Africans to the margins or entirely out of urban space.

This explosion and its aftermath, the halting but real expansion of militant trade unionism in black Durban, might have been accommodated by a renewed impetus of the old 'Durban system'. However, this proved difficult to impossible to effect. The nature of the explosion, with its new emphasis on black self-government and autonomy, worked directly against paternalist solutions. At the same time, apartheid continued. The central state expanded the empowerment of KwaZulu as an authority, blocking the administrative structures of the city from expanding into the new hinterland of shacks. Previously, despite the potential of a homeland on the city doorstep, Pretoria encouraged limitations on permits for Africans to commute regularly to town and virtually ceased to build family housing. Now more lax controls made it possible for a peripheral Durban to agglomerate on the fringe of the 'white' city.

The Liberal Hour: An Era of Transition

Less obviously but also significantly, capital's nature was also shifting. From the late 1970s, economic growth was more often linked to reducing than expanding the size of work-forces. The interest of business in a more welfare orientated urban configuration was weak. In fact, the formal organs of business in Durban, the Chambers of Commerce and Industry, were relatively undynamic and limited in their focus with little interest in change (Interviews, Crispin Hemson, 01.09.96; Andrzej Kiepela, 03.10.96). Changing tastes brought about a stagnation in the tourist industry which seemed orientated to a past era (Interview, Andrzej Kiepela, 03.10.96). Until this time, the dominant political voices in Durban had been outside the National Party but conservative on the question of race and timid about any kind of democratisation of society. This congealed in the form of the United Party in the 1940s. However, after a generation of increasingly hopeless opposition nationally, the United Party began to fissure between its conservatives and those who sought positive change.

One result was the dominant role in Durban that the liberal breakaway party, the Progressives (later the Progressive Federal Party – PFP) played from the election of 1978. For a decade, although not a majority, they constituted the dominant political voice in Durban (Interview, Crispin Hemson, 01.09.96).[27] The more energetic new councillors were eager to use their power to find means of challenging segregation and, more gingerly, reaching out to real political forces outside the white world. At the same time, they had the most positive views of business apart from those 'old fashioned' elements that seemed too parochial and wedded to a particular way of doing things. The PFP councillors rather admired the way in which the city had harnessed and controlled economic forces in Durban over time. However, they were anxious to establish a new 'modern' kind of relationship with business, one that would in fact see the regulatory role of the city government diminish. There was some tension over race but also co-operation on development issues between this new regime and the powerful figures in City Hall offices.

The period of Progressive dominance (1978–86) was marked by considerable continuity with the past and attempts to revive particular aspects of urban development, as well as experimentation that would point to the future (Interviews, Crispin Hemson, 01.09.96; Andrzej Kiepela, 03.10.96; Peter Mansfield, 11.09.96). This period can be associated with a major phase of renewal planning on the beachfront associated with the liberal Cape Town architect Revel Fox.[28] New public structures were coupled with environmental protection measures; it was assumed that cautious step-by-step racial integration of the beachfront would lead to the revival of tourism now catering to a middle class of all colours. This proved to be an impractical notion. In fact, from 1989 integration would suddenly bring a massive black working class infusion into the beachfront at holiday season, an infusion which did without most of the typical consumerism associated with beach holidays in the past. The middle class continued to opt for a less and less urban holiday preference. The beachfront was at best an interesting experiment into the making of a deracialised Durban (Interviews, Crispin Hemson, 01.09.96; Andrzej Kiepela, 03.10.96).

At the same time, there was increasing realisation that the future of the tourist industry in the city lay in the promotion of business conferences and sporting events. The city had already made considerable land available for the latter. From 1982, the availability of South African Railways & Harbours (SAR&H) land in the centre vacated by the railways was used to construct a big exhibition centre to succeed a previous one set up through city initiative on the beachfront (Interview, Gordon Haygarth, 09.09.96).[29] Railway workshop facilities were converted into an up-market shopping centre intended to revive the city centre which was beginning to lose business to commercial facilities located near the affluent suburbs north and west of the city. The terms of construction, in conjunction with the firm of Murray & Roberts, had more of the flavour of what we can deem public-private partnership (PPP) rather than the previous context where the city had arranged the terms under which specific businesses were allowed access to cheap city land.[30] Already, the main industrial new development of the 1980s on the Springfield Flats near the Umgeni was organised as a direct partnership with Anglo-American which provided the servicing (the 'offer' system) (Interview, Gordon Haygarth, 09.09.96). There were no longer requirements as to what type of enterprise could settle on the land or what kind of workers would be hired as in the past.

A British firm was brought in for advice on reconstructing the city administration, which was slowly moving towards the employment of more people of colour in other than menial positions. The result was the adoption of a classically neoliberal form of organisation whereby different units of city government were isolated from one another on a cost-recovery basis, breaking up the classic logic of accumulation and structuration identified with Gorven and the influential Town Clerk, Gordon Haygarth.[31] This potentially went against the renewal of the city's role in economic development; however, it also had the effect of breaking up informal networks and fiefdoms in such a way that would make the marriage of a new generation of black councillors and city officials willing to work with a new order more possible (Interviews, Vivian McMenamin, 30.09.97; Eddie Morton, 11.11.97).

The PFP period proved to be not only transitional but somewhat fragile in character. Attempts to break down the planning barriers between the urban authorities and the SAR&H parastatal were unsuccessful (Interview, Gordon Haygarth, 09.09.96). The excision of KwaZulu meant that the city government could rarely intervene, even if it was desirable, in the poorest parts of the metropolitan area. However, during the 1980s, the trade unions were joined by an increasingly effective civic movement (largely under the sway of a network of Indian supporters of the illegal African National Congress) which was prepared to organise against the City Council politically. Up to a point, some common ground with liberal whites was found. For example, part of the PFP delegation came to agree with the agitators that there was no excuse to bulldoze Clairwood, a small remnant neighbourhood of Indians characterised by mixed commercial, residential and industrial use (Scott 1994). In the 1970s, Clairwood was earmarked for destruction in order to allow for systematic industrial expansion of the kind that had previously taken place in Jacobs, Mobeni and other pieces of flat ground. Indian activists were successful in rallying this community to resist removal and dissolution. If white liberals at first only perceived the issue as one of racial discrimination, they could also increasingly support the civic movement without feeling that they were betraying the conventionally defined economic needs of the city.

The demand for flat industrial land was clearly less important to capital in Durban after 1980. By the middle of the 1980s, the city was moving hesitantly to identify the 'informal sector' as a source of economic growth and legitimate activity, a major historic reversal.[32] Squatter settlements became increasingly tolerated and mushroomed in areas where they had been pushed out a generation earlier, notably in parts of Cato Manor which had become a huge empty block of land in the centre of the metropolitan area. However, as the battlefield shifted towards struggles over rates and evictions and from urban questions to efforts to defy and undermine the state, the PFP was undermined by 'civic' groupings linked to the United Democratic Front, and ultimately the African National Congress (ANC), such as the Durban Housing Action Committee (DHAC).[33] Some of its councillors, such as the present director of the Management Committee, Margaret Winter, would in time in fact join the ANC themselves.

At the same time, white voters felt threatened as the tide of resistance rose. Ironically for the first time in history, the National Party gained significantly in strength and briefly in 1989–94 was a strong force in Council politics. The irony lay partly in the fact that the Nationalists, and notably their remarkable mayor Jan Venter, a one-time railway worker, were themselves as much or more committed to change and the establishment of a new order than the PFP whatever the white voters might have imagined in bringing them to power. Venter began the process of negotiating with what became after 1990 a legal opposition. A successor after Venter's death, Michael Lipschitz who joined the National Party, was critical in taking the first steps to accommodate tens of thousands of township visitors to the beachfront after the racial barriers there fell (Interview, Felicity Attwell, 01.09.96).

A parallel process, in part stimulated by the vacuum of PFP decline and the lack of effective business representation, lay in the growing emergence of business lobbying aimed at negotiating with the Inkatha Freedom Party (IFP) and the ANC to establish parameters of a new political and economic order once national negotiations had reached fruition. It was the large companies that pushed through a merger of the Chambers of Commerce and Industry in 1992 although this did not at first lead to the creation of a dynamic organisation attuned to their needs (Interview, John Bryce, 06.09.96). A crucial occasion for this was Operation Jumpstart which brought together new business leaders and politicians into a forum partly designed to consider the rapidly increasing squatter population in Cato Manor but which was more far-reaching if, in itself, not always consequential (Interview, Peter Johnston, 21.08.96).[34] One characteristic survivor of the operation was a lottery designed to provide social amenities profitably in the absence of social delivery in the transition period (McCarthy n.d.: 24).[35]

Probably the most important civic venture however, was the go-ahead for the construction of an ambitious new conference centre, the International Conference Centre, with substantial city funding. This was only to be opened in 1997 when it would still be the most impressive such facility in the country or region by a long way. Getting political consent for this expensive investment was a triumph for the shadowy growth coalition that was beginning to come together.

Another actor of growing importance in this period was Tongaat-Hulett, a corporation formed from the merger of two sugar companies with links to Anglo-American. Tongaat-Hulett owned valuable sugar land and stood to gain immense profits from the northwards movement of the city. The KwaMashu and Phoenix townships, for instance, had been taken over by the state from Tongaat land and Tongaat had originally owned the Prospecton estate on which Toyota was built, as well as the wealthy suburb of La Lucia (Interview, T. Chetty and Neels Brink, 16.01.97). For years, the property dimension of its interests had been relatively marginal while the company had focused on retaining its sugar land intact as much as possible.[36] This was in large part a response to the negative tax implications of large-scale property sales in that period. In 1989, the company began to engage in a major planning exercise – the Tongaat-Hulett Planning Forum – aimed at considering the future of the city and its spatial configuration.[37] The expansion of KwaMashu, and Inanda beyond it, as well as Phoenix, was increasingly creating a situation where the population of Durban lived north of the Umgeni River but the majority of jobs lay to the south. The greatest expansion potential lay in the north, so much of it owned by Tongaat-Hulett. Moreland, the Tongaat estate division, would emerge from its formation in 1991 as a major source of profits for this company with its focus strongly in and around Durban.[38] By 1995, it was the 'largest developer of real estate in KwaZulu-Natal'.[39] Jumpstart and Tongaat-Hulett, the emergence of new business interests attempting to think through a new political order in Durban, heralded the dawn of the present age.

Key negotiators, some of them 'progressive' planners and other go-betweens who had links to the extant city apparatus, played a critical new role as consultants as the old order lost legitimacy and the new one emerged in embryo. At the provincial level, in the context of the violent confrontations in many rural areas between the IFP and ANC, a Regional Economic Forum was set up in 1993 to allow political antagonists to discuss and come forward with development plans (Interview, Gareth Coleman, 21.11.97). Ex-trade unionists were key figures in this forum, and ANC exiles with little history of involvement in local struggles were sometimes significant. A wide range of fixers attempted to 'facilitate' development between politicians, bureaucrats and popular forces of all sorts, the so-called community. The radical civics movement, itself perhaps looking in other directions for the future of its leadership, was not a major factor; its vision of the city was largely swept aside (Interview, Pravin Gordhan, 23.01.98). The civics organisation fell into a dramatic decline following 1994 with little clarity or legitimacy remaining after three or four years (Interview, Alan Murrin and Hayden Osborne, 15.10.96).

Metro Durban: The Democratised City in an Era of Globalisation

The new Durban was still incomplete at the time of national elections in 1994. Only two years later, in mid-1996, were the first elections held for the new metropolitan area. Thus the era of the democratised city is only just dawning. Nonetheless the 1996 regime was the product of several years of negotiation and tentative institutional change itself. What were its principal characteristics?

Perhaps one needs to suggest firstly that surprisingly what has emerged is an increasingly 'strong' state. It is implied below that so-called globalisation and trends in international capitalism are impacting on the city in ways which make regulation by the local state difficult. However, there is so far little sense that a deregulated society is falling more and more out of control from any centre.[40] New black representatives in the political sphere are anxious to promote social and economic change and effectively to displace the 'civic' organisations and non-governmental organisations (NGOs) whose continued role as intermediaries between the state and so-called communities, so critical in the historic phases of resistance and negotiation, is now being effectively marginalised (Khan 1997). Moreover, the local authorities are enjoined by Pretoria to see development as a central, or the central, activity in which they are involved. In fact, in some respects, development could do with considerably more decentring in order to offer more to a broader cross-section of the population.

The most obvious shift, following the careful negotiation of new boundaries, was the creation of Metro Durban. Some 60 separate government units were restructured into a two-tier system of metropolitan and local governments (six local governments with their own elected representatives) that cut across the previous racial boundaries established under apartheid. The possibility has now come about of creating a level of metropolitan co-ordinated planning that had never before been feasible (Interview, Peter Johnston, 21.08.96).[41] In addition, the city was able – and of course also obligated – to provide services to large numbers of poor people on a more equitable basis. Delivery for the masses entered the agenda at a new level that no longer represented a continuum with the paternalist traditions of the past. It was equally true, however, that the tactics developed under the United Democratic Front aimed at encouraging non-payment to the illegitimate state no longer held any validity and the bureaucracy could hope to start collecting rate payments and bills (Interviews, Hercules Hattingh, 26.08.96; Sbu Sithole, 23.09.97).

Secondly and less officially, the possibility now exists for a new relationship between capital and the state. Out of the Tongaat-Hulett planning exercise and Operation Jumpstart emerged the possibility for what is usually termed a corporatist 'growth coalition' between capital, the state and labour.[42] The new language of public-private partnership seems increasingly pervasive. Perhaps the key actors on the private side, Terry Rosenberg of the McCarthy group and the property managers of the Tongaat-Hulett configuration, represented the wealthiest and most powerful interests that were moored definitively in Durban in the middle 1990s. They seem anxious to bring together an array of interests and to establish links to key new political actors that will promote issues central to the growth of the city (Interviews, T. Chetty and Neels Brink, 16.01.97; Peter Mansfield, 11.09.96). Of course this kind of coalition is different from the sort of intimate and organic relations between urban officials and entrepreneurs that are often particularly efficacious in the sustenance of Marshallian industrial districts. Perhaps, however, in a metropolitan area as big as Durban, such a coalition represents the limits of the possible.

Thirdly, and by contrast with the situation in many urban centres in South Africa, the initial pervasive mistrust between activists and establishment figures has to some degree been resolved. While the city bureaucracy has committed itself along a (moderate) redistributive path and is well able, as a result of the Capital Development Fund, to finance new infrastructure without raising rates as unduly as elsewhere, the new generation of black politicians have committed themselves to making use of existing expertise and retaining key bureaucrats, going easy on the 'affirmative action' policies that have elsewhere had a dramatic deleterious effect on urban change (Werlin 1965, for the example of Nairobi; Interviews, Mark Lowe, 23.09.97; Roger Sishi, 25.08.97; Sbu Sithole, 23.09.97).[43] In the new order, development has been officially enshrined as a key objective of local government.[44] It can certainly be argued that Durban is unusually well placed to carry through development policy and that a remarkably powerful and effective economic tradition can now be translated into new times and serve people of all colours equitably.

The management restructuring of the late 1980s with its creation of incoherently linked cost centres has been a spanner in the works to a degree. The new regime has however sponsored the creation of a small Economic Strategy Unit under the leadership of an economist with a strong activist background, Vivian McMenamin. The Unit has not sat easily with the existing structures under the capable hands of a long-established service but in late 1997 it was upgraded into an Economic Development Directorate which will not only receive more resources but which has the potential, together with an enhanced part for the City Treasurer's office, to create a new integrated development policy building on the actors in the Durban growth coalition (Interviews, Eddie Morton, 11.11.97; Margaret Winter, 03.09.97). McMenamin would like to see this department itself become the focus of a Metropolitan Economic Forum that would tie public and private partners together effectively (Interview, Vivian McMenamin, 30.09.97). Town Clerk Eddie Morton argues that the private sector is already more effectively engaged than before (Interview, Eddie Morton, 11.11.97).

In some respects, this department can build on the work of previous generations. Certainly the most spectacular new physical manifestation of the city economy was the centrally located International Convention Centre in which the city invested some R200 million. This really represented the fruition of the work of older bureaucrats such as Gordon Haygarth and the political foundation laid by Operation Jumpstart (Interview, John Bryce, 06.09.96). The present site of Durban International Airport, inadequate for inter-continental travel, can potentially be converted into industrial ground or even, as some propose, dredged to create a second harbour (Interview, Margaret Winter, 03.09.97).

However, it is around new transport linkages rather than industrial land that the big issues of the late 1990s are gathering steam (Interview, Terry Rosenberg, 24.11.97). One is the construction of a new and larger airport north of the city, on the drawing boards since the 1970s when Tongaat-Hulett was obliged to sell the land to the state. This airport has enormous potential for making Durban an international tourist destination and for gathering to itself a network of commercial and service activities in what is increasingly the focus of where the population of the metropolitan area is expanding (Interviews, John Bryce, 06.09.96; Peter Johnston, 21.08.96; Keith Matthias, 10.10.96).

Equally critical are potential developments connected to the port and harbour. With the breakdown of sanctions, the harbour has attracted more container traffic than it can contend with (Interview, John Bryce, 06.09.96).[45] Expensive decisions need to be made as to whether to develop Durban further as a container hub, thus potentially competing with Indian Ocean ports such as Dubai and Colombo or diverting container traffic elsewhere, perhaps to Richards Bay on the north coast which is now the main export terminus for coal and other minerals of the South African interior. The harbour itself needs replanning in such a way as to establish an appropriate division between commercial and tourist activities (Interview, Terry Rosenberg, 24.11.97). This brings in the problem of relations between the city and Portnet, itself possibly subject in future to a national ports authority rather than to the administration of the city of Durban with which it intersects so vitally (Interviews, Mark Lowe, 23.09.97; Vivian McMenamin, 30.09.97; Margaret Winter, 03.09.97).[46]

These infrastructural issues create problems that need adjudication between the Metro government of Durban and other sections of the state (Khan 1997; Interview, Eddie Morton, 11.11.97). The old boundaries between municipalities, the province, the KwaZulu homeland and parastatal actors have broken down or can now be challenged. Despite the formal desire to encourage spontaneous growth on the part of regional and local economic forces, the national government is reluctant to put too many cards in the hands of such a strong player as the city of Durban, which is wealthier than the province of KwaZulu-Natal as a whole. There is some feeling that the construction of attractive airport facilities in Durban will precipitate a decline in Johannesburg which remains the main access point for air travel to southern Africa as a whole. There is also the view that harbour and port development needs to be equitably distributed between coastal centres stretching from the impoverished Eastern Cape Province through KwaZulu-Natal where the ANC government is anxious to gain support and, beyond the frontier, into Mozambique (Interview, Gareth Coleman, 21.11.97). Conflict between Pretoria and Durban is potentially structured along these fault lines (Interview, Vivian McMenamin, 30.09.97). The South African government does not really welcome any new logic of regional growth patterns unfolding independently of national planning. The Spatial Development Initiatives (SDIs), or development corridors, are very much along the lines of classic European dirigiste planning of the post-Second World War generation. They attempt to move big projects into underdeveloped areas as a growth stimulus and political reward, although they are supposed to include relevant 'stakeholders' including regional and urban governments.[47]

Other problems of adjudication are also significant. The unification of the metropolitan region around Durban has represented an impressive rationalisation. However, a system has yet to be put into place for establishing the balance between the Metro government and the local governments, which have, especially in some cases, very limited capacity (Interviews, Vivian McMenamin, 30.09.97; Margaret Winter, 03.09.97).[48] At present, some critical areas (for instance, use of land) are left for discussion on a stakeholder basis where it is not very clear who has the last word. Co-ordination, under the jurisdiction of the Metropolitan Joint Steering Committee, probably works due to easy informal ties, rather than to any set of rules adopted (Khan 1997). One report aimed at input for the Government Green Paper on Local Government highlights battles over turf involving staffing, administrative and development issues (Khan 1997). This is very much less acute a problem in Durban than in other South African cities but it will be settled at a national level, in part because the demands for and against Unicity single-tier government elsewhere are so aggrieved.

While the Metro government has already begun delivering facilities, especially water and electricity into the township and squatter perimeter of what was once KwaZulu, there remains another problem of jurisdiction over such areas as the construction and maintenance of housing. Before the political transition, KwaZulu land was placed under the Zulu king as the Ingonyama Trust; land administered in this way cannot readily be accessed by the city without a process of political negotiation that continued after 1996 (Khan 1997). In effect, this means that various aspects of the administration of most formerly black areas are under the control of the province of KwaZulu-Natal with its IFP majority government.[49] There was not only a problem in terms of political conflict here, but one in terms of an administrative legacy that is shambolic and inept, based at best on personalised patronage networks and stronger on avoiding costs than delivering any services. Thus only from the creation of the Unicity in 2000 could a unified urban state form claim to be effectively in charge of the entire metropolitan space, and particularly with regard to key economic issues facing the poorest half of the population.

Perhaps more fundamental, however, are shifts in the whole economic order which will ironically, just as the city has come under the control of forces that in theory represent the bulk of poor and previously under- or unrepresented people, make it hard to deliver in the way that delivery was made for the core white minority in a virtuous Fordist cycle of production and distribution.

A striking absence in the language of the 'growth coalition' is production. In 1991, McCarthy noted that with some 213 000 workers, manufacturing remained the largest single employer in the formal sector in Durban (compared to 164 000 workers in commerce, the next largest sector, for instance) (McCarthy n.d.: 12). The national government sees Durban, facing as it does east towards Asia, as the most logical site for developing industrial production with an export orientation. This is very much how the Ministry of Trade and Industry envision the core of the future South African economy as mineral export inevitably fades.[50] Nevertheless, industrialists among others question whether this represents a serious industrial policy with direction and backbone (Interview, Ted Waldburger, 04.02.97). In Durban certainly the impact of factory insurgency and the very successes of unionisation seem to be important discouraging factors. While Durban industries increase their share of manufacturing employment nationally (especially since 1980), the pie that is being sliced is a diminishing one. The growth industries in the city are paper, sectors of auto components and metal products and, especially, chemicals.[51] These are largely capital intensive industries; the re-equipment and modernisation of plant in auto components and other industries from Durban's diversified base tends to involve downsizing that will lead to deconcentration of workers and greater control over them, and into shedding jobs, not increasing them (Interviews, Terry Rosenberg, 24.11.97; Ted Waldburger, 04.02.97). Of the few jobs industry creates, most are not in the dominant big firms (McCarthy n.d.: 16). One industrialist interviewed specifically remarked on and deplored the virtual disappearance of manufacturing from the plans of the 'growth coalition' (Interviews, Gareth Coleman, 21.11.97; Ted Waldburger, 04.02.97).[52]

McMenamin shares with Metropolitan Council Executive Committee chair Margaret Winter (1996–2000) or predecessors from the old regime the view that the most important economic function of city government is to create and sustain jobs (Interviews, Gordon Haygarth, 09.09.96; Vivian McMenamin, 30.09.97; Margaret Winter, 03.09.97). Yet the old familiar system whereby the city made available flat land on favourable terms to industrialists prepared to employ large numbers of Durban residents, the central basis for what I have called 'racial Fordism' in the city, has lost its purchase. The principal exception could be found in what is now termed the Inner West local government zone, with the former municipality of Pinetown at its core. Pinetown's enterprising Town Clerk continued to offer favourable land deals and rates rebates to firms prepared to relocate there. Much of his success, tied to what was formerly the KwaZulu Finance Corporation, has been linked to attracting Taiwanese firms, often aiming to evade restrictions on goods entry to the USA, to manufacture (or perhaps just add limited value) in South Africa and who are attracted to a location near a major port.[53] Some of this success, quite significant in the early 1990s, may be attributed to favourable fiscal measures no longer in place.

In general, contemporary land users do not need such extensive sites in the age of flexible specialisation in production. They are well able to service uneven land surfaces without unreasonable costs and they are very much more likely to be orientated to commercial, transshipment and warehousing purposes than to constructing facilities for the production of manufactured goods (Interview, Alan Murrin and Hayden Osborne, 15.10.96). Rail links have lost much of their importance. Given the changing nature of manufacturing, moreover, it may well be that today such purposes are apt to lead to the employment of more individuals than conventional factories (Freund 1992; Interviews, T. Chetty and Neels Brink, 16.01.97; Keith Matthias, 10.10.96).

Critical to the relationships embedded in 'racial Fordism' was the construction of council housing, significantly to the white working class but on a particularly big scale to Indian and Coloured families.[54] Housing provision is now confined either to those who can purchase reasonable quality housing or to the construction of absolutely basic structures with a small state subsidy (Interview, Keith Matthias, 10.10.96). Indeed, where long-term employment is an economic phenomenon to be avoided when possible by capital, the role of housing construction except for immediate profit is enormously diminished. It has become far less desirable for capital to intervene in the provision of the means of reproduction for a proletariat.

A number of interviewees from both business and government (thus including ANC spokespeople) made it clear that it was critical to start downsizing the local state itself and shift much of the service work actually performed by the city to contract firms.[55] This represents a large change. Representatives of the old regime are proud of their success in enskilling large numbers of workers of all colours and having had on hand an impressive range of hands-on expertise and skill in infrastructural work critical for the city (Interviews, Gordon Haygarth, 09.09.96; Margaret Winter, 03.09.97).[56] One wonders whether privatisation would not disperse and diminish a historically generated potential.

Otherwise, the city has had only limited means of intervening in the training and education of its citizens in the past (Interviews, Crispin Hemson, 01.09.96; Margaret Winter, 03.09.97).[57] One informed source referred to contemporary Durban as a 'skills desert' (Interview, Alan Murrin and Hayden Osborne, 15.10.96).[58] A weakness for Durban in future development certainly lies in its relatively low skill, low design component work-force: there is little sense yet that the city can take steps to alter this even though critical international literature suggests that inter-locking high skill, small to medium enterprise industrial nexuses may have the best chance of taking advantage of the changing nature of international capitalism (Piore and Sabel 1984).

Labour leaders are respectfully consulted by business and the state and co-operate effectively in making the big plans happen (Interview, John Bryce, 06.09.96). But organised labour noticeably lacks a vision for urban transformation (Interview, Vivian McMenamin, 30.09.97).[59] Despite the great organisational strength and loyalty built up by the labour movement in the 20 years after the great strike of 1972, the failure to evolve a genuine working class politics, a sense of direction for the city or ability to impact on plans made elsewhere represents a notable historic absence (Interview, Gareth Coleman, 21.11.97).

New political representatives are sometimes naively anxious to redistribute the traditional benefits of urban economic life, for instance in tourism, to the traditional locales of residence of black people who were formerly marginalised.[60] It is obviously not very realistic to imagine that complex economic activity, still less that orientated to middle class consumer services, will prefer to relocate to an atmosphere of poverty, squalor or insecurity. And yet such representatives are right to worry about what French urbanists call the *désenclavement*, perhaps best translated as integration, of isolated, solipsistic poor communities, into the general life of the city. Continued advocacy in planning circles of 'densification' is limited in application so far.

There is a growing spatial decentring of Durban, if less advanced than in many other parts of the world, which is difficult if not impossible for city authorities to control. This could be enabling for some poor communities (burgeoning of produce markets and clothing manufacture in the largely Indian working class neighbourhoods of Chatsworth), but the main tendency is for economic activity to move into 'edge city' complexes on the American model, best accessed from new frontiers of affluent suburbia. Mt Edgecombe-Umhlanga Rocks, in good part propelled by the entrepreneurial activities of Tongaat-Hulett, is the northern hub for that kind of movement overtaking Durban.

A key struggle in contemporary Durban must be for the future of the city centre. The centre has been vacated by the commercial bourgeoisie (high class shops, boutiques, restaurants, etc.) but thus far it retains its importance as a financial headquarters while maintaining an extremely lively hive of activity for the working class/lower middle class bulk of the population of whom only a small percentage are white (Interviews, Keith Matthias, 10.10.96; Eddie Morton, 11.11.97). The Workshop shopping complex, constituted a decade ago for an affluent white clientele, is busier than ever today. The fate of the growing number of hawkers, whom the bourgeoisie find a noisome nuisance, is always in the balance: benevolent plans to confine them in suitable quarters of town are somehow never quite effected (Interviews, John Bryce, 06.09.96; Mark Lowe, 23.09.97; Roger Sishi, 25.08.97; Sbu Sithole, 23.09.97). How this city centre which controls access to the port and the Golden Mile will evolve is very uncertain. Its decline could have significant consequences for the financial basis of city rates.

The trajectory of the emerging growth coalition in Metropolitan Durban may well represent the best possible plans that can be promoted in the age of globalisation, offering an expansion of the economy based above all on Durban's location and infrastructure. This may promote jobs indirectly far more than directly and also create the financial basis whereby services can be delivered to poor people (Interviews, Keith Matthias, 10.10.96; Sbu Sithole, 23.09.97).[61] However, I would argue that these plans may do little to affect the historic peripheralisation of the poor.[62] One can worry about the poor diffusion of skills, especially those which can be the basis for generating new economic activities.

Moreover, public-private partnerships can become a mask, if the state is weak, for simply subsidising the initiatives of powerful private interests (Interview, Margaret Winter, 03.09.97). Growth coalition strategies may reinforce the power of a relatively small number of big firms, allow for some others to come forward, whether through advantages already held within a part of the city community or through for instance, shifts in who gets city tenders, on a basis open to all colours. Yet Durban badly needs to become the site of a process by which accumulation is far more spread out spatially and in class and race terms.[63] The reproduction of existing patterns of accumulation – social and economic – and the fact that, so far, it is big capital that is most able to take advantage of the limits globalisation is placing on the regulatory capacity of the state remain the dominant aspects of economic development in Durban. How the state, even if captured by a different array of forces, could turn this around more effectively, remains to be seen.

NOTES

1. Mayor's Minute, 1974/75, 3.
2. Natal Archives Depot. Archives of the Town Clerk, 5/2/7/4/1-2. *Post-War Development Reports, 1943*, A.L. Barns, chairman.
3. It remains a major employer in Durban although corporate headquarters are in Johannesburg.
4. I am also indebted to Jeff McCarthy for ideas on this.
5. Durban Boundaries Commission file, 3/DBN 14/4/1-3, Natal Archives Depot; Archives of the Town Clerk.
6. The centrality of Durban High School, a large boys' high school that followed the social model of the private boarding schools in rural Natal, has been mentioned in this connection.
7. See Purcell (1974: 192) for the role of the Durban Club which excluded not only women and men of colour but also Afrikaners and Jews from membership.
8. See also Padayachee in this volume.
9. Mayor's Minute, 1981/82.
10. Although Crispin Hemson (Interview) pointed out that the tendering process continued to be a site where special influences could be exerted.
11. For the power of the white unions, such as the tramway workers', see McCarthy 199l.
12. Purcell argues that the political power of municipalities is considerably greater in many American cities. However, a purposeful directive bureaucracy may make the economic influence of the city administration in the context all the greater.
13. Mayor's Minute, 1974/75. These kinds of figures are and remain problematic. How to actually assess the real economic significance of tourism remains unresolved and unexamined figures still attract media attention and are often uncritically repeated.
14. See for example the Mayor's Minutes, 1970/71, 9 on shark nets, 17 on clearing 'hippies' from the beachfront.
15. Gordon Haygarth (Interview) pointed to the lease granted to the high-rise Elangeni Hotel, replacing an older structure, the Torquay, as critical in the renewal of the Golden Mile for instance.
16. 'After 1909 beerhall revenue was ploughed into the maintenance and establishment of migrant worker barracks, beerhalls, hostels, and beer breweries, as well as into the costs of police and Native Administrations in the town. Until 1929, the year in which a mass boycott of Durban's municipal beerhalls was instituted, Durban was the only town in South Africa with a self-supporting Native Revenue Account' (La Hausse, 'Drink and Cultural Innovation in Durban: The Origins of the Beerhall in South Africa, 1902–16' in Crush and Ambler 1992: 79).
17. Natal Archives Depot. Archives of the Town Clerk 5/2/7/4/1-2. *Post-War Development Reports*, A.L. Barns, chairman.
18. Natal Archives Depot. Archives of the Town Clerk 3/DBN 14/4/1-3, *Durban Boundaries Commission*, memorandum by Councillor H.H. Kemp.
19. Ibid.
20. Natal Archives Depot. Archives of the Town Clerk. 5/2/7/4/1-2. *Post-War Development Reports.*
21. Mayor's Minutes for 1970/71 for instance. After 1972 the city lost control of facilitation in those areas transferred to KwaZulu.
22. Freund 1994, especially chapter 5.

23. Purcell, 1974: 221.
24. For the endless war fought against hawkers, see Mayor's Minute, 1975/76, 29 and Nesvåg in this volume.
25. For recent comment see the writing of Knut Nustad, 1996 and 1997. The harsh perspective of some of this work is in glaring contrast to the typical modernist thrust of South African state thinking which gears itself by and large on classic development ideology.
26. See the case of the gypsies highlighted in Amor Vieira, 'Housing for Diversity: Roma-Gypsies in Madrid' in Beall 1997, as an example. Vieira shows that the best of modernist intentions were unable to accommodate this distinctive, wayward section of the population.
27. At their peak, they included 11 of the 30 city councillors.
28. For the creation of the Beach and City Steering Committee operation through a 'new willingness to act in co-operation with the private sector', see Mayor's Minute, 1984/85, 2.
29. The possibility of hosting an international orchid show led to the first conference facility being erected in 1977. Mayor's Minute 1984/85, 1986/87 where the success of this venture begins to be attested, 68.
30. Mayor's Minute, 1985/86. Construction of the Workshop was initially opposed as a threat by the traditional city commercial interests (Interview, Gordon Haygarth, 09.09.96). The city effectively invested R150 million in this project (Interview, Andrzej Kiepela, 03.10.96).
31. Only finally put into effect in 1991–92.
32. Mayor's Minute, 1985/86.
33. The 'civic movement' certainly took up economic issues. It devised an alternative rent formula suitable for the large amount of council housing in Indian and Coloured working class neighbourhoods and proposed alternative budgets. Whether one could actually support claims that it had evolved a holistic alternative and radical economic outlook on the city is less clear; there was little real consideration of growth, as opposed to redistribution, issues. This is nonetheless what some activists would claim (Interview, Pravin Gordhan, 23.01.98).
34. Robinson and Boldogh 1994. Peter Johnston (Interview) saw the composite negotiation process as one whereby business experimented with and abandoned development plans in response to 'community' reactions while working to construct a new system of 'trade-offs'. He sees this as the foundation-stone for the growth coalition that would emerge after the democratisation of local government in 1996.
35. See also Terry Rosenberg talk, Durban Metro Business Conference, 27.10.97.
36. See Annual Reports for 1971 and later which show opposition to demands for land from the state, for instance, for the construction of an airport site at La Mercy which went through in 1978.
37. Ibid.
38. Property sales represented in Tongaat-Hulett turnover 1.9 per cent, 3.5 per cent and 3.8 per cent rising between 1995 and 1997 but 4.4 per cent, 8.1 per cent and 9.2 per cent of total profits for those years. Tongaat-Hulett Corporation, Annual Reports.
39. Annual Report, 1995.
40. One could for instance draw a dramatic contrast with the typically African portrait drawn by Mohamed Halfani in 'The Challenge of Urban Governance in Africa'

in Swilling 1997: 'The pervasiveness of "informalism" has reduced the scope of formal management to a very minimum sphere of urban life', p. 16. Or see Stren and White 1989.

41. The Unicity structure created in 2000 eliminated sub-structures. This number of old units reflects the 20 000 boundary.
42. Harvey Molotch, 'The City as a Growth Machine', *American Journal of Sociology*, LXXVII, 1976. Molotch's work, highly critical of American style boosterism, is a touchstone of looking critically at growth coalitions.
43. Khan 1997, explains the process by which local government was established in terms of the Leadership Accord of 1993, the boundaries decisions of 1994 and the subsequent resignation and re-hiring of staff.
44. See, for example, the Green Paper on Local Government issued by the Ministry for Provincial Affairs and Constitutional Development, October 1997 or the speech of Durban Mayor Obed Mlaba, *International Conference on Economic Policy Issues*, University of Durban-Westville, 24 April 1997.
45. Speech by Murray Grindrod, chairman of Grindcor, Durban Metro Business Conference, 21.10. 96.
46. See Nicholas Falk, 'Turning the Tide: British Experience in Regenerating Urban Docklands' and other contributions in Hoyle and Pinder 1992, who make the point that establishing an agreement between different authorities is the most critical and difficult aspect of renewing dockland areas in Europe.
47. Whether the corridors will be backed by actual capital investment is less clear. The planning is relatively notional and depends on private sector commitment to a predominant extent. For the continued salience of development backed by government and orientated to capital-intensive projects manipulating and beneficiating heavy materials (ultimately using the mining industry as their model), see Fine and Rustomjee 1996.
48 . Margaret Winter and Sbu Sithole (Interviews) were, however, reasonably positive about the present inter-relationships.
49. Sbu Sithole (Interview) was especially important in explaining the ramifications of this situation. But I am also grateful to Glen Robbins for his perspective on the issue and Keith Matthias (Interview).
50. Speech of Minister Alec Erwin, Durban Metro Business Conference, 21.10.96.
51. For an interpretation of what continues to be the dominant thrust in South African industrial development see Fine and Rustomjee 1996.
52. Gareth Coleman suggested that industrialists are far less apt to get involved with the politics of the local economy.
53. This initiative operates on circuits quite independent of the growing economic initiatives emanating from City Hall. It is linked to funding from the KwaZulu-Natal Marketing Initiative which comes in large part from the province (Interview, Ossie Gorven, 08.12.97). For a stimulating and suggestive introduction to the driving force of Taiwanese industrial investment in South Africa, see Hart 1996.
54. See for instance Bailey 1987.
55. For instance, Mark Lowe, Alan Murrin and Hayden Osborne, and Terry Rosenberg expressed significant misgivings here.
56. Margaret Winter (Interview) pointed out some continuing potential here.
57. Limited initiatives such as the ABET basic skills programme reveal the lack of sophisticated training schemes rather than the obverse (Interview, Alan Murrin and Hayden Osborne, 15.10.96).

58. Craft skills are rarely present in the ex-township schools although informal knowledge is beginning to be passed down in resident families, largely amongst men. The attempts by the KwaZulu government to engender craft skills formally have not been very successful. The diffusion of craft and business skills amongst white, Indian and Coloured men and to some extent women makes them far better able to cope with a corporate economy anxious to limit access to secure employment in the interests of profitable flexibility.
59. One interviewee argued that the Congress of South African Trade Unions (COSATU) had in fact been the backbone behind the original ANC economic views on the city typical of the early 1990s. However, these views had been subtly relegated to the background over time (Interview, Andrzej Kiepela, 03.10.96).
60. Tourism, historically so important in the way city officials cast their sense of the developing economy of Durban, retains some of its allure. But there is uncertainty about what direction to take tourism. Clearly, the historic patterns are of limited relevance (Interviews, Felicity Attwell, 01.09.96; Andrzej Kiepela, 03.10.96; Mark Lowe, 23.09.97; Peter Mansfield, 11.09.96; Vivian McMenamin, 30.09.97).
61. An ANC representative claimed that some 43 per cent of the capital budget for 1997 went to previously disadvantaged areas. See Michael Sutcliffe, MPP, in *Business Day*, 02.09.97. Khan (1997: 15) reports that a new rates system is to be instituted by 2002 that will be based on real market value of all land and the replacement costs of the built property.
62. It is far easier to develop plans to assist the improvement of amenities in established townships than to service the tumultuous and disorganised (or unofficially organised) squatter communities, which seem in effect to *get in the way* of orderly planning (Interview, Alan Murrin and Hayden Osborne, 15.10.96).
63. The Economic Strategy Unit has recognised this problem to the extent of creating the Tekweni Business Service Centre aimed at black small businesses that might be enticed into production and tendering activities. There is an enormous way to go here. Vivian McMenamin (Interview) estimates that the city government itself represents some 12 per cent of the urban GNP.

REFERENCES

Bailey, D. 1987. 'The Origins of Phoenix 1957–76: The Durban City Council and the Indian Housing Question'. M.A. thesis, University of Natal.

Beall, J. 1997. *A City for All: Valuing Difference and Working with Diversity*. London and New Jersey: Zed Press.

Bjorvig, A.C. 1994. 'Durban 1824–1910: The Formation of a Settler Elite and its Role in the Development of a Colonial City'. D.Phil. thesis, University of Natal, Pietermaritzburg.

Cohen, M.A. et al. 1996. *Preparing for the Urban Future: Global Pressures and Local Forces*. Washington: Woodrow Wilson Center Press.

Cronin, W. 1991. *Nature's Metropolis: Chicago and the Great West*. New York: W.W. Norton.

Fine, B. and Z. Rustomjee. 1996. *The Political Economy of South Africa: From Minerals-Energy Complex to Industrialisation*. London: Hurst.

Freund, B. 1992. 'A New Industrial Revolution? Technological Change and its Implications for South African Labour'. *Social Dynamics*, 18, 1.

——. 1994. *Insiders and Outsiders: The Indian Working Class of Durban, 1910–1990.* Pietermaritzburg, Portsmouth and London: University of Natal Press, Heinemann and James Currey.

——. 2000. 'The City of Durban: Towards a Structural Analysis of the Economic Growth and Character of a South African City'. In D. Anderson and R. Rathbone (eds). *Africa's Urban Past.* London and Portsmouth: James Currey and Heinemann.

Green, L.P. 1957. *A History of Local Government in South Africa.* Cape Town: Juta.

Hart, G. 1996. 'The Agrarian Question and Industrial Dispersal in South Africa: Agri-Industrial Linkages through Asian Lenses'. In H. Bernstein (ed.). *The Agrarian Question in South Africa.* London: Frank Cass.

Hoyle, B.S. and D.A. Pinder (eds). 1992. *European Port Cities in Transition.* London: Belhaven.

Jay, R. 1981. *Joseph Chamberlain: A Political Study.* Oxford: Clarendon Press.

Katzen, M. 1961. *Industry in Greater Durban, Part 1: Its Growth and Structure.* Pietermaritzburg: Town and Regional Planning Commission.

Khan, F. 1997. 'The Case of Durban: From Forty Odd Local Councils to Six Local Councils and a Metro or from Forty Odd Councils to Seven Local Councils'. Metropolitan Case Study as Input to Local Government Green Paper.

Kuper, L., H. Watts and R. Davies. 1958. *Durban: A Study in Racial Ecology.* London: Jonathan Cape.

Maharaj, B. 1992. 'The Spatial Impress of the Central and Local States: The Group Areas Act in Durban'. In D. Smith (ed.), *The Apartheid City and Beyond.* London: Routledge.

McCarthy, J. 1991. 'Planning Issues and the Political Economy of the Local State: An Historical Case Study of Durban'. *Urban Forum,* 2, 2.

——. 'Durban: South Africa's Global Competitor?' Unpublished.

Molotch, H. 1976. 'The City as a Growth Machine'. *American Journal of Sociology,* 56.

Nustad, K. 1996. 'The Politics of Development: Power and Changing Discourses in South Africa'. *Cambridge Anthropology,* 19, 1.

——. 1997. 'The Ends of Development: Comments on an Obituary'. *Forum for Development Studies,* 1.

Piore, M. and C. Sabel. 1984. *The Second Industrial Divide.* New York: Basic Books.

Purcell, J.H.F. 1974. 'Durban, South Africa: Local Politics in a Plural Society'. Ph.D. thesis, UCLA.

Roberts, R. 1994. 'Business, Politics and Municipal Socialism'. In J. Turner (ed.). *Businessmen and Politics: Studies of Business Activity in British Politics.* London: Heinemann.

Robinson, J. and C. Boldogh. 1994. 'Operation Jumpstart: An Urban Growth Initiative in the Durban Functional Region'. In R. Tomlinson (ed.). *Urban Development Planning.* Johannesburg: Witwatersrand University Press.

Scott, D. 1994. 'Communal Space Construction: The Rise and Fall of Clairwood and District'. Ph.D. thesis, University of Natal.

Stren, R.E. and R.R. White. 1989. *African Cities in Crisis.* Boulder, San Francisco and London: Westview.

Swilling, M. 1997. *Governing Africa's Cities.* Johannesburg: Witwatersrand University Press.

Tongaat-Hulett Corporation (previously Tongaat Group). Annual Reports.

Werlin, H.H. 1965. 'Nairobi City Council: A Study in Comparative Local Government'. *Comparative Studies in Society and History*, 8.
Wilson, E. 1991. *The Sphinx in the City*. London: Virago.

Primary Sources

Durban. Mayor's Minutes.
Natal Archives Depot.
Archives of the Town Clerk.
3/DBN 14/4/1–3 Durban Boundaries Commission.
5/2/7/4/1–2 Post-War Development Reports.

Interviews

Felicity Attwell, Durban Unlimited, 01.09.96 (telephone).
John Bryce, Durban Chamber of Commerce and Industry, 06.09.96.
T. Chetty and Neels Brink, Tongaat-Hulett, 16.01.97.
Gareth Coleman, Regional Economic Forum, 21.11.97.
Pravin Gordhan, MP, ex-civic activist, 23.01.98.
Ossie Gorven, former City Treasurer, 08.12.97.
Hercules Hattingh, Town Clerk, Inner West local government and Director, KMI, 26.08.96.
Gordon Haygarth, MPP (ex-Town Clerk, Durban), 09.09.96.
Crispin Hemson, University of Natal, ex-councillor, 01.09.96.
Peter Johnston, Urban Strategy Unit, Durban Metro, 21.08.96.
Andrzej Kiepela, Consultant, 03.10.96.
Mark Lowe, Councillor, 23.09.97.
Peter Mansfield, consultant (ex City Council, ex-chair MANCO), 11.09.96.
Keith Matthias, Director, Growth and Development Facilitation, Metro Durban, 10.10.96.
Vivian McMenamin, Director, Urban Strategy, 30.09.97.
Eddie Morton, Town Clerk, 11.11.97.
Alan Murrin and Hayden Osborne, Kuphuka, 15.10.96.
Joe Nene, Councillor, South-central local government, ex-trade unionist, 17.12.97.
Terry Rosenberg, McCarthy Group, 24.11.97.
Roger Sishi, Councillor, 25.08.97.
Sbu Sithole, Councillor, 23.09.97.
Ted Waldburger, Turner and Newall, 04.02.97.
Margaret Winter, chair MANCO, 03.09.97.

Public Conferences

Durban Metro Business Conference, 21.10.96.
——, 27.10.97.
International Conference on Economic Policy Issues, 24/25.04.97.
Second Tourism Strategy Workshop, 13.06.97.
Tekwini Business Service Centre Workshop, 01.10.97.

CHAPTER TWO

Economic Development for a New Era

An Examination of the Adoption of Explicit Economic Development Strategies by Durban Local Government since 1994

PETER HALL and GLEN ROBBINS

South Africa's 1994 democratic national elections and the subsequent local government elections launched the country into a period of far-reaching institutional restructuring. If this was not enough of a challenge, the political changes also ended the country's isolation and heralded an intensified exposure of the region to global economic processes. It is in this context that South African cities have been forced to engage in serious soul-searching about their role in a new political order while facing up to complex and dynamic global economic forces. While the South African local state has certainly been an influential economic player in the past, it is only now that an attempt is being made to ensure that economic development is not merely the consequence of traditional local government activities (regulation, service provision, infrastructure maintenance and planning). Rather, economic development has become a guiding rationale behind the myriad of existing, and a host of new, responsibilities. Concepts relating to the city's role as an economic agent, a mediator of economic processes and a provider of economic services have been central to the post-apartheid policy formulation. Clauses relating to the economic development responsibilities of local government in the new constitution and local government legislation have formalised this new arena of operation for the local state. However, the policy tools to fulfill these mandates are weak, and the possibilities and limits of the new focus need to be understood as products of the political and bureauractic context in which they were created.

This chapter explores the new focus through an examination of the economic development strategies adopted by the Durban Metropolitan Council as outlined in the Durban Metropolitan Council Green Paper on Economic Development (DMC 1996). It is suggested that this framework document is the product of a rather untidy Hegelian dialectic process. At times contradictory influences have been moulded into a set of strategies in an attempt by the authors to deal adequately with the complexity and uncertainty of the economic development terrain confronting local government. The complexity of the influences referred to above can be seen in references the document makes to issues such as the varied impacts of globalisation, pressures to confront problems related to poverty and the necessity of facilitating a more conducive environment for capital accumulation. In such an environment an understanding of the relationship between structure and agency is critical both in terms of policy makers identifying appropriate strategies and in terms of a critique of the resultant policies.

A secondary goal of this chapter is to add to the small but growing literature on the local state and on local economic development in South Africa. In an article reviewing the development of the local state in Durban until the 1970s, McCarthy (1991) suggests that the political economy of the local state has been under-explored because of an assumption 'that South Africa is relatively unique in having a highly dependent set of local political processes and local political structures' (40). His historical review of urban planning and local state boundary restructuring suggests that the local state did indeed play a more independent role under apartheid than was previously thought. This view is supported by Pillay (1994) who reviews the period 1984–94 to conclude that 'the experience of Durban has to be looked at in terms of the local conjunction of different restructuring forces (deriving from and operating at different spatial levels) with the specific social, cultural, political and institutional circumstances of the locality itself' (83).

This Durban literature connects with the work on other South African cities, including Parnell's (1988) study of housing in Johannesburg in the 1930s, Western's (1981) classic book on the impact of the Group Areas Act in Cape Town, and Nel and Rogerson's (1995 and 1996) work on the history of local economic development. Mabin (1995) has reviewed the process of local government negotiation in Johannesburg, pointing to the way in which a new metropolitanism was articulated during this process, while Nel (1997) charts an emerging local economic development movement. All this work points to the importance of analysis of the local dimensions of policy responses to the changes impacting on South African cities. Hopefully this chapter also begins to address Parnell's (1997) call for 'attention to the internal struggles within and between government departments . . . the import of these sometimes petty battles for the future of cities is great in uncovering assumptions and objectives of state officials vested with the powers to transform the cities' (903).

This work has gained further importance by virtue of the new constitution of South Africa which establishes local authorities as an equal sphere of government.[1] The constitution explicitly tasks local government with social and economic development (RSA 1996a: 152(1e)) within an overall context of co-operative inter-governmental relations; this is often referred to as the 'social and economic development' clause. National government policy statements, and recent legislative reforms, have lent continued support to this formal role. The *White Paper on Local Government* (RSA 1998a) makes considerable reference to local government's need to get involved in economic development work, although it remains very vague as to how this should happen. Legislation following the Municipal Structures Bill (RSA 1998b) vested more executive power in the hands of mayors and created mega- or unicities that ended the two-tier metropolitan system. These constitutional and legislative changes have elevated the importance of analysing inter-city variations in developmental capacities, policies and outcomes.

The chapter begins with a narrative describing the emergence of economic development strategies in the Durban Metropolitan Council and a discussion of the context within which this policy work occurred. This will be followed by a presentation of the theoretical tools which are deemed most appropriate in analysing policy processes within the local state environment. These tools will then be applied to the Durban local government environment in an attempt to unpack the dynamics which have been at the core of a process which, while having universally recognisable elements, is also the product of a unique set of circumstances and actors which are likely to be at the heart of Durban's growth into the new century.

Local Government Restructuring

The apartheid system of local government was weak and highly fragmented. Greater Durban was administered by over 60 separate authorities. For white residents, local authorities were directly elected, but the powers of local authorities were limited. The largest and most powerful local authority was the Durban City Council. As the economic core of Durban expanded in a T-shape, to north and south along the coast and to the west along the corridor leading to the interior, new white local authorities were created around the expanding suburbs (for example, Pinetown, Amanzimtoti). Some of these jurisdictions, notably Pinetown, started to challenge the old core city in terms of economic importance. The administration of the Indian and Coloured areas (for example, Chatsworth, Phoenix, Merebank) fell to a combination of white local authorities and local management committees. Apart from the oldest townships of Chesterville and Clermont, most of the African townships of greater Durban fell within the homeland of KwaZulu (for example, Inanda, KwaMashu). The failings of local government fed directly into the concentration of poverty and absence of basic urban services in informal settlements such as greater Inanda (see Hindson, Byerly and Morris 1993).

Not only did apartheid local government fail to deliver basic urban services; it was also not equipped to meet the economic challenges resulting from South Africa's renewed exposure to global economic forces. For example, the direct impacts of trade liberalisation vary considerably from sector to sector. Coetzee et al. (1997) suggest that output and employment will decline in the clothing, textiles, wood and wood products and motor vehicle sectors, all of which are strongly represented in the Durban local economy (DCC 1995). Organised business and labour in these sectors have generally looked to national government for assistance. However, of particular local concern is the fact that many of these sectors are employment intensive, certainly considerably more so than the petro-chemical sector which is apparently doing very well under the new trade regime.

Globalisation does not only impact directly on local productive sectors, but also indirectly creates new dilemmas for economic development. For example, positive effects of increasing trade can be seen in the increased activity levels in the Durban harbour. The location of Durban on the Indian Ocean is also seen as particularly beneficial in terms of trade with south- and east-Asia and Australasia (Robbins 1997). However, the increased prominence of the port in the local and national economy sets up its own set of difficult issues; pressure for expansion of harbour facilities has required a major re-evaluation of the physical and economic space the port occupies in the city. This has added to the uncertainties confronting Central Business District (CBD) businesses, property-owners and those in the tourist industry. The fact that port-specific decisions are made almost exclusively at a national level has left little opportunity for local government to make an input into strategic processes which are likely to have a major impact on its future (such as the location of a new generation container handling terminal). Proposed moves by national government toward the restructuring of South Africa's transport parastatals are likely to have a profound impact on the local economy in the years that follow implementation.

The changing macro-economic context does not necessarily point to reduced growth performance; in fact there are some very positive signs for the Durban economy (CDE 1996). However, the changes do point to some very hard decisions about the future of the local economy. The old series of small, weak and fragmented local governments was especially ill-prepared to meet these challenges.

In 1996, the new Metropolitan Council area of Durban covered 1 366 km^2 and included over 2.3 million people (DMC 1996). The metropolitan boundaries were influenced by provincial and national political factors, which kept certain tribal authority areas functionally part of the city and out of the Metropolitan Council area. These boundaries were significantly expanded before the December 2000 local government elections (by approximately an extra 1 000 km^2 and including almost one million extra people), but, at least initially, an important portion of the peri-urban poor were excluded from the metropolitan jurisdiction.

Politically, the erstwhile Metropolitan Council was comprised of proportionally elected councillors from across the whole area, and indirectly elected representatives of six local councils which fell within the Metropolitan Council area. The ceremonial head of the Council was an indirectly elected mayor, while the Executive Committee acted as the highest decision-making body apart from a full session of the Council. The Council operated through a series of standing committees, to which departments reported. Following the 1996 elections, the balance of power was held by the African National Congress (ANC), with representation from the National Party, Democratic Party, Minority Front and Inkatha Freedom Party, candidates representing Ratepayers Associations and some elected as independents. Subsequent to the December 2000 elections there has been the introduction of a single Unicity Council, where, under the provisions of the Municipal Systems and Municipal Structures Acts the Executive Committee has full Council powers and is chaired by the mayor. However, as the focus of this chapter is on the late 1990s little detailed reference will be made to the post December 2000 period.

As noted in the introduction, post-apartheid local government is tasked with a range of social and economic development objectives in the new constitution. Functional areas of concurrent national and provincial/local competence and of exclusive provincial/local competence are respectively listed in Schedules 4 and 5 (RSA 1996a). Part B of each schedule lays out the areas of concurrent and exclusive local government competence. Exclusive areas of local government competence include important areas for local economic intervention, such as street trading, markets, beaches and public recreation infrastructure, and a range of urban amenity services. Concurrent areas of local government competence include municipal planning, tourism, some public works, harbours (excluding international shipping matters) and trading regulations. The new constitution thus creates considerable space and responsibility for local economic development strategy-making and implementation.

While constituting local government as a more powerful sphere of governance, there has been a complementary tendency to structure local government into relatively large units that combine richer white and poorer African residential areas. This was informed by the desire to achieve redistribution within a common tax base. However, it is important to note that the idea of a metropolitan tier of government had already acquired some powerful support in Durban before the constitutional changes.

First, one of the reforms of the late apartheid era (after 1976) was the formation of regional structures responsible for bulk service delivery – called Joint Services Boards (JSBs). The Port Natal-Ebodwe JSB established a fund to support tourism development projects, and thus precedents for intra-metropolitan redistribution and support for economic infrastructure were established. Second, local businessmen and land-owners supported regional economic research and policy-making processes which gave rise to the notion of the Durban Functional Region (DFR). The DFR is larger than the existing Metropolitan Council area, and included much of the tribal authority areas that fell outside the metropolitan jurisdiction between 1996 and 2000. A leading institution in this process was the Tongaat-Hulett Planning Forum. It is no accident that Tongaat-Hulett, a sugar company, is the major owner of land to the north and west of the city and that future expansion of the city will take place on former sugar-cane land. The Tongaat-Hulett Planning Forum's other significant contribution to defining the new system of local government was the sponsoring of a local fiscal policy framework and financial planning model for the city. It is also worth noting that in 2000 the Durban Metropolitan Council and Moreland (Tongaat-Hulett's property arm) entered into a joint venture to work towards the development of a Marine Theme Park at Durban's Point and a mixed land use node to the north of the city at an area called Effingham Avoca.

Even though there was wide support for the notion of metropolitan government in Durban, it would be incorrect to over-emphasize the local specificity of the impacts of the JSB and DFR. Across South Africa in the early 1990s, decentralised city-level negotiation forums advanced the idea of strong metropolitan government in parallel with the national constitutional negotiations.[2]

When the Durban Metropolitan Council Green Paper on Economic Development (DMC 1996) was written, local government restructuring in Durban had resulted in a two-tiered system. The Durban Metropolitan Council, which consisted of directly elected and indirectly elected representatives of the local councils, was responsible for bulk services and other issues which were seen as cutting across jurisdictional lines. The sphere of economic development had been identified as a key metropolitan function, although as we shall see, some uncertainty remained around the allocation of strategy and implementation functions. The six local councils were responsible for a range of local amenity and planning functions. Local councils consisted of indirectly proportionally elected and directly elected Ward Councillors.

The re-organisation of local government proceeded in an uneven way. The local councils differed considerably in terms of their socio-economic strength, and organisational or bureaucratic capacity. The North and South Central Local Councils shared the CBD and contained the port and much of the industrial base of Durban. They also shared the bulk of the administration of the former Durban City Council; this included departments responsible for informal trade (which regulates the city markets and street trading), parks and recreation (which looks after key tourist infrastructure) and city planning officials. In the Inner West Local Council, the administration of the former City of Pinetown dominated the bureaucracy. These relatively strong administrations resisted any tendency by the Metropolitan Council to control their activities. In the other, generally poorer, local council areas, the administrations were re-constituted out of various existing administrations, and in many cases, staffing and other capacity levels were clearly inadequate for the tasks at hand. For example, in 1997, the North Local Council had only one relatively junior planner to deal with development in the most rapidly growing portion of the city. In such cases, the provincial authorities played an active role in supporting local council planning processes.

The Metropolitan Council had taken over the staff and functions of some key large service-delivery departments of the former JSB and Durban City Council, including Durban Water, Electricity and the City Police. However, the Metropolitan Council generally did not seek, nor was it able, to dominate the local councils. This reflected the ongoing bureaucratic restructuring, and the fact that the Metropolitan Council was unable to raise funds beyond cost-recovery for service delivery; it was thus dependent on property tax revenue collected by local councils. The ex-JSB business levy did generate substantial income for the Metropolitan Council although its use to cover operating expenses was highly contested and uncertain.

The strengthening of the metropolitan tier since December 2000 through the creation of what is referred to as a uni- or megacity, with a single integrated tax base, has changed some of these financial and functional allocations.[3] This has certainly removed some of the constraints on policy implementation, although, as we will argue below, the complexities of metropolitan economic development extend well beyond the functional allocation of competencies between the metropolitan and local council tiers. For example, the bureaucratic space for direct economic intervention is limited by the fact that the most powerful entities within local government are the service-delivery departments. These departments control substantial budgets and are structured around a strong professional identity.

It is also worth recalling that local government is one of many local actors that has the potential to influence the trajectory of the local economy in one way or another. For example, the references made earlier to parastatals such as the port, and to land-owners such as the Tongaat-Hulett Group remind us that these players can have a significant impact on the economic development agenda within the local state. The democratisation of local government may have had an impact on the terms and conditions under which such impacts might occur, however, in a context of a local state opening itself up to an economic development agenda, corporate and other influences also gain points of systemic influence. Thus, talk of procurement reform, public-private partnerships and other 'economic development-isms' is more widespread in local government today compared to a decade earlier.

What this discussion points to is the considerable fluidity of the context within which the Metropolitan Council's economic development strategy emerged. How then are we to make sense of the strategy and what it tells us about the changing nature of the local state in Durban? Before describing and analysing the strategy, we review some theoretical tools to aid this analysis.

Theoretical Tools

Political economy approaches to understanding the local state – specifically urban regime theory – have come to occupy a dominant position in writings on urban politics (Lauria 1997). This view of urban economic development 'emphasizes how the actions and behaviours of key institutions and actors are responsible for determining how urban structures develop' (Holupka and Shlay 1993: 176). Holupka and Shlay identify three central characteristics of this approach. First, the approach recognises that 'a constellation of specific local actors and institutions play key roles in determining how local development occurs' (177). Second, the approach takes as a premise that the benefits of urban development are highly skewed. And third, it suggests that urban development decisions tend to be undemocratic; 'critical decisions are hidden from the public view and the public serves to legitimate decisions rather than to play a material role in making them' (178). Writers using this approach include Logan and Molotch (1987), Cox and Mair (1988) and Mollenkopf (1983). Certainly this approach provides useful tools for analysing urban economic strategy, since it provides some guidance as to why pluralist local polities almost invariably 'choose' competitive, or entrepreneurial growth models. Quite justifiably, many authors remain profoundly skeptical about the possibilities for high-road, equitable development through such 'bootstrap' approaches to local and regional development (Eisenschitz and Gough 1993).

Notwithstanding the limitations of local interventions, the attention to local political economy has gained salience in the current context of profound change within the global economy and the state, specifically the weakening of the nation-state. These arguments resonate through a literature that emphasises the increasingly important role of regional institutions and actors in the global economy (Cox 1997; Scott 1998; Storper 1997). Eisinger (1988) argues that subnational economic development is becoming more important for various reasons. First, traditional competitive policies were becoming less effective as they became more widespread. Second, central government transfers to localities have declined and thus incentives to find ways of fostering local growth have increased. Third, global economic changes impacting on localities have increased competitive pressures, but have also increased opportunities for exports and the re-orientation of local economies. At the very least, the second and third explanations are directly applicable to the Durban case. These changes demand a response by the local state, and in this sense, 'globalization makes states' (Kiel 1998).

And yet, while the political economy approach offers important insights into the structural context of change, it under-emphasizes the bureaucratic and organisational dimensions of the economic development task. In particular, it seems that a direct reading off economic strategy from particular interests, or (more subtly) from the articulation of particular interest groups and global forces, is unable to deal with the fact that the Durban economic development strategy was also part of the process of establishing the new local government administration, and a new set of local 'governance' practices. As we shall see, the economic development goals of the local state can only be achieved through a complex array of organisational interdependencies. Thus, a more institutional analysis of strategy-making processes, organisational form and bureaucratic identity would add usefully to the political economy analysis.

It would, however, be incorrect to characterise life in the bureaucracy of Durban's local government in strictly Weberian terms. Certainly, during the period under discussion, there was no 'iron cage' constraining the actions of individual bureaucrats (DiMaggio and Powell 1991). Rather, this was a period of intense uncertainty, to which the work of later organisational theorists speaks more clearly. Rather than understanding bureaucratic organisation as a way of promoting efficiency, we might regard it as a way of reducing uncertainty. This perspective derives from the tradition of Cyert, March and Simon, which sees complex organisations as problem-facing and problem-solving phenomena (Thomson 1967). The key variables that establish the extent of uncertainty facing an organisation concern the problem-solving technologies available to organisations and the environment in which they operate. Organisations will attempt to define their sphere of operation, their boundaries, to reduce uncertainty. Thus 'organisations cope with uncertainty by creating certain parts specifically to deal with it, specialising other parts in operating under conditions of certainty or near certainty' (Thomson 1967: 13).

Following Christensen (1985), it can be argued that the local economic development arena is profoundly uncertain, since there is both a lack of agreement on what we mean by economic development (goal uncertainty) or how to achieve it (technological uncertainty). This view has been elegantly stated by Beauregard (1993) who argues that economic development 'is greatly influenced by the need for action and a corresponding reliance on actors whose decisions are only partly motivated by analytical knowledge, resistant to government command, and tenuously linked to the spatial arenas in which policy makers operate. As a result, the path between knowledge and action is murky and discontinuous' (280). In this uncertain environment, multiple decentralised policy experiments seem to be a good approach but this fits uncomfortably with two dimensions of the economic development policy environment, specifically the problems with redistribution at the local level and the large scale of impact required to influence economic development outcomes.

The implications of this (admittedly de-contextualised) line of argument are relatively clear. In comparison to the more clearly defined tasks of service delivery, we should expect local economic development strategy to occupy the bureaucratic periphery. We might also expect a form of policy intervention, or practice, in which complex inter-organisational relationships provide the context for policy interventions. The term 'governance' has come to describe many of the practices associated with this type of government (Stoker 1998). Writers such as Healey et al. (1995) embrace this role for public servants, for example, regarding strategic spatial planning, not only as reflecting local development interests, but also as a key institution that provides the certainty, information and legitimating framework required to ensure investment. This view also emphasizes the importance of negotiation and flexibility as desirable features of the system for both developers and other (local) interests. Others remain more skeptical about the self-organising capacities of an approach to government in which the lines between public and private spheres are often blurred (see for example Jessop 1998).

Our theoretical approach thus recognises a certain tension within economic strategy-making at the local level. On one hand, local economic strategy must be understood as reflective of sectional interests within, and impacting upon, the local economy. Strategy documents may be employed as a device to legitimate pro-growth interests, or to signal to similar interests elsewhere, that the locality is a good place to do business. We will show how key aspects of Durban's economic development strategy can be seen as addressing the concerns of local and national business interests, while trying to create space for a developmental local government.

On the other hand, we need to understand how the macro-economic context, and complex political and institutional pressures, condition local economic strategy. Economic strategy-making is thus also about the creation of an institutional context within which uncertain economic development goals may be pursued. In this regard we will examine inter-departmental, local metropolitan council, and other complex inter-organisational relationships to reflect upon the formulation and implementation of economic strategy in Durban. The result is that local economic development strategy does not simply reflect singular interests. In part, this tension is reflected in a disjuncture between the symbolic aspects of economic strategy and what happens in practice.

Durban Economic Strategy and the Durban Local State

The 1996 Green Paper on Economic Development was written as one part of a wider metropolitan strategic planning process. The strategic planning process was driven by a Joint Steering Committee (JSC) consisting of two senior councillors and the Chief Executive Officer (CEO) from each of the six local councils and the Metropolitan Council, and two representatives each from organised business and organised labour. The JSC initiated a metropolitan strategic planning process to prepare a policy framework to guide the formation of the Durban Metropolitan Council (at that stage, the CEO was the only person formally appointed to the Durban Metropolitan Council).

At a workshop in February 1996, the JSC adopted a broadly inclusive vision, mission and set of guiding principles, as well as draft strategic plans for key metropolitan functional sectors. The key sectors were management, housing, infrastructure (for example, electricity, water and sanitation), urban form, community services (for example, public amenities and city policing) and economic development. Despite the fact that many of these documents had a rather different content and feel, the breadth of the metropolitan vision was such that political differences could be easily accommodated. Revised strategic papers were adopted as Green Papers at an October 1996 workshop. These then formed the basis for an April 1997 Integrated Development Plan (DMC 1997) which guided the implementation of metropolitan government in Durban.

The Green Paper on Economic Development contains three substantive sections. The first is an analysis of the economy of the Durban Metropolitan Area. This section examines the economy of Durban in international, national and provincial context, and the key characteristics, trends and challenges facing the local economy (on a sectoral basis). Using a SWOT-type analysis it suggests that the key challenge facing Durban *is to be globally competitive* in order to attract investment, to create substantial sustainable jobs, to address the uneven spatial distribution of economic activity and to grow in an environmentally sustainable way.

The second substantive section of the document analyses the historical impact of local government activities on the local economy. It argues that local government did have important direct and indirect impacts on the local economy, as planner, regulator, service provider, employer and consumer. The strengths of local government in maintaining the environment and infrastructure required for development of the core of Durban (CBD and beachfront) are recognised, as is the success of Pinetown in attracting inward investment. However, racial biases in many policies, the lack of a coherent economic policy framework, restrictive bureaucracy, lack of co-ordination between physical and economic development, and lack of attention to distributional issues are noted as weaknesses. This analysis places considerable emphasis on the indirect economic impacts of all the activities of local government, not just those that explicitly address themselves to economic goals.

This leads directly into the third substantive section that makes the case for the role of local government in meeting the challenges facing the local economy. Its recommendations are contained in five clusters. Cluster one recommends a high-level commitment to economic development. This entails the establishment of economic planning and policy-making capacity at the metropolitan level, and of economic implementation capacity at local council level. It also points to the need for improved co-operation between departments that perform functions with economic impacts. The section dealing with economic development capacity reflects the emerging division of functions between the metropolitan and local tiers, as well as the co-ordinative or strategic, rather than actively interventionist, thrust of the metropolitan economic function.

Cluster two speaks to the need to make the city attractive to local and international business. This entails the maintenance of local fiscal discipline and the establishment of investor information and reception services. Other elements mentioned include flagship infrastructure investments (such as the International Convention Centre), tourism planning and CBD upgrading. In other words, this section contains commitments to key local economic interests.

The third cluster addresses extending access to economic opportunities for disadvantaged communities. Included here are procurement and tendering policy reform to encourage small businesses, changing council employment practices to encourage labour intensive activities, infrastructure to support small business, and support for economic development in disadvantaged communities. However, this section is certainly not a commitment to a fully-fledged bottom-up development strategy.

Fourthly, as part of making the city attractive to international investors and extending access to the disadvantaged, the strategy suggests the need to work towards an efficient urban system. Proposals include support for integrated spatial planning, joint port-city-airport planning, development of key corridors, reduced travel-to-work distances and crime reduction programmes.

In both the third and fourth clusters, the indirectly interventionist, or 'governance' paradigm implicit in the economic development strategy becomes clear. Local government will *monitor* the environment for job creation opportunities, it will *investigate* its role in education and training, it will *introduce* economic criteria into land use regulations and other planning systems, it will seek greater *co-ordination* between the different transport authorities, and it will *become involved in* national and provincial development initiatives (DMC 1996: 25–6). Where metropolitan government's directly interventionist role in the local economy is recognised, for example, in the purchasing of goods and services, note that this impact occurs through the powerful, substantially independent service departments.

Finally, the fifth cluster notes the problems of environmental degradation and says that economic development needs to be sustainable. A combination of regulatory and incentive approaches are suggested, although it is not clear what legislative or fiscal powers are available to achieve this.

Seen within the context of the Growth, Employment and Redistribution (GEAR) policy,[4] the Durban strategy reflects tight fiscal constraints and the prioritisation of economic growth. The strategy contains important advocacy or symbolic commitments to key local interests, especially the concerns of local businesses. However, these commitments are largely symbolic; the strategy was written with the presumption that there would not be significant resources for direct business support. Similarly, the strategy does not make any substantial proposals for resource redistribution, partly because few welfare functions, including education, fall under the influence of local government.

The tensions arising from the GEAR policy framework can only be partially resolved within the institutional context that has emerged; for example, new electricity connections to businesses have become 20 times more costly as a way of generating funds for household electricity connections. Recommendations from the Fiscal and Finance Commission on the provision of an effective subsidy for basic services have received a cool reception from local government as they are part of a financial restructuring exercise which will significantly reduce total state transfers to local government (in the form of transport subsidies, township management grants, etc).

Thus one of the results of the GEAR framework is that it limits resources for businesses as much as it confounds the service-delivery demands that have been deflected to the local level. Furthermore, in the absence of a social welfare safety net, Durban's economic strategy does not significantly advance the linkage of local economic development efforts and welfare provision (for example in targeted training and employment schemes) which increasingly characterise local partnerships in Europe and elsewhere (see Sabel 1996).

However, within the context of the wider metropolitan strategic planning process, it may be argued that the economic strategy was primarily oriented towards meeting the needs of the local business constituency (including the emerging black business interests), while other strategies, specifically the one dealing with housing (see DMC 1997), were orientated to the needs of poor, African constituencies. The authors of the economic strategy needed to present an argument that would find currency with major stakeholders in the region, while at the same time advancing the argument that local resources for redistribution were primarily generated through charges on business and wealthier communities. The emphasis in the paper on growth should therefore be seen in the context of the need to increase the size of the proverbial cake in a sustainable manner, while at the same time ensuring a flexible enough approach was taken towards the recipe to enable emerging black businesses to gain a slice of opportunity. Economic strategy thus formed part of the wider process of defining and legitimating the new shape of local government in Durban.

This analysis is enhanced by the recognition that the strategy also defined, and was shaped by, the organisational context for economic development intervention. As noted above, requests for capacity (i.e. bureaucratic resources) in the strategy were essentially limited to a call for greater co-ordination at metropolitan level. This can be contrasted with the fairly grand proposals in terms of levels (if not targets) of service delivery contained in other strategy papers. A more institutional analysis that takes account of the way in which the economic development function emerged in this particular organisational context helps to explain why this occurred.

The key elements of this context are the considerable uncertainty over how to achieve local economic development, made more difficult by the fact that the most direct economic development interventions could only be pursued through the actions of the relatively powerful service providing line function departments, the local councils, and other agencies. It is thus not surprising that the economic development function should have been created in a meta-organisational form. In other words, these bureaucratic or intra-governmental interests also acted to define the boundaries that would structure the institutional context for local economic development.

In reflecting on this institutional environment, the strategy paper recognised a role for 'economic capacity' to assist in the process of redefining existing arenas of council work as well as in carving out entirely new arenas of activity for local government. There is a strong pragmatic thread to the manner in which these capacity changes are presented. This can be ascribed both to the marginal position of the authors in a budgetary and organisational sense (something which has changed since the document was first written), as well as a recognition of the value of powerful, efficient and well organised service providers in actually achieving the above-mentioned economic ends.

In the post-1998 period much of the influence and positioning, deemed necessary for the effective implementation of an economic development agenda for the city, has been secured. The original Metropolitan Economic Development Department is required as a matter of course to be at the heart of strategic city-wide, and in some cases even national, processes such as budgeting and decisions on major projects. There are a number of possible explanations for this. These include the fact that as a relatively new department it has not been tainted as being 'representative of the old order' and hence carries some legitimacy with political leadership. Furthermore, the leadership of the department also has a relatively strong political track-record in the pre-1994 era and has therefore been able to link into influential networks that are so prevalent in bureaucracies. An ability to illustrate the success of micro-projects and increased acceptance of involvement in strategic macro-processes has also opened up space for the department and its programmes, which in turn has meant a more effective and tangible role for local political leadership in economic processes.

Reflections

If economic strategy-making is also about the structuration of an organisational and institutional environment, what does a brief review of the implementation of the strategy reveal? The analysis presented here is necessarily speculative since we are dealing with very recent events. During the transition period, the economic development function was a unit within the metropolitan Urban Strategy Department and the Economic Development Department was only formally constituted in 1997. The department, during the period under consideration, did not control a substantial project budget or other resources, except for the tourism project fund (R5 million) inherited from the JSB, and a new small, medium and micro-enterprise (SMME) and township development fund (R5 million).

Virtually everything that was done had to be achieved in collaboration with one or more organisational partner. Collaboration has depended on the building of personal and professional relationships, across a range of stakeholders, which in turn diluted the efforts of economic development staff as well as related agendas of the dominant party. Urban economic strategy has thus been less about delivery, and more about co-operation, co-ordination and cajoling. This forced the department to operate in a very complex institutional environment when it wanted to achieve things and was exacerbated by ongoing restructuring, power plays and capacity constraints. What then were the contours of this institutional/organisational environment?

Economic strategy recognised that many decisions with important economic consequences are taken by functional departments such as Electricity, Housing, Water and other service providers. One example of work in this area has been the Council's Affirmative Procurement and Tendering Policy that seeks to advantage smaller, labour intensive, black owned firms when council money is spent. The policy has been drawn up by an inter-departmental committee co-ordinated by the Economic Development Department. It is, however, important to note that this organisational mechanism was created to implement what was a clearly defined policy goal, backed by strong political commitment.

Under the pre-December 2000 system the six local councils remained responsible for key functions which had economic impacts, for example, the management of street traders, beachfront and other amenity development, land releases and development, granting planning permission, writing integrated planning frameworks and so on. There were many examples of co-operation between the metropolitan and local councils on specific projects, but attempts by the Economic Development Department to be involved in, for example, establishing the criteria for local council land sales were generally coolly received. Strategic releases of local council land represented one of the key arenas in which local government could act as a direct mediator in economic processes.

However, where changing political and economic demands have exposed a vacuum in the bureaucracy, the Economic Development Department managed to offer increasingly sophisticated services in some areas. Nevertheless, it remains to be seen how large a role other arms of government will allow the department in providing economic policy guidelines, particularly in arenas that are likely to entail conflict and uncertainty over distributional equity issues. It also remains to be seen how the unicity proposals will impact on these intra-governmental relationships. The Unicity transitional process is likely to take more than 18 months; however, the setting up of transitional mechanisms has seen a key role being carved out for economic development.

Virtually all actual delivery of economic services, from tourism marketing, support for small businesses, or training programmes, occurs through non-governmental or parastatal agencies. In some cases, the Metropolitan Council is represented in the Board of Directors of these agencies but these agencies have their own interests and reporting relationships. National and provincial government and departments also continue to have a major impact on the city. For example, in South Africa, virtually all important industrial policy decision-making and funding mechanisms remain at national level. The Department of Trade and Industry is currently pursuing an investment promotion strategy known as the Spatial Development Initiative (SDI). In Durban, the proposed SDI has been the centre of considerable local-central conflict, which is closely related to ongoing conflict between the port and the city. The city signalled to the port that it would go to court to stop certain proposed developments which would have affected properties near the harbour. This conflict, and the intervention by national government in the SDI, was used by the city to create a port-city forum which should promote joint decision-making. It seems that the formation of a strong Metropolitan Council, with a focus on economic development, contributed to this shift.

Although organised labour and organised business are formally represented in many Metropolitan Council decision-making forums, the general experience is that labour does not have the capacity to play an active role in local policy formation, while business remains well organised and actively involved. For example, there are close links between the Economic Development Department and the National Business Initiative around local economic development training, and active involvement of business representatives in metropolitan spatial development framework planning process. The Metropolitan Council also now co-hosts an annual investment conference with the support of the local Chamber of Commerce and sponsored by a major daily newspaper.

This complex inter-dependent style of operation means that particular interests are involved in economic development interventions, which further dilutes the goals of economic strategy in various ways. However, this improves the prospects for experimentation and a diversity of responses in the face of goal uncertainty. Also, the fact that the idea of metropolitan government has been accepted as legitimate means that some local economic issues are approached with a metropolitan-wide perspective. In general, this is a positive development.

Furthermore, the manner in which much of the work of the

Economic Unit, and subsequently the Economic Development Department, has been undertaken has struck a positive chord with senior politicians. There is often an insistence by politicians that the director of the Economic Development Department offer advice on issues that extend beyond narrowly or bureaucratically defined economic functions. This close association with political power and an ability to tap into the agenda of the political elites has further enhanced the space for the Economic Development Department to assert itself and its mandated agenda. As mentioned previously this trend of increasing influence has been sustained beyond 1998 and in some instances intensified.

Conclusion

A political-economy analysis can show how urban economic development strategy played an important symbolic role in reinforcing the idea of metropolitan governance in Durban, in defining an identity for the metropolitan level of local government, and in offering certain promises to key business sectors, political constituencies and other role players. In important respects this symbolic role has been reinforced by the mode of institutional networking that characterises the interventions of the local state in the economic arena. By working with and through other agencies, departments, authorities, across the public-private divide, metropolitan economic strategy continues to play an integrative role and contributes significantly to the transformation of local government into a conscious economic actor. The combination of a high approval rating from a range of constituencies and access to decision-making structures in local government have contributed to the view that the Economic Development Department is different from other levels of the bureaucracy.

However, to some extent this approach to urban economic strategy reflects the absence of policy tools and resources through which to achieve economic development goals, and thus points to a less successful role as a mediator of economic processes. This is a problem insofar as local economic strategy is about more than satisfying symbolic goals. There are very real changes in the wider economic context, as well as the socio-economic challenges of poverty and unemployment. These are exacerbated by the impact of globalisation which demands a re-configuration of the organisation of production; dealing with the impact of trade liberalisation on specific local sectors, becoming export-oriented, managing the need for change in the harbour and in its relation to the city, and creating a city that is attractive to global investors. Attempts to mediate these processes through the provision of economic services have thus far been limited to investment facilitation, support for small, medium and micro-enterprises and the provision of economic development training; further work in this area is constrained by resources and the complex organisational terrain.

Thus, an institutional analysis that focuses on the difficulties of achieving economic development through conscious policy-making and planning interventions adds considerably to the political-economy analysis. Metropolitan economic strategy-making therefore also needs to be understood as a part of the process of defining an institutional context, a modus operandi, for action. Such an analysis has to explore the ways in which different spheres of government, powerful bureaucratic sectors, and other agencies, participate in this process. In the face of considerable goal and technological uncertainty, economic strategy has been pursued through a meta-organisational, less directly interventionist form. This result, for better and for worse, conforms with the constrained fiscal context, and with the interests of some of the most powerful local government agencies and sectors of the local business constituency, including the emerging black business constituency.

NOTES

1. The constitution establishes local government with 'the right to govern, on its own initiative, the local government affairs of its community, subject to national and provincial legislation as provided for in the constitution' and with the proviso that the 'national or a provincial government may not compromise or impede a municipality's ability or right to exercise its powers or perform its functions' (RSA 1996a: 151 (3) and (4)).
2. For a case study of the Central Witwatersrand Metropolitan Negotiating Forum, see Mabin (1995).
3. For more information, see the *White Paper on Local Government* (RSA 1998a) and Municipal Structures Bill (RSA 1998b).
4. GEAR is a macro-economic policy of structural adjustment and fiscal restraint; it contains a commitment to cutting the deficit to three per cent of GDP by the year 2000 from its 1993/94 level of six per cent, foreign exchange liberalisation, export-promotion and investment incentives (RSA 1996b). One of the impacts of this policy is a real cut in inter-governmental transfers, which means reduced resources for local economic development spending given that municipalities have limited borrowing powers.

REFERENCES

Beauregard, R. 1993. 'Constituting Economic Development: A Theoretical Perspective'. In R.D. Bingham and R. Mier. *Theories of Local Economic Development*. Newbury Park: Sage.

CDE (Centre for Development and Enterprise). 1996. 'Durban: South Africa's Global Competitor?' CDE, Johannesburg.

Christensen, K. 1985. 'Coping with Uncertainty in Planning'. *Journal of the American Planning Association*, Winter.

Coetzee, Z.R., K. Gwarade, W. Naude and J. Swanepoel. 1997. 'Currency Depreciation, Trade Liberalisation and Economic Development'. *South African Journal of Economics*, 65, 2.

Cox, K.R. and A. Mair. 1988. 'Locality and Community in the Politics of Local Economic Development'. *Annals of the Association of American Geographers*, 78.

Cox, K.R. (ed). 1997. *Spaces of Globalization: Reasserting the Power of the Local.* New York: Guildford Press.

DiMaggio, P.J. and W.W. Powell. 1991. 'The Iron Cage Revisisted: Institutional Isomorphism and Collective Rationality'. In P.J. DiMaggio and W.W. Powell (eds). *The New Institutionalism in Organisational Analysis*. Chicago: University of Chicago Press.

Durban City Council (DCC). 1995. *The Greater Durban Metropolitan Area: Understanding our Economy*. Durban: Durban City Council.

Durban Metropolitan Council (DMC). 1996. 'Economic Development (Durban Metropolitan Council Green Paper on Economic Development)'. Report prepared by the Urban Strategy Economic Unit and local council officials for the Joint Steering Committee.

——. 1997. *Integrated Development Plan 97/98*. Durban: Durban Metropolitan Council.

Economic Development Department (EDD). 1997. *Investment Profile*. Durban: Durban Metropolitan Council.

Eisenshitz, A. and J. Gough. 1993. *The Politics of Local Economic Policy: The Problems and Possibilities of Local Initiative*. London: Macmillan.

Eisinger, P.K. 1988. *The Rise of the Entrepreneurial State*. Madison: University of Wisconsin Press.

Healey, P., S. Cameron, S. Davoudi, S. Graham and A. Madani Pour (eds). 1995. *Managing Cities: The New Urban Context*. Chichester: John Wiley.

Hindson, D., M. Byerly and M. Morris. 1993. 'From Violence to Reconstruction: The Making, Disintegration and Remaking of an Apartheid City'. Centre for Social and Development Studies Working Paper 10. University of Natal, Durban.

Holupka, C.S. and A.B. Shlay. 1993. 'Political Economy and Urban Development'. In R.D. Bingham and R. Mier. *Theories of Local Economic Development*. Newbury Park: Sage.

Jessop, R. 1998. 'The Rise of Governance and the Risks of Failure: The Case of Economic Development'. *International Social Science Journal*, 50, 1.

Keil, R. 1998. 'Globalization Makes States: Perspectives of Local Governance in the Age of the World City. *Review of International Political Economy*, 5, 4.

Lauria, M. (ed.). 1997. *Reconstructing Urban Regime Theory: Regulating Urban Politics in a Global Economy*. Thousand Oaks: Sage.

Logan, J.R. and H.L. Molotch. 1987. *Urban Fortunes: The Political Economy of Place.* Berkeley: University of California Press.
Mabin, A. 1995. 'Urban Crisis, Growth Management and the History of Metropolitan Planning in South Africa'. *Urban Forum*, 6, 1.
McCarthy, J. 1991. 'Planning Issues and the Political Economy of the Local State: An Historical Case Study of Durban'. *Urban Forum*, 2, 2.
Mollenkopf, J.H. 1983. *The Contested City*. Princeton: Princeton University Press.
Nel, E. 1997. 'Evolving Local Economic Development Policy in South Africa'. *Regional Studies*, 31, 1.
Nel, E. and C. Rogerson. 1995. 'Incipient Local Economic Development in the Eastern Cape, 1909–1947'. *Contree: JSA Urban and Regional History*, 37.
——. 1996. 'The Application of Local Economic Development in East London, South Africa, 1927–1955'. *Urban Forum*, 7, 1.
Parnell, S. 1988. 'Racial Segregation in Johannesburg: The Slums Act'. *South African Geographical Journal*, 70.
Parnell, S. 1997. 'South African Cities: Perspectives from the Ivory Tower of Urban Studies'. *Urban Studies*, 34, 5–6.
Pillay, U. 1994. 'Local Government Restructuring, Growth Coalitions, and the Development Process in the Durban Functional Region, *c.*1984–1994'. *Urban Forum*, 5, 2.
Robbins, G. 1997. 'Global Competitiveness and Port Cities on the Indian Ocean Rim: Some Thoughts from Durban, South Africa'. *Indian Ocean Review*, 10, 3, Perth, Australia: Indian Ocean Centre.
Republic of South Africa (RSA). 1996a. *The Constitution of the Republic of South Africa, 1996. (Act 108 of 1996)*. Pretoria: Government Printer.
——. 1996b. *Growth, Employment and Redistribution: A Macroeconomic Strategy*. Pretoria: Government Printer.
——. 1998a. *White Paper on Local Government*. Pretoria: Department of Provincial Affairs and Constitutional Development.
——. 1998b. *Municipal Structures Bill*. Pretoria: Government Printer.
Sabel, C. 1996. *Ireland: Local Partnerships and Social Innovation*. Paris: OECD.
Scott, A. 1998. *Regions and the World Economy: The Coming Shape of Global Production, Competition, and Political Order*. New York: Oxford University Press.
Stoker, G. 1998. 'Governance as Theory: Five Propositions'. *International Social Science Journal*, 50, 1.
Storper, M. 1997. *The Regional World: Territorial Development in a Global Economy*. New York: Guildford Press.
Thompson, J.D. 1967. *Organisations in Action: Social Science Bases of Administrative Theory*. New York: McGraw-Hill.
Western, J. 1981. *Outcast Cape Town*. Minneapolis: University of Minnesota Press.

Part Two

Durban's Economy

The urban economy is not easy to comprehend using conventional economic indicators. Its boundaries are relative but not absolute and the key feature seems to be networks and nodes rather than hard and fast structures. Urban analysts tend to abandon earlier efforts to construct input-output models for cities and instead are focusing on cities as centres for the generation and transmission of knowledge and co-ordination of multiform but related activities.

Durban has been a successful industrial centre – and it is relatively easy to capture industrial activities statistically – but even its industrial growth really has depended on location. The most fundamental thing about the city is its site where land and sea routes meet. Durban is a capacious natural bay connected by road via relatively accessible passes to the rich mineral interior of South Africa where the densest and richest consuming population came to be found in the twentieth century. Durban industry, while originating in the presence of a local market, really depended for its emergence on the viability of a location ideally accessible to the populous Rand (and east of the country more generally), as well as to the cheapest water route to sources of raw materials and machinery outside the country.

The biggest obvious economic questions about contemporary Durban are in fact questions about the harbour, the road and rail system, the possibility of constructing a major international airport rather than about industry itself. Yet the economics of transport does not simply take care of itself. The efforts in Victorian times, crowned with success early in the twentieth century, to make the bay a safe ocean-linked harbour, were fundamental to Durban's growth. In the following chapter Trevor Jones explores the impact of the port, undoubtedly the most important single feature in the city economy, and the dilemmas and opportunities that it is facing as traffic expands and the nature of international shipping changes. The port is administered, moreover, by Portnet, a national parastatal which does not co-ordinate its interests very effectively with those of the city, a point also made by Morris et al. Jones suggests the importance of co-ordinated thinking that can maximise

Durban's advantages in adapting to expansion and change. It could be argued (a) that further research on other transport features such as roads, rail and air links need to complement Jones' analysis directly; and (b) that the port's development perhaps needs to be dovetailed with that of export-orientated industry looking out to the world, including the new markets to the East, as opposed to simply utilising imported materials.

At peak, Durban industry in the 1980s employed almost 200 000 workers. Its health is thus quite critical to the welfare of Durban's people. Manufacturing activity in Durban has been extremely diverse and it has involved internal networking and, to some extent, the creation of cluster activities that belong with one another. Yet the logic of most of this activity has lain in the creation of a national captive market with Durban as a suitable inexpensive receptacle for imported inputs. In the 1960s, the golden age of import-substitution behind tariff walls, with South African industry also benefiting from the growing state emphasis on security and self-sufficiency, Durban industry grew very fast – faster in fact than the national average. This pattern now belongs to memory. Growth is slow and the industrial work-force is declining in size.

Morris et al. consider the performance of Durban firms to be 'patchy'. They focus on the efforts of particular producers and local associations to try to cope with the undermining of import-substitution strategies that were profitable and hungry for the absorption of labour in the past. They propose aiming at international competitiveness as the most reliable means of uncovering new strategies that work, echoing the position by Hall and Robbins emanating from the local state. Garments and textiles are used as one case study and automotive parts as another. In fact, while both constitute spatial clusters in the sense of industrial concentration, neither so far have the impetus or synergy to qualify as more than that although this research is optimistic about the surfacing of some positive signs. The local state or local associations, perhaps aided by the state, might play a role in providing some of that impetus, but the mechanisms for making such structures effective are yet to come to life.

The disinterest of the big players in Durban in industrial development and growth, likely to have political and social causes, as well as the decline in industrial protection, need also be taken on board. Is there then a Durban capitalist class – a core around which local accumulation can be shaped? Padayachee carefully explores the extent to which Durban has been and is a centre in which capital can be raised. Successful capital acquisition appears to depend upon the location of companies within the larger structure of South Africa's conglomerate world. For those outside these powerful networks, the raising of capital can prove to be a huge obstacle. In general, while the advantages of Durban have brought investment, the local business community, with one or two notable exceptions, has not really shown itself capable of developing a financial engine and innovative capacity that can self-direct further development to the advantage of the city. In his chapter, Padayachee delineates what is in most respects 'a branch economy', although not lacking entirely in financial resources. Still the absence of a locally orientated financial nexus militates against the effectiveness of any Durban based *growth coalition*, whether urban or provincial.

Economic research on Durban must consider more than transport, industry and finance. There is, for instance, the historic importance of tourism. The Durban beachfront is generally considered the traditional focal point of domestic tourism in South Africa, but there is room for more dynamic and penetrating analyses of its present impact and main features. Some of the contemporary literature on cities, looking at technopoles, science centres and electronic commerce, highlights skills and the attraction of particular cities to the highly skilled (Castells and Hall, 1994). The skills – or lack of them – of Durban workers and others active in the economy could be featured and could potentially be the subject of significant intervention by the local state.

CHAPTER THREE

The Port of Durban

Lynchpin of the Local Economy?

TREVOR JONES

The port of Durban is presently standing at the crossroads. After establishing itself as the major general cargo port of the African continent, the container hub port of the western Indian Ocean and in most respects the dominant port of the southern hemisphere, Durban's pre-eminence is now challenged by a number of factors. These include further development and diversification of facilities in the port of Richards Bay; investment in the Maputo corridor; and possible new port development at Coega in the more politically correct Eastern Cape. In the Durban area itself an increasingly vocal environmental lobby opposes expansion in an already saturated port area, while an apparent identity crisis on the part of the port authority has placed urgently needed capacity extensions in a state of virtual suspended animation. This inaction is ill-timed, for it coincides with a policy shift of the South African state, away from a reliance on high-mass primary product exports and towards growth driven by manufactured exports in a low-tariff globalised world. This growth trajectory requires world-class general cargo facilities, rather than world-class bulk facilities, in the nation's ports (Department of Transport 1998).

These domestic pressures play themselves out against a backdrop of an international sea transport industry that is itself in a state of flux and transformation. These changes have overturned the old order in liner shipping, which is now dominated by a thoroughly globalised container shipping industry, structured around complex interconnected regional and round-the-world services, rather than traditional point-to-point (and largely north-south) liner routes. This can have massive repercussions for individual ports. The large global consortia that command international container shipping could focus their Indian Ocean operations on hub ports as far afield as Aden, Salalah or Singapore, in the process threatening to relegate Durban and other southern African ports to subordinate spoke cargo recipients as opposed to genuine hub generators of regional and transshipment traffic (Palsson 1998). A consequence of the interplay of these many influences is that pivotal capacity and investment decisions in the South African ports sector must be taken as a matter of urgency. These will largely determine whether Durban suffers a final millennial eclipse, or whether it moves strongly into the twenty-first century as the unchallenged hub port of the Indian Ocean Rim.

The port's future expansion or stasis is also a factor of immense importance for the local Durban economy and for the community that metropolitan economy supports. The nature of the economic linkages between the port of Durban and the local economy forms the central focus of this chapter. This central theme will be explored at two levels: in a static sense by attempting to examine the impact of the present activities of the port on the economy of the Greater Durban Metropolitan Area (GDMA); and rather more ambitiously by endeavouring to assess the dynamic gains that are likely to be reaped by investing in capacity sufficient to attract additional port traffic to Durban, or the dynamic losses that would result if potential traffic should be diverted to other ports or transport corridors.

The first section briefly sketches the historical development of port facilities and then examines in rather more detail the evolution and shape of the traffic base of the port of Durban within the context of other southern African and southern hemisphere ports. In the second section, the focus shifts to the central question of the impact of the port's activities on the local economy. It seeks to examine the activities both of direct port-ancillary (or port-dependent) industries and of those port users whose fortunes are more indirectly but nonetheless unambiguously linked to the port. Particular attention is directed to the role of the port authority itself, and the extent to which port management arrangements permit the incorporation of local interests in investment decision-making. The third section attempts to assess the related question of the likely impact of traffic diversion (either in favour of or against Durban) on the economy of the GDMA. Finally, I seek to identify the comparative advantages or disadvantages possessed by the port of Durban *vis-à-vis* other regional ports in respect of different broad categories of cargo, in an endeavour to establish rough guidelines as to the most appropriate future path of expansion for the port.

The Facilities and Traffic Performance of the Port of Durban

The story of the historical development of modern deepwater facilities in the port of Durban is essentially a twentieth-century story. Before the development and innovation of modern dredging techniques in the late nineteenth century, vessel entry into the Bay of Natal was severely limited by water depth in the main approach channel, to a point where larger vessels were forced to work passengers and cargo in the open roadstead off the port (Heydendrych 1985; Pearson 1995). The early development of the port was consequently dominated by the many campaigns that were waged in the 'battle of the bar' against the accretion of sand formed by the natural littoral drift that flows up the eastern seaboard from south-west to north-east (Bender 1988). By 1904,[1] the sand had been vanquished (or at least semi-permanently subdued) to a point where the largest deep sea vessels then deployed on the southern African trades were able to enter the port. Thereafter, expansion of port facilities proceeded apace, although water depth in the main port fairway remains a limiting factor to the present day,[2] since the available water depth of –12.8 m on chart datum[3] effectively restricts port access to fully laden vessels up to approximately 65 000 deadweight tons (dwt).[4] The larger cohorts of both dry-bulk carriers and tankers have long been prevented from entering Durban, at least when in a loaded condition, while over the last decade the largest cohorts of 'post-Panamax' container ships have joined the ranks of vessels for which the Bay of Natal is inaccessible.

Following the defeat of the sand, port facilities developed and expanded in three distinct areas of the port: the Point area adjoining the present Central Business District; the Bluff area, where the port's first genuine bulk-handling facilities were established in late-Victorian and Edwardian times (and remain relatively unaltered today) to handle coal exports from the Dundee-Vryheid coalfields; and in the Maydon Wharf/Congella area, which handled its first working vessels in 1910. This latter area developed in a manner significantly different from that of all other port segments in South Africa, insofar as private enterprise was able to establish and entrench a presence, on a long-term leasehold basis, in land areas in the immediate quaywall hinterland. The Maydon Wharf area consequently witnessed the development of the first true private port terminals in the South African port sector, and to date it retains a form of split personality, with sophisticated private terminals sharing the terrain with common-user facilities controlled by the port authority. The epicentre of Durban's ship repair and (now largely dormant) shipbuilding industry is also located in the Congella area.

The inter-war years and the immediate post-war period were accompanied more by a qualitative deepening of these existing facilities than by major new infrastructural developments, with the notable exception of the Island View area around the old Salisbury and Farewell Islands on the south-eastern perimeter of the Bay of Natal. The original *raison d'être* for the development of port facilities in this area was the need to service the burgeoning international trade in oil and petroleum products, which had overtaken coal as the pre-eminent marine and industrial energy source by the 1940s. For more than 20 years the principal focus of this port segment remained the import of crude oil, the export and regional distribution of refined petroleum products (boosted by the construction of two major oil refineries in the Durban area) and the supply of bunker fuel to transit callers. This focus was, however, to change quite radically from the late 1960s when technological advances in shipbuilding permitted the construction of increasingly large tankers offering hitherto unanticipated economies of scale in liquid-bulk transport, but the resultant vessels (Very Large Crude Carriers or VLCCs) were draft-restricted in ports such as Durban. To exploit the freight cost advantages offered by large tankers, a single-buoy mooring (SBM) was installed offshore south of the port, and now serves as the principal maingate for the importation of crude oil for the Durban area, for the industrial heartland of Gauteng (to which oil is delivered by pipeline) and for the southern African sub-region. Of Durban's annual crude oil imports, which have fluctuated between 13–16 million tons in recent years, almost none is now handled through the port facilities within the Bay of Natal, hence the focus of the Island View port area has shifted to cater for a more diversified gamut of liquid- and dry-bulk cargoes, including a lucrative trade in chemical cargoes. During the 1990s this port segment sustained a consistently high level of activity, to a point where excess demand for chemical and refined petroleum product berths, in particular, has produced persistent congestion. Consequently, it is now one of the areas of the port where an expansion of physical capacity, or the re-location of activities to alternative sites, is required. By the mid-1960s, the *perimeter* of the Bay of Natal was already quite heavily saturated with port development, to a point where further expansion around the rim of the Bay was severely constrained. At this point, the centre of gravity of Durban's general cargo activities was firmly located in the Point docks, while minor bulks and coastal traffic were handled at Maydon Wharf, and major wet- and dry-bulk traffic was concentrated at the Bluff and Island View. Also at this stage, the facilities of the port were still essentially those of a classical 'railway' port in which conventional and most dry-bulk cargo was handled either directly between rail wagons and vessels, or from vessels into wharfside cargo sheds and thence into rail wagons (and road vehicles) for distribution.

These cargo-handling techniques required a considerable input of stevedoring labour but relatively little open space, and could be handled quite successfully in the narrow and cramped hinterland behind the working berths of the Point and Maydon Wharf areas. Such strictures proved, however, to be near-fatal for modern cargo-handling techniques. The handling of conventional general cargo is now dominated by unitised techniques that require large open spaces for the stacking of containers, while certain neo-bulk[5] cargoes such as steel, granite and forest products (which loom large in Durban's traffic base) now require large open spaces for consolidation and pre-assembly prior to loading. The old configuration of the port's general cargo berths made immediate adaptation to these techniques difficult if not impossible, and essentially required both that existing facilities be re-modelled and that entirely new terminals be developed, particularly for container traffic.

Such expansion posed immediate problems and the dense clustering of facilities around the perimeter of the port left only one viable alternative: to thrust out into the water area of the Bay of Natal through the construction of quaywalls and cargo working areas on virgin sites reclaimed from tidal sandbanks and mangrove swamps. The natural area of expansion was the southern perimeter of the Bay, where two large piers – Pier 1 and Pier 2 – were constructed in the late 1960s and mid-1970s, respectively.

These two developments, which increased the port's overall berth capacity by nearly 40 per cent, now represent the centre of gravity of the modern port. The principal focus of Pier 1 is the handling of neo-bulk cargoes such as steel and ferro-alloys, while Portnet has recently refurbished several berths to function as the port's first true 'combi' terminal. This concept is predicated on the need to service the growing category of multi-purpose vessels at a single terminal capable of handling a mix of conventional general cargo, unitised cargo and parcel bulk cargo.

The real 'commanding heights' of the modern port of Durban, and the key to its position as the dominant maingate for southern African general cargo traffic, are located in the port's main container terminal in the Pier 2 complex. Paradoxically, this terminal is also Durban port's greatest potential weakness, since upward pressure on containerised traffic volumes has driven demand above inherent terminal capacity, with the inevitable consequences of vessel and cargo delays, increases in the final distribution costs of sea transport, and the spectre of traffic migration to other southern African ports.

Containerisation was slow to overtake southern African seaborne commerce. The carriage of general cargo in standard freight containers

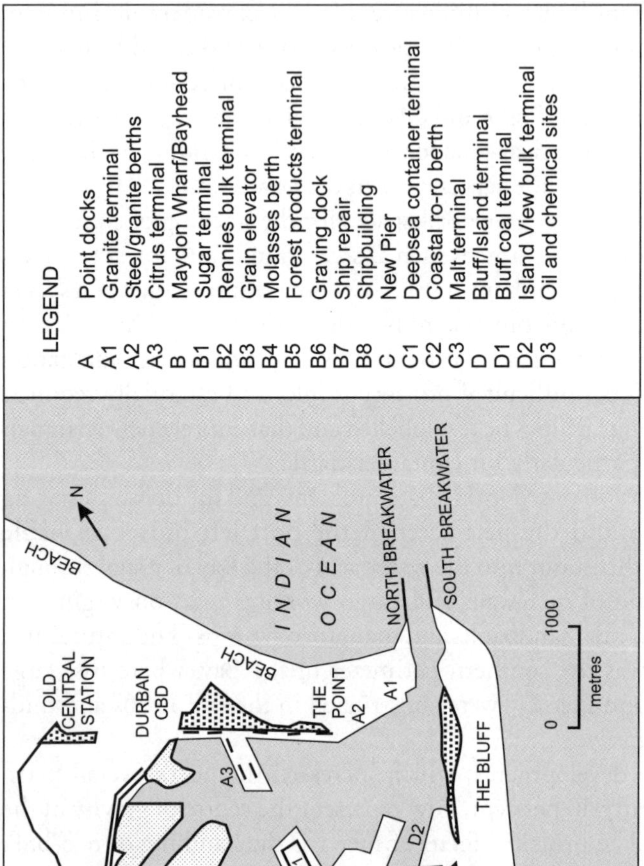

Figure 1 Durban harbour layout.

transported in dedicated cellular container vessels began to convulse international liner shipping from the late 1960s, and rapidly established an unassailable position on the principal liner trade routes. The 'container revolution' finally pulled South African carriers, cargo owners and port planners in its wake as somewhat reluctant fellow travellers in the 1970s, as the major Conference Lines serving southern Africa committed themselves to invest in the requisite cellular vessels, while the ports of Durban, Cape Town and Port Elizabeth were equipped with the necessary berth infrastructure and cargo-handling superstructure. In all the ports, container terminal operations remained strictly under the umbrella of the public sector port authority, and in the Durban terminal container handling remains an effective Portnet monopoly. Durban's container facilities took the form of an eight-berth terminal constructed on a pristine site adjacent to Pier 1, and from the official 'switch on' of South African container facilities in July 1977, Durban immediately established itself as the dominant container-handling port of southern Africa, accounting for some two-thirds of the sub-region's aggregate seaborne box moves.

From 1977 to the present, the basic marine infrastructure of the terminal has remained essentially unchanged in terms of berthing capacity, but both cargo-handling equipment and container stacking areas have been extended. As container traffic has grown, the terminal's designed capacity of 650 000 teus[6] was surpassed in the early 1990s but the installation of more efficient equipment, extended stacking areas for containers and more sophisticated computer based container-tracking systems, have stretched its inherent maximum annual capacity to some 1.3 million teus. This capacity stood perilously close to sea trade demand levels of approximately 1.2 million teus in 2000; hence if the traffic needs of southern African cargo owners are to be satisfied, additional container-handling capacity has to be installed as a matter of considerable urgency. That capacity could be installed either within the port of Durban or elsewhere within the range of eastern seaboard ports that compete for the trade of the industrial heartland of Gauteng. The Department of Transport's 'Moving South Africa' initiative recommended the 'densification' of existing transport corridors, which would point to Durban as the obvious candidate for deepened general cargo activity, but the creation of additional terminal capacity will not be easy. The options are either via new or reconfigured sites within the already saturated Durban port area, or via the more ambitious creation of a 'dig out' port in another area of the GDMA, such as the existing Durban International Airport (DIA) site.

The first of these options to be exploited will be a reconfiguration of the present saturated port area. In October 2000, the Transnet Board approved a three-phase plan to widen and deepen a four-berth segment of the Point Docks into a new 'combi' terminal, suitable for multi-purpose traffic and neo-bulk activities. When this traffic migrates to its new home, it will free up the existing Pier 1 'combi' terminal for full container operations, in the process raising annual container-handling capacity to approximately 1.9 million teus. This will be the first new investment in basic container-handling *infrastructure* since 1977 and will go some small way to mitigating the historic under-investment in general cargo facilities that was identified in the 'Moving South Africa' study (Department of Transport 1998). The implementation of this scheme will provide at best a breathing space for cargo owners and port planners; it leaves the question of the long-term capacity of the eastern seaboard ports unanswered.

The composite port facilities that have been outlined, and which are shown schematically in Figure 1, are those of a multi-purpose port, par excellence. In terms of overall facilities, Durban provides a total of 66 berths for deep sea vessels, spread over 15 km of quaywalls, distributed across five major spatial segments of the Bay of Natal. No other ports in southern or sub-Saharan Africa come remotely close to matching these facilities (Fair and Jones 1991): Table Bay harbour in Cape Town boasts some 35 berths for cargo-handling and ship repair (plus extensive facilities for the commercial fishing industry); Port Elizabeth has 12 working berths; Buffalo harbour in East London has 10; and Richards Bay offers a total of 17 berths, several of which are suitable for the larger cohorts of Panamax and Cape-sized dry-bulk vessels[7] that would be draft-restricted in Durban and the other general cargo ports. Further afield, the Mozambican port of Maputo has a fairly extensive physical infrastructure that nominally includes a total of 26 berths but, despite recent refurbishment of the port area, not all facilities are effectively operational. Other ports on the African east coast are considerably smaller; indeed, the only other ports anywhere in sub-Saharan Africa to offer anything approaching the capacity of the South African ports are the chaotically inefficient port of Lagos in Nigeria (with 36 berths), and little-used Dakar in Senegal (with 40 berths).

The diversity of Durban's physical port facilities is mirrored in the traffic base those facilities support. From its inauspicious beginning as a sand-choked lagoon in the mid-nineteenth century, Durban had evolved to a point where it became the dominant South African port by the time of the First World War, handling more traffic than all the Cape ports combined by 1915. This dominance was to continue throughout the inter-war years when the economic base of the South African economy was widening and diversifying and it was maintained through and beyond the Second World War. Total traffic volumes shipped and landed through Durban passed the three million ton threshold by the early 1920s, topped five million tons by 1928, sagged somewhat during the depressed trading conditions of the early 1930s, and recovered to the five million ton mark by 1940. Traffic levels were maintained at roughly this level during the war years of 1940–45, whereafter volumes of cargo handled grew at a steady if unspectacular rate for the next decade, reaching seven million tons by the mid-1950s. The pace of traffic growth was to accelerate markedly over the period 1956–75, with aggregate cargo handled doubling to reach 14 million tons by 1964, and doubling again to 29 million tons by 1970. Further traffic gains were recorded in the first half of the 1970s, to a point where Durban handled 35 million tons of cargo of all types in 1975. Thereafter, the growth trajectory of Durban port traffic is less easy to interpret, although a lower trend rate of growth has been recorded over the last two decades, with total traffic fluctuating between 40 and 46 million tons of cargo of all types (including previously classified oil products) annually. The explanation for this apparent turning point from a higher to a lower secular rate of traffic growth is largely to be found in the events that overtook the international sea transport industry and the South African port sector during and after the 1970s.

The decade of the 1970s was to mark a major watershed in South African port development and inter-port performance. Certain developments, notably the decision to introduce advanced container-handling techniques, served considerably to strengthen the competitive position of the port of Durban. Others, particularly the decision to invest in new deepwater port facilities in virgin (or at least largely undeveloped) harbour sites, were to see a decrease in Durban's dominance of the South African port league table, at least in terms of the crude arithmetic of recorded cargo volumes. The development of Saldanha as an export conduit for iron-ore had minimal impact on the eastern seaboard ports, but the establishment of deepwater facilities in Richards Bay 100 nautical miles to the north of Durban has exerted a huge influence on the activities of its southern neighbour.

The initial *raison d'être* for the establishment of the largest and most ambitious bulk port in the southern hemisphere was to serve as an export 'vent for surplus' for the Mpumulanga coal industry (Jones and Cawood 1974), and while coal remains the single dominant prop of Richards Bay's traffic base, the port has widened and diversified this base significantly since the 1980s, most notably so in the broad categories of bulk minerals and neo-bulk commodities such as steel, forest products and ferro-alloys. In all these categories, significant traffic diversion from Durban has occurred, and more may follow in the future. None of this migration is in any way surprising, as the greater availability of space in the Richards Bay port area allows the use of modern, space-hungry, cargo-handling techniques that are difficult to apply in the densely developed port areas of Durban. Cargo types that are less obvious candidates for migration include higher value general cargoes, container cargo and chemicals, where there is little impetus to utilise larger vessels that would be draft-restricted in Durban, and where the cargo makes heavy demands on the complex web of port-ancillary industries that the Durban area possesses in abundance, but with which Richards Bay is poorly endowed. The question of the respective comparative advantages of the two KwaZulu-Natal ports will be explored more fully later in this chapter, hence for the moment it suffices to assert that the two ports should be viewed as offering complementary rather than competing facilities.

In 1997, the port of Durban handled a total of a little over 46 million tons of cargo of all types, or some 30 million tons of cargo other than oil and petroleum products. The most obvious characteristic of Durban's port traffic is its diversity: Figure 2 indicates that all four major categories of sea trade – oil and petroleum products, containerised cargo, conventional breakbulk cargo and bulk traffic – are well represented.

In purely volume terms, the oil trades are the single dominant category, accounting for some 15 million tons or 34 per cent of overall port tonnage; containerised cargo contributes a 30 per cent (and rising)

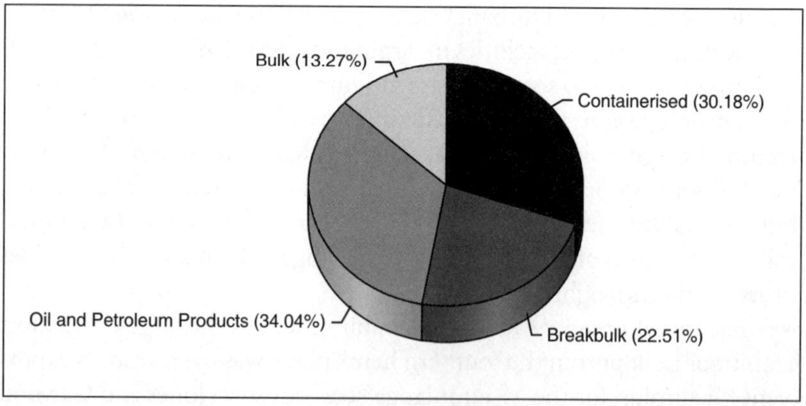

Figure 2 Major components of Durban port traffic, 1997 (% total cargo: total traffic 46.1 m tons).

share; and labour intensive breakbulk cargo makes up a little less than a quarter of the total traffic cake. The smallest relative weight is wielded by non-oil bulk cargoes which account for about 13 per cent of total freight volumes but still amount to a substantial 6 million tons. Below the surface of aggregate port traffic, Figures 3 and 4 show that the broad shape of cargo shipped (essentially exports) differs significantly from the shape of cargo landed (essentially imports).

Even the most cursory examination of these graphics reveals that Durban is the principal port of a developing region. The matrix of exports is dominated in volume terms by primary products (maize, coal, sugar, fruit and granite); by semi-beneficiated mineral products (ferro-alloys); by processed petroleum products and chemicals; and by intermediate goods or semi-manufactured goods (paper, woodpulp and steel). By contrast, finished goods and more sophisticated manufactures are largely absent from this volume rather than value based account, although the weight wielded by intermediate and manufactured goods can be expected to rise as the economy's planned reliance on manufactured exports increases.

By contrast, the pattern of imports is more diverse. Although dominated to an overwhelming extent (in volume but of course not in value terms) by the single item of crude oil, Durban's imports reflect the South African economy's continued reliance on imports of finished goods such as machinery, motor vehicles and components for the domestic assembly industries, textiles and general cargo (captured by the residual 'miscellaneous' category). With the exception of crude oil, bulk imports are limited, with principal commodity classes including the broad group of generally high-value chemicals, other liquid-bulk animal and vegetable oils, and rice. Something of a wild card in the import matrix over the last decade has been the broad family of cereals and foodgrains. With the exception of fairly stable volumes of rice, and some steady importation of wheat (much of it overborder cargo destined for the landlocked Southern African Development Community (SADC) countries), maize imports have fluctuated wildly. With regional cereal harvests decimated by successive *El Niño* episodes during the early 1990s, the South African ports switched from net exporters to substantial net importers of maize, but from the mid-1990s the pendulum has swung back towards net exports.

Although total traffic through Durban has been stable between 40 and 46 million tons over the last decade, some types of cargo have been anything but static in their performance. Indeed, no account of the traffic performance of the port of Durban would be complete without some

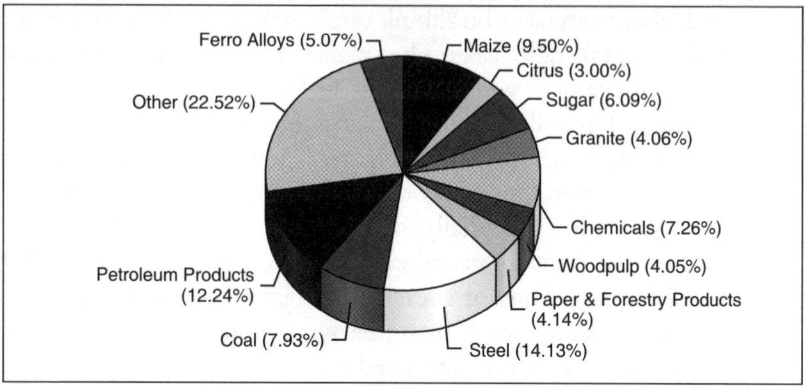

Figure 3 Principal exports shipped in the port of Durban, 1997.

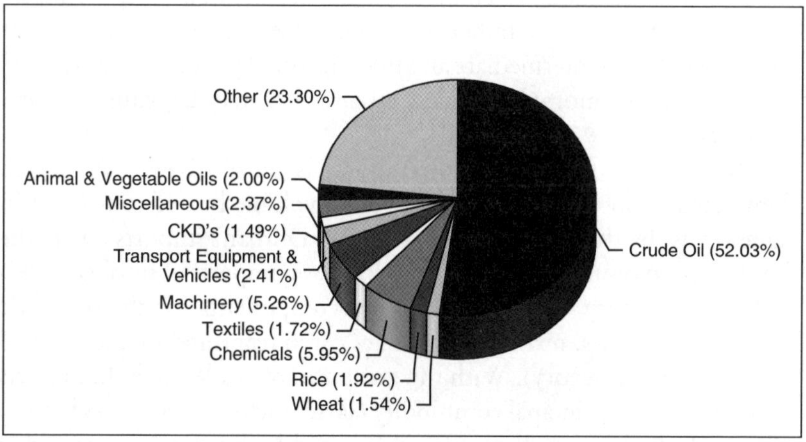

Figure 4 Principal imports landed in the port of Durban, 1997.

specific attention to the growth of containerised traffic, since this has become both the source of Durban's continued domination of southern African general cargo sea trade, and the principal source of stress for the port.

Since South African maritime transport joined the 'container revolution' in 1977, containerised traffic has appropriated an increasing share of regional general cargoes. Mainstream container facilities were established only in the three principal 'liner' ports of Cape Town, Port Elizabeth and Durban, and in all three, capacity well beyond the traffic parameters of the late 1970s was installed. In the port of Durban, this capacity (both in terms of the basic berth infrastructure of the container terminal and the cargo-handling superstructure required to move boxes between the terminal and its hinterland) proved adequate for the first decade of its operations. Durban's container traffic passed the 200 000 teu threshold in 1979, doubled to reach 400 000 teus by 1981, and then languished around this level until 1987, whereafter an upward growth trajectory resumed. By 1993, the throughput of 635 000 teus was still below the original capacity of the terminal, and there were few portents of the surge in container volumes that were soon to place these facilities under siege. As Figure 5 indicates, the rate of growth surged from 1992 to 1995, increasing by 11.5 per cent from 1992 to 1993; by a massive 20 per cent from 1993 to 1994; and by a further 12.5 per cent to 1995, to reach a record annual level of 860 000 teus. This once again threatened to overwhelm the capacity of the terminal, which had been expanded to an estimated 880 000 teus via the acquisition of higher capacity gantries plus an emergency extension of the container stacking area. Thereafter, runaway growth was reined in somewhat, with volumes stabilising between 900 000 and 1 million teus between 1996 and 1999, although 2000 witnessed a further growth spurt of almost 20 per cent, to reach nearly 1.2 million teus. The reconfiguration of Pier 1 into a full container terminal will keep capacity ahead of demand for the moment, but if the eight per cent steady state growth in container volumes experienced since 1993 is sustained, then the augmented container-

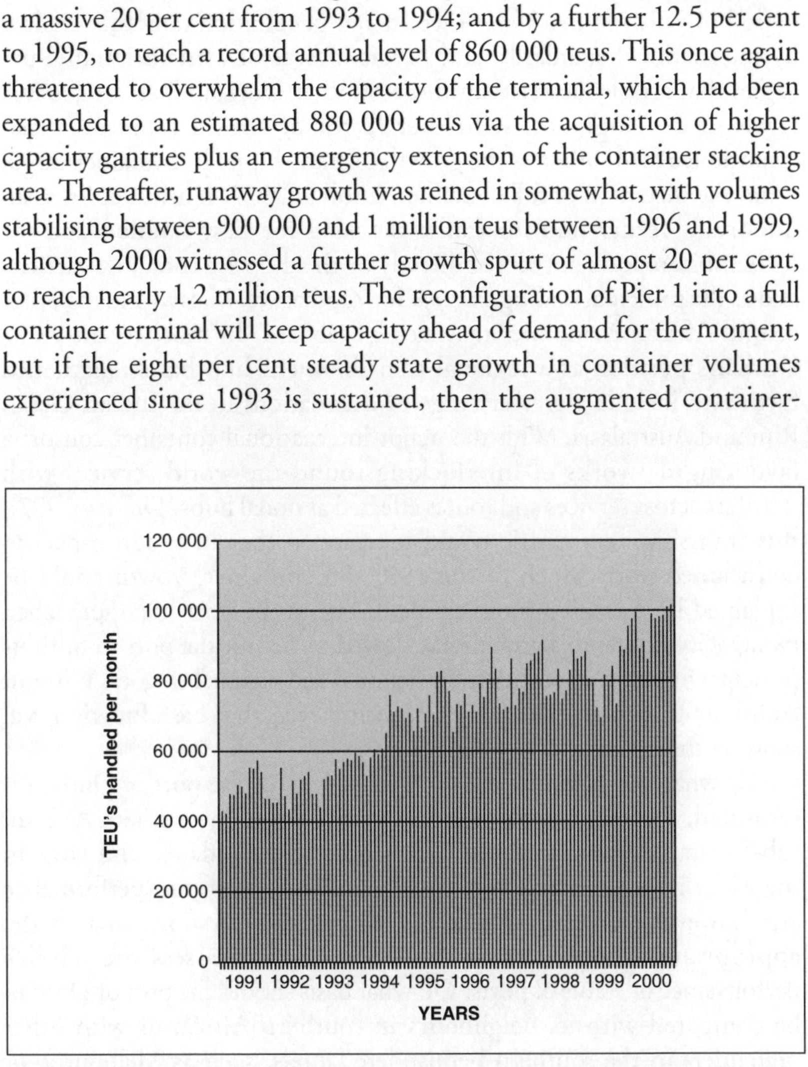

Figure 5 Containers handled in the port of Durban 1991–2000 (teus).

handling capacity of 1.9 million teus will be overwhelmed by 2007/08. By that time, sites for more substantial capacity expansion will have to be created if Durban is to retain its present share of southern African containerised sea trade, let alone pretend to any kind of regional 'hub' status.

The basis for this traffic growth, which initially caught both the port authorities and the carrying lines on the back foot, is not well understood. Factors advanced include the 'catching up' that the South African liner trades were faced with once the economy ended its long period of isolation in 1993/94; container penetration rates that are low by international standards; and heroic indices of container traffic per capita that are also lower than those of other economies at comparable levels of development. A further factor of considerable potential importance for Durban is the growth of transshipment container cargo. From the inception of full containerisation in 1977, Durban acted as an important feeder hub for traffic destined for East London and for Mozambican ports not served directly by the deep sea container carriers, and as the principal trading *entrepôt* for Zimbabwe, Malawi and the other central African economies that lack a seaboard. In more recent years, Durban's position as a regional transshipment hub has strengthened further to include a greater range of destinations in the Indian Ocean Rim and Australasia. With the major international container consortia favouring networks of interlocking round-the-world services with transfers across services and routes effected at nodal hubs (Drewry 1997), this transshipment traffic could increase further in a non-capacity-constrained port. Much of the 1993–95 container growth could be explained by increased transshipment, but as the port has approached its capacity limits, this growth has slowed to permit the port to fulfil its principal function as a conduit for national and regional cargoes. Without additions to container-handling capacity, even that base function will soon be threatened.

By whatever yardstick the size and activity of the port of Durban is measured, it emerges as a significant port: colossal by southern African, sub-Saharan African and southern hemisphere standards, and large in the wider international league table. Comparisons of port performance are, however, not easily made and all beg the question: what is the appropriate numeraire that should be used to assess the relative performance or status of ports? On what basis should the port of Durban be compared with its neighbours in southern Africa, or with other pretenders to the southern hemisphere laurels, such as Melbourne or Sydney?

Several poor but commonly used aggregate indicators include the physical size of port facilities (in terms of numbers of berths); the numbers of annual vessel callers; and the total tonnage of cargo handled. All of these measures ignore crucial dimensions such as the value, type and composition of cargo handled, and cargo-handling technology used. Some attempts have been made to construct 'real' measures of port activity (Suykens 1984; Charlier 1996) by deflating various types of port traffic to a common base of conventional breakbulk.[8] Charlier applied this technique to the traffic base of the South African ports to produce a more credible ranking that promotes Durban to top spot but none of these simple measures capture the richness of economic activity associated with highly diversified, multi-purpose ports. Consequently, what is suggested in this chapter is a different approach to assess port performance.

This approach views a port as an interface in a wider multi-modal transportation and service process, and as an organism which, when operating successfully, adds value to commodity trade and to the community it serves. This value, and hence the 'real' performance of a port, could be measured, at least in part, by the employment generated directly and indirectly by the port; by the linkages it forges with other industries and sectors; by the revenues it generates in these associated economic activities; and by the expenditure patterns required to sustain the fabric of those activities. In essence, therefore, a port is viewed as a crucible for the creation and maintenance of jobs, revenue, investment and wealth in a host of port-related areas.

The principal focus of the next major section (and the real guts of this chapter) will seek to do just that in the context of the port of Durban and the linkages it creates in its host community, the GDMA. But before that exercise is attempted, it may be useful to summarise relative performance on the basis of the available quantitative indicators of port activity, however imperfect these may be.

In terms of total harbour traffic in nominal tonnage terms, Durban emerges as the second most active port in southern Africa, with its approximately 40–45 million tons of cargo of all types representing about 28 per cent of the total annual cargo base of all the South African ports. On the same basis, Durban holds this position in sub-Saharan Africa, where the competition is admittedly thin. Indeed, elsewhere in southern Africa it is desperately thin, as Maputo presently handles annually some 2.7 million tons of cargo of all types, Beira 2.3 million tons, the deepwater port of Nacala less than ten per cent of that, and Dar es Salaam between 4 and 5 million tons. More notably, in the southern hemisphere, Durban outperforms all the South American ports, while the traffic bases of Durban, Melbourne and Sydney emerge as broadly similar in quantity terms, but with the ranking in the order noted above. In terms of container traffic only, the same ranking emerges (ISL 1997).

A final possible benchmark to employ would be to examine the command of various ports over the value as opposed to the physical volume of cargoes passing across the wharfside. Here, in a South African context, the port of Durban stands supreme. Two earlier exercises (Pearson 1995; Jones 1990) indicate that approximately 65 per cent by value of the cargo handled by all the South African harbours passes through Durban. This is understandable, and reflects Durban's dominance of the region's traditional 'liner' trades, whether these are organised by way of containerised or conventional shipping services.

In overall terms, Durban's claim to be the leading port of southern Africa, sub-Saharan Africa and the Indian Ocean Rim is immensely strong. Indeed, it has few serious rivals anywhere in the southern hemisphere. That claim rests on the size and diversity of its facilities, the size and diversity of its traffic base, and the myriad of ancillary industries associated with that traffic base. It is towards an understanding of the impact of the activities of those port-related industries that the next section is directed.

The Impact of Port Activities on the Durban Metropolitan Economy

The objective of this central section is to attempt to quantify the influence of the activities of the port on the Durban community at a recent specific level of port performance. The exercise, though based on fairly extensive legwork, is therefore essentially a piece of static analysis, insofar as only one single time slice (based on 1994 port activity levels) is presented.

In attempting to examine the impact of the activities of the port on the local economy, three very broad categories of port-dependent economic activity can be identified. The first, which may be termed the family of directly port-related activities, are those ancillary industries that service vessels, cargoes and persons passing through the port. These activities owe their existence directly to the port, and would not exist in its absence. The second category, which may be termed the family of indirectly port-related activities, has two components. The first is the group of port users or cargo owners (sources of export cargo and consignees of cargo landed) that are located in the Durban area, wholly or partly because of the locational advantages the port confers. The second is the group of industries that are backwardly linked to the direct port ancillary players, by supplying goods, services and factor inputs. The third and final broad category, which may be termed the set of induced effects, arises as a result of the local economic ripples generated via the multiplier effects of the purchasing power created by all the enterprises dependent on the port.

The methodology used was to interview as many of the major associated firms and industries as possible. During the mid-1994 to early 1995 period, just short of 100 such interviews were conducted. In each case (with varying degrees of success) an attempt was made to elicit information concerning, inter alia, employment levels, the associated wages and salaries bill, other major items of cost, revenue generated, and linkage effects with other Durban based or regionally based businesses. In the process, this exercise produced a reasonably comprehensive and robust picture of the activities of the direct port ancillary industries, including both their linkages with other locally based enterprises and the induced multipliers generated by their spending injections into local circular flow of economic activity. However, apart from obvious candidates such as the oil refineries, the motor assembly industry and the paper industry, a far less satisfactory coverage of the family of local port users emerged, largely because of the extreme difficulty of identifying local sources and sinks of cargo (particularly within the important category of heterogeneous general cargo) from within the port's overall cargo matrix. The analysis that follows consequently attempts to quantify the impact on the local economy of the port purely as a transport interface – that is, as an entity that handles vessels and their cargoes – and largely ignores the impact of the activities of Durban based importers and exporters who use the port.

Directly port-related activities

When vessels call at a port or when cargo passes across the wharfside, economic activity is energised at several levels. The simple questions posed here are: when ships are serviced or when cargo is handled in the port of Durban, where and in what numbers are persons employed; where is revenue generated and in what pursuits; where are costs incurred: and how much spending remains in the Durban community?

Port ancillary industries perform two basic tasks: one quite complex set of activities services vessels that use harbour facilities, while a more extensive and certainly more lucrative daisy chain of economic activities is associated with the physical handling, management, logistic tracking and distribution of cargo. The former includes the marine infrastructure and services provided by Portnet; the ships' husbandry functions of the ships' agency business; the ship repair industry; the bunker fuel industry (where Durban is one of the largest and most inexpensive bunker supply centres in the southern hemisphere); the family of ship chandlers supplying victuals and stores to vessels patronising the port; locally based shipowners and operators; and several state departments. The richer array of cargo related economic functions includes a host of cargo services supplied by Portnet; the activities of the 13 private terminal operators in Durban port; the labour intensive stevedoring industry engaged in physical cargo handling; the freight-oriented business of the ships agents; the complex gamut of financial and management services provided to cargo owners by the clearing and forwarding industry; the specialised services supporting container traffic; Spoornet's port-related rail services; the many road hauliers involved in the long- and short-haul distribution of cargo; and certain other state departments, most notably the Customs and Excise division of the Department of Finance. These two chains of activities obviously interlock at several points but all the links in these chains (plus several more that have not been listed) are necessary to maintain the fabric of a modern port.

An attempt was made to assess the performance of virtually all the major enterprises in these two closely related if not interbred families. The results of this exercise are summarised in Table 1, and indicate that the activities of the port sustain over 360 establishments in both the private and public sectors, and that in excess of 24 000 jobs are created in the Durban area in first-round activities immediately linked to the port. The establishments listed in Table 1 cover a huge spectrum, ranging from the two Transnet colossi, with combined local employment of more than 8 500 persons, to the smallest independent clearing and forwarding agencies with three or four employees. Not surprisingly, Portnet itself emerged as the largest employer, with a work-force that had stabilised around the 5 400 level in the mid-1990s, after a period of falling numbers. Portnet employment levels in the port of Durban may also be used as a vehicle to illustrate some of the fundamental differences between Durban and Richards Bay. While the traffic base of the latter exceeds that of Durban by some 75 per cent if the full traffic bases of the ports are considered, total Portnet employment in Richards Bay stands at only some 1 440 persons. In the port of Durban, one local Portnet job is created for roughly each 7 500 tons of cargo handled annually, while in Richards Bay some 47 000 tons of cargo (or approximately six times as much) are needed to generate one workplace. While this heroic exercise abstracts from the complex differences in the terminal structure of the two ports, it nonetheless underscores the vastly increased employment creating potential of a multi-purpose port as opposed to an essentially bulk oriented port.

Other significant crucibles for local jobs include the private terminal operators (who control annually between 9 and 10 million tons of cargo or about 40 per cent of the total non-oil traffic of the port); the labour intensive and highly diffuse clearing and forwarding fraternity (130 firms employing over 3 500 persons); the stevedores; the ships agents; and the road hauliers. Several of these industries also offer interesting opportunities for small businesses, insofar as low to insignificant barriers to entry permit small-scale entrepreneurs to share the market with larger firms in areas such as clearing and forwarding, ship chandling and road haulage. In other areas, notably in the terminals and ships' agency, industries operate on more oligopolistic lines.

Estimates of the expenditure on wages and salaries of this work-force must be seen as more speculative, as not all the respondents furnished coherent wage and cost information, but if the assumption is made that average wages in the unspecified instances are similar to those reported, then the gross remuneration of the directly port-related labour force emerges at approximately R950 million in 1994 prices, or an average gross annual remuneration (including all benefits and contributions) of some R39 600 per employee.

Both these employment and wage estimates should be seen as conservative, since some quite significant interests associated with sea transport are excluded. These include the insurance and legal fraternity associated with the maritime sector; the wide-ranging financial and banking services supporting shipping; the transport and travel industry associated with crew transfers and the seasonal cruise industry; medical services; linkages with the entertainment industry (some clearly in the informal sector); and smaller but notable services such as the provision of laundry facilities, specialist equipment repairers and others.

The estimates of employment and expenditure enumerated in Table 1 are conservative for two far more powerful reasons. Firstly, the employment and wage levels indicated represent only the immediate, first-round influence on the local economy. In practice, the effect of expenditure (on wages and salaries or other inputs) on the community is not felt in a one-shot fashion; rather any injection into the circular flow of economic activity has a multiplied impact on final income and output. The size of the local community multiplier is determined by the consumption propensity of wage earners, the tax leakage factor and the extent to which expenditure leaks out of the Durban area. With the majority of port-related employees in the low- to middle-income brackets,

Table 1 Establishments, employment and wages in Durban port ancillary industries (all data at 1994 levels).

Industry/Sector	*Number*	*Employment*	*Wage bill (R million)*
Portnet	1	5 400	240
Portnet dredging	1	112	6
Spoornet	1	3 217	115
Terminal operators	11	2 213	90
Liquid bulk terminals	3	275	16
Clearing and forwarding agents	138	3 600	135
Ships' agents	37	1 350	65
Ship chandlers	17	400	ns
Container depots	3	366	13
Container parks	7	260	ns
Container logistics	3	140	6
Shipowners and operators	5	1 100[2]	ns
Ship repairers and builders	5	960[3]	34
Stevedores	24	1 650	45
Cargo equipment suppliers	2	200	ns
Road haulers	>75	1 500[1]	ns
Bunker services	2	110	5
Offshore services	3	80	3
Tallying services	5	120[4]	ns
Security	3	300[1]	ns
Marine contractors	2	114	5
Customs and excise	1	300	ns
Other state	3	100[1]	ns
Total	>360	23 867	~R950[5]

Notes

1. The employment magnitudes shown in these cases should be seen as very rough estimates, and must be interpreted with appropriate caution.
2. This figure includes sea-going and shore based personnel.
3. This figure includes the personnel of the large pleasure-craft builders, but excludes any employment in industries backwardly linked to the repair industry, however close those linkages might be. The dockyard workers of Portnet are excluded, as these are shown in the broad Portnet entry.
4. The total number of persons engaged in tallying operations is almost certainly greater, but several of these are included in other listed categories, such as the terminal operations of cargo principals like ISCOR, and the ships' agencies.
5. The estimate of aggregate remuneration is, once again, a very rough estimate, as by no means all respondents, particularly those in the smaller establishments, furnished wages and salaries data.

a relatively high marginal propensity to consume and a relatively low effective tax rate are likely, making a high multiplier plausible. For the purposes of this exercise, an average tax rate of 20 per cent, a marginal propensity to consume out disposable income of 0.85, and an expenditure retention of 85 per cent in the Greater Durban Area have been assumed. This yields an overall multiplier of approximately 2.4 and implies that the R950 million paid to persons in direct port employment in the Durban area would generate an increase in local expenditure of some R2.3 billion, all at 1994 prices. This exercise is admittedly crude, but a more detailed distribution of earnings across income ranges, that would be required for a more convincing stab at an effective tax rate, was simply not forthcoming from respondents. A similar set of assumptions underpins all subsequent multiplier applications in this chapter.

As a more comprehensive measure of the real impact of the activities of the port of Durban on the local economy, the information in Table 1 is conservative for a further major reason. Wages and salaries are not the only costs of port-related enterprises; other substantial costs (or expenditures) pass into the hands of those Durban based industries that supply inputs and services to the direct port ancillary establishments. An attempt was made during interviews with the latter to establish these somewhat broader patterns of expenditure. In most cases where the relevant information could be gleaned, between 45–55 per cent of total costs represented remuneration of employees. Of the remaining categories of cost, most respondents reported a high incidence of Durban sourcing, particularly in the case of property costs; services; paper; timber products (extensively used in stevedoring and lashing); ropes, hooks and simple cargo-working equipment; building materials; and consumable stores. Principal inputs not obtained locally comprised transport equipment; computer equipment; more specialised cargo-handling equipment such as forklifts, stackers and gantry cranes; and other machinery and capital items. Cost details supplied were admittedly impressionistic, but with a weighted average of 48 per cent of total costs incurred in areas other than wages and salaries, together with the relatively conservative assumption that Durban based enterprises absorbed 60 per cent of this expenditure, a further R500–550 million of essentially port-related spending entered the circular flow of economic activity in the GDMA in 1994. Once again, this is a first-round influence only, and with an assumed multiplier of 2.4, will generate overall annual expenditure of some R1.2 billion. If labour intensities in these support industries are (heroically) taken to be similar to those in the direct port ancillary industries themselves, then the basis for a further 6 500 to 7 000 jobs in the Durban area is established.

The port of Durban therefore emerges as a substantial source of both employment and expenditure, supporting a minimum of 31 000 jobs in the GDMA (or about seven per cent of formal sector employment), and generating aggregate annual local expenditure of some R3.5 billion at constant 1994 prices, or R5.2 billion in 2000 prices. It must be stressed that these magnitudes reflect the activities of the port solely as a transport interface between land and sea transport, and *exclude* the economic activities of port users (exporters and importers) located in the Durban area. In some cases, the distinction between port users and the direct port ancillary group of enterprises is so fuzzy as to be practically non-existent. Obvious candidates for inclusion into the immediate ambit of the port would include the commercial fishing industry that uses a Durban base to exploit northern KwaZulu-Natal and Mozambican waters; the recreational fishing and boating community; and the Durban naval base. A more heavy weight candidate is the petroleum industry, centred around the SAPREF and Engen refineries but also including a host of ancillary activities associated with the blending and distribution of oil products. The refineries alone provide employment for some 1 800 employees and daily contractors, while the oil products processors, most of whom are located in the Island View area of the port, create another 500-plus jobs. All of these activities owe their day-to-day livelihood to the port and would not exist in its absence. If these activities and their linkages are pulled into the port ancillary net, they raise total port-related employment towards the 40 000 mark.

A final pivotal dimension of the relationship between ports and their host cities centres around the organisational structure and operational performance of the port authority. Models abound internationally (Goss 1992): some of the world's major ports, such as Rotterdam and Antwerp, fall under the jurisdiction of municipal port authorities; others, such as Hamburg, Bremen and several American ports, are essentially controlled by regional, state or provincial authorities; while yet others, including what is arguably the world's leading port – Singapore – operate under the aegis of national port authorities.

In South Africa, the ports have always been administered as national assets, initially by the Harbours division of the South African Railways & Harbours; later by the Harbours division of the South African Transport Services; and most recently by Portnet, the semi-autonomous Harbours division of the state owned Transnet Ltd. What is unusual about the South African ports is not the centralised nature of control, but rather its parameters, which extend to a far wider gamut of facilities and services than is the norm in most developed market-type economies.[9]

These cover not only the provision and management of the ports' basic marine- and cargo-working infrastructure, but also include the cargo-handling superstructure and many cargo services, including physical cargo handling and distribution. In a port like Durban, with a substantial set of private terminals, this produces a messy set of arrangements, whereby Portnet retains an overarching landlord role over the port as a whole, while the operating terrain is shared with private terminal operators. The port authority is consequently in a very real sense both player and referee, carrying out cargo-handling operations in its own right, but also making and administering the rules for private-sector competitors.

In the Working Group that was established in 1995 to advise the Ministry of Transport on maritime policy issues as part of the groundwork for the production of the recent Green and White Papers on transport policy, there was much discussion over various models of port authority jurisdiction. South Africa's practices were acknowledged to be unhealthy and the essential separation of landlord and operating functions was strongly favoured, with recommendations that the former responsibilities be entrusted to a statutory body quite separate from any operating entities. These recommendations have, in part, been followed by Portnet, which effectively 'unbundled' itself during the course of 2000 into a port authority or landlord division and an operating division. For reasons of convenience, the national headquarters of the latter have been located in Durban, although this physical move does not betoken a devolution of decision-making power to the local level.

There was also much discussion in the Working Group over various local, regional and national port authority models. The Transport White Paper leaves this question open, but there is little realistic prospect of a change in the ruling view of ports as national rather than local assets.

This is an important question for the port and city of Durban, not least because Durban port has been historically, and presently remains, a highly profitable venture. Under the present dispensation, the surplus generated by individual ports does not necessarily redound to the advantage of the host communities, but has effectively disappeared into a centralised Transnet 'black hole'. For many decades, port profits were utilised, against all the efficiency rules of micro-economics, to cross-subsidise other loss-making transport operations. Although the extent of this cross-subsidisation has decreased significantly since the mid-1980s, there is still a considerable net transfer of surplus or profit out of a port community such as Durban. The precise details of profitability have been difficult to estimate since the 'commercialisation' of Transnet in the early 1990s, but if Durban's financial performance relative to the other ports is assumed to have remained roughly the same as it was in the late 1980s, when fuller data were last available, then Durban is likely to remain the major contributor to overall Portnet profits, which stood at some R1.7 billion in 1997/98.

The consequences of the present model of port management for the Durban community extend far beyond mere control over financial resources. More seriously, the Durban community has been historically and still is excluded from the decision-making process in the port, including decisions over tariff policy (and therefore over the relative competitiveness of Durban port) and major investment decisions that affect the shape and use of the port/Bay area, as well as alternative sites for port expansion. Over the years, the responses of both local commerce/industry and local government to this exclusion have been surprisingly muted. The Durban Chamber of Commerce has frequently registered its unhappiness over tariff issues and periodic bouts of port congestion, but has seldom confronted the peripheral position of Durban in the decision-making process. Local government has in recent years tackled the latter issue, but has found central government ministries in a democratic South Africa to be no more receptive than those of the former regime to a greater role for the local community in port decision-making. Indeed, during the course of 1997 the Durban Metro battled to secure permission to conduct a mere *investigation* of alternative port sites in the Greater Durban Area, against a backdrop of the state's preference for transport corridors to Richards Bay or Algoa Bay.

Such effective anti-Durban bias has since diminished, but any formal shift of port-planning power to a genuine municipal port authority remains a remote probability (and may also not even be desirable in terms of optimal national transport resource allocation). However, whatever the future formal port authority and operational structures may be, the inclusion of metropolitan and community interests in serious port-related decision-making is nothing less than basic good sense.

From Statics to Dynamics: The Effects of a Changing Port Traffic Base on the Metropolitan Economy

The previous section sought to examine the *overall* impact of the activities of the port of Durban on the local economy *at a particular level of port activity*. That impact was shown to be significant, revealing the port to be a major crucible for both jobs and expenditure flows. In a situation where certain segments of the port are under considerable demand and capacity pressure, a more pivotally important set of questions may rather be those that explore the economic impact of *changes* in port activity on the local economy. If additional vessel calls or cargo flows can be captured by the port, what output, employment and expenditure gains will be conferred upon the Durban community? Conversely, if traffic is lost to other regional ports, how many potential local jobs will be sacrificed as a result of this diversion, or how much local expenditure will be foregone?

These questions are most relevant in those areas where port facilities are under stress or where traffic growth prospects are high. The prime and overwhelming candidate for attention is therefore plainly the broad area of container traffic, where recent growth has stretched port capacity up to and beyond its elastic limits. This section will consequently be directed almost exclusively at containerised and unitised traffic.

The local Durban economy has the advantage of an established infrastructure capable of supporting the traffic base of the port. An increase in the volume of traffic, be it containerised, general or bulk, consequently does not necessarily require the establishment of entirely new facilities or activities, although it certainly will do so as ultimate capacity limits are exceeded. This has already occurred in container handling, where sustained demand pressure has finally generated an investment response, albeit a limited one. Within the network of port ancillary industries, a larger volume of traffic directly and quickly affects certain activities such as stevedoring; warehousing; road cartage; rail transport; the container depots, parks and logistics operations; the relevant terminal operators; the freight departments of ships' agents; and the documentation processing functions of the clearing and forwarding business. The impact on other entities, such as the marine division of Portnet; the ship chandlers; the repair industry and others may be less immediate, particularly if the increased traffic performance comes from vessels working larger volumes of cargo per port call. In sum, however, a larger volume of traffic generates additional activity across a broad gamut of enterprises, and ultimately translates into more spending, more facilities and more jobs in the Durban area. But how much more?

The simple arithmetic of the exercises carried out in the previous section suggests that Durban's total annual traffic sustains, on the basis of admittedly conservative assumptions, a total of over 30 000 jobs as a result of the activities of direct port ancillary industries. Very crudely, therefore, a job appears to be created for every 1 300 tons of cargo handled. Quite obviously, different types of traffic may have markedly different influences on employment creation, and the isolation of the impact of specific categories of cargo would be virtually impossible. An exception is the category of containerised traffic where previous work by the author (Jones 1996) showed the port's container trades to be responsible for some 9 000–10 000 workplaces in directly port-related industries, plus a further 3 000 in industries backwardly linked to these direct container enterprises. This suggests that a full-time job is created in the Durban area for every 70 containers passing through the port. To extend either of these simple relationships uncritically onto an expanding or contracting traffic base would be simplistic to the point of absurdity, and indeed it is difficult to measure marginal benefits in terms of employment creation with any precision. Rather, the method used here was to attempt to quantify the additional *spending* injected into the local economy when a typical container vessel passes through the port of Durban.

Much of the information used in this exercise was drawn from local ships' agents, several of whom supplied information relating to the typical expenditure patterns of different types of vessels using the port of Durban. Not all spending is captured by the disbursement accounts of the ships' agents. Notable exceptions include direct outlays by cargo owners as opposed to shipowners (particularly in respect of clearing, forwarding, warehousing and inland transport charges), while certain vessel costs such as the costs of ships' supplies furnished by ship chandlers, bunker costs and certain repair costs are also excluded. In these cases, shipowners generally negotiate directly with the service suppliers. Estimates of these expenditure categories were attempted on the basis of information gleaned directly from the various industries involved.

Specifically within the spectrum of container activities, data gathered covered vessels ranging in size from the 3 000-plus teu cellular vessels running on the South Africa/Europe Container Service (SAECS) to small feeder container vessels distributing transshipment boxes along the East African coast. For the purposes of this exercise, however, a 'standard' container vessel was taken to be a vessel working between 400–500 teus through the port's main container terminal on a single call to the port of Durban, since this conformed roughly to the parameters of the 'average' container terminal caller as estimated by Portnet in 1994.[10] On this basis, an attempt was made to construct a typical expenditure profile per 'standard' port call. The results are shown in Table 2.

One very important category of cost/expenditure has been left out of the arithmetic reflected in the Table. This is the category of *ad valorem* wharfage levied on the value of cargo passing across the wharfside.[11] This is the single most important source of revenue for Portnet, and is particularly significant in the case of container cargo, which tends to fill the upper end of the cargo value spectrum. The reason for the omission is quite clear. The objective of this undertaking is to estimate the impact of port activities on the *local Durban* economy. This is complicated by the fact that a substantial proportion of both revenue and ultimately profit generated by Portnet in Durban is not contained within the metropolitan area but is leaked away into the central Portnet/Transnet coffers. It is to compensate for this haemorrhage that wharfage revenue has been omitted. For the same reason, customs charges have been ignored. Other items covered by the Portnet harbour tariff structure are included, as they can more tangibly be associated with economic activities on the ground, or on the water, in the Durban area.

This exercise should be seen as an impressionistic indication rather than as a precise snapshot of economic activity. Some of the magnitudes enumerated should be interpreted with caution, most notably the road and rail expenditure sums. The private road haulage industry is notoriously difficult to penetrate, both in terms of cargo volumes and tariff levels. The resultant estimates are consequently highly tentative although they are also conservative. In the case of rail spending, the net impact on the metropolitan economy may be overstated somewhat, as not all port-generated rail revenue ultimately translates into economic activity and jobs in the Durban area. These qualifications should not, however, deflect attention from the substantial level of direct Durban based expenditure generated from a typical container ship call: this exercise reveals that an 'average' box ship handling 400 containers in a single call at the port of Durban is responsible for direct first-round expenditure in port activities and port ancillary industries of approximately R788 000 in 1994 prices, or some R1 970 per box. Like all other injections into the circular flow of economic activity, this expenditure affects the economy in a multiplied way. If the same multiplier as that associated with overall port activity is applied to the container-handling industry, then this injection ultimately produces an increase in Durban based income or output of a little under R1.9 million. Further economic linkages are obviously also experienced in industries supporting the direct port ancillary enterprises.

As Table 2 indicates, first-round expenditure is split roughly equally across the private and public sectors, with the major beneficiaries being the two large Transnet divisions. Portnet marine, container terminal and cartage services absorb a little less than one-third of spending, while a further 13.3 per cent finds its way into Spoornet's coffers. Other major items of expenditure that flow into more unambiguously private and largely Durban based pockets are clearing and forwarding charges (10.8 per cent); road haulage (12.7 per cent); bunkering services (13.1 per cent); ships' agency fees (5.7 per cent); ship repairs (5.1 per cent); the

Table 2 Major categories of expenditure by a typical container vessel using the main container terminal of the port of Durban (1994 tariff and cost levels).

Item/Service	*Expenditure*	*% total*
Portnet marine services	20 000	2.5
Portnet container charges	180 000	22.9
Portnet container cartage	30 000	3.8
Stevedoring and lashing	5 000	0.7
Tallying	1 000	0.1
Ships' agency[1]	45 000	5.7
Medical	1 000	0.1
Crew transfers	2 000	0.3
Security	1 000	0.1
Clearing and forwarding	85 000	10.8
Ship chandlers	30 000	3.8
Ship repair services[2]	40 000	5.1
Container depots	35 000	4.4
Container logistics	5 000	0.6
Bunkers and fuel[3]	103 000	13.1
Rail charges[4]	105 000	13.3
Private road haulage[5]	100 000	12.7
Total expenditure	R788 000	100.0

Notes

1. Ships' agency charges comprise two components – agency fees in respect of port husbandry operations, and freight commissions. The latter dominates.
2. Ship repair activities tend to be large and indivisible but for these purposes the heroic assumption has been made that repair expenditure is averaged equally over all callers. The major clients of local repair yards are the large container carriers.
3. Based on the purchase of 240 tons of marine fuel oil per port call, at $100 per ton. This assumption may be highly conservative, as some of the larger container vessels take as much as 4 000 tons of bunkers during a single call.
4. Based on what Spoornet claims its share of inland container carriage is, and on the Durban/Gauteng rates for a 6 metre container. Not all of this expenditure is contained within the Durban area.
5. Little useful data on road movements and rates were forthcoming, hence this item is little more than a rough (though conservative) guess.

packing/unpacking and storage services provided by container depots (4.4 per cent); and ship supply services provided by ship chandlers (3.8 per cent).

This exercise reveals that the gains to be made by the Durban community from the attraction of additional container traffic are substantial. Conversely, the losses that would result should container vessels be diverted to other ports are equally significant. The basis for the magnitudes set out in Table 2 is a 'standard' container vessel working a relatively modest number of boxes; clearly, the expenditure gains or losses resulting from the retention or diversion of the largest container vessels currently deployed on the South African trades (that work over 2 000 boxes per call), would be commensurately greater. If a steady eight per cent growth in container volumes is sustained in the foreseeable future, an additional annual 80 000 teus will pass through the port of Durban. On the basis of the above methodology, the annual cost to the Durban community of not having the facilities to handle such incremental traffic would amount to some R135 million (in constant 1994 prices) in the form of direct foregone revenue for port-related industries; or a multiplied expenditure sacrifice of R310 million. Further, if the very loose equation is accepted that one direct job in the local port sector is created for every 70 containers handled, the anticipated annual growth of traffic would produce approximately 1 200 additional jobs per annum.

It is important to note that the exercises carried out in this section, and the economic benefits that have been identified, are largely independent of the ultimate destination of imported container cargo, or the source of containerised exports. The expenditure estimates, multipliers and linkages relate solely to activities associated with the actual handling, husbandry and management of container vessels, and the physical handling, distribution and administration of their cargoes. Economic activity associated with cargo owners (importers and exporters) in the Durban area has been ignored. This is an important qualification as it underscores the argument that even where the port of Durban does act as a 'clearing house' for Gauteng traffic or as an *entrepôt* for overborder cargo originating in or destined for areas elsewhere in southern Africa, major expenditure and employment benefits are still conferred upon the local Durban economy. Equally obviously, where cargo is generated or absorbed in the Durban area (and up to 40 per cent of container traffic has been estimated to be essentially 'Durban based' cargo), the multiplier effects on the local economy are significantly greater.

Indeed, the only container traffic in respect of which local economic impacts are more limited is the category of transshipment cargo that essentially remains in the port area between discharge and eventual on-carriage. The vessel-related spending associated with a transshipment caller is similar to that of a vessel carrying national or overborder cargo, but in respect of cargo-related expenditure, the local linkages are significantly smaller, since the cargo does not impinge on the clearing, forwarding, warehousing, logistics or distribution industries. Portnet, the carrying lines and the purveyors of vessel-related services, are consequently the principal beneficiaries of any value-added that is generated. On this basis, it may be tempting to suggest that growth in the demand for transshipment cargo may not be the most compelling reason to increase the overall container-handling infrastructure of the port since the costs of traffic diversion to other ports are not enormous. Such sentiments have been expressed with some vigour by the environmental lobby and other interested parties who oppose further encroachment of port facilities into the water area of the Bay of Natal. Unfortunately, this view is also highly simplistic, since the operation of modern container shipping does not permit a simple separation of national and transshipment cargoes. Instead, the container trades are increasingly organised around global services that interconnect at hub ports. There are consequently few or no container callers carrying *exclusively* national cargo and equally few if any that transport *exclusively* transshipment boxes. For a port such as Durban that aspires to hub status, there would appear to be no alternative but to provide the requisite facilities for all 'normal' hub-and-spoke container traffic which the carrying lines estimate should incorporate about a 30 per cent transshipment share.

The key traffic for the metropolitan economy, however, remains national or regional container cargo whether or not this traffic is Durban based. It has been demonstrated that an increase in the port of Durban's container-handling activities in these categories will have a massive impact on the local economy. Similarly, should capacity sufficient to attract and sustain additional containerised business not be installed in the port, the Durban community will bear the costs in the form of fewer potential jobs, lower local spending and less wealth.

The Comparative Advantage of the Port of Durban

This chapter has shown that the port of Durban is a highly diversified multi-purpose port. However, implicit in much of what has gone before is the presumption that the way forward for the port is to strengthen its position as a general cargo-handling hub port, rather than as a maingate for bulk or neo-bulk cargoes. The purpose of this section is to question that presumption in a number of ways, by posing a series of questions relating to the future of economic activities within the Bay area.

These include questions such as: are the advantages associated with expanded general cargo activity greater than the benefits that would be generated via an extension of other kinds of cargo handling? Or would an extension of container facilities, or the redevelopment of existing port areas to handle a larger volume of containers, not shut off other even more beneficial opportunities for the port and the local community?

These other opportunities may also involve alternative recreational or tourist uses of the port and Bay area. These latter activities, which have largely been ignored here, are already an important feature of the Point area of the port, and are likely to expand. The expansion of port facilities should be planned with the realities of such developments in mind, with an optimal future path clearly being one that combines the benefits of a vibrant and expanding port with those of a city that is striving to optimise its tourism potential. These options should be seen as complements rather than substitutes, and can only be realised if Durban exploits its comparative advantages in both spheres. The likelihood that the Durban community will be able to exploit the full potential of the port/Bay area will also be improved if a closer relationship could be forged between the port authority and the city, in the process giving the latter a larger role to play in strategic port planning. Consequently, this final section tackles the broad question of where the real comparative advantages of the port of Durban lie in the context of both the traffic base of the southern African region and the characteristics of the eastern seaboard ports.

Within the range of southern African ports, Durban is the dominant port in the handling of crude oil and refined petroleum products; other bulk liquids, including chemicals, conventional breakbulk cargo, and containers. By contrast, Durban has already been thoroughly eclipsed by Richards Bay in the handling of high-volume, low-value bulk staples such as coal, woodchips, phosphates and sand products. Within the category of neo-bulks such as paper, woodpulp and other forest products, steel and granite, Durban has yielded some of her earlier dominance in these cargoes to Richards Bay, to the point where the two KwaZulu-Natal ports now share in this traffic.

If the future competitive position of Durban is considered, the port's pre-eminence in respect of petroleum products is likely to be retained. Apart from refined products, these commodities are largely not handled through the central port area, and have relatively little impact on the central Bay area.

Within the realm of dry-bulk cargoes, physical limitations and restricted water depth prevent the larger categories of bulk vessels from entering the port in a loaded condition. The high-volume bulk trades are therefore to all intents and purposes closed to Durban, and even traditional staples such as cereals may be lost if larger vessels associated with lower freight rates are employed. The road ahead for the port of Durban is thus clearly not in the arena of traditional bulk cargoes, although just as clearly certain smaller bulk operations will remain an important dimension of its operations. The high-volume, low-value bulk trades are also those with the lowest linkage and multiplier effects in the local port economy, hence Durban's limitations in this market segment are no great tragedy for the local community.

Within the sphere of traditional general cargoes handled by conventional breakbulk techniques, Durban is likely to remain the dominant regional port. However, this category of cargo is on a secular decline and represents a shrinking residual of the region's overall traffic base as various forms of unitisation make inroads into general cargo. In many respects, this is an unfortunate direction of change for traditional port communities, since conventional general cargo remains the most directly labour intensive in terms of jobs created in traditional stevedoring and other cargo-handling activities. The imperatives of transport efficiency have forced ports all over the world to adapt to a relative decline in breakbulk cargo activities; the South African ports are no exceptions. Although Durban's supremacy in this area is likely to remain unchallenged for the foreseeable future, an increasing reliance on the broad area of conventional general cargo does not therefore emerge as the obvious road ahead.

The future position of Durban in the neo-bulk arena is more difficult to predict. The author's view is that Richards Bay is likely to appropriate a higher relative share of this traffic in the years ahead, although the overall base of steel, granite and forest product cargoes will almost certainly continue to be shared by the two ports for some considerable time. The reason for Durban's relative disadvantage lies in the nature of modern cargo-handling techniques, which require the storage and pre-assembly of these cargoes on open areas in the immediate hinterland behind working berths. This secures vastly increased cargo-handling rates and improves both port and vessel efficiency. It is also demanding of space in the immediate port area. These handling techniques are easier to effect in areas such as Richards Bay or in other greenfields developments where ample space remains, but they are problematical for a port such as Durban where the immediate port area is already highly saturated. Certain areas of the port of Durban have been adapted very successfully for these cargoes but it is doubtful whether further large increases in traffic could be accommodated without putting pressure on scarce land.

Durban already enjoys a position of considerable dominance in the areas of chemicals and other non-oil, liquid-bulk cargoes. This dominance should continue, although such cargoes are likely to remain confined to such remote port segments as Island View, and the hazardous nature of some products makes them inappropriate for expansion into port areas adjacent to high-class tourist or public access sites.

This leaves the category of containerised and unitised cargo. Unitised/palletised cargoes such as fruit and paper are relatively aesthetically pleasing and non-polluting, and remain as good candidates for handling in port segments close to residential, recreational or tourist areas. Containerised cargo is also non-polluting, non-hazardous and relatively immune to pilferage. Container handling is also demanding of space, but it is argued to be a more appropriate candidate for scarce port space than other bulk or neo-bulk cargoes that offer lower economic linkages and multipliers. The physical limitations of the port of Durban are also less likely to impede the container trade. Although certain 'post-Panamax' container vessels currently in service or on order would be restricted in their access to the port of Durban, these vessels represent a tiny minority of the world's container fleet, and they are expressly designed for deployment on a limited number of high-volume global routes.[12] Durban's inability to accommodate these vessels is also shared by many medium-sized container ports, hence the risk of a container fleet dominated by vessels too large to use the facilities of the port of Durban is small.

Recent important developments in international container shipping also greatly strengthen Durban's hand in the regional container-handling derby. Virtually all the major carrying lines now organise their activities around global 'hub-and-spoke' services that interlock at sub-regional transshipment nodes. As such, carriers strongly favour the concentration of their eastern seaboard southern African activities in a single port, and even more strongly oppose a split of mainstream container-handling facilities across neighbouring ports such as Durban and Richards Bay, thereby requiring two port calls within a 100 nautical mile range. At present, Durban is the only southern African container port with any remote pretensions to hub status, and is overwhelmingly supported by the carriers as the choice for future terminal expansion. The reason for this choice is quite simple: Durban is a genuine terminal port in its own right, insofar as between 35 and 40 per cent of container cargo is associated with the Durban Metropolitan area itself. There is consequently a clear reason for container vessels to patronise the port of Durban. By contrast, Richards Bay is not a terminal port for general cargo, and there is consequently no pressing reason for container vessels to utilise that port. Other eastern seaboard options simply do not exist. Maputo is an insignificant element in the container-handling equation, with draft parameters far more restrictive than Durban, a maximum terminal capacity currently equal to roughly a single year's container growth in Durban, and significant deviation costs for vessels on round-the-world routes. Its present feeder status is likely to continue. Port Elizabeth has handled some container overspills precipitated by recent Durban congestion, but its weak and circuitous land side links with the industrial heartland of Gauteng, together with the limited size of the local market, make sites in Algoa Bay poor choices as genuine terminal ports or as container *entrepôts* for the sub-continent. The apparent interest in establishing the potential new port of Coega as a regional container hub is therefore surprising.

Since other eastern seaboard ports are likely ultimately to out-compete Durban in the areas of bulk and neo-bulk cargoes, the expansion of container handling emerges as the most appropriate way forward for Durban's port community. Reasons include the extensive network of port ancillary industries that already exist in the Durban area and the existence of ample spare capacity on the Durban-Gauteng rail artery.[13] Growth prospects in containerised trade also exceed those in other seatrade segments, and the carrying lines are keen to concentrate that trade in a single sub-regional port. Above all, container handling has also been shown to be rich in generating employment and expenditure.

Conclusion

This chapter has attempted to drive home five fundamental dimensions of the relationship between the port of Durban and the Durban community. The first and most fundamental is that the original establishment and subsequent development of the port *is* the reason why a diverse community and economy has located itself around the shores of the Bay of Natal; without Durban harbour this Bay would resemble many of the other picturesque but ultimately irrelevant tidal lagoons that proliferate on the KwaZulu-Natal coast.

The second is that port activities remain a massive source of overall employment, expenditure and investment, both in the family of direct port-ancillary industries, and in economic activities more indirectly associated with the port. Port activities associated with the handling of general as opposed to bulk cargoes are richer in generating local economic linkages but it is also in respect of these former activities that Durban port is most severely under demand pressure, to a point where additional container-handling capacity is urgently required. Durban's needs are congruent with national needs, as investment in general cargo facilities in the South African ports as a whole have been well below long-term capital needs, yet it is specifically in this area that world-class facilities must support the economy's export-led growth trajectory.

The third is that key planning and operating decisions relating to the port have been historically, and continue to be, taken by persons and institutions outside Durban. This has generated tensions between local authorities and local commerce and industry on the one hand and national government departments and the centralised Transnet management on the other.

The fourth is that the diversion of port traffic, particularly containerised traffic, would have a potentially devastating effect on the local economy by stripping it of potential increases in employment and spending.

The fifth and last is that the present and future comparative advantage of Durban port lies increasingly in the realm of containerised cargoes, conventional general cargo and liquid-bulk petro-chemicals. Of these, container traffic offers the greatest potential opportunities, given the desire of the carrying lines to patronise regional 'hub' ports, as well as the greatest potential employment and expenditure gains for the metropolitan economy.

The fullest exploitation of these comparative advantages in the new millennium will not be easy. The prize that beckons for the Durban community is the strengthening of its historic position as the dominant general cargo port in the southern African sub-region. In an increasingly globalised international trading community, the influence of 'hub' ports, particularly for container traffic, should increase significantly, but in the case of Durban this status will only be secured if several hard investment and capacity-building decisions are taken as a matter of some urgency. A major task facing port and city planners then becomes to chart a way forward for the port in a manner that maximises the potential gains and minimises the potential risks to the Durban community.

NOTES

1. The final defeat of the sand in the 'battle of the bar' is conventionally dated as June 1904, when the first large mail steamer, Donald Currie's *Armadale Castle*, crossed the bar to berth alongside the Point wharves.
2. Although sand no longer presents an insurmountable barrier to Durban port entry, Portnet nonetheless is compelled to undertake continuous prophylactic dredging to maintain the integrity of the main entrance channel. This dredging is carried out by the Portnet Dredging Services (a separate profit centre within the Portnet organisation) and involves the extraction of several hundred thousand cubic metres

of sand annually from the 'sand trap' behind the south breakwater. Considerable volumes of this pristine, deep sea sand are then sold to the city of Durban and pumped out onto the city's beaches to maintain their width and profile, thereby establishing a further economic linkage between the port and the city.

3. The measurement of water depth on chart datum gives an indication of the minimum water depth available for passing vessels at low water on ordinary spring tide conditions.
4. Two measures of vessel size or capacity are conventionally used in the international sea transport industry. So-called 'gross' registered tonnage (grt) provides a volumetric measure of (certain portions of) enclosed vessel space, while so-called 'deadweight' tonnage (dwt) crudely measures cargo-carrying capacity of vessels. The latter is consequently the more appropriate one in measuring the cargo-carrying capabilities of bulk carriers, oil tankers, etc.
5. The category of 'neo-bulk' cargo occupies an intermediate position between the traditional category of bulk cargo, which refers to parcels (usually full shiploads) of homogeneous cargo without individual mark or number, and the category of heterogeneous breakbulk cargo, where individual units generally can be identified by discrete marks or numbers on bales, tea chests, boxes, pallets, etc. Classic 'neo-bulks' would include partially differentiated steel cargoes, different types and sizes of paper rolls, different blocks of granite and the like.
6. The teu or 'twenty-foot-equivalent-unit' is the internationally accepted *numéraire* for the measurement of container traffic flows. One teu corresponds to a 20 foot by 8 foot by 8 foot 'standard' container. The feu or standard forty-foot container (equivalent to 2 teus) is increasingly supplanting the 20 foot box as the dominant carrying unit.
7. Panamax bulk carriers are vessels constructed with maximum dimensions permissible for transit of the lock systems of the Panama Canal, and are generally in the 60 000–85 000 dwt carrying capacity range. 'Cape-sized' bulk carriers are too large to pass through the Panama Canal, and are generally in the 120 000-plus dwt capacity range.
8. Charlier's approach applies the following weights or deflators to the cargo base of the ports: conventional breakbulk cargo carries its full weight; containerised cargo is deflated by a factor of 3; bulk cargo by a factor of 6; and the liquid-bulk trade in oil and petroleum products by a factor of 12.
9. In many of the leading international ports, such as Rotterdam and Antwerp, the operating role of the port authority rarely extends beyond the landside edge of quaywalls. Port authorities are thus generally landlords and custodians of the marine infrastructure of ports, while all or most cargo-handling operations are in the hands of private terminal companies.
10. The 400–500-box basis for a 'standard' container caller is based on estimates by Portnet's Ton Bestenbreur. Traffic growth, and the deployment of somewhat larger container vessels, most notably by the non-Conference independent carriers who previously relied on smaller units, make this 'standard' vessel a conservative one in the context of 1998.
11. *Ad valorem* wharfage has historically been the most controversial of the various harbour charges levied in the South African ports. Based on commodity value (and charged at a rate of 1.8 per cent on imports and 0.9 per cent on exports), wharfage is designed to finance the cargo-working infrastructure of the various

ports. From the perspective of the port authorities, it has performed this task with meteoric success as the revenues generated have exceeded the associated costs by a factor of some 4:1. Port users and economists have always taken a less sanguine view of this tariff item on the grounds that it represents the very antithesis of a cost-related tariff. Since it has historically also generated the bulk (some two-thirds) of total harbour revenue, it has been viewed by users as a *de facto* tax on cargo owners, and one of the principal sources of intra-Transnet cross-subsidisation.

12. Over the last several years, a series of 'post-Panamax' container vessels has been constructed to dimensions too large to permit transit of the Panama Canal, and too large to permit entry into most of the world's general cargo ports. These vessels, the largest of which have capacity for some 8 000 teus (or more than twice the capacity of the largest cellular vessels on the South African trades), represent a huge gamble for the container majors, since they are so inflexible in their trading options. The likelihood that these vessels will dominate southern hemisphere container trades is slim, hence the draft limitations of the port of Durban are unlikely to shut off significant potential container callers.
13. On the Durban-Gauteng rail line, the highest utilisation is experienced on the Durban-Pietermaritzburg segment, while on other segments utilisation levels of 28–30 per cent are the order of the day.

REFERENCES

Bender, C. 1988. *Who saved Natal?* Durban: Colleen Bender.

Bestenbreur, T. 1994. 'Container Handling in the Port of Durban'. Proceedings of Intermodal Africa 94, Baltic Conventions, London.

Charlier, J. 1996. *Le système portuaire sud-africain á l'aube du 21eme siècle.* Brussels: Royal Belgian Marine Academy.

Department of Transport. 1997. *Draft White Paper on National Transport Policy*. Pretoria: Department of Transport.

——. 1998. *Moving South Africa*. Pretoria: Department of Transport.

Drewry. 1997. *Short Sea Container Markets: The Feeder and Regional Trade Dynamo.* London: Drewry Shipping Consultants.

Fair, D. and T. Jones. 1991. *The Ports of Sub-Saharan Africa and their Hinterlands: An Overview.* Pretoria: Africa Institute of South Africa.

Goss, R.O. 1990. 'Economic Policies and Seaports: The Diversity of Port Policies'. *Maritime Policy and Management*, 17, 3.

Guest, B. and J. Sellers (eds). 1985. *Enterprise and Exploitation in a Victorian Colony.* Pietermaritzburg: University of Natal Press.

Heydendrych, L. 1985. 'Port Natal Harbour, *c.*1850–1897'. In B. Guest and J. Sellers, *Enterprise and Exploitation.*

Horwood, O.P.F. (ed.). 1968. *The Port of Durban, Natal Regional Survey,* Vol. 15. Durban: Department of Economics, University of Natal.

IEM Study Group. 1996. 'Port of Durban Container Handling Integrated Environmental Management (IEM) Study'. Unpublished report, Durban.

ISL 1997. *Shipping Statistics Yearbook 1997.* Bremen: Institut für Seeverkehrs-wirtschaft und Logistik.

Jones, R.E. and C.H. Cawood. 1974. 'Planning of the New Deep Water Harbour at Richards Bay'. Paper presented at International Havenkongres, Amsterdam.

Jones, T. 1987. *The International shipping Industry and South Africa's Seaborne Trade.* Pretoria: Council for Scientific and Industrial Research, National Institute for Transport and Road Research.

——. 1990. 'The Ports of South Africa: Durban and Richards Bay'. *Africa Insight,* Journal of the Africa Institute of South Africa, 20, 4.

——. 1991. 'The Ports of South Africa: The Cape Ports'. *Africa Insight,* Journal of the Africa Institute of South Africa, 21, 1.

——. 1996. 'The Impact of the Port of Durban's Container Activities on the Economy of the Greater Durban Metropolitan Area'. *Proceedings of Intermodal Africa 96.* Baltic Conventions. London

Lumby, A.B. 1991. 'The South African Economy and the Development of the Port of Durban during the Inter-War Years'. *The Great Circle, Journal of the Australian Association for Maritime History,* 13, 1.

Palsson, G. 1998. 'Multiple Ports of Call vs. Hub and Spoke: Containerized Maritime Trade West Africa and Europe'. *Africa Transport Technical Note* No. 12. Washington DC: The World Bank.

Pearson, T. 1995. *African Keyport.* Rossburgh: Accucut Books.

Peters, H. 1993. 'The Maritime Transport Crisis'. World Bank Discussion Paper No. 220. Washington DC: The World Bank.

Portnet, Port of Durban. 1994. *Port of Durban: Statistical Overviews, 1994, 1996, 1997 and 1998.* Durban: Portnet.

Ports of South Africa and Mozambique 1994. Florida: Industrial Publishing Corporation.

Republic of South Africa. 1993. *Report of the Committee of Inquiry into a National Maritime Policy for South Africa (Floor Report).* Pretoria: Government Printer.

South African Railways & Harbours. Various years 1949–79/80. *Annual Reports.* Pretoria: Government Printer.

South African Transport Services. Various years 1980/81–89/90. *Annual Reports.* Johannesburg: South African Transport Services.

Stopford, M. 1995. *Maritime Economics.* London: Routledge.

Suykens, F. 1984. *Havencapaciteit: Een Relatief Begrip.* Antwerpen: Havenbedrijf van de gemeente Antwerpen.

Wiese, B. 1981. *Seaports and Port Cities of Southern Africa.* Wiesbaden: Bruno Verlag.

CHAPTER FOUR

From Import Substituting Industrialisation to Globalised International Competitiveness

Industrial Restructuring in a South African City

MIKE MORRIS, JUSTIN BARNES and NIKKI DUNNE

As the second largest city, with the biggest port, Durban has a major role to play in the economic development of South Africa. As the conduit for most of the goods being exported, major emphasis is often placed on its role in the era of globalised integration into the world economy. Finally, as the gateway facing the east, hopes are often pinned on Durban becoming the major opening to a new flourishing traffic from India, where it is twinned with Mumbai, as well as with South East Asia.

For Durban, key locational features have been the presence of a large natural harbour, abundant manpower, a relatively large consumer market, and the city's geographical position as the hub of a region rich in raw materials and water resources (DPA 1982; Harrison and Morris 1996). Durban is more dependent on manufacturing than other major South African cities with manufacturing contributing 30 per cent of its GGP (South Durban SEA Project Team 1998). This emphasis on manufacturing represents both a strength and, potentially, a weakness in Durban's economy. An excessive reliance on primary products places any developing economy in a vulnerable position *vis-à-vis* world markets, and Durban's relatively strong manufacturing base serves to diversify this risk. However, the environment facing manufacturers, both globally and domestically, is changing rapidly, and it remains to be seen whether Durban's industries will respond to these changes.

The post-apartheid government's acknowledgement of global trends towards reduced trade barriers is reflected in a fundamental shift from import substituting industrialisation (ISI) to trade liberalisation, with a strong focus on export promotion. ISI has historically been extremely important, and the shift in policy makes this an era of both crisis and opportunity for domestic industry. The city's relatively developed industrial base quite clearly stands at a crossroads, dependent on the new industrial policy. However, developing and implementing a successful industrial policy is a complex issue, located in decisions taken at the transnational, macro-, meso- and micro-levels, as reflected in international, national, regional and local policies. In addition, the response of industry itself to changes in the operating environment will determine its ongoing success.

This chapter examines the present structure of industry in Durban and considers the effect both the changing domestic policy agenda and global industrial trends are likely to have on its industrial structure. Initially we briefly outline Durban's current industrial structure and the forces which shaped it. This is followed by a consideration of Durban's future industrial prospects – i.e. trends within the global economic environment, the current domestic policy environment of trade liberalisation, and the shift in industrial policy from demand-side to supply-side support measures. The prospects for Durban's industry in light of the new criteria governing industrial development and competitiveness are then analysed. Finally, the general issues presented in the broad analysis are concretised by considering in greater detail two industrial sectors in Durban in order to ascertain the extent to which they are responding to the challenges of the global and domestic environment.

Durban as a Port City

Historically city ports have played an important role and been accorded a special status as regional economies have emerged. They have tended to play a catalytic function in the development of localised regional economies, fostering economic activity and trade in their immediate hinterland (Hoyle and Pinder 1981). In this sense they have historically played a significant role in less developed countries (LDCs) following an ISI growth path. However, containerisation and subsequent changes in the structure and operation of the shipping industry, the emergence of alternative means of transport, the increasing relative importance of the service sector and heightened concern with environmental issues have changed the importance and impact of ports in regional economies (Hall 1999). Consequently, internationally famous ports such as San Francisco (or Cape Town) have been transformed from breakbulk cargo nodes into centres of tourism, whilst Oakland (or Durban) have remained as critical nodal points for transport and conventional purveyors of commodities through becoming successful container ports.

The demise of import substituting industrialisation has opened new economic opportunities for city ports as gateways for globalised and export based manufacturing operations. Changes in shipping technology, containerisation and the fact that goods can be moved on ships, road and rail has dramatically reduced costs. Furthermore, in the new era of globalised flexible production systems, with its emphasis on reducing lead times, increasing flexibility, frequent and reliable delivery schedules, and Just In Time (JIT) production, cost has also become less important than efficient supply logistics. Port efficiency and flexibility have become more important than simple freight costs.

Since transport based city ports still play a central role in regional development efforts, this has proved a major source of local, regional and national power as different economic and social interests have jockeyed for a share of the benefits derived from economic and trading opportunities. Where ports fall under the direct control of a local or regional state authority, they are major revenue earners for local tax jurisdictions. Furthermore, policy over the ports' future direction and utilisation can be synchronised with local and regional state led economic policy interests, land use, and tourist or industrial led growth strategies.

Where ports are not controlled by local authorities, harmonisation of local and national economic interests becomes a critical institutional issue. If control over the port is dislocated from local or regional state interests and instead concentrated in distant national hands then there is massive potential for substantial political and economic conflict over long term trajectories. A key question that is therefore thrown up in respect of a particular port city is: who controls the port politically and institutionally?

Durban provides an interesting case study of some of these tendencies applicable to the changing role of port cities. As the major port in southern Africa and the concentrated locus of major industrial activity, it would appear to be the major beneficiary of a government led export promotion industrial strategy. However Durban is caught in a serious fault line flowing between the city and the port. Political authority over the port is not vested in the local city authority or the regional state. Historically the port was, and still remains, controlled by a parastatal politically answerable to the national government. Interests that are not in any sense representative of local or regional state concerns therefore dominate it.

There has been little attempt at harmonisation of local and national interests, of city and port policy and practice. Indeed this has often resulted in direct conflict between the economic policy implementation plans of the city authorities and the views of the port authorities. It results in crucially absent institutional linkages between port, city and key local industrial sectors. This fundamental fault line governs and fractures the ability of the city to locate and take advantage of itself as a dynamic port city. The city is only half a port city, and the port only half related to the city. Instead of local purposive institutional action being the driving force of this port city's industrial activity, external forces dominate industrial decisions and activity.

The Development of Durban's Industry

There are a number of inter-linked and mutually reinforcing factors that historically created favourable circumstances for particular industries in Durban. The port has always been key. Durban's port has long handled more cargo than all South Africa's other ports combined, and as such the city was the logical place to establish industries that depended on imported production inputs. Although ISI aimed to *replace* imports, much of the associated industry was built around imported *inputs*. This gave rise to the establishment of the chemical, textile, clothing, automotive assembly and component, food and beverage, printing and stationery, metal and engineering, paper and pulp industries. In addition, lower duties on bulk or unprocessed imports encouraged the development of packaging (tea) and assembly (vehicle and machinery) industries around the port.

Access to *domestic* raw materials has been another important factor in Durban's industrial development: early industrialisation centred on the utilisation of natural resources and agricultural produce, especially food and beverages (Harrison and Morris 1996). Durban's position in the centre of the sugar belt was particularly important in this regard, while its position near to forestry areas contributed to the establishment of the wood and furniture industries (Katzen 1961). Once again, the port played an important role, this time in encouraging the establishment of industries based on processing raw materials for export.

Ancillary policies also played a role in the establishment and location of sectors – a lower minimum wage payable at the coast was key to the location of labour intensive clothing firms in Durban. Similarly, local content requirements in the motor industry promoted the growth of a host of input suppliers around Toyota, which had initially established in Durban to benefit from access to imports provided by the port (Harrison and Morris 1996; Jones 1997). A policy emphasis on strategically important industries encouraged the growth of capital and technology intensive industries such as paper and pulp, and the petro-chemical industrial complex. This dual approach of the government – to encourage the substitution of imported consumer goods as well as more sophisticated strategic goods – led to the establishment in Durban of a large, low-wage, labour intensive manufacturing segment alongside a capital intensive, higher wage segment (Harrison and Morris 1996).

Currently, in terms of contribution to total manufacturing employment and output, the six most important industries in Durban are: food, clothing, chemicals, textiles, metals and paper. Of the six most important industries, clothing (0.63), textiles (0.57) and metals (0.55) can be regarded as labour intensive industries, with a salaries to net output ratio[1] of greater than 50 per cent. There are no local auto statistics since Toyota SA were historically omitted from government data for reasons of confidentiality. The national labour intensity for automotive vehicle assembly is, however, 0.47.

The port remains the hub of Durban's industrialisation and settlement pattern, which forms a T-pattern radiating out from the port (Day 1993). Industry extended south, establishing in Jacobs, Mobeni, and later Prospecton (Day 1993; DPA 1982; Katzen 1961). The industrial core of this Southern Industrial Basin (SIB), was leading firms in heavy industries, particularly those dependent on imported inputs, such as paper and pulp, food, textiles, chemicals and heavy metals, and later the automotive industry (DPA 1982).

A shortage of industrial land in the immediate vicinity of Durban resulted in a noticeable decentralisation, or suburbanisation of industry, by the 1960s (McCarthy 1993). The major beneficiaries of this suburbanisation process were the satellite towns of Pinetown and New Germany to the west of Durban. These towns benefited both from a natural advantage in terms of their location on the most direct route between Durban and Gauteng and from planning and support functions undertaken by the Pinetown Municipality (Day 1993; Watkinson 1996). Despite the advantages of cheaper land, mainly smaller, less capital intensive firms were drawn to these areas. The most apparent clusters which developed in these areas were textile firms; chemicals, paints and pharmaceuticals; metal, machinery and engineering; and automotive components (Young 1976). Most recently, some industrialisation has occurred to the north of Durban in areas such as Phoenix and Springfield Park although this area remains essentially underdeveloped (McCarthy 1993; Siyakhana 1998). Finally, the industrial decentralisation programme of the central government encouraged labour intensive industries to relocate to the west and north of Durban. Consequently, a significant cluster of textile firms has developed at Hammarsdale (Harrison and Morris 1996).

Global, Domestic Trends and Post-Apartheid Policy

Here we examine the post-apartheid prospects for Durban's industry particularly in the context of the *external* economic environment. Firms operate at the nexus between the global and local environments, between domestic trade and industrial policy, and between policies developed and implemented at the national, regional and local level. Given the rapid reduction of protective tariffs at the national level, it is clear that the future of Durban's manufacturing sectors depends on being able to compete internationally in the new global environment.

The current era can be referred to as one of global, knowledge intensive, technologically sophisticated capitalism. The main force driving recent changes in the pattern of industrial development is globalisation. Globalisation centres on an increase in communications and other links that bind the distant reaches of the world together. The effects of this process are felt in a number of arenas:

- The *globalisation of consumer tastes*, reflected in more rapidly changing patterns of consumer demand, and a demand for more varied products.
- The *globalisation of trade*, reflected in trade agreements limiting the extent to which any country can insulate its economy from foreign competition.
- The *globalisation of competition*, reflected in individual companies at any particular national location facing a dramatic increase in competitors domestically and simultaneously, in order to maintain market share, looking to target a global marketplace.

These, plus general increases in disposable incomes have led to a change in the basis of competition. While price competitiveness is still important, consumers are increasingly demanding better product quality, greater variety and more rapid innovations. Conformity to standards and more reliable delivery are other features of the new competitive environment (Kaplinsky 1994).

As the nature of demand and competition has begun to shift, the inadequacies of the existing mass production system in meeting the needs of the global consumer have become apparent. New forms of production arrangements better suited to the production of smaller batches of more specialised products have arisen. Production is increasingly set up to best capture economies of scope, with an emphasis on small batch production, flexible technology and smaller production units. Specialisation encourages unbundling and downsizing, with a concomitant growth in small firms. The design and marketing aspects of production have gained prominence, encouraging closer links between the various parts of the production process, from conception to execution. Flexible production requires multi-skilled workers able to make ongoing contributions to quality and innovation. Inter-firm organisational relationships are becoming closer, as ongoing innovation of product and process requires greater co-operation between suppliers of inputs and services, and their manufacturing clients. Similarly, inventory reducing arrangements aimed at increasing flexibility make close proximity between suppliers and manufacturers essential.

What then are the key requirements for industrial success under this new industrial paradigm? The human resource requirements of flexible production, particularly of sophisticated products, are high (Brown 1996). Process and product innovation require a work-force with good technical and creative skills, while even the basic requirement of a productive labour force able to contribute more broadly to production, requires a literate and numerate work-force. JIT production and simultaneous engineering require a strong network of producers and suppliers in close proximity to each other, connected by good transport and other communication infrastructure. In certain instances this mitigates against the decentralisation of production based on low wages (Kaplinsky 1994). The trend towards smaller production units has led to an increased demand for smaller premises. In some sectors the more reciprocal relationship between design and production has led to an increasing demand for combined office-production premises. The greater emphasis on design and marketing makes proximity to final markets an important aspect of competitiveness. However, there are simultaneously conflicting tendencies in some sectors separating design and marketing from production and locating the former in industrialised countries, with concomitant shifts in power relations. (Humphrey et al. 1998). The globalisation of markets means an increase in trade requiring better export facilities for manufacturers. Moreover, in order to compete successfully, industry requires favourable institutional arrangements, where trade and industrial policy, and national, regional and local policy are co-ordinated to create an operating environment conducive to international competitiveness. Institutionally this requires a co-ordinated nexus between national and local strategic initiatives (Kaplinsky and Morris 1997).

The over-riding policy concern of the current government is the need to balance the 'redistribution of income and opportunities' with the development of a 'competitive fast-growing economy', achieved, in part, through 'employment creating international competitiveness'. Post-apartheid trade policy reflects a fundamental shift to an outwardly oriented, export promoting economy. This has meant a reduction in the number of tariff barriers, with remaining tariffs being phased down, in many cases faster than required by the World Trade Organisation (Kaplinsky and Morris 1997; Valodia 1997). While these moves provide South African industry with access to competitively priced inputs, they also serve to rapidly expose industry to increased international competition.

Current industrial policy focuses on the need to generate employment, increase investment, raise productivity and improve trade performance (i.e. increase exports). The principal change is one from demand-side support, which is aimed at creating demand for domestic producers, to supply-side support, which is aimed at lowering the factor costs that contribute to manufacturing inefficiency. These supply-side measures aim to assist firms and clusters to re-organise production to be more in tune with the new demands of international competitiveness. Thus policy aims to encourage industrial innovation, human resource development, improvements in productivity, technology transfer, import-export complementation schemes, specialisation and movement up the value chain. A tax holiday scheme to stimulate new investment, small and medium firm development, a strengthening of competition policy and the development of industrial cluster support programmes are amongst the policy initiatives, as is encouraging a more flexible labour market. Increasing competition in protected or monopolistic industries, developing forward linkages, moving up the value chain and supporting labour intensive and light industries are seen as key components of successful sectoral policies.

Competitive Potential in Durban's Current Industrial Structure

Durban faces the twenty-first century with a number of strengths and weaknesses in its industrial structure. The most obvious weakness is the heavy reliance on sectors that have developed under tariff protection and are now facing rapid liberalisation. The textiles, clothing, automotive and food industries are all expected to be negatively affected. Together these vulnerable industries account for 31.7 per cent of Durban's net manufacturing output, and 43.7 per cent of manufacturing employment. On a more positive note, other important industries such as paper, printing and publishing, and chemicals are expected to benefit from liberalisation (South Durban SEA Project Team 1998). Job losses remain a major problem – labour intensive sectors, such as clothing, and other large employers (e.g. automotive) are under threat due to a lack of international competitiveness. Conversely, the sector with probably the greatest international potential is the capital intensive chemical industry. Employment is being eroded in a range of industries, both labour and capital intensive, and in general the opportunities for unskilled workers are declining.

Some of the city's leading manufacturing sectors, including food, chemicals and paper, are already considered internationally competitive (Harrison 1995). Non-ferrous metals, food and textiles are significant exporters and earners of foreign exchange. Exports through Durban's port are dominated by primary products, semi-beneficiated mineral products (ferro-alloys), processed petroleum products and chemicals, and by intermediate or semi-manufactured goods such as paper, woodpulp and steel. Given that several of Durban's industries feature in this list, and that moving up the value chain is the path chosen by the national government for industrial development, this may prove problematic for the future growth of Durban's industry.

If Durban is to compete internationally in line with the requirements of the new competition, then a crucial issue will be access to skilled workers as well as management (Barnes 1998a). One of the legacies of apartheid is the relatively low level of skilled labour in the country: in KwaZulu-Natal 55.7 per cent of the labour force are classed as unskilled or semi-skilled (DRA 1995). In Durban itself the situation is more positive. The emphasis on skilled labour in flexible production is likely to favour centralised localities where levels of education and skills tend to be higher and this will benefit Durban over other industrial locations in KwaZulu-Natal. More specifically, Durban is said to have a particular comparative advantage in its large Indian population: the success of the Indian educational system, even under apartheid, has led to a pool of skilled labour lacking amongst the non-white majorities of other major industrial centres (CDE 1996; Tomlinson 1993). This issue is likely to become increasingly relevant as affirmative action is introduced into the economy by way of the 1999 Employment Equity Act.

One of the most encouraging opportunities within the framework of flexible production (particularly for developing countries), is the ground it opens for small firms to operate, in networks or individually, as suppliers or contractors to larger firms (Kaplinsky 1994; Piore and Sabel 1984). Durban supports a number of industrial sectors where the average size of firms suggests that the sectors may be dominated by small or medium enterprises. While only the metals industry currently contributes significantly to employment or output, the potential exists for these small firm-dominated sectors to serve as a basis for a dynamic small and medium sized enterprise (SME) sector.

Associated with this is the issue of closer inter-firm relations, a key feature of flexible production. While there is little to suggest true networking between small firms, and room to improve relationships between firms and suppliers, existing sectoral clustering within Durban lays a foundation for closer links. The most obvious clustering of industry is within the Southern Industrial Basin (SIB), and at Pinetown/New Germany to the west of Durban. Recent research suggests strong linkages between firms located in the SIB, particularly within the chemicals and automotive industries (South Durban SEA Project Team 1998). Similarly, a study of Pinetown firms found that linkages were well developed, with most service functions performed within Pinetown itself or within the Durban Metropolitan Area (DMA) (Watkinson 1996).

Geographic clustering is not, however, the same as strategic networking (Best 1990). While clustering may offer firms benefits in the form of access to a skilled labour force and locally based suppliers and services, networking implies co-operative relationships between both competitors and links in the supply chain. The evidence suggests that clustering in the DMA predominantly reflects incidental linkages built around business services, rather than strategic linkages based on capturing economies of scale and developing a comparative advantage (Aniruth et al. 1998). A notable exception has been the sustained momentum of a cluster of auto components firms that belong to the KwaZulu-Natal Benchmarking Club, which is aimed at increasing internal operational competitiveness (Barnes and Morris 1999).

Seemingly the core of Durban's economy (the port) can be expected to feature prominently in the era of globalisation and export orientated growth. Export led growth can be expected to benefit Durban giving it an advantage over Gauteng, South Africa's current industrial heartland (Harrison and Morris 1996; Tomlinson 1993). In addition, as Gauteng's most accessible port, Durban will form a critical trade link with international trading partners in the East and in Europe. As the most efficient port in Africa, and highly competitive in Indian Ocean terms, Durban has the opportunity to become a key hub port serving Indian Ocean markets (CDE 1996).

The export thrust of current government policy can be positively linked to the emphasis on niche markets apparent in flexible production. By specialising in a narrower product range and targeting world markets, South African industries could stand to capture economies of both scale and scope. A World Bank study has identified specific export niches for South Africa in the medium to high-end garment industry, and in the production of polymers, polyethylene and polypropylene used in the manufacture of plastics. Both industries have a strong presence in Durban (Tomlinson 1993).

However, internal competitiveness issues may themselves prove insufficient for firm-level success. In certain industries, notably auto components, issues of connectivity are just as important as those issues concerning internal competitiveness (Humphrey et al. 1998). The success of certain industrial sectors in Durban may, for example, be reliant on locally owned firms connecting themselves into global networks as a mechanism for penetrating exports markets and acquiring the requisite technology. This is because ISI did not only lead to the development of generally uncompetitive industries in Durban, it also led to certain domestic industries having very different ownership structures from the global industries into which they are now increasingly integrated. The multinational corporations (MNCs) that control these industries globally are not only dominant in terms of the advanced production systems that they use, they are also dominant in terms of the control of technology, innovation and marketing networks (Humphrey et al. 1998). Locally owned firms in certain industries have little alternative but to connect into these MNCs through equity arrangements.

Notwithstanding the importance of the broad context, predictions concerning the success of manufacturing do not take account of 'strategic responses to sectors within industries. There is nothing inevitable about predicted growth and decline' (Harrison 1995: 47). The question really is how industry will react in light of changing opportunities and threats, and act to mitigate weaknesses and capitalise on strengths. The second part of this chapter will look at two of the city's key manufacturing industries, the labour intensive clothing sector and the more capital intensive automotive sector, to answer this question. Both are under enormous pressure as a result of the liberalisation of the domestic economy. The manner in which these two important local industries face up to the challenges confronting them is obviously of critical importance, not only in terms of their own survival but also as examples of the types of challenges confronting Durban industry more generally.

The Clothing Sector

The Durban Metropolitan Area represents the largest clothing cluster within KwaZulu-Natal. Of a total of approximately 525 clothing firms in KwaZulu-Natal, 416 firms (employing 32 409 employees with 229 working proprietors) are based in the Durban, Pinetown, Inanda and Chatsworth areas. These produce 79 per cent of the gross output and pay 76 per cent of the provincial industry's production wages. Significant firm clustering occurs within central Durban, in the Southern Industrial Basin and in the northern metropolitan area. At least 320 of these firms are Cut, Make and Trim (CMT) operations concerned solely with the production process in clothing manufacturing as opposed to full manufacturers who focus on both the pre-production and production aspects of manufacture, and design houses and independent retailers who specialise in pre-production functions and distribution activities.

The reasons underpinning the development of an important local clothing industry are multifarious: the existence of a relatively skilled labour pool, cheaper wage rates, and a large local textile industry. Importantly, however, all these factors were grounded in the previous government's ISI policies. The growing and highly protected domestic clothing market generated a demand for clothing manufacture, thus creating a strong impetus for the development of a local clothing industry. The relatively low barriers to entry into the clothing industry allowed capital strapped Indian entrepreneurs ready access, thus creating an industry with a very different ownership profile from the clothing industry in the Western Cape, as well as other, more white dominated Durban industries (Harrison 1996).

The dynamic development trajectory of Durban's clothing industry is now one of its major weaknesses. Unlike the clothing industry in the Western Cape, which is closely tied to the major retail chains, the local industry is largely wholesale based, focused on lower value added segments subject to severe price competition. It is the segment with the highest level of import penetration, both legal and illegal, and most sensitive to wage rates (implicit in its low value added, labour intensive structure). It is also the sector that has been targeted by very price-competitive firms from India, China and Taiwan in their assault on the rapidly globalising international clothing industry.

These threats become clear when one considers the industry's performance through the 1990s which has witnessed the sharpest decline in new establishments of full manufacturers in Durban. While new CMT establishments have started operating, the growth in the number of CMT operations has not compensated for the loss of employment in full manufacturers owing to the small size of many of these firms. The numbers of new CMT establishments are also affected by the footloose nature of many of these firms, opening and closing as they do depending on orders, creditors and seasons.

Of the clothing firms recently surveyed in Durban (Harrison and Dunne 1998), the majority of firms that did show increasing profits and turnover over the three years, 1994 to 1996, operated within the upper income market. The middle income market is regarded as the fastest growing domestic market and firms feeding into this market also recorded adequate economic performance results. The firms feeding into the low-end market, still the largest South African domestic market, have been virtually wiped out with the increasing penetration of cheap foreign imports. Finally, the export market is still extremely small and limited to the large trading houses within the metropole and a few large full manufacturers in South Africa.

Firms that experienced increasing turnover and profit accredited their success to high productivity levels as a result of a skilled work-force, effective management, updated technology, and access to cheaper imported trim material and textiles.[2] Firms in decline blamed high input costs, poor industrial relations and low skill levels for their plight, in addition to a more competitive market experienced through shrinking order sizes and fewer orders. Significantly, it was largely those firms that migrated from the lower end into the upper end of the market that showed increased profit and turnover whilst firms in the low income market segment survived by sacrificing profits for turnover.

Owing to the labour intensive nature of the production process, CMT firms feel vulnerable to competition from enterprises operating outside the statutory wage regulated areas with current wages about 40 per cent below those typical of Durban. Increasing numbers of CMTs in low income markets are consequently resorting to 'informalisation' in an effort to compete in the market place (Fakude 2000). There are also allegedly hundreds of unregistered firms in Durban producing for registered firms in an effort to compete on the basis of price.

Despite the increased competition in the local market, few manufacturers appear to have shown any attempt to restructure (Harrison and Dunne 1998). Firms that are migrating into upper market segments are shifting their customer base but very few firms appear to be meeting the production demands of their respective customers. Although firms operating in this market were generally more competitive than firms in the lower end, there were still gaps between their customers' demands and what they were able to deliver. Gaps between supply and demand were also evident down the supply chain between suppliers to the clothing industry and the manufacturers.

With changing market demands, the importance of non-price factors in determining a firm's competitiveness is increasingly significant for the Durban clothing industry. Although price remains important within all markets (more so in the lowest segments), other factors such as quality, delivery times, innovative capacity, quick response, and flexibility are becoming important qualifiers within the industry, particularly in the higher income market segments. Failure to meet delivery times and to operate on a quick response basis within the clothing supply chain has resulted in high average levels of inventory, particularly raw material inventory, low frequencies of stock turns, and long lead times. Failure to meet quality requirements through poor production practices, and the purchasing of cheap textiles to lower input costs, has resulted in a high average percentage of defect rates within the industry (Kaplinsky and Morris 1997; Harrison and Dunne 1998).

Globalisation and the associated shift in consumption patterns, and consequently, in production systems offer a number of opportunities and threats to Durban's clothing sector. For the Durban clothing sector, traditionally structured to capture mass production economies of scale, and orientated to price based competition, these shifts represent a distinct threat. On the other hand, closer relations with the global economy have improved access to updated technology and encouraged closer adherence to international clothing trends, making domestic clothing firms potentially more internationally competitive. Furthermore, globalisation and the devaluation of the currency, brings increased opportunity for exporting and access to huge, but very competitive, international markets.

On the domestic front, tariff reductions are rapidly intensifying competition, a problem exacerbated by the state's inability to halt illegal imports. This is particularly problematic for Durban clothing firms concentrating on the lower end of the market, where competition from imports is now most fierce. The more segmented and demanding domestic market which is developing under outward orientation, offers the opportunity to encourage improved domestic firm performance and the development of international competitiveness. Finally, a crucial threat arising from the domestic environment is the gap between government policy formulation and implementation. While increased competition is essential for promoting firm efficiency and international competitiveness, inadequate emphasis on firm restructuring will leave industries vulnerable, potentially leading to huge losses in both employment and output. Government policy acknowledges the need for both, but clothing sector tariff reductions are being implemented far more rapidly than are support programmes for the restructuring of the clothing industry.

In the final instance, the future of the Durban clothing industry will depend on the way in which the industry itself reacts to the threats and opportunities of the external and domestic environment. CMT costs are competitive relative to the industrialised countries, while quality is better than that supplied by low cost competitors in Asia. At the same time, the styling capacity of full manufacturers, retailers and designing houses is better than that of their Asian counterparts. Durban's small manufacturers are relatively flexible compared to the performance of large manufacturers. Furthermore, Durban operators have a reputation for responding competitively and ingeniously to changing market demands. Strong clustering patterns in the Durban clothing industry provides a basis for the development of more collaborative inter-firm relationships. Finally, the industry's strong union and employers' association puts it in a positive position to lobby for state support for the industry.

The weaknesses of the industry relate to a failure to reorganise production relationships. Unstable suppliers, and uncommitted, arms-length relationships make developing closer, more co-operative, supply chain relationships difficult. Gaps between supply and demand in the clothing supply chain (such as late delivery, high domestic textile costs, poor quality), continue to interfere with efficiency and competitiveness. While some firms are migrating to upper market niches, many firms are responding to increased competition by attempting to reduce costs (through informalisation or automation), rather than improving other aspects of competitiveness such as quality, innovation and quick response through training, the use of advanced informational technologies and improved inter-firm relationships.

Durban's Automotive Industry

Durban is an important automotive vehicle and component manufacturing centre, ranked behind Pretoria and Port Elizabeth/Uitenhage, dominated by the single assembler, Toyota SA. As the leading domestic automotive vehicle manufacturer, Toyota SA holds an important position in the South African automotive industry. Many of the component firms that supply Toyota are located in close proximity to it in the Southern Industrial Basin, although the importance of the industry extends well beyond, with a number of engineering firms, fabricated metal producers and steel merchants located in close vicinity to the automotive component firms. The Southern Industrial Basin and Pinetown/New Germany, with 35 per cent and 33 per cent respectively of auto component firms, are without doubt the most important automotive localities in the province.

Globally automobile assembling companies (known as original equipment manufacturers or OEMs) are presently suffering from massive overcapacity. This has resulted in the industry becoming increasingly competitive, with the world's major auto companies looking at ways in which to cut costs and get new products to the market sooner. Vehicle production life spans have as a consequence diminished significantly over the last decade to cycles of about four years only. In order to increase the scale of production for such models there is also a move towards the global sourcing of particular models from a shrinking number of suppliers.

The net result of these pressures is massive change in the automotive components industry. The world's leading component firms are consolidating their positions by acquiring their smaller competitors, whilst at the same time moving towards modular production. In order to cut costs and lessen design lead times OEMs are transferring responsibility for the design and development of certain parts of their vehicles to selected multinational component manufacturers. As a reward for their development activities they are assured of long term sole supplier contracts with the OEMs. This is leading to a distinct tiering of the automotive industry. OEMs no longer have 2 000 component suppliers. They now have 200 first tier suppliers responsible for the production of particular modules (or sub-assemblies) that require the supply of components from the other 1 800 second tier component suppliers.

These global trends have a significant impact on the automotive industries of developing economies. Whilst South African OEMs were, for example, protected by tariff barriers of 115 per cent prior to the launch of the Motor Industry Development Programme (MIDP) in September 1995, real protection levels, if all the mechanisms of the programme are factored in, are currently estimated at lying between 0 and 5 per cent. A critically important dimension to the MIDP is its Import/Export Complementation (IEC) scheme devised as a mechanism for subsidising exports and increasing the competitiveness of South African automotive products in the international automotive markets. The scheme allows both OEMs and component manufacturers to earn duty credits through exporting which can be used to offset duties incurred through importing or sold to other firms in the industry at a slightly discounted rate.

This has opened up the highly insulated and internationally

uncompetitive South African automotive industry to international competition extremely quickly. A large number of automotive retailing companies and OEMs are now importing vehicles directly. Approximately 12 per cent of the vehicles sold in the local market in 1997 and 20 per cent in 2000 were fully imported units. The South African OEMs are therefore being placed under enormous pressure by the increased sale of imported vehicles into the small domestic market of approximately 380 000 passenger, light, medium and heavy commercial vehicles – constituting less than 0.5 per cent of global sales. Exports are however rising significantly. Over 20 per cent of vehicles manufactured in South Africa are currently exported. Some domestic OEMs, particularly Toyota SA, are however restricted in their export endeavours because of their licensing agreements with their foreign licensors.

The components industry has been under extreme pressure with turnover having stagnated over the last couple of years (Barnes and Kaplinsky 2000). The reasons underpinning this are (a) the poor performance of the domestic market; (b) increased foreign sourcing from domestic OEMs; and (c) the flood of imported components into the domestic parts and accessories aftermarket. However, whilst the industry is in general struggling, various sub-sectors are performing well. This is clearly evident from Table 1, which highlights the extent of export growth from various sub-sectors of the national industry between 1994 and 1999.

The problem associated with this growth in exports, however, is the extent to which low value added components dominate the make up of the exports. Leather seat covers and catalytic converters hardly qualify as high technology components. As the export of these products increases so it becomes easier to import higher value added components from foreign companies, thus eroding the technology base of the local industry.

Notwithstanding some of the negative implications of the industry's rapid assimilation into the global automotive environment, a number of positive implications have also emerged.

- Domestic vehicles prices have decreased in price in real terms since the launch of the MIDP, thus making them more affordable to South African consumers.
- Domestic firms (both OEMs and component manufacturers) have generally improved their internal performance thus improving their competitiveness (cf. Barnes 1997a, 1997b, 1998b, 1999, 2000).
- Firms are selling equity to foreign multinationals, thus linking themselves into global networks – e.g. with regard to Durban, Federal Mogul has purchased T&N plc and hence controlling interest in

Table 1 South Africa's most important auto component exports: 1994, 1996 and 1999 (R million).

Component	*1994*	*1996*	*1999*	*% of Exports: 1999*
Catalytic converters	197	485	2 569	26.6
Seat parts, leather seat covers	464	1 259	1 888	19.5
Tyres	132	296	639	6.6
Silencers, exhaust pipes	181	170	598	6.2
Road wheels and parts thereof	77	227	518	5.4
Engine parts	61	137	383	4.0
Wiring harnesses	0	92	304	3.1
Tooling	165	279	264	2.7
Glass	59	71	147	1.5
Radiators	44	107	111	1.1
Other[3]	711	928	2 253	23.3
Total	2 091	4 051	9 674	100.0

Source: Department of Trade and Industry (1997, 2000)

T&N Holdings, the largest Durban based component manufacturer, and the second largest automotive component company in South Africa.

It is clear then that the national industry, whilst struggling, is not being completely eroded. The new operating environment in which domestic firms find themselves has shifted the terrain somewhat and there are almost certainly going to be casualties, especially in the short term. However, there are also possibilities for future expansion in the industry, although perhaps not from some of the traditionally strong sub-sectors that owe their existence to previous ISI policies. The shape of the industry in the Durban locality is likely to change and it may even contract somewhat in the short to medium term (due to both national and international factors), but it is still likely to remain an important industry. Its importance will not only be conspicuous in terms of employment and output figures but also by its strong linkages to other manufacturing sectors such as textiles, plastics, ferrous and non-ferrous metal fabrication, electronics, etc.

Toyota SA has traditionally been the most successful of the South African OEMs in the domestic market. In South African terms, it is an extremely well run company with a clear understanding of the domestic automotive market. Despite its strong domestic showing, it has probably the weakest global networking abilities which is critically important in terms of the manner in which the MIDP has been structured. Toyota SA has the lowest level of foreign equity of any of the South African OEMs. Toyota Japan only has a 27.8 per cent equity stake in Toyota SA with the majority of its shares being owned by Wesco, a South African company listed on the Johannesburg Stock Exchange.

The fact that Toyota SA's export markets are restricted by its franchise agreements with Toyota Japan limits the company's ability to generate benefits from the MIDP. Furthermore, the fact that Toyota Japan has not as yet adopted a global sourcing strategy means there are also only limited opportunities for even the most competitive component firms supplying Toyota SA to access export contracts. This stands in stark contrast to the German owned domestic OEMs located elsewhere in the country, where component export contracts have been widely facilitated – primarily in order to generate duty rebates via the IEC component of the MIDP. In 1999, 46.1 per cent of all component exports from South Africa were destined for Germany (DTI 2000), whilst BMW SA has increased its production of the 3 series model in SA from 60 to 200 units per day, because of its new export contract for right hand drive models. Given the duty credits it will earn, as well as the economies of scale benefits that it and its component suppliers will reap, the export order will place BMW SA in a very strong strategic position both domestically and internationally.

If Toyota SA is to compete in the long term, it needs better access to Toyota Japan's global networks, and it similarly needs to help facilitate significant export contracts for its domestic component suppliers. Between 70 and 80 per cent of a vehicle's value added takes place at component manufacturers, and so if Toyota SA wishes to improve its own competitiveness it is imperative that its component suppliers improve accordingly. Given the limited economies of scale that component suppliers are able to generate in the small domestic market, it is therefore imperative that they access export markets (Black 1993, 1994).

Toyota SA's unstable strategic direction has a direct impact on the numerous component suppliers situated in Durban. However, not all the component manufacturers in the metropole are reliant on Toyota SA for their survival. Many Durban based firms (especially the larger component manufacturers) also supply to other domestic OEMs and/or are aftermarket focused. Some of the component firms in Durban are also expanding their exports significantly, particularly into the European parts and accessory aftermarkets, thus limiting their reliance on the domestic market. Durban's automotive components industry has generally, however, not shown any dynamism lately. Much of the significant foreign investment that has taken place in the components industry nationally has been directed towards the Eastern Cape and Gauteng.

The problems experienced by component firms in Durban are largely generic and they follow some of the national issues quite closely. As highlighted in Figure 1, in line with national and provincial trends (cf. Black 1994; Barnes 1997a, 1997b, 1998, 1999, 2000), average internal performance indicators amongst automotive component firms in Durban in the late 1990s did not compare with international best practice indicators. Inventory levels, internal defect rates and absenteeism levels were excessively high, pointing to manufacturing inefficiencies and problems associated with the external economic environment in which Durban firms operated.

Through successful interventions such as the KwaZulu-Natal Benchmarking Club, Durban based automotive component manufacturers have, however, made significant competitiveness strides over the last three years. The KwaZulu-Natal Benchmarking Club exemplifies the supply-side support measures available to industry in that it is a national government (Sector Partnership Fund) supported continuous improvement network for automotive component manufacturers in the region. The possible success of such initiatives is highlighted in Figure 2, which outlines the competitiveness progress of the eight Durban based members of the KwaZulu-Natal Benchmarking Club. As revealed, the Durban based automotive component manufacturers improved their inventory holding, customer return rates and absenteeism rates by 19, 47 and 27 per cent respectively between 1997 and 2000.

Generally, then, although Durban based automotive firms are not internationally competitive in terms of their operational competitiveness and are losing domestic market sales to foreign imports and subdued domestic demand (in both the assembly and aftermarkets), they are responding aggressively. This is evident in terms of their significantly improved competitiveness, their gradual adoption of advanced Informational Technology infrastructures (Moodley 2001) and their increased levels of exporting. This process needs to be further consolidated, however, with firms also needing to improve their connectivity into the global automotive markets as a mechanism for ensuring long term sustainability.

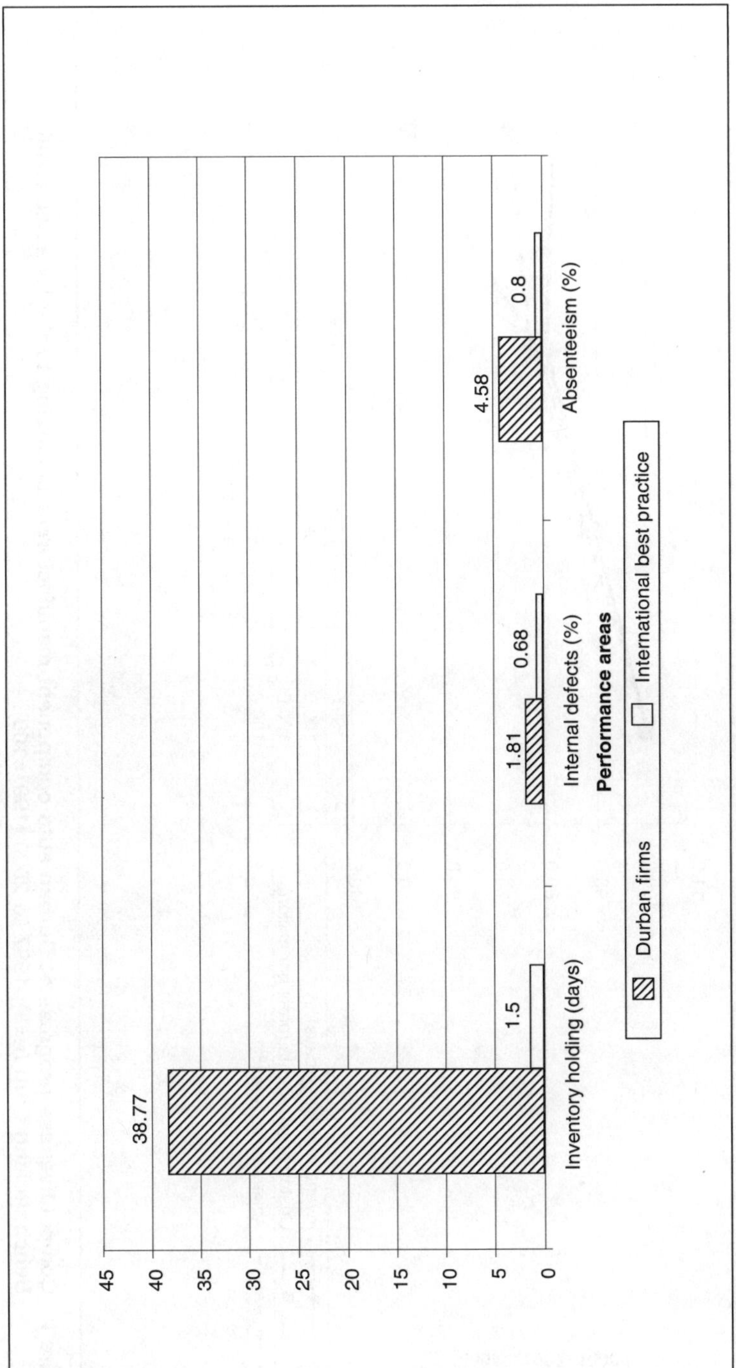

Figure 1 Operational competitiveness: Durban firms (n=23) versus international best practice indicators.

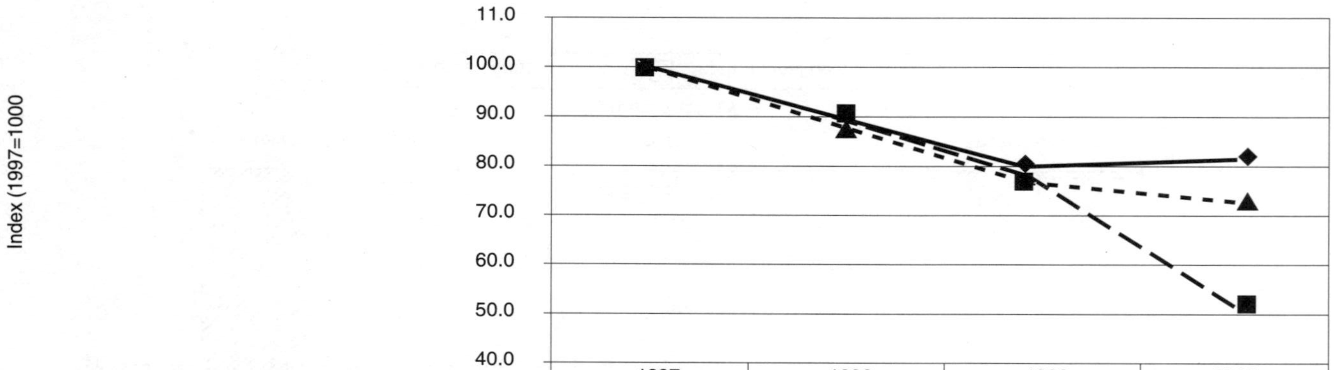

	1997	1998	1999	2000
Inventory holding (days)	100.0	89.7	79.9	80.9
Customer return rate (parts per million)	100.0	89.6	77.7	52.5
Absenteeism rate (%)	100.0	87.7	77.0	73.2

Years

Figure 2 Competitiveness progress at Durban auto component manufacturers belonging to the KwaZulu-Natal Benchmarking Club (n=8): 1997 to 2000 (1997=100).

Conclusion

Durban owes its substantial industrial sector and its national manufacturing significance to a number of historical factors. Principal amongst these was the role of the port and a trade regime based on import substituting industrialisation. The latter no longer prevails but the former has a major role to play in the new trade regime, notwithstanding the crippling fault line over its status as a city port discussed earlier in the chapter. The impact of globalisation and a government sponsored export oriented trade liberalisation programme with supply-side support measures, places the manufacturing sector as the central economic driver and creates new opportunities for the city.

Whether the city can respond accordingly depends on how firms, industrial sectors, key stakeholders, national institutions controlling the port, and local government react to this new scenario. The institutional response is patchy. The city government has limited manoeuvreability in using the port as a driving force. It still has no control over this key economic instrument which plays an extraordinarily important role in influencing economic life in the city, and the prospect of this changing seems highly unlikely. However, key local departments, associations and stakeholders are attempting to tackle the new challenges.

Ultimately, however, the key to becoming more internationally competitive lies with the particular responses of firms and industrial sectors. In this respect, our focus on the clothing and automotive industries has highlighted a number of pertinent issues for consideration which would seem to be generic to manufacturing in Durban generally.

The automotive sector in Durban presents a useful case study of a local industry reconfiguring itself in the face of the government's present trade liberalisation policies. Domestic firms are being forced to compete with foreign firms with many suffering economically as a result of the new competitive demands that have emerged out of this new interface between the global and national industry. The success of the automotive sector is contingent upon a multiplicity of factors. Some of these, such as internal competitiveness issues, are under the control of the domestic firms, whilst others are far more powerful than any domestic firm could deal with and fall within the ambit of decisions made at the international and national levels. A key factor here is the issue of global connectivity which restructures the world auto stage and through locking component firms into structured relationships with particular OEMs guarantees them a continued sourcing and exporting role. However, the local industry has demonstrated that it is possible to respond to the harsh winds of trade liberalisation and significantly raise levels of international competitiveness through a focused application of the new government's supply-side support measures. The significant competitiveness progress made by the Durban based auto component manufacturers that belong to the KwaZulu-Natal Benchmarking Club verifies this.

The clothing industry in Durban faces similar challenges with respect to the new trade regime. However, the threat, and possible advantages, of being excluded or included in favoured status arrangements with global players does not apply in this industry in the same way as in the auto components sector. Issues of internal competitiveness therefore predominate in the local clothing sector. This industry is both dynamic and threatened. The lower end of the market is severely threatened by cheap imports from India and South East Asia and in this respect the port plays a negative role since it facilitates the legal and illegal inflow of cheap lower end clothing into the market. However, the fact that some firms are surviving through migrating into upper market segments is of major importance. Strategies that assist in encouraging firms to make improvements in their organisation of production and management at a firm level, and that improve the relationship between firms within the clothing supply chain are therefore fundamental to the industry's success. Although there is pressure on the industry with retailing agents looking elsewhere for suppliers within the increasingly globalised context, Durban firms do have the ability to be competitive in the middle to upper market segments if creative strategies are pursued. Coupled with the advantage that the proximity of the port creates within the context of the new trade regime, this produces the possibility of an expanding export oriented clothing sector. A focus on exports through institutional support to firms within Durban could assist firms in breaking into new markets and escaping the competitive spiral of a shrinking domestic market.

NOTES

1. This ratio will give an indication of the *relative* labour intensity of sectors. A salaries to net output ratio of 50 per cent implies that 50 per cent of value-added is accounted for by salaries and wages.
2. Half of the cost of clothing production is the cost of textile inputs.
3. All component categories with export sales of less than R100 million for 1999 are classified as 'other'.

REFERENCES

Andersen Consulting. 1993. *The Lean Enterprise Benchmarking Project*, Andersen Consulting.

Aniruth, J., J. Barnes and M. Morris. 1998. 'Providing Institutional Support for International Competitiveness: Evidence from the Clothing, Automotive, Textile and Furniture Sectors in KwaZulu-Natal'. Report for the KwaZulu-Natal Regional Economic Forum.

Barnes, J. 1997a. 'Market Gaps and Firm Performance Levels: The State of the Automotive Industry in KwaZulu-Natal'. Report for the KwaZulu-Natal Industrial Restructuring Project, mimeo. Centre for Social and Development Studies, University of Natal, Durban.

——. 1997b. 'Facing up to the Global Challenge: The State of KwaZulu-Natal's Automotive Components Industry'. CSDS Research Report No. 11. Centre for Social and Development Studies, University of Natal, Durban.

——. 1998a. 'An Investigation into Middle-Management's Understanding of International Competitiveness in KwaZulu-Natal's Manufacturing Sector'. CSDS Research Report No. 12. Centre for Social and Development Studies, University of Natal, Durban.

——. 1998b. 'Competing in the Global Economy: The Competitiveness of the South African Automotive Components Industry'. CSDS Research Report No. 13. Centre for Social and Development Studies, University of Natal, Durban.

——. 1999. 'What Chances International Competitiveness in the South African Automotive Components Industry? Evidence from an International Benchmark Undertaking'. CSDS Research Report No. 20. Centre for Social and Development Studies, University of Natal, Durban.

——. 2000. 'The Competitiveness of the South African Automotive Components Industry: Findings from the 1999 Follow-up Study'. CSDS Research Report No. 27. Centre for Social and Development Studies, University of Natal, Durban.

Barnes, J. and R. Kaplinsky. 2000. 'Globalisation and the Death of the Local Firm? The Automobile Components Sector in South Africa'. *Regional Studies*, 34, 9.

Best, M.H. 1990. *The New Competition: Institutions of Industrial Restructuring*. Cambridge: Polity Press.

Black, A. 1993. 'Economies of Scale, Flexibility and Industry Restructuring: The Case of the South African Automobile and Components Sectors'. Unpublished Paper, School of Economics, University of Cape Town.

——. 1994. *An Industrial Strategy for the Motor Vehicle Assembly and Components Sectors*. Cape Town: University of Cape Town Press.

Brown, S. 1996. *Strategic Manufacturing for Competitive Advantage: Transforming Operations from Shop Floor to Strategy*. New York: Prentice Hall.

CDE Research. 1996. *Durban: South Africa's Global Competitor*. The Big City Series. Johannesburg: Centre for Development Research.

Central Statistical Services. 1993. *Census of Manufacturing 1993 Principal Statistics on a Regional Basis*. Pretoria: Government Printer.

Data Research Africa (DRA). 1995. 'A Study of Key Economic Sectors in the Durban Functional Region'. Phase 1 – Draft Report.

Department of Trade and Industry. 1997. *Monitoring and Implementation of the Motor Industry Development Programme*. Pretoria: Government Printer.

——. 2000. *Current Developments in the Automotive Industry.* Pretoria: Government Printer.

Durban Publicity Association (DPA). 1982. *Durban: A Review of Commerce, Industry and Tourism.* Durban: A.C. Braby (Pty) Ltd.

Fakude, G. 2000. 'Informalisation in KwaZulu-Natal's Clothing Sector'. Research Report No. 37. Centre for Social and Development Studies, University of Natal, Durban.

Harrison, K. 1996. 'KZN IRP Clothing Study: Changing SA Markets and Supply Chain Developments'. Report for the KwaZulu-Natal Industrial Restructuring Project, mimeo. Centre for Social and Development Studies, University of Natal, Durban.

——. 1997. 'Migrate, Innovate or Evaporate'. Draft Report for the KwaZulu-Natal Industrial Restructuring Project, mimeo. Centre for Social and Development Studies, University of Natal, Durban.

Harrison, K. and N. Dunne. 1998. 'KwaZulu-Natal's Clothing Industry: The Importance of Firm-Level and Pipeline Competitiveness Issues'. CSDS Research Report No. 14. Centre for Social and Development Studies, University of Natal, Durban.

Harrison, P. 1995. 'Global Transformations and the Changing Geography of Production in KwaZulu-Natal'. Report for the Town and Regional Planning Commission. Interim Report No. 5.

Harrison, P. and M. Morris. 1996. 'Manufacturing in KwaZulu-Natal'. Unpublished Report for the KwaZulu-Natal Provincial Ministry of Economic Affairs.

Hoyle, B.S. and D.A. Pinder. 1981. 'Seaports, Cities and Transport Systems'. In B.S. Hoyle and D. Hilling (eds). *Cityport Industrialisation and Regional Development: Spatial Analysis and Planning Strategies.* Oxford: Pergamon Press.

Humphrey, J., A. Mukherjee, M. Zilbovicius and G. Arbix. 1998. 'Globalisation, Foreign Direct Investment and the Restructuring of Supplier Networks: The Motor Industry in Brazil and India'. In M. Kagami, J. Humphrey and M. Piore (eds). *Learning, Liberalisation and Economic Adjustment.* Tokyo: Institute of Developing Economies.

Jones, T. 1997. 'The Port of Durban and the Durban Metropolitan Economy'. Research Monograph No. 10. Economics Research Unit, University of Natal.

Kaplinsky, R. 1994. *Easternisation: The Spread of Japanese Management Techniques to Developing Countries.* London: Frank Cass.

Kaplinsky, R. and M. Morris. 1997. 'The Formulation and Implementation of Industrial Policy in South Africa: A View from the Edge'. CSDS Working Paper No. 15. Centre for Social and Development Studies, University of Natal, Durban.

Katzen, M. 1961. *Industry in Greater Durban. Part 1. Its Growth and Structure.* Pietermaritzburg: Natal Town and Regional Planning Commission.

Management Today. 1994. *Britain's Best Factories.* London: Haymarket Business Publications.

McCarthy, J. 1993. 'Planning for Industrial Growth in the Durban Region: Current Trends and Future Prospects'. Report to the Physical Planning Directorate of the Natal Provincial Administration.

Moodley, S. 2001. 'E-business and Supply Chain Management in the Automotive Industry: Preliminary Findings from the Eastern Cape and KwaZulu-Natal

Benchmarking Club Pilot Surveys'. Research Report No. 35. Centre for Social and Development Studies, University of Natal, Durban.

Nishiguchi, T. 1989. 'Good Management is Good Management: The Japanization of the U.S. Auto Industry'. *The JAMA Forum*, 7, 4.

Piore, M. and C. Sabel. 1984. *The Second Industrial Divide*. New York: Basic Books.

South Durban SEA Project Team. 1998. 'South Durban Strategic Environmental Assessment – Option 1: Existing Situation'.

Tomlinson, R. 1993. 'Durban Functional Region: Strategic Urban Perspective'. Discussion Paper. Development Bank of South Africa.

Watkinson, E. 1996. 'Evaluation of the Regional Industrial Development Programme in KwaZulu-Natal: Pinetown Survey Area'. Report to the Board for Regional Industrial Decentralisation as part of an evaluation of the performance of the Regional Industrial Decentralisation Programme in KwaZulu-Natal.

CHAPTER FIVE

Financing Durban's Development

1970–99

VISHNU PADAYACHEE

A study of the financial institutions operating out of, or in Durban, and of the ways in which these institutions have contributed to the development of the city has not been attempted. Part of the reason for this arises out of the extreme difficulty in obtaining reliable, comparable data and information on a city-level basis. The South African literature on the relationships between finance, industry and development at national level is limited both in extent and scope – the major works rarely probe beneath the surface and are lacking in imagination and in methodological and analytical power. Few useful reference points exist to guide a study such as this. This chapter represents a first attempt at describing and analysing some aspects of Durban's financial scene in the period 1970–99; it also attempts to come to an impressionistic view of the kinds of development – industrial, commercial and infrastructural – that the local, national and international financial and corporate sectors made possible in this city.

The central argument advanced in this chapter is that access to finance in the city of Durban over the last 25–30 years appears to depend upon whether and how potential borrowers are locked into the larger structure of South Africa's corporate world (the mining-industrial-finance network). The insiders, like Tongaat-Huletts and other large corporations, have had no difficulty raising finance, either from within (retained earnings, group borrowing) or (using their power and influence) from outside through new rights issues or support from the private banks and development finance corporations. Those outside the conglomerate structure, including small and medium-sized companies owned by white as well as emerging Indian and African businessmen, are the ones who have experienced the greatest difficulty in raising capital, especially in the post-1984 era of high interest rates and slow or declining national growth.

The chapter describes and assesses the major characteristics of, and trends in, Durban's financial world in two periods, 1970–90 and 1990–to date. The following section examines the main sources of new finance that have been, and are, available to the borrowing institutions of the city (both large, medium and small). Later sections shift the focus to the lending side of the finance equation and describe in some detail the origins, objectives and scope of the activity of the major financial institutions, both private sector and developmental, that have either been based, or had a major presence, in Durban since 1970. In the penultimate section the role played by the local state in developing innovative instruments to finance infrastructural and other development in the city is examined.

Durban as a Financial Centre

Understanding something about the history, nature and dynamics of the urban economy is crucial to a proper analysis of the structure, strengths and weaknesses of any city as a financial centre. I begin with such an overview of the Durban economy since 1970, in which key features and trends which impact upon Durban as a financial centre are highlighted.

Durban is the dominant centre of economic activity in the KwaZulu-Natal Province, contributing over half of the region's production and about a third of the region's employment for most of the period since 1970. Its economy is fairly diversified, with major strengths in manufacturing, commerce (tourism being the largest sub-sector here), transport, community and social services, and increasingly, finance. Within manufacturing the most important sub-sectors over this period have been clothing, textiles, food, chemicals and fabricated metal products. In the long post-war period, the chemical and automobile industries have become crucial to industrial growth in the city.

Using Development Bank data, Smith (1993) has estimated that, in terms of economic value, the financial sector in KwaZulu-Natal (which is heavily concentrated in Durban) grew faster than any other sector outside agriculture. However, more recent data examined by Hornby suggests that, although the sector is still significant in terms of value added to the economy, its growth in the 1980s was more modest than Smith proposed (memo n.d). The sector is highly capital and technology intensive and is not a major employer, especially of poorer and less skilled workers.

The key companies in greater Durban in the post-1970 period have been Toyota, Tongaat-Huletts, Frame, Metal Box, Kingsgate, Bakers,

Dunlop, Unilever, SAICCOR, McCarthy, Beacon, Rennies, Grindrod, Suncrush, ABI, CG Smith, Romatex, the Coastal Group and NBS. These companies straddle a wide variety of industries, but as Freund points out 'they cannot really be said to rest on a virtuous circle of mutual attraction or on a competitive pool of particularly skilled labour' (Freund 2000). Strong links have, however, existed between some of these companies (for example, NBS, McCarthy and Tongaat-Huletts), as we shall see later.

Although it is a relatively mature, complex economy with a spread of firm size and type, one distinctive trend has been the steady drain (mainly) to Johannesburg of the headquarters of some of the city's major companies. Large companies, including CG Smith, Thomas Barlow and Romatex have moved their headquarters from Durban to Johannesburg since the late 1950s. Others such as Tongaat-Huletts and McCarthy, although Durban registered, have significant non-Durban based shareholding.

The major international companies which have some presence in Durban include AEG, BMG International and Siemens (Germany); Alusaf and Nestlé (Switzerland); BP, Dunlop, Protea Asphalt, Shell, and Smith and Nephew (UK); Masomite (USA); Toyota (Japan); and Belgotex (Belgium) (Pillay 1995: n.p.). The South African head offices of all these companies are, however, based elsewhere in the country, mainly in Gauteng. Only two major international companies – Unilever (Netherlands) and T&N Holdings (UK) – have their South African headquarters in Durban.

The presence of a company in a city, however, does not automatically suggest that its fortunes are tied to that of the city in any direct way. Companies such as Rennies and Grindrod, given their connections to the shipping industry, have tended to be very concerned about the future economic prospects of the city of Durban. Others, such as Tongaat-Huletts and McCarthy, have acted in ways which have demonstrated their interest in the wider development of the city, but their interests are also provincial and national in character. Yet others such as Metal Box, whose Durban branch is bigger even than their Johannesburg headquarters, sell nationally and internationally, and have tended not to devote much of their energies into city developments.

Most commentators have characterised Durban as a 'branch economy', a term implying that although the area has many international and national companies, it is really home to the ancillaries of such companies rather than being headquarters to them. Terry Rosenberg, CEO of the McCarthy Group puts it this way:

> The statement that Durban tends to be a branch economy is a fair statement. You've got a lot of either very small or relatively small local businesses, or you've got subsidiaries of main businesses which are headquartered mainly in Johannesburg. It's [Durban] not like Cape Town which you can say is the head of the insurance industry, you know Sanlam, Old Mutual, they're all headquartered there. The oil industry . . . Caltex, BP, Mobil, they're all in Cape Town. We just have a scattering . . . (Interviewed by U. Pillay, 01.06.94).

This 'branch' status of the Durban economy clearly has had a major impact on the development of Durban as a financial centre. The absence of a substantial core of company headquarters has meant that at least one major reason for locating the headquarters of major financial institutions here does not exist. To this has to be added certain developments at the national level, including the downturn in the economy after 1973, the increasing sanctions campaign against the country in the 1980s, and intensifying political and labour unrest since the mid-1970s. All these factors combined to further stifle the growth and development of Durban as a financial centre.

The Durban functional region is by far the largest financial and business centre in the province, accounting for 66 per cent of regional value added in the sector, and significantly more than half of the region's financial infrastructure (Smith 1993). This dominance is reflected, among other things, in the decision in 1991 of the South African Reserve Bank to close its Pietermaritzburg branch, and to consolidate its regional activities in the newly built Durban branch (Smith 1993).

Despite this regional dominance, however, the city, reflecting the branch nature of its economy, is very much a secondary financial centre in national terms, compared with Johannesburg, Cape Town and even Pretoria. Very few financial institutions were headquartered here between 1970–90, as is evident from Table 1.

Durban's financial scene remained rather static for most of this period, with only the small (Indian-focused) Albaraka Bank having just arrived on the scene as a new player by 1990. The Natal Building Society (NBS), the most significant of Durban's financial institutions in this time, was relatively small by national standards, and targeted a niche market in small and medium-size enterprises. Furthermore, as Hornby points out, up to three-quarters of the NBS's investing clients are in Johannesburg with another 15 per cent in Cape Town. Similarly only about 30 per cent of NBS's corporate loans are in Durban, about 5 per cent in the Free State, 15 per cent in Cape Town and the remainder in Johannesburg.

Table 1 Durban registered and headquartered banks and building societies.

1970	*1980*	*1990*	*1999*
NBS Provincial NRB	NBS Provincial NRB	NBS Provincial NRB Albaraka Bank	NBS-Boland NRB Albaraka Bank HBZ Bank Marriott Merchant McCarthy Bank Bank of Baroda

Source: South African Reserve Bank, Bank Supervision Reports, various; information from interviews; and press reports.

The Provincial Building Society was established in Durban in 1929, and as we shall see later, was distinguished by its willingness to extend mortgage loans to Indian and African clients, even as early as the 1940s, at a time when few other financial institutions in the country were prepared to do this. It was taken over by Investec Bank in 1991. The New Republic Bank (NRB) was set up (initially with the assistance of the Standard Bank) in 1970 and has for most of the period focused mainly on relatively small Indian depositors and borrowers.

No merchant banks, whose business is mainly at the long-end of the capital market, were located in Durban in the 1970s. Only two small insurance companies were registered in Durban in the period until 1990. These were the NBS linked NBS Insurance Company (1977) and the New India Assurance Company (1972). A few property and equity unit trusts associated in the main either with the NBS or Russell Marriott Boyd Trust (RMBT) were registered in Durban from 1983 onwards (Financial Services Board letter dated 02.12.96).

Although not registered here, most national banks have had a major presence in the city for many decades. These include the 'Big Four': Barclays (later First National Bank, FNB); Standard Bank of South Africa; Amalgamated Banks of South Africa (ABSA); and Nedcor/Nedbank. Smaller national and international banks (Bank of Lisbon, Bank of Athens) also had branches in Durban over time. All the major building societies (before they registered as banks following the 1988 changes to the Banks Act) were represented here, including the Permanent, United and Allied. The major insurance companies, including Sanlam, Liberty Life, Southern and the Old Mutual had important regional offices in the city.

All the state linked development financial institutions, including the

Industrial Development Corporation (IDC), Development Bank of South Africa (DBSA), Small Business Development Corporation (SBDC), and the Independent Development Trust (IDT) had a presence in the province. The IDC (which was set up nationally in 1940) only opened its Durban office in the early 1970s (Interview, Ian Halliday, 23.04.97). Only two development financial institutions were headquartered in Durban after 1970. These were the Indian Industrial Development Corporation (IIDC) which was established under the guidance of the IDC in the early 1970s, and which later merged with the SBDC; and the KwaZulu Finance Corporation (KFC) which was established in 1979.

Signs of greater activity in Durban's financial scene became evident from the early 1990s, as is shown in the last column of Table 1. In December 1991, the Provincial Building Society was taken over by the Johannesburg based Investec Bank, ending the business life of one of Durban's oldest financial institutions, but heralding the more active presence in the city of one of South Africa's most aggressive and internationally competitive banks. In October 1994, Marriott Merchant Bank was launched as a wholly owned subsidiary of Marriott Holding Limited, a company whose history in the city stretches back to 1862 when Samuel Marriott joined George Russell to establish Russell and Marriott. HBZ Bank Limited, a wholly owned subsidiary of HBZ Bank AG Zurich, opened its South African headquarters in Durban in November 1995, targeting in the first instance the city's large Indian community.

The NRB was effectively taken over by a Malaysian group headed by Dato Samsudin Abu Hassan, who through Redbridge Assets Limited (registered in the Virgin Isles) and SMG Holdings, acquired a 41.9 per cent interest in the NRB in March 1996. Sanlam with 12.4 and SA Mutual with 5.2 are the largest of the minority shareholders. Late in 1996 the NBS merged with the predominantly Afrikaans, Cape based Boland Bank, to create NBS-Boland, a national niche marketed retail bank, now one of the top five finance houses in the country. In August 1997, the Indian based Bank of Baroda opened its South African headquarters in Durban, its 2 500th branch in the world, with a initial investment of R50 million. In November 1997, the Reserve Bank granted McCarthy Motor Holdings a banking license to launch McCarthy Bank, a niche bank specialising in corporate and vehicle financing.

The 1990s also saw the emergence, following the restoration of greater normalcy in the national political situation, of a number of new finance companies headed by locally based Indian and African businessmen, sometimes in association with Malaysian, Indonesian or other East Asian backers. The most prominent of these new 'black empowerment' companies which originated in Durban was (former Robben Island prisoner) Mzi Khumalo's Capital Alliance. These developments represent a far greater level of activity in what had been up to then Durban's rather dull and risk-averse financial world. Whether and how these changes affected the city's industry and development will form part of the subject of the following sections of this chapter.

Retained Earnings, Equity and Debt

I now examine aspects of finance and development from a borrower's perspective. There are basically three sources of new finance available to companies to fund their capital expenditure and other regular activities: internal sources (retained earnings), share issues (equity) and borrowings from banks and other financial institutions (debt/loans). The balance and choice among these three broad categories differ between companies and countries, and can change over time, depending on such factors as the prevailing interest rate structure and trends, national tax policy, company dividend policy and the like. Companies financing with borrowing get a tax break because interest repayments are deducted from profits before tax. This benefit does not accrue in the case of raising capital via, say, new share issues.

In the UK, during the short period between 1986 and 1990, the share of bank and other borrowing as a source of new finance for British companies just about doubled (from 21 to 40 per cent). However, new finance raised from internal sources (51 per cent) remained the single most important category (Pike and Neale 1993: 275). This kind of analysis for South Africa, let alone Durban, is severely limited by the absence of reliable data, and the account which follows has therefore to be impressionistic, intuitive and suggestive rather than definitive. Where possible, available data for selected Durban companies including Tongaat-Huletts, McCarthy, T&N Holdings, Marshalls, AM Moolla (and the Richards Bay based Bell Industries) are used to illustrate particular points.

Decisions about what particular package of retained earnings, borrowings and share issues are to be used to finance any particular project, expansion, or acquisition are inter-linked, and although the discussion which follows attempts initially to separate out each of these sources, it must be appreciated that a neat compartmentalisation is not possible.

Little reliable aggregate information is available from published sources that enables us to say much about the relative significance of retained earnings as a source of new finance for Durban companies. However, it is clear from interviews with leading bankers and company executives, retained earnings seem to be the most important source of finance in Durban, certainly for funding the normal capital expansion programmes of the larger corporations. Investec's former Durban Chief Executive, Neil MacNeillie, has pointed out that 'company borrowing from banks are limited, the most important sources of capital come from retained earnings and the Johannesburg Stock Exchange' (JSE) (share and rights issues) (Interview, 11.03.98).

The annual reports of a large company like Tongaat-Huletts from 1976–97, for example, regularly refer to the fact that capital expenditure was, or is to be, funded in the main by some combination of retained earnings, depreciation retentions and existing (borrowing) facilities (see for example, Annual Reports 1990: 34, 1993: 34). T&N Holdings also sets out its financing of expected capital expenditure. Its 1996 Report, for example, points out in Note 19.1 to the financial statements that 'total budgeted capital expenditure is expected to be approximately R24 million. This expenditure will be funded using existing cash resources, funds generated within the group and borrowing from third parties' (1996: 44). From this it is also clear that intra-group funds are an important source of internal financing.

Most medium and small business, for very different reasons, have been forced into using internal sources to start up, and expand their operations. Only a handful of medium-sized companies in the Durban area are listed and so have no access to share capital. For many others, especially those owned by Indian and African entrepreneurs, redlining (the practice of not extending bank loans to certain defined groups or areas) and/or the high cost of borrowing, have cut them off from the formal banking and financial institutions. Exceptions here are developmental organisations like the SBDC and the KFC, which are, to some extent, more attuned to the needs of small business, although there are disturbing signals of late that even these institutions are increasingly being driven by normal commercial lending considerations.

Thus, for example, a comprehensive, cross section survey of 650 small and medium enterprises (SMEs) in KwaZulu-Natal (including Durban) conducted by Data Research Africa in 1995 revealed that banks were the main source of start-up capital for only 5.4 per cent of the operators surveyed. Less than a quarter attempted to obtain a bank loan for working capital and investment purposes, and less than half of these had been successful. Bank procedures were perceived to be too complicated and finance charges too high, leaving most entrepreneurs to rely on their own funds and savings or that of family and friends (ERU and BEES n.d.: 42ff). These results are similar to those obtained by Morris et al. (1997: 88–91) from a survey of 26 informal tavern operators in the Western Cape. There, 81 per cent of the initial capital was obtained from personal savings, 12 per cent from family loans, none from banks and only one respondent indicated that he obtained a loan from the SBDC.

McGregor's 1997 edition records 32 Durban registered companies, as being listed on the Johannesburg Stock Exchange. Tongaat-Huletts is also listed directly on the London Stock Exchange. The stock market over time has been an important source of new capital for these listed companies, and certainly outranks borrowing from banks and other financial institutions. The stock market is particularly important in raising funds for really large capital projects and also for acquisitions. We can get some indication, using various issues of McGregor's, of the importance of share issues (relative to borrowings) by examining the gearing or debt-equity ratios of four listed companies over a period of time. (The figures are to be read as the proportion of debt for every unit of equity.)

Table 2 Debt-equity (gearing) ratios of selected Durban registered companies, 1985–95.

	1985	*1990*	*1995*
Tongaat-Huletts	1.20	0.50	0.45
T&N	0.71	1.58	1.34
Marshalls	0.20	0.19	0.26
McCarthy	1.44	1.18	2.54

Source: McGregor's (various years)

McGregor's uses company financial statements (balance sheets) rather than market values of debt and equity to calculate these ratios for each year. This is not the most accurate way of ascertaining these ratios (for reasons we need not go into here). However, the trends over time are likely to be a fairly accurate indication of the relative financing situation in respect of loan and equity financing.[1]

What they reveal is that Tongaat-Huletts and Marshalls have a relatively low gearing ratio, with the ratio for the former company dropping rapidly over the period, and the latter being relatively stable. For Tongaat this is a reflection of its relatively strong position as part of a large conglomerate stable (Anglo-American). This has facilitated relatively easier access to internal and intra-Group funds. The low gearing is in line with the company's view (expressed by Chairman Chris Saunders in respect of the funding for two new capital projects in 1995) that 'at no stage will Tongaat allow gearing to exceed 40%. Current projections for the two main capital projects indicate gearing should not exceed 25% within 10 years' (*Financial Mail* 04.08.95). These projects provide an important illustration of the ways in which a large Durban based company like Tongaat finances its capital development projects. As far as can be ascertained, Tongaat raised part of the funds for these two projects via a new share issue (R400 million), the proceeds of a sale of half of Huletts Aluminum to Amic-IDC (R300 million), internal funds (R200 million) and some amount from borrowings (*Financial Mail* 04.08.95).

McCarthy and T&N Holdings, on the other hand, have a relatively high gearing ratio, one which, for McCarthy, has risen sharply in recent years, in the wake of growing intra-Group problems. For T&N this situation was a result of the agreement with their UK parent (T&N plc)[2] – that the parent would always retain a 51 per cent controlling shareholding. This has meant that the local company has not been able to raise more capital via share issues unless T&N plc agreed to raise its own shareholding proportionately to maintain the agreed 51 per cent controlling interest. This is something that the UK parent has explicitly ruled out. The situation has forced T&N Holdings to make relatively greater use of loans/debt financing or retained earnings. However, as Finance Director Chris Good has observed, the arrangement was one with which the local company was happy – the 'constraint' had not limited the local T&N's access to finance. Good also pointed out that the company's Johannesburg Stock Exchange listing in 1986, was in any case, mainly to make the shares more marketable, not to raise significant new capital (Interview, Chris Good, 11.09.97).

Our research has revealed that larger companies, especially those backed by a local or international conglomerate, are able to sustain relatively large debt-equity ratios, especially if they maintain relatively robust profit margins, and have a good mutual understanding with the banks or other lenders about re-financing the debt. The situation is eased further (through, for example, preferential interest rate charges) if the local borrowing company and the financing institution belong to the same conglomerate stable. In short, for larger Durban based companies, it would appear that raising capital, from whatever source (share issues, borrowing or internal funds) was no problem, even if at times, high interest rate levels or changes in tax policy, affected the cost of the financing. Most of these financing decisions were however, taken in Johannesburg, and not in Durban (Interviews Brian McCarthy, 22.10.96; David Marshall, 02.10.96; Chris Good, 11.09.97).

Large debt-equity ratios do appear to have caused problems for smaller Durban companies. Those companies with debt-equity ratios over 2.00 could find (and in cases like Scotts Stores did find) themselves squeezed and then shut out by the banks (Interview, Brian McCarthy, 22.10.96). In general, medium and small business, including emerging Indian and African enterprise, are faced with greater challenges when it comes to financing their growth and expansion.

Some 'non-conglomerate' businesses such as the 'Indian owned' clothing giant, AM Moolla (owners of Kingsgate Clothing) recognised the importance of listing on the JSE as a way to raise capital. Reflecting the emergence from a 'corner-shop culture' AM Moolla, which owns six factories in KwaZulu-Natal, raised some R130 million in a private placing of 65 million shares in September 1997. The issue was taken up by some of South Africa's major financial institutions, including Norwich and the Board of Executors. The new capital, it was claimed, would be used to offset borrowings, pursue acquisitions within South Africa and beyond and broaden the ownership spread (*Natal Mercury* 18.09.97).

Given the culture that has existed among Indian owned firms to retain as much ownership and control within tight family networks, the AM Moolla decision was something of a landmark. When the company started business in 1955, and for many years thereafter, AM Moolla was forced, by limited capital, to borrow heavily. Two-thirds of its capital requirements during this period came from borrowing. Given the customary reticence of the major financial institutions to lend to Indian business (attributable both to poor accounting records and racial discrimination), the cost of such borrowings were usually high. That only changed for AM Moolla in the mid-1980s but its decision to further expand its business (including internationally) in the mid-1990s meant that the stock exchange listing was a logical step in its development and maturation as a company (Interview, Sadek Vahed, 22.10.97). However, falling share prices (the result of poor corporate results and, arguably, a hostile take-over-bid by the Coastal Group in late 1998) led the core (family) shareholders first into a 10 for 1 share consolidation followed by a total withdrawal from the JSE.

Although it is located in Richards Bay, Bell Industries exemplifies other sorts of financing problems faced by some medium-sized companies in Durban.[3] The company has been forced to carry the costs of a high positive real interest rate (approximately eight per cent in the mid-1990s).

Because it has no links to any of the banks or conglomerates, it was forced to pay high market rates of interest. This is a major problem for many companies as Kaplinsky and Mhlongo point out:

> . . . the high concentrated pattern of industrial ownership in South Africa . . . has meant unequal access to funds and differential interest charges to different parties. By its very nature this type of imperfection is difficult to document but our own discussions with the senior strategist of one of the major conglomerates confirms its existence (1997: 76).

In addition, Bell's capital needs in the early 1990s drove the company into the hands of banks 'which demanded that it float on the stock exchange to provide the banks with capital gains on their equity-linked funds'. This situation forced Bell in a later period to postpone expansion plans, precisely because it did not want to issue new shares and so lose its independent status (Kaplinsky and Mhlongo 1997: 77). So, although Bell is now a listed company, and can raise capital in this way, it remains constrained by virtue of its desire to retain some degree of independence. Neither, given the costs and the fact that it does not have the financial muscle of a conglomerate parent, can it easily obtain bank loans at favourable rates. Despite its needs for capital, therefore, these factors have limited its borrowing. Its debt-equity gearing ratio in 1996 was 0.65 (Kaplinsky and Mhlongo 1997: 76–7).

Financing difficulties such as these prompted debate in 1997 about the value of a regional KwaZulu-Natal Stock Exchange. However, the idea, originally proposed by Anglo American's Clem Sunter, and backed by the Inkatha Freedom Party (IFP) led regional government, was strongly opposed by the regional African National Congress (ANC) as a political ploy in support of the IFP's federalist policies. It is also hard to see why local companies would be more successful in raising finance through such a regional bourse, as compared to the JSE. The idea has not been debated or developed further.

Let us look briefly at where some of this finance has been applied for broader development purposes, i.e. outside narrow industrial expansion projects and acquisitions. Access to information and confidentiality commitments were an obstacle to our research. So an illustrative example will have to suffice. The Tongaat-Huletts case, admittedly an exceptional one, is instructive. Tongaat-Huletts, through its property company, Morelands Estates, has become a significant developer of industrial, commercial and residential land in the northern corridor of the Durban Metropolitan Area, including Mt Edgecombe and Umhlanga.

Concerned with the possibility that the previous government was about to develop a black township in a 'white lung' near its backyard in the mid-1980s, the Group activated a planning process that led to the formation of the Tongaat-Huletts Planning Forum, the revitalisation of its property division in 1988, and finally to the development of the land itself, initially in partnership with the (old) Mt Edgecombe Local Authority. The relationship between Morelands and the local authority was innovative and dynamic – a member of the company's planning division, for example, doubled as the Town Planner for some time (Interview, T.C. Chetty, 25.02.98). Tongaat provided (from its own sources) the bridging finance to the local authority to build up the infrastructure. These loans were repaid annually from the rapidly escalating ratable income of the local authority, as development followed the laying down of infrastructure. The company laid out R150 million in four years for such infrastructural development (Interview, Neels Brink, 16.01.97).

Morelands followed this initial investment with flagship residential developments including the Mt Edgecombe Country Club Estate, Umhlanga Ridge, as well as Sunningdale, La Lucia Ridge and Umhlanga Manors. In the process, and given its leading role as planner and financier, it was able to impose aesthetic, architectural and materials controls over these residential developments. In the industrial and commercial sectors, it developed the Red Hill Industrial Park, Briardene Industrial Park, the Activity and Old Mill Industrial Park at Mt Edgecombe and the Moreland Industrial Estate in Canelands, near Tongaat. The company was also involved in the development of the Zimbali coastal resort on the North Coast of Durban. Further office developments have been completed, including the Umhlanga Gateway and La Lucia Office Park, the first decentralised office park development in the Durban area (Interview, T.C. Chetty, 25.02.98).

Morelands funded most of these projects either from its own resources or by factoring funds from within the Tongaat Group. It did not use Anglo-American Corporation, its controlling shareholder, as a source of funds for these purposes. Funding via bank borrowing was rare. In fact, neither private sector nor development financial institutions with one or two exceptions 'came to the party', to use T.C. Chetty's phrase. Thus, for example, Morelands' attempt (with the International Hilton Hotel group) to raise local finance to develop a hotel at Zimbali was ultimately to fail. They tried the KwaZulu Finance Corporation, the Development Bank of South Africa, the Industrial Development Corporation, and among the private banks, Standard and ABSA. These and other institutions declined to co-finance on the grounds that the project was too large and too risky an investment for them to undertake. Morelands experienced similar problems with a development of a very different type, the low cost housing scheme at Mt Moriah in the north west of Durban. Only Nedcor agreed to change its mortgage lending criteria to make loans available to prospective home-owners in this scheme. Some of the other banks, including Standard and First National, only entered this market later, and with some hesitancy. Chetty concluded that these experiences were a 'damning indictment' of local South African finance.

These Tongaat-Huletts led developments have already radically altered working and living patterns in the city, by halting, then slowly reversing, the concentration of economic activity in the Southern Durban industrial basin. Until recently 34 per cent of Durban's population lived in northern Durban, but the area provided only 14 per cent of the city's employment (Interview, Neels Brink, 16.01.97). The case study illustrates the power of a large company, using mainly internal financing sources, to physically reshape the working and living space of a city, through its own (profit-seeking) initiatives.

Private Financial Institutions

Natal Building Society

The Natal Building Society (NBS) began business in 1882. Its Act of Incorporation passed by the Natal parliament on the eve of Union in March 1910 limited its activities for many decades to Natal, so inhibiting its growth at a time when non-Natal building societies were beginning to 'encroach' into this province. Much of the credit for the financing of white residential property in and around Durban from the 1920s especially must go to the NBS. Although the NBS first went national in the late 1950s, it retained its strong Natal identity, and until very recently it was a tradition that its chairman had to be a Natalian.

In the late 1950s the NBS began to make an effort at attracting Indian business. It opened its first 'all-Indian' sub-branch in 1959 in the heart of the Indian business centre in Durban' (Wilks 1982: 99). The extension of its business to Africans occurred in 1981, when a branch was opened in Umlazi on Durban's southern flank. However, the NBS offered only savings facilities to Africans.

Changes in the banking legislation in the late 1980s made it possible for the NBS to become a fully-fledged bank, until the control of NBS

Holdings. Although the NBS grew nationally to become one of the top five financial institutions in the country, it retained its small corporate culture and followed a deliberate strategy of not spreading its forces too widely. The NBS made a not very successful attempt to challenge First National and Standard's stranglehold of Natal's sugar farmers (Interview, Tony Ardington, 26.02.97), and although it did succeed in acquiring a small part share of the ordinary banking business of some of Durban and Natal's bigger companies, it still lagged behind FNB, Standard, Nedcor and ABSA, even in this respect.

However, it continued to be closely linked to some of Natal and Durban's bigger companies like Tongaat-Huletts, and McCarthy through old school tie, club, sports and other social networks, as well as more formally through interlocking membership of corporate boards. Thus, for example when Brian McCarthy of the McCarthy Group stepped down as the chair of the NBS Board in 1996, the non-executive leadership 'baton' was passed on to Cedric Savage, who was then CEO of the Tongaat Group. Executive leadership went to another well connected Natalian, Tony Norton. McCarthy retained his position as Chair of McCarthy Retail. The *Natal Mercury* observed at the time that 'these links are interesting, because these three men are leaders of arguably the three most powerful groups with headquarters in KwaZulu-Natal – Tongaat-Huletts with a market capitalisation of R6 billion, the NBS right behind with R5.7 billion and McCarthy Retail with R4.5 billion. (15.08.96).

The merger of NBS Holdings and the Afrikaans-dominated Boland Bank (headed by Christo Wiese) in early 1997 caught even some informed observers by surprise. There were concerns that one of the NBS's greatest strengths as a small corporate entity, a flexibility and management structure which facilitated quick decision-making, would be lost (*Finance Week* 13–19.02.97). Although the move represented in some sense a logical culmination of its efforts stretching back to the late 1950s to go national, there was concern that its history and perceived identity as a Natal, and Durban, financial institution would be irrevocably lost. But the merger option may well have been one of the few open to the NBS after 1990, when following positive developments on the national political front, small niche international banks, new Durban based banks and aggressive national players invaded its traditional turf. Changes in banking legislation also accelerated a process of 'rationalisation' in the financial services sector, of which the NBS-Boland deal was one of many in the post-1994 period.

Provincial Building Society

The Provincial Building Society (PBS) was established in Durban in 1929. The PBS did most of its home-loan business with lower-income and middle-class whites. Although it was not official policy, the PBS supported and was more 'dynamic and active' in Natal, especially Durban, than elsewhere in the country (Interview, John Russell, 19.02.97). But it is perhaps best known for the fact that it was the first building society to lend to African and Indian clients. As early as the 1940s it was also willing (when most other financial institutions were not) to go through the laborious process of applying to the Department of Native Affairs in terms of Section 1 of the 1913 Native Land Act for permission to grant mortgage loans to Africans (Personal archives, John Russell, former Managing Director, PBS).

The PBS opened offices for Indian clients in Ajmeri Arcade (in the core of the Grey Street area) in 1958. In 1966 it absorbed the business of the small Liberty Building Society, which had been established in Albert Street to cater for Indian investors and borrowers (PBS Annual Reports 1958, 1966). Provincial was able to extend its loan activities to these kinds of clients (who were regarded by others as 'risky') because, as a relatively small institution, it was able to devote more attention to investigating potential borrowers and the sites on which they wished to build.

By 1990, as competitive pressures mounted in the financial sector, however, it had become clear that the PBS would not be able to offer the diversified financial products and services which some of the other (newer, or restructured) financial institutions were offering. Older banks had also successfully penetrated the longer term investment market and the mortgage financial market, and all these factors forced the PBS, which had through the years succeeded in maintaining a profitable and well managed operation, to accept a merger with one of South Africa's newer and most aggressive financial market leaders, Investec. Whatever the merits of that move, it brought an end to the PBS's productive and close relationship with its 'small client' base (Interview, John Russell, 18.03.97).

The New Republic Bank

For J.N. Reddy, the New Republic Bank's (NRB) first Managing Director, the idea of forming a separate Indian bank or building society can be traced back to the time when South Africa became a republic in 1961. That idea was motivated by limited employment opportunities for Indians in existing banking institutions and the restrictions which (white) banks and building societies placed on lending to Indians. The NRB opened its doors in Goodhope Centre in the Grey Street area on 1 February 1971. It later moved to new headquarters in Field Street.

The bank's main business for much of its early existence was in receiving deposits from individual Indian professionals and workers and lending mainly to small and medium sized Indian firms. The predominant part of this early business was conducted in Durban, and its adjoining Indian controlled municipalities and suburbs such as Verulam, Tongaat, Chatsworth and Stanger. The bank opened a corporate office, later division, to cater for larger business clients in Durban in 1986, and later extended this division to Cape Town and Johannesburg. The NRB was able to raise its asset base and profits from this kind of business quite substantially, even winning the JSE non-listed company award in 1993.

However, the NRB ran into liquidity problems in the early 1990s when, following the collapse of a few smaller banks nationally, sentiment turned against smaller financial institutions. The NRB did not escape this changed mood, and some of its clients, including corporates and municipalities, took their business to the major banks. That situation forced the NRB into a restructuring process that eventually saw its listing on the JSE in 1993 and (later in 1997) its take over by the Malaysian businessman Dato Samsudin Abu Hassan, through Redbridge Assets Limited. By then the NRB had eight retail branches and three corporate lending offices in South Africa and an office on the Isle of Man.

By this time, the NRB had not only gone 'international' it also, controversially in some circles, shed its predominantly Indian identity and focus. The Managing Director of the bank, Mac Mia, resigned in August 1996 reportedly on the grounds of dissatisfaction with the NRB's new direction. (Mia later became a director of the First Asian Investment Corporation, see below, and in October 1996 joined the board of Tongaat-Huletts.) The *Business Day* (09.08.96) put it this way:

> Informal talks, aimed at setting up a new bank with an Indian business focus, indicate some prominent Durban businessmen feel NRB is moving away from its original focus on this market. This however, may fit in with the longer-term refocusing of NRB as it aims to achieve a wider geographical spread and more of an international flavour.

Late in 1998, Dato Samsudin, arguably in the wake of the Asian financial crisis, announced his intention to sell-off his controlling shareholding in the NRB. This coupled with the collapse in February 1999 of negotiations with a black empowerment company led by Mzi Khumalo to buy the Malaysian stake precipitated a new crisis for the NRB, and led to its eventual liquidation. In general, these developments raised concerns about the sustainability of the huge inflows of new Malaysian investment in the immediate post-apatheid era (see, for example, Valodia and Padayachee 1998).

Marriott Merchant Bank

In October 1994, Russell Marriott Boyd Trust (RMBT), which can trace its links to the Durban economy back to 1862, underwent a 'massive restructuring' – including the formation and registration of Marriott Holdings Limited as a bank controlling company. Marriott Merchant Bank (MMB) was set up as its wholly owned subsidiary. At the time Tony Ardington, who has been associated with the sugar association for many years, and was from the mid-1970s also a member of the Regional Board of Standard Bank, resigned from the latter position to become Chair of MMB.

There is a clear sense that Durban and Natal are important to the MMB. Vice-Chair Kevin Moore and Executive Director Mick Hyatt stressed the importance to local clients of making decisions in Durban, rather than in Johannesburg. Head officed in Durban, Marriott Merchant Bank, its newsletter proclaims, 'is able to understand the local conditions and meet the needs of our clients with efficient service' (MMB Newsletter October 1996). The major national banks, they argue, have low regional lending limits making it necessary for all major decisions to be made at the head office, usually in Johannesburg. As most investment managers are located in Johannesburg (and Cape Town) it is natural, they pointed out, that these managers would be more likely to divert investments to their own backyard. That was a situation that MMB wanted to address and reverse to some extent.

So too was the perception (false in their view) that Durban and Natal, have a long and violent history, which makes the region unattractive to investors. The bank has invested the energies of some of its top officers in conducting research into crime in this city and province. MMB also demonstrated its commitment to the city by co-hosting and co-funding the highly successful Durban Business Metro Conference in 1996. A further indication of its focus on the province and city came with the appointment of Marriot Asset Management, as asset managers of the KwaZulu-Natal Development Fund in August 1998. The Fund was set up specifically to divert a percentage of the retirement fund contributions made by the people of KwaZulu-Natal towards investment in the province, thereby potentially creating a major source of development capital.

The bank is heavily involved in the flotation of property and equity unit trusts. RMBT had in fact floated property unit trusts for some time. These included the Umdoni Property Fund (1983), the Tamboti Property Fund (1986), Higate Property Fund (1989), and the Highstone Property Fund (1990). In 1995 MMB listed the Ukhozi Property Fund. The Marriott Property Equity Unit Trust, the first specialist property equity fund in South Africa, followed in September 1996. Through these finance vehicles, RMBT and MMB have been able to raise capital from pension funds, insurance houses and other sources in Johannesburg and Cape Town for investment largely in Durban, a reversal of the trend that saw Durban based capital being used elsewhere in the country.

National Banks with a Durban Presence

South Africa's Big Four banks (First National, Standard, ABSA and Nedcor) have a major presence in Durban. First National Bank's history in Durban can be traced back to 1854 when one of its predecessors, the Natal Bank (later taken over by Barclays DCO) opened its head office in the city. Standard's links go back to the early 1860s when a branch of Standard Chartered was opened in the city (Morrell et al. 1993: 163–4). Volkskas which was established nationally in 1929, and is now part of the ABSA Group, arrived just before the Second World War, and Nedcor much later still.

Between them the Big Four hold the regular banking accounts of most of Durban's JSE listed companies. Of the 32 JSE listed, Durban registered companies (as reported in McGregor's 1997) eight banked only with First National, five only with Standard, four with other banks, and 15 held accounts with more than one bank. Some of Durban's leading businessmen serve on the main or regional boards of some of these banks. Tongaat-Huletts' Chris Saunders has served on Standard's main board for many years, and (to take a different example) AM Moolla's Sadek Vahed, was appointed to the main Board of Barclays/FNB during Chris Ball's tenure as Barclays CEO in the mid-1980s.

Durban is not very highly regarded as a financial centre by these national banks. In the 1980s, for example, only about 20 per cent of Barclays' profits were generated out of Natal, mainly Durban, as compared to about 60 per cent from the (then) Transvaal. At the time, the Natal Regional Manager for Barclays, Terry Field, tried to persuade the Barclays Board of Directors to move the bank's Barclaycard Division to Durban, to give the city some greater identity as a financial centre, in much the same way as Barclay's (UK) moved their Barclaycard Division from London to Liverpool. He was unsuccessful.

Regional bank managers and regional boards have had relatively low limits of authority in respect of lending to Durban clients. While estimates about this limit vary (they are not often disclosed), it would appear that in the 1980s regional managers had an authority limit of a few million Rand (perhaps between R4–10 million). Most decisions on financing Durban capex and development projects have had to be made at headquarters in Johannesburg.

Standard Bank provided facilities to companies and organisations to finance some or all of the following major commercial or development projects in Metropolitan Durban since the 1960s: the sugar terminals near the port, Kings Park Stadium, the Toyota factory in Prospecton, the Sugar Refinery, Umgeni Water Works, the International Convention Centre (ICC) and extensions to the Port. Barclays/FNB were involved in a housing development project for Beacon Sweets employees with more than three years service, and the Expo Centre in the heart of the city (which was called the FNB Expo Centre for the first eight years) among others (Letter, Jack Bush, 27.05.97; Interviews, Terry Field, 09.04.97 and 07.05.97).

The approach and activities of Investec Bank, a relatively recent national player on the Durban scene, is a good illustration of some of the dynamism apparent in the local financing scene in the early 1990s. Investec began life as a small finance company in Johannesburg in 1974. It acquired a banking license in 1980, and engaged in a dramatic round of mergers, acquisitions, take-overs and strategic alliances over the next 10 years, and went international in a big way, especially after 1990 (Annual Report 1996: 1–2). It opened its Durban/Natal office in 1984, and Zululand-born executive, Neil MacNeillie, returned to Natal from Johannesburg to head up the office. When they arrived they were called 'cowboys on the hill' by some of Durban's more established financial institutions, who did not expect them to survive long in the city.

Investec's strategy for breaking into Durban was simple: they targeted a clearly defined market – on the investment side they went for individuals and organisations with high net worth (individuals had to have unencumbered assets of over R3 million). In terms of financing development, the company first identified sectors that they would not finance: hotels, trucking companies, motor garages/stations, and certain geographic areas, including the more crime and violence-ridden townships. Investec then moved into the social networks of the city, its clubs, societies and business organisations, and adopted an aggressive, confident approach which was directed to adding value to a client, rather than competing on the basis of price. Banks like First National and Standard, MacNeillie argued, are no competition for Investec within the parameters of its niche market. For the first six years at least this comprehensive strategy worked well, and the local business grew rapidly. By 1989/90, Durban made up a quarter of Investec's total business.

Since Investec arrived on the Durban financial scene they have been involved in a wide variety of project financing, including commercial property development and industrial development. They have financed many factories in Springfield and Phoenix Industrial Parks and in Pinetown. They provided the finance for the City Council's Ocean Sports Complex, an initiative that has collapsed, according to MacNeillie, mainly because of the crime in the area. Investec thereafter took a decision not to engage in any project financing on Durban's beachfront.

However, it is significant to note that MacNeillie is pessimistic about Durban's future prospects, arguing that the enthusiasm and excitement, which many financial institutions displayed about Durban in the early 1990s, has dissipated. Crime, corruption, a lack of initiative by the City Council, the tardiness of getting developments like the airport and the Point moving, have all contributed to this. There are 'dark thunder clouds' over Durban's Central Business District (CBD). Tongaat-Huletts' success in luring big companies like Deloitte and Touche to Umhlanga, and the attempt (in some quarters) to move the financial district out of the CBD to the new Kingmead Office Park, may lengthen these clouds. By 1998, Investec had higher hopes for its Cape Town and (then) newly opened Port Elizabeth branches, than it had for Durban (Interview, Neil MacNeillie, 11.03.98).

Other Financial Institutions

A number of other financial institutions operated in Durban during 1970–99. Throughout this period, the insurance conglomerates, SA Mutual and Sanlam, occupied pre-eminent positions in the commercial property development sector. Many of these commercial development projects, including the shopping centre phenomenon which reached Durban in the 1960s, were co-funded or co-managed with some of South Africa's major retail chains such as Pick 'n Pay and Checkers. Although such development in the 1960s and 1970s occurred mainly within the CBD, these institutions pursued what were referred to as their 'greening' initiatives by developing office blocks and shopping centres in Durban's suburbs. Overport City, initially developed by Hoffman Bense, financed by Trust Bank (part of the Sanlam stable) and opened in 1972, was one of the first of these. Like Commercial City in the CBD, Overport City was taken over by Sanlam in *c.*1983, after the owners ran into financial difficulties (Interview, Dallas Reed, 30.03.98). This was followed by further such development: the up-market Musgrave Centre (acquired by Sanlam in November 1980 and redeveloped in the early 1990s), the Pavilion (owned by the Eskom Pension Fund and the Cape based company, Conwest), and the La Lucia Mall (owned by the Mines Pension Fund). Other Sanlam properties include the Chatsworth and Phoenix Centres situated in the large 'Indian' townships of Durban and the major R110 million city centre office development, The Embassy, which opened in 1992. Together with Tongaat-Huletts, Sanlam was also involved in industrial property development in Phoenix, north of Durban (in the mid-1980s). SA Mutual was involved in a number of major commercial development projects in the CBD, including its massive, new Durban office which opened in 1996, and other commercial sites in Winder and Field Streets in central Durban, and Pinetown. It was involved in the financing of several industrial development schemes in New Germany and Prospecton in the 1970s (*Financial Mail*, various, 1970–97; Interview, Dallas Reed, 09.06.98).

By the 1990s a few international banks, with Asian connections, opened their South African head offices in Durban. These included the HBZ Bank Limited, which is the South African subsidiary of Habib Bank AG Zurich (and which has former Barclays Regional Manager for Natal, Terry Field, on its five-person Board of Directors). London based Vice-President of HBZ, M. Yacoob Chowdhury, indicated that the decision to locate the bank's South African head office in Durban, was based on the significant presence in the city of businessmen of Indian origin. This potential clientele, he pointed out, would form the foundations of HBZ's initial activities here. But, as they did in Kenya where they also began with a focus on Kenyan Asians, HBZ intended expanding its client base among African businesses (Interview, M.Y. Chowdhury, 09.04.97).

In August 1997, India's Bank of Baroda opened its South African head office in Cowie Road, on Durban's Berea Ridge. The bank which in India focused on financing and developing small and medium-scale industries in rural areas, aims to do something similar here eventually, though it would initially engage in wholesale banking, trade finance, money market operations and retail lending. Its decision to locate in

Durban was motivated by its assessment that the city 'is ready for major growth', and by potential links with Indian businessmen (*Daily News* 04.08.97; *Business Day* 13.08.97).

Political developments after 1990 have facilitated the emergence, from the ranks of previously disadvantaged communities, of a few new finance and development organisations. Perhaps the best known is Mzi Khumalo's Capital Alliance Bank, which originated in Durban, and which has become a significant financial services group. Capital Alliance was a co-developer (with Malaysian partners) of the ICC Hilton Hotel, built adjacent to the flagship International Convention Centre. The South African Hindu Association (SAHA) Business Forum which includes an investment wing, counts among its supporters Edison Power CEO Vivian Reddy, who is also Chair of Sam-Sisonke, an Indo-African joint venture with a Malaysian company.

Early in 1997 a new black empowerment investment fund, First Asian Investment Corporation (Fasic) aimed mainly at the Indian community in Durban was launched with a capital of R100 million. The Group includes among its members former New Republic Bank MD Mac Mia, AM Moolla's CEO Sadek Vahed, Edison Power's Vivian Reddy and Standard Bank regional board member and Universal (Web) Printing MD Haresh Metha (whose company was awarded the lucrative contract to print Telkom's directories from the year 2000). In mid-1998 Fasic bought out one of Durban's oldest companies (established 1900), the South African Breweries owned Lion Match Company, for R584 million, signalling its entry into the corporate finance world of the city (*Leader* 12.06.98). Fasic has also been involved in discussions with another powerful local businessman (and former IFP secretary-general), Oscar Dhlomo, the chair of another Durban based finance empowerment group, Dynamo Investments (*Business Day* 21.02.97).

Development Finance Institutions

KwaZulu Finance and Investment Corporation

The KFC was a relatively important player in the city. Its head office is now in the heart of the sprawling Umlazi township south of Durban. The KFC was a provincial development agency and financier which has injected some R2.2 billion into the province since its establishment in 1979 (*Sunday Tribune* 27.04.97). It operated divisions in business property, housing, small business (in which it claims to service a higher risk, mainly African township and 'black spot' based clientele than the SBDC), industry, commerce (including tourism) and rural development. It also ran Ithala Bank, a savings institution which (ostensibly) provides banking' services to rural communities not catered for by the larger commercial banks. It had little revenue capacity of its own (outside the small deposit-taking activity of Ithala) and relies on national and provincial government funding for the bulk of its revenue. As of 31 March 1994 the KFC was reported to have created some 100 000 jobs, established 9 000 enterprises, trained 49 000 people and extended 18 526 housing loans in the period of its existence in the province as a whole.

Information obtained in a confidential study conducted for the national government into the KFC by the DBSA in 1995 provides some facts about the spatial distribution of the KFC's investments in the province. In the cluster of its activities labelled 'medium and large industry' only 20 per cent of its investments occurred within the Durban functional region, the largest proportion (52.2 per cent) going to Isithebe/Sundumbuli in Zululand. For 'commerce and tourism' Durban received only 12.2 per cent, the rest being spread fairly evenly to the other regions, with Ulundi receiving 27.9 per cent. Durban received the largest share (42.0 per cent) of the KFC's investments in the 'micro and small business' cluster. However, even this information does not say much about the spatial development impact of these investments in Durban (or elsewhere) as crucial information, such as the size of the investments, is not provided (DBSA Report 1995: 24–5).

Prior to 1994, the KFC also acted as an investment promotion agency, in which it appears to have focused on attracting mainly Taiwanese investment to its industrial estates in areas such as Isithebe, Ezakheni and Madadeni, largely on the basis of their cheap labour resources. It was not very successful in raising foreign capital for Durban. Since 1994 this function was taken over by the KwaZulu Marketing Initiative (KMI) (for which the KFC provides the infrastructural and management support). In the context of positive national political developments, the KMI has attracted some new foreign investment to Metropolitan Durban. These include investments in 1997 from Malaysia (R1 million investment in plastic bags manufacture); Russia (R5 million for motor cycle manufacture); Taiwan (R12 million for yarn products); and India (R5 million for stationery production). In 1996 these foreign investments included a R88 million investment by the UK construction company BR Hodgson, as well as three smaller foreign investments (Minerals and Energy Centre 1998).

The KFC was for long dogged by accusations that it was linked too closely with the IFP (more specifically that it favoured IFP members in making its investments). Since 1994 various proposals were put forward to restructure the KFC and to bring its Ithala banking operations in line with the requirements of the Banks Act. Some minor changes, including a name change (to Ithala) were completed by the end of 1999.

A number of other nationally based financial institutions (whose activities cannot be dealt with here in any detail) contributed to financing development projects in the Durban region in the period of this study. These included the Industrial Development Corporation (IDC) established in 1940; the Indian Industrial Development Corporation established by the state in 1979 and which was created with the 'idea of helping [Indian] business to move forward in the field of industry' (Desai 1986: 137, 186); the Small Business Development Corporation, set up by the state in 1981; and the Development Bank of Southern Africa which was officially opened in September 1983.

The Local State's Capital Development Fund

Like city governments in most parts of the world, the City Council of Metropolitan Durban has been an important player in financing urban infrastructural development, including roads, electricity, water reticulation, even low cost housing. These expenses have tended to be financed from a combination of ratable income and external borrowing. The Durban City Council has also used these sources of income to finance capital expenditure; in addition it has been a pioneer in the establishment of innovative schemes to supplement its income, in ways which have created its status as one of the few debt-free cities in the country, and beyond.

Thus, for example, it was only in the mid-1970s, after some 90 years, that the scheme to use the city's Superannuation Fund to grant first mortgage loans to members of the public on normal commercial terms, finally ceased.[4] The city, in this way, acted as a building society or bank, and profited from the lending like other financial institutions. But the city is perhaps best recognised for its creation in 1957 of the (Consolidated) Capital Development Fund.

The (Consolidated) Capital Development Fund

In 1957 the City Council established the Capital Development Fund in order to obtain the benefits of financing its capital expenditure largely from internal sources. The scheme was the brain child of Ossie Gorven, who eventually became City Treasurer in 1962, and remained in that position until 1985 (Interviewed by Bill Freund, 08.12.97). Separate funds exist for each major service (for example a Water Capital Development Fund), and although some cross-subsidisation has occurred, the accumulated amount in each fund has been used to finance capital expenditure in that service area. The various separate funds together make up the Consolidated Capital Development Fund (CCDF). The fund has been built up in three essential ways: first, by the transfers of a small proportion of the income (about three per cent) received from each of the main services (water, electricity, transport, the market, airport) to this separate fund; second, from the sale of assets (such as that of the Post Office building, formerly the town hall, to the national Department of Posts and Telecommunications); and third, from interest plough-backs. With the exception of the Water, and Rate and General Services Capital Development Fund, 50 per cent of the interest earned is transferred annually to each service to offset their operating expenses, with the rest being put back into the fund. In 1983 the city was granted permission to invest a portion of the CCDF in property (and property unit trusts) both within and outside Durban (Interviews with Prakash Silal, 18.02.97 and 29.05.97). The city's decision to make such investments outside Durban was criticised in some circles, especially at a time, when anti-apartheid civic groups were increasing their protests against the lack of services within the city's disadvantaged townships and settlements.

The Consolidated Fund stood at just over R1 billion in 1993, rising to R1.5 billion by mid-1997. From its inception (to 1993), the CCDF has financed capital expenditure of approximately R657.8 million. This reliance on internal funds has resulted in interest savings in the order of some R1 190 million since the inception of the fund (Epitome of the City's Accounts 1993: 12; Annual Report 1997: 23). Although initially some of the CCDF was used to reduce the city's debts, from 1957 to 1983 it was also a critical source for funding the city's capital expenditure in its various infrastructural projects.

The CCDF has more recently been used (partly) to finance one of Durban's major flag-ship investments, the R280 million International Convention Centre. Recognising the importance of such a world class centre to the city and after failing to obtain significant financial support from private sources, the City Council financed the project (on a loan basis) itself. Of the total cost of R280 million, some R70–80 million came directly from the CCDF. A significant part of the rest came from the sale of some of the property unit trusts, which itself had been initially funded from the CCDF (Telephonic interview with City Treasury Official, Lawrence Gibson, 02.06.97). The city also raised some money from land sales and borrowed the rest on normal commercial terms from the private sector financial institutions (including the Standard Bank, its regular banker). Although this total amount is ostensibly to be repaid with interest by the ICC (from its operating income and other sources), Ridsdale has speculated that the Council may well write-off the construction debt after a few years (1997: 71).

Since 1983 the loan contribution of the CCDF to financing the city's regular forms of infrastructural capital expenditure has declined, as the fund was increasingly used for rent and dividend-earning investments in immovable property and property unit trusts respectively, as well as for such projects as the ICC. Thus, for example, in 1984 the CCDF contributed R247.7 million out of a total capex of R1.3 billion. By 1993, the CCDF contribution was a (massively lower) R18.8 of a total capex of R3.5 million. Since then the reliance on external borrowing (from institutions including the Development Bank of South Africa, and private banks such as FNB, ABSA, Imperial, MLS, Nedbank and the NBS) and other internal loan sources for funding capital expenditure has therefore increased concomitantly (Epitome of the City's Accounts 1993: 6; Annual Report 1997: 85).

Beginning on 1 July 1991, new contributions by each of the services to the CCDF was suspended for a period of five years. This development reflects the growing pressure on each of the services in the changing political climate of the 1990s. Some of these services had in fact begun to run into deficits even earlier and had received exemptions for short periods of time. While up to 1991 the city's finances were both sound and growing, it has for most of the 1990s been under increasing pressure. The city's commitment to keep rates as low as possible has closed off revenue-raising possibilities. Even though Durban is still relatively strong financially, it has been forced to use some of its reserves in recent years (Interview, Prakash Silal, 18.02.97) while raising rates steadily.

ANC head of local government in KwaZulu-Natal, Mike Sutcliffe, has recently made the following observations:

> There is a lot to be proud about in looking at Durban's model of effective government delivery. Much of this has been accomplished relatively recently, although Durban is fortunate in being able to build on the positive effects of a long history of financial discipline and innovation (*Business Day* 02.09.97).

The challenges of extending development across all of Durban's citizens in the post-1990 period will test the innovative capacity of the city to its limits, but it will certainly need to draw on this history and tradition, if it is to retain its status as a 'model of effective government delivery . . . tomorrow and beyond' (Sutcliffe, *Business Day,* 02.09.97).

Assessment and Conclusion

The major features, trends and conclusions that arise out of the study may be summarised as follows:

- that the local financial scene, including all the financial institutions located here, has tended to be rather static, stagnant and unimaginative for most of the period with which this study is concerned;
- that, with minor exceptions, most financing decisions, both private and developmental, tend to be made in Johannesburg headquarters, rather than in Durban;
- that the large, local corporations, have had little difficulty in accessing finance for their capital expenditure and development needs from a combination of internal and group sources as well as the share market and (to a lesser extent) from bank borrowing;
- that smaller and medium sized business has faced more difficulties with raising finance from the formal banking institutions, and have had to rely mainly on their own internal and family resources;
- that some Indian businesses (an important feature of the local economy) have graduated out of the 'corner-shop' culture into the world of stock markets and large-scale bank borrowing;
- that bank borrowing in general, for both large and smaller companies, has been used for only limited short-term purposes, rarely being available on its own for the financing of larger capital and development projects;
- that the major development finance institutions have been important in funding larger development projects in the city, although they too have tended to do this as part of a larger financing package (including share issues, internal funds and some limited borrowing from private sector financial institutions);
- that some development finance institutions, like the KFC and the SBDC have, of late, moved their operations onto a more commercial basis, raising questions about their 'developmental' status and mandate;
- that the city of Durban, via its innovative Capital Development Fund, has been able to muster a significant amount of finance for the city's infrastructural development (albeit in racially skewed ways), while maintaining sound fiscal discipline;
- that concerns have been raised in some corporate circles about city governance, which may both directly and indirectly affect the prospects for further growth and diversification of the financial sector.

For a few years after 1990 there appeared to some hope that the newer, internationally connected finance institutions which were setting up in South Africa, would make some positive impact on servicing the financing requirements, especially of small and medium sized business. However, only a few of these have set up their headquarters or branches in Durban. Those which have, are mainly Asian linked institutions seeking to use the local Indian business presence as a bridgehead into South Africa. However, they have not developed either a locally generated balance sheet or an effective retail network, and have offered no new financing instruments or facilities which are, in any significant way, an improvement on the existing, largely cartelised local and national banking institutions.

All indications suggest that Durban will remain a secondary branch economy and financial centre. The window of opportunity and optimism created by *political reform* which characterised the first half of the 1990s could have been opened wider had the democratic government undertaken some of the far-reaching *financial reforms* proposed in some quarters. The Macroeconomic Research Group (MERG) proposals, for example, were specifically designed to reduce those elements in the national financial system which 'were an inheritance from British practice, and move the system to the German model', in a way which would have actively involved the 'financial institutions in financing the new social infrastructure and industrial development' (MERG 1993: 243ff). These kinds of changes may well have led to the more rapid transformation of the industrial, commercial and financial life of the country, and Durban's distinctive locational, human resource and other advantages could well have placed it in a position to benefit even more than the rest of the country.

NOTES

1. I am grateful to Professors Jeremy Lord and Lindsay Mitchell of the University of Natal's department of Accounting and Finance for clarifying for me the use and meaning of these selected financial ratios. The interpretation of the data is mine.
2. T&N plc was bought out by the US auto-components giant Federal Mogul in 1998.
3. This example is used here mainly because information on this point is available from the work of Kaplinsky and Mhlongo (1997). No other equivalent study of a Durban based company is available.
4. In 1963, to take one example, a Mrs Gladys Maud Cyrus was granted an additional

loan of R1 200 on first mortgage for 25 years at six per cent on a property at 407 Manning Road, repayable in monthly installments of R8.00 including principal and interest (Documents of the City's Superannuation Fund).

REFERENCES

City of Durban. 1993. *Epitome of the City's Accounts*. Durban: City of Durban.

City of Durban. 1997. *Annual Report*. Durban: City of Durban.

Desai, A. 1987. 'The State and the South African Indian Council'. M.A. thesis, Rhodes University, Grahamstown.

Development Bank of South Africa (DBSA). 1995. 'Appraisal Report into the KwaZulu Finance and Investment Corporation'. Confidential Working Draft, Midrand.

Economic Research Unit and the Black Entrepreneurship and Enterprise Support Facility (ERU and BEES). n.d. 'The Characteristics and Support Needs of Black Small and Micro-Enterprises in KwaZulu-Natal'. Durban.

Fine, B. 1997. 'Industrial Policy in South Africa: A Strategic View'. Unpublished memo, London.

Fourie, L.J., H.B. Falkena and W.J. Kok. 1992. *Fundamentals of the South African Financial System*. Halfway House: Southern Book Publishers.

Freund, B. 2000. 'The City of Durban: Towards a Structural Analysis of the Economic Growth and Character of a South African City'. In R. Rathbone and D. Anderson (eds). *Africa's Urban Past*. London and Portsmouth: James Currey and Heinemann.

Harris, L. 1994. 'Financing Post-Apartheid South Africa: Theoretical Aspects'. Paper presented at the American Economic Association Annual Meeting, Boston.

Hirsch, A. 1986. 'Banking on Discipline: The Development Bank of Southern Africa'. In *South African Review 3*. Johannesburg: Ravan Press.

Hornby, D. n.d. 'Financial Sector, Comparative Advantage and Contribution to the Province'. Unpublished memo, Durban.

Kaplinsky, R. and E. Mhlongo. 1997. 'Infant Industries and Industrial Policies: A Lesson from South Africa'. *Transformation*, 34.

Marlin, J. 1968. 'Financial Institutions and Economic Growth in South Africa, 1956–66'. Ph.D. thesis, The George Washington University, Washington DC.

McCarthy, J.J. 1993. 'Planning for Industrial Growth in the Durban Region'. Report.

McGregor's, various. *Who Owns Whom*. Cape Town: Juta.

MERG. 1993. *Making Democracy Work: A Framework for Macroeconomic Policy in South Africa*. Bellville: Centre for Development Studies and Oxford University Press.

Mineral and Energy Centre. 1998. 'Export Promotion in KwaZulu-Natal'. Report prepared for the Department of Trade and Industry, Durban.

Morrell, R., V. Padayachee and S. Vawda. 1993. 'Banking, Capital and Credit in Colonial Natal'. In G. Austin and K. Sughihara (eds). *Local Suppliers of Credit in the Third World, 1750–1960*. London and New York: St Martin's Press.

Morris, M.H., P. Jones and D. Nel. 1997. 'The Informal Sector, Entrepreneurship and Economic Development'. *Journal of Developmental Entrepreneurship*, 2, 2.

The 1961/62 Natal Review. 1962. *The Annual Economic Review of South Africa – from Natal*. Eighth edition, Durban.

Pike, R. and B. Neale. 1993. *Corporate Finance and Investment*. New York: Prentice-Hall.

Pillay, U. 1995. 'The Local Dimensions of the Durban Functional Region: An Assessment of the Proclaimed Uniqueness of this Locality'. Unpublished paper, Durban.

Ramburuth, S. 1997. 'The IDC, Equity Market and the Megaprojects'. Masters Research Proposal, Department of Public and Development Management, University of the Witwatersrand.

Ridsdale, G. 1997. 'Durban's International Convention Centre: A Case Study of a Public-Private Partnership Initiative'. M.A. thesis, Centre for Social and Development Studies, University of Natal, Durban.

Sitas, A., J. Stanwix and C. Shaw. 1984. 'Trade Unions, Monopoly Power and Poverty in Natal's Industries'. Carnegie Conference Paper, No. 108. Cape Town.

Smith, G. 1993. 'Services and Financial Sector'. Working Document for input into the Synthesis Report into Economic Development Strategies for Region E. RDAC, Pietermaritzburg.

Stanwix, J. 1985. 'A Study of the Natal Regional Economy'. Natal Town and Regional Planning Report, No. 66. Pietermaritzburg.

Stiglitz, J. 1998. 'Redefining the Role of the State'. Paper presented on the 10th anniversary of the MITI Research Institute, Tokyo.

Valodia, I. and V. Padayachee. 1998. 'Malaysian Money, Sustainable Investments?' *Economic and Political Weekly*, 19 September.

Wilks, T. 1982. *One Hundred Golden Years: A History of the Natal Building Society, 1882–1982*. Durban: King and Wilks.

Interviews

Ardington, Tony, Chairman, Marriott Merchant Bank, former member of the Regional Board of the Standard Bank, and Chair, South African Sugar Association, 26.02.97.

Blem David, Advocate and former Barclays Bank Executive, 13.08.97.

Bush, Jack, Retail General Manager for Natal, Standard Bank, 10.04.97.

Brink, Neels, Planning Executive, Morelands/Tongaat-Huletts, 16.01.97.

Chetty, T.C., Planning Officer, Morelands/Tongaat-Huletts, 16.01.97 and 25.02.98.

Chowdhury, Yacoob, Vice President, HBZ Bank, 09.02.97.

Field, Terry, former Regional General Manager, Barclays/First National Bank, 09.04.97.

Gibson, Lawrence, City of Durban Treasury, 02.06.97.

Good, Chris, Finance Director, T&N Holdings, 11.09.97.

Gordhan, Pravin, Former Civic Activist, 23.01.98.

Gorven, Ossie, Former City of Durban Treasurer, interviewed by Bill Freund, 08.12.97.

Hyatt, Mick, Executive Director, Marriott Merchant Bank, 24.02.97.

Halliday I, former Managing Director, Industrial Development Corporation, 23.04.97.

MacNellie, Neil, former Executive in Charge, Natal Region, Investec Bank, 11.03.98.

Marshall, D., Chair, Marshalls Holding, 02.10.96.

McCarthy, Brian, former Chair of the Natal Building Society and Chair, McCarthy Retail, 22.10.96.

Moore, Dana, Chief Economist, KwaZulu Finance Corporation, 23.04.97.

Moore, Kevin, Vice-Chair, Marriott Merchant Bank, 24.02.97.

Pillay, Rajen, Group Managing Director, Coastal Group, 11.05.98.

Reddy, J.N., former Managing Director and Chair, New Republic Bank, 08.10.96.

Reed, Dallas, former Regional Manager, Sanlam, 30.03.98 and 09.06.98.
Rosenberg, Terry, Chief Executive Officer, McCarthy Group, Interviewed by Bill Freund, 24.11.97.
Russell, John, former Managing Director, Provincial Building Society, 19.02.97 and 18.03.97.
Seedat, Mohammed, City of Durban Pension Fund, 18.02.97.
Silal, Prakash, Assistant City Treasurer, 18.02.97.
Vahed, Sadek, Chairman and Chief Executive Office, AM Moolla, 22.10.97.
Van Rooijen, Izak, Executive, KwaZulu Finance Corporation, 23.04.97.

ACKNOWLEDGEMENTS

I would like to thank Paddy McDowell, former Managing Director, Marshalls Confirming, and Ian Ballack, First National Trust and Asset Management, for helping me make contact with many of the financial bosses of the city, past and present. Thanks also go to my research assistant, Buntu Siwisa, for his painstaking trawling of some of the financial journals and newspapers from 1970–97.

Part Three

Society and Governance

Part Three surveys the sociology of the city of Durban and highlights the relationship of society to natural environment in the light of the political transition and its consequences. Maharaj focuses on the creation and dismantling of spatial boundaries. He thus provides us with an overview of the most dominant theme of South African urban literature. He takes up the theme of deracialisation which can be said to have begun to affect urban life from the early 1980s and was then marked by the abolition of the pass laws and the weakening of the Group Areas legislation. After the political transition this led to the end of all racial laws. Only in 1996 was a democratic local government election held in Durban and even then it was democracy with some qualification until the second local government election in 2000.

In the Durban that is emerging, there are obvious differences between squatter settlements, hostel accommodation and settled family housing based on the council houses established by the state on a large scale in the 1950s and 1960s amongst the African population (Hindson and McCarthy 1994). These differences became especially noticeable when the political violence that peaked in the early 1990s revealed significant fissures that often showed hostility between insiders and outsiders as they have sometimes been called (Morris and Hindson 1994).

The deracialisation of space is occuring in significant ways within the new and enhanced Metro Durban that unifies what was a white city with varied other former political units. The city centre has become markedly less white while retaining commercial vitality. People of colour have moved into concentrated areas of urban flatland such as Albert Park on the CBD periphery and have taken advantage of the slack white property market to expand into the fringe of areas formerly defined as white, both affluent areas now sought after by the Indian middle class and those white working class suburbs into which new buyers can enter the market more easily. What were once controlled hostels for migrant workers become unserviced slum quarters occupied on a more or less permanent basis. Council house tenants turn into shacklords filling up backyards with huts.

Change does not mean, however, that race – and other categories developed before 1994 – has lost all importance. Indeed, one could emphasize at least as much restructuring and re-definition of group boundaries. White business has flown from the city centre to reconcentrate in new select shopping centres while a whole new affluent suburbia has expanded from limited roots to the north of the city. This shift, powerfully fuelled by the commercial activities of the sugar and property giant Tongaat-Hulett, is beginning to decentre Durban to an unprecedented extent.

Much of the deracialisation of white suburbia actually involves redrawing (now invisible) social boundaries to meet pent-up demand. Black demands on facilities in what were Indian townships, notably schools, clinics and sports fields, cause tensions and new lines of conflict. Apartheid was both cause and consequence of a process of encapsulation defining South Africans by race, a process which was not terminated in 1994; the racial sense of belonging is an enduring one.

The battle to desegregate the city has given way to the battle to provide services and a better life for different 'communities', communities that are to a large extent but not entirely defined racially. The state, moreover does not actually have any real plan to deracialise society in Durban. To a significant extent it recognises *communities* which are largely racially defined. This emphasis on community, that extremely difficult word to define, is critical. Change is intended to benefit groups and be governed by communication amongst (collective) stakeholders. In the construction of new housing, for instance, conflicts have been spun out and, to some extent, resolved as Maharaj shows, through intra-community negotiation, often delicate and long-enduring. This is unsurprising given that political resistance often focused on rates and services. It is revealing that, while individuals apply for houses, the bulk of the provision has been about the movement of *communities* from inadequate and squatter shelter to this new built environment. The language of community in South Africa is as legitimate and pervasive as the language of racial differentiation used to be, but sometimes the two refer to the same thing.

At most, the local state has been careful and so far relatively successful in preventing 'community' power-brokers from getting out of hand and transforming themselves into immovable local bosses – despite the increase of what Wiley et al. have called the 'explosion in the number of consultative structures'. What this team felt, in an important consideration of conflict between corporate imperatives and the environmental demands of long shunted aside residents, is that while the rules of the game are now at least in line with internationally acceptable practice, corporate power remains very much more important than community power where the two clash directly. The chemical industry, located near the sea on flat land for strategic reasons, is far more dynamic than other sectors of manufacturing and continues to be greedy in its need for land and polluting to the extent that causes serious problems for the residents established nearby in the context of the Group Areas Act of 1950 and the removals of the following two decades. The assumption is that Metro Durban has in essence bought into the dictates of globalisation. Thus far, however, environmental policy in the city is incoherent and shows the influence of middle class environmental pressure groups as well as business needs.

The same could be said for the allied theme of the labour market taken up by Hemson. The shattering event that broke up the old Durban system here was the wave of spectacular strikes in early 1973 (Friedman 1987; Institute of Industrial Education 1974). These strikes challenged the old work hierarchies and began the process by which Durban became a key site for an incendiary labour movement in the 1980s. But this era of dramatic, politicised confrontation has come to an end. The labour market is now shorn of any racial legislation or definition but the realities of skill, custom and competitive pressure in a slowly growing economy weigh on the life of the large section of the population at the disadvantaged end of the market. At the same time, Hemson demonstrates in this volume the extent to which Durban is beginning to de-industrialise and the problems that this poses a working class population which had in the previous generation started to establish control over space in the urban context and annex parts of the city for its own. This theme emerges insistently in the international literature under the rubric of globalisation, and especially in the literature on Africa as the related story of structural adjustment. He explores it while providing examples of state-society interaction in Durban that reveal the contradictory strands facing a reforming left of centre government at the turn of the century. Both Maharaj and Hemson provide us with important case studies that highlight the limited but real efforts of the state, national and local, to intervene effectively in a transformation process. They keep an eye on the relationship of state and society (focusing on the local state), while emphasizing three key themes: the nature of community, shifting boundaries in the wake of deracialisation and the provision of basic services to the mass of the population. Wiley et al.

spotlight the way these themes impact on an important aspect of city life – the classic 'brown' environmental issues – in a politically democratic but unequal social context.

This book sheds light on the changing social structure of Durban in particular, but its inadequacies in this regard are fairly manifest. Further research is badly needed on many other milieux in South African society. As this volume can demonstrate, for instance, the remarkable terrain of Cato Manor gets a lot of deserved attention (see also Maylam and Edwards 1996). This erstwhile farm was divided into Indian smallholdings and became the site of a massive African shackland in the 1940s. It was the scene of the worst incidences of violence in the so-called race riots between Africans and Indians in 1949, in fact it was largely a struggle by Africans, perhaps under the sway of enterprising individuals, to drive Indians out of this quite central area. Then Cato Manor residents were resettled in Indian and African Group Areas apart from small remnant populations. The strategic central state idea to turn this area into a white residential core proved totally impractical. Eventually, the large district was conceded to the Indian administration but, in good part due to the machinations of speculators, it only began to be demarcated for a new Indian settlement pattern in the dying years of the apartheid regime. Displaced Indians and Africans continued to view Cato Manor as theirs and wanted to return under a freer system. Large numbers of African squatters in fact did settle in sections of Cato Manor as the regime weakened from the end of the 1980s, exactly as the Indian House of Delegates did begin construction of new housing for its own constituents. Unsurprisingly Cato Manor is the locus of a growing body of research as it is a pilot project for the ANC government nationally and a unsurpassed magnifying glass for observing the new Durban. By contrast, there are no systematic social surveys on the big black townships such as Umlazi and KwaMashu. In a previous work, Freund has emphasized the rather dramatic nature of class formation and re-formation in the key Indian population; again there is no systematic study of different fractions of the Indian population (or *community*?) going into the post-apartheid era (Freund 1995).

Social research in South Africa, when it is there, has unconsciously followed the tide by concentrating on the inner life and dynamics of racial communities; there is a need to refocus on research that concentrates on the relationships *between* communities and is willing to problematise the concept of community itself. There is also a need to consider women, children, the elderly, other cross-cutting categories and place their urban agendas to the fore.

CHAPTER SIX

Segregation, Desegregation and De-Racialisation

Racial Politics and the City of Durban[1]

BRIJ MAHARAJ

This chapter examines the origins, implementation and the demise of racial segregation in Durban through an abstraction of specific moments in the history of the city. Like many South African cities Durban does not function efficiently, 'largely due to the legacy of apartheid' (Williamson 1996: 3). In fact, Durban was a pioneering 'exponent of group race policy' (Swanson 1968: 142), and as Maylam (1996, 26) has emphasized:

> much of the history of Durban in the twentieth century has been about the contesting of space. The local state consistently tried to control space in the service of the city's predominantly white middle class. Residential space has been manipulated through various mechanisms with a view to banishing the black underclasses to the city's periphery and so insulating and immunising whites from the supposed dangers that accompanied the black urban presence. The closing down of physical space for the underclasses also served to limit their access to other forms of space, economic, cultural and political.

Conceptually, this chapter is influenced by the view that any realistic analysis of urban structure must recognise that the city is an embodiment of the political, economic and social structure of society. There are numerous conflicts over the control of urban space around such issues as urban development plans, political influence, land use controls and the socio-spatial distribution of resources within the city. These conflicts cannot be explained from a single perspective as they are influenced by local specificities and contingencies. However, a common feature of such conflicts is the battle for 'political power and participation in the decision-making process' (Leitner 1992: 112).

The chapter will reveal that in Durban the perceived economic threat from Indians consolidated an historical alliance between the white working class and the local state, and influenced the development of segregation policies which culminated in the Group Areas Act (1950). By the 1970s the socio-spatial structuring of the apartheid city of Durban was complete. Economic imperatives influenced the development of 'grey areas' in the early 1980s. Social movements with strong grassroots support demanded the transformation of the apartheid local state. The local authority was also forced to deal with land invasions and the development of informal settlements.

Political contestation between the African National Congress (ANC) and the Inkatha Freedom Party (IFP) resulted in the Durban region being racked by endemic violence since the 1980s (Morris and Hindson 1992). The high levels of crime and violence in the region had a major impact on growth and development. The development crisis in the Durban region is illustrated by the rapid population growth, a slow economic growth rate, housing backlogs, an increasing number of informal settlements, rising poverty, high unemployment rates and an inadequate supply of basic services to the majority of the population (Pillay 1996).

After the unbanning of the liberation organisations in 1990, civic organisations began a campaign for a democratic city. This initiated the restructuring of local government and culminated with the election of a non-racial, democratic local authority. The democratically elected Metro Council faced a number of challenges, not least of which were land restitution claims from those who had been dispossessed, promoting local economic development, and addressing the historical backlog in infrastructure and service provision in previously disadvantaged areas.

Historical Perspectives[2]

In Durban the local state has historically played a critical role in facilitating the growth and development of commerce and industry. In fact economic and industrial growth has featured prominently on the agenda of the local state since its very inception. Every attempt was made to market the city as a 'premier borough' in terms of its potential for development in order to attract capital to Durban. There is evidence of a 'growth coalition' between the local state, the Railways administration and local capital, which co-ordinated attempts to market the city as an industrial and tourist centre (Maharaj 1996b), whilst the harbour was the key factor attracting industries to the city.

Frequent references were made in Durban to economic competition with other urban centres and the mobility of capital.[3] In order to further ensure that Durban was attractive to investors, the local state became heavily involved in the provision of the social means of reproduction – especially housing for working class whites. There were frequent requests for the Council to provide housing for poor whites. For example, although the Council's entry into the housing arena would disturb market forces, the Town Clerk argued that the supply of housing would be increased and rents would therefore be lowered. Overcrowding and its attendant social problems would also be reduced.[4] In November 1927 the Public Health Committee stated that there was an urgent need for the provision of houses for the poor class 'Europeans' and called for the initiation of a housing scheme to improve their living conditions. The Council agreed that poorer class whites were not adequately housed, and urged the government to assist in the provision of housing for this group.[5] The ultimate concern was to cater for poor whites who were forced to live next to Indians. This concern with the problems of working class whites permeated the discourse of the Town Council.[6]

In Durban there was a strong alliance between the Council and the white working class. The Council bureaucracy, many of whom were recruited from this group, were particularly sympathetic to white working class interests. This was one of the factors influencing the local state to adopt a racist discourse which peaked in the 1950s (Maharaj 1996b). The perceived 'social menace' associated with the presence of Africans and Indians in Durban compelled municipal officers to wrestle constantly with 'problems' of crime, disease and sanitation (Swanson 1983). It was not merely by chance that the police and health authorities were largely pre-occupied with the urban 'Native' question. Municipal law identified such functions, apart from controlling trade licences and maintaining roads, as the chief function of local government. Furthermore,

> the nature of urban labouring led white society to perceive public order and personal security, overcrowding and slums, health and sanitation, in terms of racial differences. Whites found it easy to deal with the labour question as a police problem and to debate the social consequences of African urbanisation in the imagery of a health menace (Swanson 1976: 166).

A local debate ensued about whether the African proletariat should be accommodated in compounds and barracks close to their place of employment or in locations outside the city. Employers (industrial capital and the municipality) supported the former, while the native affairs bureaucracy and the superintendent of police supported the latter. There was a great deal of concern about the rapid growth of *togt* (casual) workers, who commanded high wages and refused to be regulated by living in municipal barracks. The local state had to appease the white electorate without endangering the supply of cheap labour into the city or imposing any additional financial burden upon the white ratepayers or capital (Maylam 1982, 1985).

The local state was not prepared to finance African housing from the municipal budget. It developed a unique system whereby African workers contributed to the cost of their own reproduction. It established its own African eating houses as well as a monopoly on the sale of beer. A separate Native Revenue Account was established which was used to finance the native affairs bureaucratic administration (Swanson 1976; La Hausse 1984). Since very little housing was provided by the municipality, there was a proliferation of squatter settlements in the peri-urban areas, which further subsidised the costs of the reproduction of labour (Maylam 1982).

Since the turn of the century, industrial capital required more land to expand its activities, and there was some concern about the need to increase control over the bulk of the labour force which was living in informal settlements in the peri-urban areas. The local state responded by expanding its boundaries in 1932 which almost doubled the black population in the borough. However, since they were not enfranchised, they could not influence the allocation resources, nor change the composition of, the local white power bloc (McCarthy 1991).

The view that the local state needed to expand its boundaries to expedite industrial expansion was reinforced during the 1940s, a period characterised by rapid growth of urban based industrial capital. To plan for the anticipated economic growth the local state appointed a special sub-committee to investigate a 'programme of post-war development'. In his evidence to the sub-committee, the City Evaluator and Estates Manager emphasized the need to plan for industrial expansion as well as racial residential segregation, arguing that it would be in the interests of whites, Africans, Indians and Coloureds to be housed separately.[7] It was therefore evident during this period that city councillors as well as municipal officials supported racial residential segregation of the labour force, an issue which was later to be taken up vigorously by the central state.

Although racial residential planning was introduced in the 1950s, restrictions on Indian acquisition and occupation of land in Durban dated back almost to their arrival in South Africa in 1860. The origin of South African Indians can be traced back to the agricultural labour requirements of colonial Natal in the mid-nineteenth century. The indentured labourers were followed by 'passenger' Indians who were mainly traders. As Indians progressed economically they were perceived to be a threat to European interests. There was a conflict between white and Indian capital, and this was being expressed in racial and ethnic terms. During this period trade was the main economic activity of local whites, and was also a symbol of social status. Indian merchants challenged white economic hegemony and status. Durban whites retaliated to this threat in racial terms (Wyley 1986). The local state in Durban, representing the white ruling class, was at the forefront of calls for the segregation of Indians. In 1940 white civic organisations and the Durban Chamber of Commerce complained about the increased Indian encroachment into white residential areas, and this led to commissions of enquiry into Indian 'penetration' in 1941 and 1943 (Bagwandeen 1991; Maharaj 1995). As a result of pressure from white residents the Durban City Council (DCC) played a significant role in the initiation, development and promulgation of segregation laws, for example, the Pegging Act (1943), the Indian Land Tenure and Representation Act (1946) and the Group Areas Act (1950). The local state regarded the Group Areas Act as a life line by which Durban could be preserved as a 'European' city. The Council almost matched the National Party in their defence of the Group Areas Act, arguing that it provided opportunities for blacks to develop on a parallel basis to Europeans, as well as offering them new economic opportunities.

Given the almost unanimous acceptance of the Group Areas Act by the Council, it immediately set machinery into motion to implement the act. A Technical Sub-Committee (TSC), comprising different municipal heads of departments, was appointed on 20 November 1950, which drew up detailed race zoning plans for Durban. The TSC's views on the implementation of the Group Areas Act had far reaching implications for the rest of the country. This was because neither the central state bureaucracy nor the executive had given thought to how the Group Areas Act would actually be implemented. The TSC believed that each group area must have effective boundaries, and each race group must have access to its place of employment without traversing the area of another group. In making these recommendations, the TSC went beyond the legal requirements of the Group Areas Act from conviction rather than compulsion (Kuper et al. 1958; Maharaj 1997a).

The pattern of zoning favoured by the TSC was that of locating each race group as conveniently as possible in terms of its relation to other groups and access to places of employment. The TSC argued that this approach would utilise as far as possible existing natural topographical boundaries, as well as considering the type of development which had occurred in each area, the needs of each group in terms of employment, transport, etc. Planning in this context would lead to racial residential ribs or radii, extending from a spinal working area.[8]

The different race zoning plans drawn by the Council ensured that white interests would be entrenched at the expense of displacing settled Indian communities. Collaboration with the government resulted in the Group Area proclamation of 6 June 1958, in terms of which Durban was zoned a 'white' city. As a result, about 75 000 Indians and 81 000 Africans would be uprooted from settled communities.[9] Consequently, integrated communities like Cato Manor were destroyed, with Indians being relocated to areas like Chatsworth and Phoenix and Africans to KwaMashu and Umlazi. African and Indian communities unsuccessfully resisted relocation. There was a lack of organised protest action and resistance (Edwards 1989; Maharaj 1994); but the main reason for the failure of resistance was the repressive state apparatus.

Another reason for the failure of resistance was that residents realised resettlement was inevitable, and they therefore joined the queue for new housing as soon as was possible. Furthermore, for Africans allocation to a municipal house would give them rights to live in the urban area and end their feelings of insecurity (Maasdorp and Humphreys 1975: 63). In the Indian community segregation affected the different classes in disparate ways. Segregation laws seriously affected those Indians who could afford to buy land in white areas. It reduced opportunities for investment and commercial expansion for the wealthy, and there was also a possibility of financial loss. The less affluent of the elite faced the possibility of moving into working class neighbourhoods. It did not have any immediate effect on the majority of working class Indians who could not afford to move out of the Indian ghettos. Segregation represented a double edged sword for the underclasses – with increasing rents and slum clearance some would become homeless, while others could possibly be housed in municipal housing schemes (Johnson 1973; Swan 1987; Freund 1995).

By the 1970s racial residential planning in Durban was complete, with only one inner city integrated area remaining, the Warwick Avenue Triangle (Maharaj 1999). However, particular ambiguities still remained, for example, the failure of Cato Manor to develop as a white group area, and unsuccessful attempts to relocate the Indian central business district.[10]

Desegregating the City: 1980

Against the background of the post-1976 era, the material and social conditions in the relocated townships soon provided the impetus for civic movements to pressurise the Council for concessions and political changes. In the periphery and buffer zones land invasions escalated and informal settlements were burgeoning. Also rigid race-space divisions were blurred as blacks began to infiltrate white residential areas.

In the 1980s, *de jure* white residential exclusivity was being contravened as large numbers of blacks began to move into designated white group areas, and this led to the formation of so called 'grey areas' in most major urban centres in South Africa (Elder 1990). Three factors contributed to the development of 'grey areas' in Durban and other South African cities:

- With the process of suburbanisation, whites were moving from the inner cities to the suburbs, even before the influx of blacks into the area. There was a declining interest in inner city flatland as well as a movement to areas that had once been rural.
- There was a surplus of accommodation for whites, and landlords were forced to accept black tenants, who were experiencing a tremendous shortage of housing. Hence, landlords and black tenants were responding to market forces. The Group Areas Act created an artificial shortage of land and housing for blacks.
- With improvements in socio-economic status, blacks were seeking a better quality of life, away from dormitory, strife-torn townships (Maharaj and Mpungose 1994: 30).

In Durban black tenants living in 'grey areas' were subjected to constant threats of eviction. The Durban Central Residents' Association was formed in 1984 to oppose eviction of such tenants. It played a key role in mobilising, organising and protecting the rights of black tenants in Albert Park and other parts of the city.

The reaction of Council to the development of 'grey areas' in the city can best be described as ambivalent and contradictory. In May 1986 it resolved to request the government to scrap the operation of the

Group Areas Act in the city. Failing this, the Council requested that it be granted the authority and flexibility to implement the act in the city (Maharaj and Mpungose 1994). Conservative councillors argued that the repeal of the Group Areas Act was a matter for the central government to decide, and that it should not be discussed by the Council. Liberal councillors referred to the possible implications if the Council dragged its feet over the matter, warning that the Council could 'get rid of Group Areas voluntarily, and make a small contribution to relations, or wait for violence, consumer boycotts, and commerce in chaos to force us' (*Natal Mercury* 20.05.86). In August 1987 the Council protested to central government against the eviction of blacks from white areas in Durban.

The issue ended in deadlock when none of the above options were accepted. The stalemate reflected the clear divisions in opinion held by the different power blocs on the Council. Councillors on the political left supported a motion to declare the whole of Durban a free settlement area. Such a move, they argued, would demonstrate to the government that the Council supported a reform policy which would ultimately lead to the abolition of the legislation. Councillor Bruce Boaden maintained that 'Durban should be able to show its face to the rest of the world as the city which has cast aside apartheid.' Councillors on the political right maintained that no existing residential areas should be opened, in accordance with the mandate they had received from the municipal elections of October 1988. The primary concern was to protect the interests of the white working class. Their views were summarised by Councillor Arthur Morris who contended that 'it was all very well for the upper class of the Berea who had high walls and security systems' to call for total residential desegregation. He expressed concern about the white working class who would be forced 'to live cheek by jowl with lower class people' of other races (*Natal Mercury* 04.04.89). The debate was interpreted as the beginnings of a move for a non-racial city. It had separated those who favoured a democratic city and those who supported the status quo. However, while whites spent a great deal of time discussing the integration of facilities, such changes only emerged as a result of initiatives from blacks (Maharaj and Mpungose 1994).

The 1980s also witnessed a massive influx of migrants into the Durban region. During apartheid planning, large vacant land, known as buffer zones, separated white suburbs from black townships. During the 1980s the black townships had experienced an increase in backyard shack dwellings, which expanded on vacant land on the peripheries of white suburbs. Given the shortage of formal housing for the poor, the only accommodation available in Durban was in informal settlements.

Also, violence and crime in the townships and rising unemployment precipitated movement of people to vacant land in the inner city, and open land occupations and invasions replaced clandestine squatting (Hindson et al. 1994; Hindson and McCarthy 1994; Cunnan and Maharaj 2000). In June 1987 the DCC debated the problems of squatter communities and accepted the Housing and Health Committee's recommendation that the settlements should be accepted as permanent. However, squatters in Wenthworth, Clare Estate and Reservoir Hills had their shacks demolished by the police, and many were arrested and charged for trespassing. According to Councillor Margaret Winter the Council was unable to prevent the eviction of squatters from private property (*Daily News* 06.06.87).

A further stage of squatting began in inner city areas such as Clare Estate and Cato Manor. While spatially the racial impress of the apartheid city was changed by this process, it had little social effect on the new black residents, as they were excluded from access to virtually all facilities and social institutions within the neighbouring white suburbs (Saff 1994: 328). Officials subsequently stated that 'the city must accept that urbanisation and the attendant squatter problems are part of its future' (*Daily News* 12.04.89).

Cato Manor itself became a highly contested terrain (Edwards 1994). All the groups removed from Cato Manor in the 1950s and 1960s staked moral claims to some form of right in the resettlement and development of the area. These claims were made on a racial basis. The few Indian families that remained in the area were able to realise this claim in the form of new housing constructed for them in Bonella by the House of Delegates at the end of the apartheid era. New groups of African invaders were also staking claims. Cato Manor had become a large and undeveloped piece of land attractive to many low-income residents in the Durban functional region. Aspirant home-owners from the metropolitan periphery were rapidly invading the area (Hindson and Makhathini 1993; Hindson and Byerley 1993). In spite of the competing interests, there was a view that Cato Manor could become the microcosm of a new non-racial society where people live in a peaceful, inter-cultural and democratic setting, contributing to nation-building and unity in the new South Africa (Gigaba and Maharaj 1996).

The illegal occupation of land raised fears and anxieties and this has led in some instances to racial and class based conflict. The expansion of the informal settlements on the fringes of affluent areas had a profound effect on the property values of these suburbs. In Cato Manor the residents of the affluent Manor Gardens suburb demanded an interfaced development instead of low cost housing in order to retain the value of their property. Although some wanted to sell their properties and move out, banks would not provide finance due to the large informal settlements adjoining their homes (Maharaj and Khan 1998).

Land invasions in Durban and other cities have largely taken place on land adjacent to existing townships on the periphery of urban areas. More recently, the urban poor began moving towards the city-core areas, mainly on land surrounding Indian and Coloured suburbs. These invasions have tended 'to reinforce the broad apartheid geography of the cities rather than fundamentally challenge it' (Mabin 1992: 21–2), despite the occasional counter-examples such as that of Cato Manor.

The last decade of apartheid rule was characterised by reform in the urban arena. The decentralisation of administrative functions to local black township councils required a massive increase in the local revenue base and was accompanied by major increases in rents, property taxation and other township revenues (Morris and Padayachee 1988; Lupton 1992; Seethal 1993). These increases precipitated widespread urban protests and rent boycotts, spearheaded by civic organisations.

Civic protests around collective consumption issues (rent, housing, transport) dominated the urban political arena in the 1980s. The urban locale, and in particular the local state, became a contested terrain. Although rent boycotts started as protest movements, they soon provided the catalyst for civics to explore alternative local government structures which would transform the apartheid city. This represented the beginnings of a move towards a more democratic, non-racial local government.

Two major civic organisations, the Joint Rent Action Committee (JORAC) and the Durban Housing Action Committee (DHAC) were formed in the early 1980s, and were 'structured largely along racial lines because of the discrete geographical area and bureaucratic structures that Africans and Indians respectively operate within, and must therefore confront' (McCarthy 1985: 11). JORAC opposed the Port Natal Administration Board rent increases in African townships around the Durban region, and resisted the planned incorporation of these townships into the KwaZulu bantustan (Reintges 1990).

The DHAC was formed in March 1980 in response to the DCC's decision to increase rents in public housing. In Durban the apartheid local state initially ignored the DHAC's request that rent increases be reviewed and the civic was branded as being radical. However, as the DHAC's capacity to mobilise thousands of residents and the reality of a rent boycott became apparent, the Council was forced to negotiate. By demonstrating its capacity for mass action, the DHAC forced the local state at various stages to defer temporarily rent increases in 1980–81, 1985 and 1987–88. Clearly, the DHAC's pragmatism and willingness to negotiate with local state officials and to participate in local state structures and forums dispelled the state's attempts to discredit it. By the late 1980s these campaigns in the Coloured and Indian areas served as a catalyst for the development of a non-racial alliance opposing the high rents for public housing imposed by the local state (Maharaj 1996a).

Housing issues, especially rents and affordability, were central concerns for civics in South Africa because blacks were denied land tenure in urban areas until 1986. In Durban, Coloureds and Indians were forced to relocate in segregated public housing estates like Phoenix, Chatsworth and Newlands East in terms of the Group Areas Act. The local state attempted to dominate residents in public housing estates by imposing unbearable rent increases. Residents opposed these increases. Hence, public housing estates constituted a 'terrain of resistance' (Routledge 1993). The housing issue also served as a catalyst for the formation of a multi-class, non-racial, populist alliance and the emergence of metropolitan integration in Durban. In consequence, local housing issues involved a challenge to apartheid at the highest levels.

Despite their geographic and seemingly racial emphasis, DHAC and JORAC worked closely together and were further aligned through their affiliation to the pro-ANC United Democratic Front in 1983. Civic organisations like the DHAC and JORAC served as important agents of social change and initiated a shift towards a non-racial local government. They also contributed towards the development of collective political consciousness across race barriers. A major factor facilitating mobilisation was material – the incapacity of the people to pay increasing rents in Durban. While the focus was on local problems, the civics were aware that these issues were inextricably linked to the apartheid central state. Hence, the civics consciously advanced non-violent strategies – mass meetings, demonstrations, marches, boycotts and petitions – that advanced the struggle for national political change. The mode of resistance was non-violent (Maharaj 1996a).

The DHAC and its affiliates were also at the vanguard of the demands for a non-racial city – a move which gained considerable impetus following the unbanning of the African National Congress in February 1990 and the commencement of negotiations for a non-racial, democratic South Africa.

The collapse of apartheid in the early 1990s and the imminent prospects of democracy brought about immense pressures for the deracialisation of South African cities. In Durban, the local state was forced to respond to a multitude of problems and demands as it attempted to come to terms with burgeoning numbers, a depressed economy, political demands for a non-racial city from civic organisations with strong grassroots, and land claims from those who had been dispossessed under apartheid.

Deracialising the City: 1990s

On 10 March 1990 a number of civic organisations including the DHAC, Westville Residents' Support Group, Berea Residents' Association, and Lamontville Residents' Association met to discuss strategies for non-racial local government in the Durban area. At the meeting many speakers highlighted the unequal allocation of resources in black areas, and attributed this to being disenfranchised. They stressed the necessity for a non-racial local government, representative of all communities in Durban and called for the boundaries of the city to be redefined.

The vehicle to achieve these objectives was the Campaign for a Democratic City (CDC). The CDC was launched on 29 September 1991 and was supported by about 75 civic groups, straddling race, class and geographic boundaries. The CDC resolved to strive for:

- the eradication of apartheid local government structures in the Durban region;
- the realisation of a non-racial, democratic and equitable local government based on a common non-racial voters roll;
- the immediate improvement in the living conditions of the people who inhabited the region (Maharaj 1996a).

The launch of the CDC was welcomed as it focused 'attention on the true meaning of democracy in municipal government' and served as 'watch dogs in this period before transition and also at all stages until democracy is truly established in municipal affairs' (*Leader* 27.09.91). Local government analysts viewed the campaign 'as the most serious attempt yet to change the face of South Africa, and really establish the "new South Africa"' (*Natal Mercury* 05.10.91).

The CDC strongly opposed the racial allocation of public housing in the city. In a memorandum, the Council was asked to formulate a new non-racial list, so that vacant dwellings could be allotted to those in need.[11] Councillor Mona Riddle, chairperson of the Community Services Committee, replied that the non-racial housing allocation had been accepted in principle, but that the municipal restructuring process had delayed its implementation (*Daily News* 27.06.91). At a meeting held on 10 July 1991 a sub-committee comprising representatives from the CDC and the Community Services Committee was formed to develop a new non-racial housing list. The CDC was satisfied with the outcome of the meeting, particularly as they would be involved in the decision-making process (*Daily News* 11.07.91). This represented a penetration of the apartheid local state by the civics.

The closer working relationship between the Council and civics led the latter to believe that there

> was a change of style in the way the Council operated, if not of heart. For example, Deputy Mayor Margaret Winter, later to join the ANC, stated the Council was more inclined to recognise civics as an important constituency in the city, whereas previously they were viewed as a nuisance.

Municipal politics in Durban in the 1980s and early 1990s was 'characterised by numerous shifts in alliances, parties enjoying short-lived majority control of the Council, and very tenuous balances (Pillay 1995: 142). By mid-1990 an alliance between the National Party (NP), right wing, and independent councillors ensured that for the first time in its history the NP gained control of the City Council. However, by October 1990, Mayor Venter was reviewing his association with the conservative alliance. Venter supported President De Klerk's reforms, and gave them a local ambience by initiating dialogue between the region's key political players (Maharaj 1997b).The challenge for Durban was to initiate processes which would not only guarantee the results of national political negotiations but would also reinforce that outcome at the local level (Mkhwanazi 1990: 2). On 15 October 1990 the Council adopted an unambiguous mission statement which 'committed itself to pursuing the restructuring of local government on a non-racial and democratic basis within the context of a unitary and democratically governed South Africa' (*Natal Mercury* 16.10.90; Council Minutes 15.10.90).

In addition to political restructuring, the employment policy of the city had to be revised. The Council had a history of racist employment practices which favoured whites at the expense of blacks. There was a clear class, race and gender stratification of the Council's labour force. Africans and Indians made up the bulk of the general staff and basic skilled staff, white women dominated as secretaries and clerks, and white males were dominant at the middle and senior management levels. Given the political changes and pressure from trade unions, the Council was forced to commit itself to adopt and implement affirmative action policies so that its staff began to reflect the race and gender composition of the communities they served (Maharaj 1997b). In September 1993 the Council adopted a 'charter of intent for an affirmative change process' which was approved by the different stakeholders in the Durban municipality (including unions). The following 'vision statement' was adopted by the charter: 'The Council, both the work-force and the body politic, reflects the demographics of the region and creates opportunity for all people to achieve their full potential' (Durban City Council 1993: 1). According to the Durban Integrated Municipal Employees' Society (DIMES) 'affirmative action will involve transforming the ethos, quality and content of local government to help reverse the legacy of inequality, under resourcing and impoverishment of an apartheid environment' (DIMES 1994: 40).

Democratic local government elections took place on 1 November 1995 in South Africa. However, elections in KwaZulu-Natal only took place on 26 June 1996 because of administrative problems and the high level of political intolerance and violence. In spite of these problems, the 26 June elections in KwaZulu-Natal was 'substantially free and fair'. As expected, the ANC was successful in the major urban areas, and the IFP in the rural areas. Against the background of the political conflict, violence and instability, the relatively peaceful local elections marked the beginning of a new era which would focus on reconstruction, development and planning. The new non-racial local authorities in the Durban region faced major challenges as they focused on urban reconstruction and development strategies to address the socio-spatial distortions of the apartheid era. Central government control over local development planning has been reduced, with an increased emphasis on local and regional economic strategies as South African cities try to alleviate the high levels of unemployment and poverty in the country (Rogerson 1995; Maharaj and Ramballi 1996). In Durban the International Convention Centre and Point Redevelopment Project were part of the DCC's strategic planning initiative to form an alliance between local government and the private sector to help save the region's ailing economy. These projects were underpinned by a protocol to address past inequalities, with policies for affirmative action, stable job creation and levelling of playing fields (Maharaj and Ramballi 1998). It was envisaged that these projects would influence a significant increase in international tourism, which would create one new job for every eleven visitors and also bring foreign currency into the country. This money would have a multiplier effect of five to seven times (*Mercury* 16.12.92).

However, all these predictions of thousands of employment opportunities did not consider the cyclical nature, low pay and unstable jobs that were created by the tourism-convention centre industry. Local examples (the Victoria and Alfred Waterfront project in Cape Town) and international examples illustrate that additional or long term, stable jobs were not created (Loftman and Nevin 1996), but were merely redistributed to white suburbanites and not the low income groups. Grant and Kohler (1996: 539) have similarly concluded that the 'unrealistic plans which characterise the Point reconstruction programme are problematic and unlikely to benefit those most in need'.

Although a number of processes have been responsible for the inequitable distribution of political power and wealth in South Africa, it has been argued that the dispossession of land was the most important for most black communities. With the demise of the Group Areas Act and the Land Act serious attention has focused on plans to reconstruct some of the areas which were destroyed by the legislation. The Restitution of Land Rights Act of 1994 provided a mechanism to address the land dispossession that occurred during the apartheid era. In an era of reconstruction, development and planning, land restitution can be regarded as an opportunity to heal the scars resulting from apartheid planning and forced removals.

In Durban, Cato Manor attracted 3 000 urban claims. However, plans are well in advance for the reconstruction and development of Cato Manor into a model non-racial environment. A non-profit Section 21 company,[12] the Cato Manor Development Association (CMDA), was formed to administer the project (Maharaj and Ramballi 1997). Section 34 of the Restitution Act allows local authorities to apply to the Land Claims Court to prevent restoration of property to original owners who were displaced by apartheid laws, if this was perceived as not being in the public interest. In August 1996, the Durban Metro made a Section 34 application to stop restoration in Cato Manor.

The CMDA's policy framework for the development of Cato Manor envisages the provision of between 30 000 to 40 000 houses for middle to low income people over a 10-year period, catering for their economic and social needs. Land restoration would impede development progress; therefore the CMDA was in favour of restitution (alternate sites) which would accommodate claimants in its land allocations policy. However, there was no mention of the historically dispossessed in the CMDA's land allocation policy. The CMDA argued that the project was in the public interest because it would deliver affordable housing, provide economic benefits, influence the environment and would be a model for the future. Although there were some impressive plans for the development of Cato Manor, there was little tangible progress in implementation. The Land Claims hearings were costly and time consuming, and the local authority was forced to negotiate with the claimants. The chief Land Claims Commissioner Joe Seremane warned that the 'claimants' rights to restitution should not be sacrificed on the altar of ambitious plans that disregard the needs and rights of dispossessed citizens' (Media Release 03.02.97). The essence of the Cato Manor agreement concluded in April 1997 was that where feasible, restoration must be incorporated in the development plans for the area as a whole (Maharaj and Ramballi 1997). In Durban the Cato Manor land claims hearings confirmed the need for negotiations and consultation before development plans are drawn for land with potential restitution claims and that there had to be a compromise between restitution and urban development projects.

Contemporary Socio-Political Dynamics[13]

While there was a new democratic council, there was concern about the lack of delivery and the great expectations of the people. Within the city there were extreme disparities: 'Well turned out suburbs adjacent to squatter camps mean that a disparate range of services is available to people living on opposite sides of the road' (*Daily News* 11.04.97). Existing levels of services were being maintained in the former white areas. Cynics would argue that this would entrench the inequalities inherited from the apartheid era. However, it should be noted that the new black elites have moved into these areas precisely because of the high standard of services. The focus in black areas was on the provision of infrastructure.

As part of its Reconstruction and Development Programme (RDP) strategy, the Council also had major plans for restructuring previously disadvantaged areas including those in the inner city zone (Maharaj 2000). For example, in November 1995 the Physical Environment Service unit of the city announced an impressive plan to upgrade the Warwick Avenue Triangle and the Grey Street areas in 'terms of safety, security, cleanliness, functionality and the promotion of economic opportunities'.[14] In supporting the plan the Durban Metro acknowledged that these areas had been 'politically marginalised in the past in terms of physical, social and economic development and investment'.[15]

However, the government's new macro-economic framework, the Growth, Employment and Redistribution (GEAR) policy, which emphasizes fiscal discipline, debt reduction and cuts in public spending, is viewed by some as a departure from the RDP (Marais 1998). In terms of this policy local authorities will be forced to generate a larger proportion of their own revenues, and there is also a strong emphasis on public-private partnerships. This raises questions about whether finances for addressing the historical backlogs in service provision in black townships would be available:

> Many councillors representing constituencies in townships have had to explain to their long-suffering electorate why the housing schemes, community halls and sprawling green playgrounds are taking so long to rise from the ashes of apartheid, three years after political liberation (*Natal Mercury* 28.08.97).

The previously conflictual relations between the Council and local communities was reduced because in a democratic area there was direct access to councillors and officials. Although there was a high level of organisation and mobilisation in the late 1980s and early 1990s, many civic organisations were weak because their leaders were now part of the Council. There was a call for a 'renewed culture of political activism and strong grass-roots leadership' that will force the authorities to listen to the views of the electorate (*Mercury* 28.08.97).

Two issues that did receive attention were the inequitable rating system, and rent and service charges arrears. The inequitable rating system and the Council's neglect in the provision of services and facilities in black areas were one reason for Durban having the dubious distinction of being the only debt free local authority in the country. The Group Areas Act had inflated the rateable value of properties in Indian and Coloured areas (Seethal 1993), and residents in areas such as Clare Estate, Reservoir Hills, Newlands and Shallcross had initiated a rates boycott between 1994–96. As the campaign mounted, the new Council responded by providing a rates rebate in former Indian areas. It also requested the provincial government to write off the rent and service charges arrears which had accrued in the former black townships since the 1980s. However, the Council warned that 'the future prosperity of our local government structures rests firmly on the creation of a culture of payment for services rendered' (Mayor's Minutes 1995/96: 10). There was concern that high levels of non-payment and reduced state subsidies would undermine the financial viability of the city. In 1997 councillors supported the Masakhane[16] campaign by appropriating most of the capital budgets to development projects in the townships. Councillor Nomvuso Shabalala, chairperson of the city's Masakhane committee, maintained that the campaign would only be successful if there was a two-way strategy: 'We need to spread the word to our communities that our budgets are people's budgets and make them understand the reason for paying rates and tariffs' (*Daily News* 01.09.97).

Councillors complained about being overwhelmed with piles of agendas and being bombarded with technical jargon and data from the bureaucrats. Open debate on Council matters, especially controversial issues, was limited.[17] Councillors were forced to support positions adopted at party caucuses even if such decisions were not favoured by their electorate. Hence, the interests of political parties superseded that of local communities. For example, perusal of the Council's minutes revealed that there was no evidence that the Council had seriously considered the impact of the Land Restitution Act in Durban. Such neglect is grossly insensitive, given the historical role of the Council in dispossessing hundreds of thousands of people. It was only after the Cato Manor Land Claims Hearings in January 1997 that the Council was forced to apply itself to the issue of restitution.

Historically, business interests were strongly represented on the Council (Purcell 1974). In the post-apartheid era the direct influence of big business on the Council has diminished. Indirectly, the influence of big business is still pronounced. Basically, business interests lobby politicians at the national and provincial levels, who then influence their caucuses on the Council to support specific business projects.

Conclusion

In the past there was a great deal of conflict and contradictions between the local state, the white elite and working class groups over labour, housing and 'race' issues in Durban. This was diffused with the adoption of a patronage style of politics which accommodated white working class interests. The increasingly racist discourse consolidated a political alliance between the local state, the white elite and the working class. The anti-Indian agitation of the Council and its white electorate played an important role in the development of segregation legislation, especially the Group Areas Act.

However, *de jure* white residential exclusivity was being contravened by the mid-1980s as large numbers of blacks began to move into designated white group areas in major urban centres in South Africa. In Durban, the local state was forced to respond to many problems as it attempted to come to terms with a rapidly increasing population, economic decline, and political demands for a non-racial city. Civic organisations resisted rent increases, opposed evictions, and initiated demands for a non-racial democratic city. The delayed local government elections resulted in Durban, one of the first cities to develop and implement racist policies, becoming one of the last to embrace the new, democratic order.

While there has been an increased emphasis on local strategies for urban reconstruction and development in Durban there is a need to implement linkage policies which guarantee that benefits are channelled directly to the disadvantaged communities. In Durban the desegregation of the apartheid city was generally taking place within the inner city and on the fringes of affluent suburbs. In the apartheid era, squatting and land invasion were generally confined to the borders of townships and the peripheries of the city. In the post-apartheid era there has been an increasing tendency to occupy vacant land within the core city. The rapid increase in land invasions and the proliferation of informal settlements in Durban demands that the pace of land reform and housing delivery processes increase significantly. The land restitution process can be used as an opportunity to eradicate the apartheid city, provide non-racial housing, compensate victims of forced removals, and contribute to the development of the post-apartheid city.

Segregation, however, has been deeply entrenched in the social fabric, and is further reinforced by the socio-economic differences between blacks and whites. Decades of institutionalised segregation will not be eliminated overnight, and the legacy of apartheid will be visible for a long time in Durban and other South African cities.

NOTES

1. I am grateful to Bill Freund for his incisive comments which contributed to a significantly revised chapter.
2. For a good analysis of the political, social and economic dynamics in Durban in the twentieth century, see Maylam and Edwards (1996).
3. For example, in 1914 the Town Council emphasized the industrial and commercial advantages of Durban which enabled 'private enterprise to develop on terms and conditions such as no other South African town can offer' (Minutes of the Durban Town Council, 01.12.14).
4. Durban's Land Problem. Report of the Town Clerk to the Mayor and Councillors of the Borough of Durban, 12 November 1917.
5. Minutes of the Durban Town Council, 07.11.30.
6. Minutes of the Durban Town Council, 07.11.18.
7. City of Durban. 1943. Post-War Development – Report of Special Committee, p. 18.
8. Technical Sub-Committee on Race Zoning, Part II, paras. 267–70.

9. Hansard of House of Assembly, 05.08.58, col. 1472.
10. Cato Manor failed as a white group area for two reasons. Firstly, there was an abundant supply of land and housing for whites in other group areas. Secondly, parts of Cato Manor had ecca shale, which would contribute to significantly higher construction costs. The government did not proceed with the relocation of the Indian central business district in order to increase the legitimacy of the state-appointed South African Indian Council (SAIC). Many members of the SAIC had business interests in this area.
11. There were about 100 vacant Council flats in white areas (*Sunday Tribune* 07.07.91).
12. Organisations registered in terms of the Companies Act which are not for commercial purposes or for gain.
13. Unless otherwise indicated, this section is based on interviews conducted with three councillors in October 1998. They requested anonymity.
14. Physical Environment Service Unit Report for Committee, Greater Warwick Avenue and Grey Street Project, November 1995, p. 5.
15. Ibid., p. 4.
16. A campaign initiated by the government to end the culture of non-payment for services. Initially the focus was on payment of services. This was subsequently extended to include the reconstruction and the provision of services and facilities.
17. In fact, towards the end of 1997 'a range of politically sensitive issues were discussed behind closed doors. These include the "financial disaster" of the World Veterans' Games and the subsequent internal inquiries into the matter, and discussions with the Airports Company about the La Mercy Airport' (*Daily News* 03.12.97).

REFERENCES

Bagwandeen, D. 1991. *A People on Trial for Breaching Racism: The Struggle for Land and Housing of the Indian People of Natal, 1940–1946*. Durban: Madiba Publishers.

City of Durban. 1995. 'Settlement Areas and Population Estimate Project Durban Metropolitan Area'. Urban Strategy Department.

Cunnan, P. and B. Maharaj. 2000. 'Against the Odds: Health Care in an Informal Settlement in Durban'. *Development South Africa*, 17.

DIMES. 1994. 'Classes of Struggle: 60 years of DIMES 1934–94'. Souvenir Brochure.

Durban City Council. 1993. 'Charter of Intent for an Affirmative Change Process'. Affirmative Change Workshop held on 30 September – 1 October 1993.

Edwards, I.A. 1989. 'Mkhubane Our Home: African Shantytown Society in Cato Manor Farm, 1946–1960'. Ph.D. thesis, University of Natal.

——. 1994. 'Cato Manor: Cruel Past, Pivotal Future'. *Review of African Political Economy*, 61.

Elder, G. 1990. 'The Grey Dawn of South African Racial Residential Integration'. *GeoJournal*, 22.

Freund, B. 1995. *Insiders and Outsiders: The Indian Working Class of Durban, 1910–1990*. Pietermaritzburg: University of Natal Press.

Gigaba, M. and B. Maharaj. 1996. 'Land Invasions during Political Transition: The Wiggins Saga in Cato Manor'. *Development Southern Africa*, 13.

Grant, L. and K. Kohler. 1996. 'Evaluating Tourism as a Policy Tool for Urban Reconstruction in South Africa: Focus on the Point Waterfront Development, Durban, Kwazulu-Natal'. In R.J. Davies (ed.). *Contemporary City Structuring*. Cape Town: IGU Commission on Urban Life, pp. 531–41.

Hindson, D. and M. Byerley. 1993. 'Class, Race and Settlement in Cato Manor: A Report on Surveys of African and Indian Households in Cato Manor'. Institute for Social and Economic Research, University of Durban-Westville.

Hindson, D. and M. Makhathini. 1993. 'Community Dynamics and Leadership in Cato Manor'. Institute for Social and Economic Research, University of Durban-Westville.

Hindson, D. and J. McCarthy (eds). 1994. *Here to Stay: Informal Settlements in KwaZulu-Natal*. Durban: Indicator Press.

Hindson, D., M. Byerley and M. Morris. 1994. 'From Violence to Reconstruction: The Making, Disintegrating and Remaking of an Apartheid City'. *Antipode*, 26.

Johnson, R.E. 1973. 'Indians and Apartheid: The Failure of Resistance'. Ph.D. thesis, University of Massachusetts.

Kuper, L., Watts, H., and Davies, R. 1958. *Durban: A Study in Racial Ecology*. London: Jonathan Cape.

La Hausse, P. 1984. 'The Struggle for the City: Alcohol, the Ematsheni and Popular Culture in Durban, 1902–1936'. M.A. thesis, University of Cape Town.

Loftman, P. and B. Nevin. 1996. 'Going for Growth: Prestige Projects in Three British Cities'. *Urban Studies*, 33.

Lupton, M. 1992. 'Class Struggle over the Built Environment in Johannesburg's Coloured Areas'. In D.M. Smith (ed.). *The Apartheid City and Beyond*. London: Routledge.

Maasdorp, G. and A.S.B. Humphreys. 1975. *From Shantytown to Township*. Cape Town: Juta.

Mabin, A. 1992. 'Dispossession, Exploitation and Struggle: An Historical Overview of South African Urbanization'. In D.M. Smith (ed.). *The Apartheid City and Beyond*. London: Routledge.

Maharaj, B. 1994. 'The Group Areas Act and Community Destruction in South Africa: The Struggle for Cato Manor in Durban'. *Urban Forum*, 5, 1.

——. 1995. 'The Local State and Residential Segregation: Durban and the Prelude to the Group Areas Act'. *South African Geographical Journal*, 77.

——. 1996a. 'Urban Struggles and the Transformation of the Apartheid Local State: The Case of Community and Civic Organisations in Durban'. *Political Geography*, 15.

——. 1996b. 'The Historical Development of the Apartheid Local State in South Africa: The Case of Durban'. *International Journal of Urban and Regional Research*, 20.

——. 1997a. 'Apartheid, Urban Segregation and the Local State: Durban and the Group Areas Act in South Africa'. *Urban Geography*, 18.

——. 1997b. 'The Politics of Local Government Restructuring and Apartheid Transformation in South Africa: The Case of Durban'. *Journal of Contemporary African Studies*, 15.

——. 1999. 'The Integrated Community Apartheid Could Not Destroy: The Warwick Avenue Triangle in Durban'. *Journal of Southern African Studies*, 25.

——. 2000. 'Urban Decline and Renewal: A Case Study of the Inner City in Durban'. Paper presented at the Urban Futures Conference, University of Witwatersrand.
Maharaj, B. and S. Khan. 1998. 'Urban Reconstruction, Development and Planning in the New South Africa: The Case of Durban'. In H. Dandekar (ed.). *Space, Urbanisation and Globalisation*. Ann Arbor: University of Michigan.
Maharaj, B. and J. Mpungose. 1994. 'The Erosion of Residential Segregation in South Africa: The "Greying" of Albert Park in Durban'. *Geoforum*, 25.
Maharaj, B. and K. Ramballi. 1996. 'Recent Trends in Local Economic Development in the USA: Policy Implications for Urban Reconstruction and Development in South Africa'. *Urban Forum*, 7.
——. 1997. 'Urban Land Claims: Contested Terrain: The Case of Cato Manor'. Paper presented at the CONSAS Conference on Land Surveying and Land Tenure, Durban.
——. 1998. 'Local Economic Development Strategies in an Emerging Democracy: The Case of Durban in South Africa'. *Urban Studies*, 35.
Marais, H. 1998. *South Africa: Limits to Change – The Political Economy of Transformation*. Cape Town: University of Cape Town Press.
Maylam, P. 1982. 'Shackled by the Contradictions: The Municipal Response to African Urbanisation in Durban, 1920–1950'. *African Urban Studies*, 14.
——. 1985. 'Aspects of African Urbanisation in the Durban Area Before 1940'. In R. Haines and G. Buijs (eds). *The Struggle for Social and Economic Space: Urbanisation in Twentieth Century South Africa*. University of Durban-Westville.
——. 1996. 'Introduction: The Struggle for Space in Twentieth-Century Durban'. In P. Maylam and I. Edwards, *The People's City*, pp. 1–32.
Maylam, P. and I. Edwards (eds). 1996. *The People's City: African Life in Tentieth-Century Durban*. Pietermaritzburg: University of Natal Press.
McCarthy, J.J. 1985. 'Progressive Politics and Crises of Urban Reproduction in South Africa: The Cases of Rent and Transport'. Paper presented at the Conference of the Association for Sociology in South Africa, University of Cape Town.
——. 1991. 'Planning Issues and the Political Economy of the Local State: An Historical Case Study of Durban'. *Urban Forum*, 2.
Mkwanazi, D. 1990. 'Contextual Development'. Paper presented at the Economic Development Conference, 7 November 1990.
Morris, M. and D. Hindson. 1992. 'South Africa: Political Violence, Reform and Reconstruction'. *Review of African Political Economy*, 53.
Morris, M. and V. Padayachee. 1988. 'State Reform Policy in South Africa'. *Transformation*, 7.
Pillay, U. 1995. 'Local Economic Development Initiatives in South Africa: The Case of Durban'. Ph.D. thesis, University of Minnesota.
——. 1996. 'The Uniqueness of Locality: The Case of the Durban Functional Region'. *Urban Forum*, 7.
Purcell, J. 1974. 'Durban, South Africa: Local Politics in a Plural Society'. Ph.D. thesis, University of California, Los Angeles.
Reintges, C.M. 1990. 'Urban Movements in South African Black Townships: A Case Study'. *International Journal of Urban and Regional Research*, 14.
Rogerson, C. 1995. 'Local Economic Strategies in South Africa: Lessons from Britain's Local Enterprise Boards'. *Africa Insight*, 25.
Routledge, P. 1993. *Terrains of Resistance*. London: Praeger.

Saff, G. 1994. 'The Changing Face of the South African City: From Urban Apartheid to the Deracialisation of Space'. *International Journal of Urban and Regional Research*, 18.

Seethal, C. 1993. 'The Transformation of the Local State in South Africa (1979–1991): Group Areas, Property Super-Taxation and Civic Organisations'. *Urban Geography*, 13.

Swan, M. 1987. 'Ideology in Organised Indian Politics, 1891–1948'. In S. Marks and S. Trapido (eds). *The Politics of Race, Class and Nationalism in Twentieth Century South Africa*. London: Longman.

Swanson, M.W. 1968. 'Reflections on the Urban History of South Africa: Some Problems and Possibilities, with Special Reference to Durban'. In H.L. Watts (ed.). *Focus on Cities*. Durban: University of Natal.

——. 1976. 'The "Durban System": Roots of Urban Apartheid in Colonial Natal'. *African Studies*, 35.

——. 1983. '"The Asiatic Menace": Creating Segregation in Durban, 1870–1900'. *International Journal of African Historical Studies*, 16.

Williamson, A. 1996. 'General Overview'. Sector reports prepared for the Joint Steering Committee, Durban Metropolitan Council.

Wyley, C.H. 1986. 'The Natal Dealers Licences Act of 1897 and the Conflict between Indian and White Capital in the Borough of Durban, 1897–1909'. Honours thesis, University of Natal, Durban.

CHAPTER SEVEN

Breaking the Impasse, Beginning the Change

Labour Market, Unions and Social Initiative in Durban

DAVID HEMSON

'The process of work is at the core of social structure.'
Manuel Castells, *The Rise of Network Society*

The analysis of labour markets, which often deals with the minutiae of change in work, appears an aspect of economics and sociology incapable of illuminating the broader process of social change and explaining society's inner workings. Yet the categories of labour supply, productivity, employment, and low-wage labour, translate into human hopes and possibilities, the prosaic and analytic concepts into human desire and aspirations; data into brothers, fathers, sisters, comrades, football enthusiasts, Zionists and Hindus, radicals and traditionalists, vegetarians and those who buy roasted meat from women selling on the street. The long columns of statistics and the detailed analysis of work data over time do not appear to offer the promise of broad explanation of historical change and the role of agency in the erosion of the old and reconstruction of social structures in a large industrial city such as Durban. In analysis we move from the abstract to the abstract, attempting to grasp the concrete, the individual, and the real through case study and the evidence of human struggle.

If national and international economies rest on the linkage of a series of cities, as has been argued, then we are witnessing this series of cities in the developing world riding the most extraordinary pressures. Following the Asian economic crisis of 1997 there has sudden rash of unemployment in countries other than the first world, even amongst those which had been previously regarded as the rising world leaders of the millennium, in the face of overwhelming pressures of capital flight and sharply depreciating currencies. What appeared to be the creation of a unique approach to development in which many Asian countries broke out of the category of underdevelopment is now under intense and relentless pressure. The labour markets of these countries are being shrunk and reshaped, and workers retrenched, retrained and redeployed. Characteristic of the period has been the tendency for unemployment to rise or remain stubbornly high despite economic growth. In South Africa figures of unemployment are generally regarded as being proportionally higher with total African unemployment estimated at four million constituting an unemployment rate among Africans of 41 per cent, with considerably lesser proportions among other racial groups. With figures such as these, the Labour Market Commission, which in 1996 set out the task of the government, has stated without risk of exaggeration: 'Unemployment is undeniably a national crisis.'[1]

These are the pressures that impinge directly on political initiatives such as the Job Summit of October 1998 in response to the criticism by workers, employed and unemployed, of rising numbers of retrenchments and the growing numbers of unemployed. These debates, conducted at the national level, are refracted through the demands being placed on local government to deliver substantial reforms in metropolitan governments and towns.

For an extended period during which the labour market in Durban took shape, the municipal authorities played a central role in determining policy and administration in relation to African workers. This emphasis on the local state appears to be swept aside by the development of autocratic controls by the national state in the subsequent period but the traditions and practices which were then established have retained an extraordinary resilience. The municipal tradition of Durban was, moreover, far from liberal, and the practices and institutions of a previous period drag on. Labour markets for casual workers persist in isolated areas such as Old Fort Road near the old Native Administration Offices and others are evident near the post office and shops in Reservoir Hills. The workers sit isolated or in small groups well separated from each other, all desperate for casual day labour.

For a whole period, roughly from the 1870s until the mid-1940s, the city itself had been the locus of decisions on the labour market. The city authority was, of course, nurtured in the arms of British imperial dominance and reinforced locally by the colonial state, but within this context it retained a certain autonomy. For some, the rise of apartheid conceptions in the city during the colonial era is a cause for surprise and appear strangely anachronistic (Swanson 1968). For others, there appears a definite line of logic between the labour coercive measures of the colonial period and the rise of race distinctions – rather than those of the urban/rural, tribe or clan, 'civilised/uncivilised' as the primary line of social demarcation (see debate on these matters in Wolpe 1972 and Legassick 1974). Whatever the precise explanation, for more than a century there has been a peculiarly repressive labour market in the history of the city. The city, the place of markets, communication and sociability in which the full range of human desires can be expressed and achieved, is the site for the warping and squandering of human labour. These distortions, in turn, have limited the potential of the city with a restricted market in housing and commodities and the accumulation of huge infrastructural demands which have been unmet over decades. A city which has been acclaimed from the turn of the century as one of the most effective city governments in the country has, for decades, rested on binding and oppressive relationships which has limited its ability to meet the human needs of the majority of its inhabitants.

The Rise of Despotic Controls over Labour

For more than a century the labour market in Durban has been shaped by the most extraordinary series of arbitrary interventions by the local and colonial state in pursuit of cheap labour for the white property-owners and the port. The beginnings of interventionist policies in the early 1870s were marked by opposition of the city authorities, amplified by the colonial state of Natal, to the rise in wages earned by daily employed African work-seekers in the city. This trend undermined the low-wage monthly contracts of permanent staff employed by white householders, commercial and other interests. The demand to repress the rise of informal daily contracts with higher wages carried, for the first time in an urban setting in South Africa, the rationale of urban apartheid (Hemson 1980: 22–8). Here lies the claim in ruling circles that the cities were the creation and preserve of whites, that the African presence should be temporary and limited to serving the interests of white citizens and that ruthless controls over African movement and contracts were the mainstay in maintaining a labour market convenient to the dominant interests in the city: in short the basis for a cheap labour system.

The process has also been discussed elsewhere (Swanson 1968) and will not be developed here beyond mentioning that the spur to racial legislation was the crisis in the labour market. The repressive features of the local state in Durban were largely funded from the registration of

African workers provided for in the regulations. From these controls the peculiar rationale was established that the African workers in the city should pay for their own social control and repression. The 'Durban system', as the set of institutions and controls were termed, was added to, expanded (particularly through the municipal monopoly of beer brewing for the African market), reproduced through legislation, and copied throughout southern Africa. This labour market, subject to distortions and racial definition from the colonial period onwards, remained in force until the fateful repeal of the pass laws on the historic first of May 1986. In the period thereafter some pillars of the old order still stood for a period but their foundations were shattered and one after another they fell. Despite this, the social characteristics of this market live on.

What remains is to describe the form of labour market that developed under such restrictions. Under the conditions of segregation and apartheid, a sharp bifurcation developed between white labour, anxious and determined to demarcate itself from the humiliations and low wages of the black worker, and black labour, which was held in a situation of semi-proletarianisation and semi-urbanisation. Between these extremes, although then not far up the hierarchy of wages from the African workers, were positioned the Indian workers. These were the racially defined elements of a highly stratified work-force and a deeply segmented labour force. Until the rapid growth of industry in the 1960s these features of the labour market were relatively stable, and even today persist in broad outline. For decades local government in Durban resisted the inevitable completion of the process of proletarianisation by attacking and attempting to annihilate the growth of African households within the city limits. The multiracial community of Bamboo Square, which evolved in the area just south of today's Addington Beach on land owned by the harbour authority, was destroyed after the outbreak of plague at the turn of the century (Hemson 1980: 94). Other developments on the Eastern Vlei were destroyed with less publicity. African settlement was forced to the fringes of the city, notwithstanding the grudging concessions of housing initiatives such as the present Chesterville and Lamontville.

The Features of Racial Segmentation

While the labour market reflected the growth of commercial and later industrial employment, large numbers of workers were also involved in the white domestic economy with servants housed in rooms outside the main home, termed 'kias'. Researchers have discovered there was a graduated labour market with younger workers and those from more distant areas starting employment in Durban as domestic servants and rising over time into jobs in the commercial and industrial sector (Smith 1950). The large numbers involved are evidence of the dedication of the city authorities to strengthen and enhance the capacity of the white domestic economy.

For a whole period the labour market described above was relatively stable. Durban was essentially a service economy dependent on the growth of mining and industry in the interior, although it did develop industries dependent on imports and certain engineering, chemical and consumer good industries. The growth in manufacturing was uneven, taking place in bursts in the mid-1920s, the mid-1930s, the 1940s, and again in the mid-1960s (Burrows 1959: 176–7). The growth in employment in industry tended to take on the contours of existing labour market hierarchies and segmentation. Yet over time there was contestation and conflict over the determination of the racial features of the labour segments and shifts in and out of industries and job categories. The overall social position and form of family life of African workers was decisive in creating a cheap labour force at the bottom of the labour market. Most of Durban's African labour was housed in single-sex compounds or hostels under close supervision. Such conditions were intended to deny family life to African workers. It is estimated that, of the 104 100 Africans living in Durban in 1946, some 77 500 were migrants, leaving only 26 600 to be classified as permanently urbanised. Most of these workers were short-term migrants or weekly commuters to the districts in the outlying areas surrounding Durban (Maylam 1996: 99).

The allocation of labour by sector tended to take a racially specific form largely determined by the choices made by private and public employers. Africans were almost exclusively the labourers in sectors such as domestic service, rickshaw pulling and the labouring work in the docks. Indians came to constitute a distinct labour market, predominant in municipal services, hotels, furniture, sectors of transport, laundry work, sugar refining and in emerging manufacturing generally. White workers were, in part, the privileged unskilled labour force in sectors such as the railways but largely the skilled workers in industry, services and transport. But even from the 1920s the African workers constituted the biggest group with 40–50 per cent of Durban's wage-earning population, while Indians and white workers each made up 25 per cent (Katzen quoted in Freund 1995: 48). There was, of course, differential involvement in employment, with African workers concentrated in the lowest wage and most dangerous hard manual work, and white workers in the same sectors involved in superior positions. Indian and African workers were often employed in similar job categories until the 1960s.

Relationships between Africans and Indians were tenuous even when they were neighbours, reinforcing the notion that in Natal close proximity is associated with social estrangement. The distance in income between Indian and African workers was not great initially. From the 1920s–30s the differential between Indian and African workers was relatively small with African workers earning 69 per cent of the average Indian wage per annum compared to 19 per cent of the average white wage.[2] Most Indian workers were labourers until the 1940s, many living in conditions of abject poverty with dysentery, malnutrition and tuberculosis being prevalent. But the wage gap between the two groups widened rapidly in the 1950s when more white collar jobs became available and Indian workers moved out of the lower wage industries.[3]

There is a complex relationship between social mobility and social action; although the segments of labour markets are often the result of coercive forces, they also gain an internal life. Freund writes that segmented markets are 'moulded from within' and in this sense have a voluntary side, and that social identity is 'asserted in work or occupational categories' (1995: 53). In this way, he argues, the rise of militancy is linked to the defence of ethnic positions in the labour market. Resistance starts from the topography of the existing society in its segmentation and division and in a complex way reinforces an ethnic resistance identity. In this way mobilisation of the Indian working class took place around Indian problems and poverty.

Despite discrimination, Freund argues, Indians could not be pushed out of key niches in the industrial labour market in favour of whites (1995: 58). The trend was in the opposite direction – towards slow upward mobility. The active processes of identity and resistance were eroded by trends in occupational mobility, which shaped and reshaped occupational and racial configurations.

> As the upliftment of whites took place and white unemployment was mopped up, Indians, whose command of English and formal schooling years was on average improving relatively rapidly, were able to advance gradually through these decades into better job grades and skills (Freund 1995: 62–3).

Still, the racial ranking of work and occupation remained relatively stable for an extended period. The repression of African trade unions when they did emerge; the rigid control over labour mobility; the conscious undermining of African skills when these tended to challenge the privileged white labour sector and drive wages upward; the strong dependence on migrant labour, firstly from the regions around the city and, in the lowest wage sectors, from those further beyond; were the elements which applied to the majority of workers. Taken together with the gradual opening of sectors for the upward advancement of Indian workers and special procedures for protection of white workers, all these measures defined the general characteristics of the Durban labour market. The labour controls and customary operations brought about a market which was grossly unequal and distorted with a small number of high-waged skilled workers and a large number of low-waged workers, so characteristic of the colonial and apartheid labour market. This was a labour market which was inflexible in many crucial ways, particularly in the restraint of upward movement of the wages of African workers and their mobility in the occupational structure.

The rise of factory production in part represented an inevitable trend towards the growth of a modern African industrial and urbanised working class which would break through all formal and informal controls through its growing experience and confidence in the factory and city. Acknowledgement of this fact was long delayed and grudgingly advanced, usually only after a long process of gradual increase in their numbers. Changes in the segmented labour market usually took place quietly and unnoticed, by, for instance, younger educated Indian workers not wanting low-wage manual labour and making openings for African workers. But a series of engagements between capital and organised labour in the 1940s demonstrated that employers, closely backed by the state, had a strategy of substituting unorganised for organised labour, or more specially in Durban's racial context, to supplant Indian workers with African workers.

The classic case is that of the Dunlop factory where Indian and African unionised workers had come out on strike in 1943 and, to break the strike, the employers brought in labour from outlying areas. The rise of an African industrial work-force under these conditions was considered sufficiently significant to be celebrated in studies by university academics (University of Natal 1950) which portrayed Dunlop as a model employer of African labour.[4] The rise of this class brought out the need for a more explicitly capitalist city with city authorities closely involved in breaking strikes of African workers during the 1930s, 40s and 50s and allowing relief from labour controls when it conveniently served the policy of support for Durban's industrial development. The role of African labour was defined by the authorities to ensure the comfort of white households and propertyholders and to feed the development of commerce and industry.

The gap between Indian and African workers widened largely because of differential access to education, job mobility, housing and legal rights. Indian workers had formally the same right to organise and to strike as white workers, and could change their jobs without official obstacles. Until the 1950s job reservation was conventional rather than statutory and the statutory regulations which were eventually enforced applied largely to skilled manual labour rather than the white collar employment to which many Indian men aspired. The possibilities for advance in white collar employment were often full of prejudice and personal hurt, but there was progress in a number of fields such as shipping, quantity surveying, commerce and in other occupations and fields. In a shipping firm in the early 1960s, Indian clerks who did essentially the same work as white women and who were also increasingly employed in the firm were physically separated in an office by a partition. They were not allowed to use the same cups for tea as the white women and had to provide their own. In this context toilets were rigidly segregated and white toilets accessed only with keys (Private discussion 1969).

The rise of a modern industry with captains of industry readily interchangeable with capitalist directors elsewhere in the English language international economy brought out fairly minor modifications in the labour bureaux which controlled the lives and mobility of the African workers and simultaneously exemplified its racial character. Cheap labour, while in the last analysis an evident contradiction to the development of a robust internal market in South Africa, was wholly appropriate to South Africa's role as a provider of mining commodities to the world. The cheap labour system was sustained for decades in its basic features by the repression of African households within the limits of the city and by opening up recruitment to the more distant rural areas from which labour could be withdrawn. Although it is now fashionable to point out that such a policy of apartheid undermined the formation of a modern economy and limited the extent of the South African market, there is surprisingly little evidence of any opposition from employers to the operations of the racial labour market even in its death throes. Any opposition tended to be based around the immediate interests of a particular segment of employment (there is no evidence at all of forthright opposition to the elaborate controls) and short-term solutions were devised to meet these interests. The racial character of the city was defined and made implicit in custom and practice and explicit in legislation as a means of regulating labour and meeting challenges to the prevailing level of wages.

While the cleavage of race in the labour market is one line of division, the complex structuring of the African work-force is another. A study of African workers in the early 1980s, (Scharff 1981), based on the records of the city's labour bureau, demonstrated the primacy of migrant labour in Durban after more than a century of commercial and industrial development. Contrary to the findings of researchers into migration in American towns, who discovered an inverse relationship between migrant labour flows and the distance of the supplying regions from the centre of employment, there was a direct, not inverse, relationship from the first four zones (1–200 km) and an inverse relationship only from areas further than 201 km from Durban (Scharff 1981: 14–15). The findings are evidence of suppressed urbanisation among the African work-force (as it can be assumed that migrants from the surrounding areas of Durban were kept from settling in Durban itself).

Yet despite the battery of regulations and extensive apparatus, a majority of workers were settled and had residential and other rights of sojourn in the urban area. Further segments within the African labour force had grown, with settled labour being supplemented by contract migrant workers constituting some 39 per cent of the total from the rural areas of Natal and the Transkei. These contract workers (regarded as 'requisitioned' by Scharff) were employed mainly in construction and service sectors. Migrant workers thus operated as a 'secondary' labour force, while the stabilised workers were part of a 'primary' or 'better-off' component of the work-force, as has been analysed in other contexts by Doeringer and Priore (1971: 164). As the urban 'outsiders', the contract migrant workers were forced to accept 'the tough, unattractive, low-paid jobs at the bottom of the economic pyramid' (Wilson 1975 quoted in Scharff). Broadly speaking the majority of the contract migrant workers were employed in the building and domestic service sector while the most stabilised workers were found in the manufacturing and government services sectors. At one level these findings are unexceptional (such rigid segmentation between outsiders and insiders is common internationally where foreign labour is engaged), but at another level there is evidence of long term and fairly permanent lines of division which would persist well beyond the end of the apartheid system which enforced them.

The Death Throes of the System

Durban, which has been characterised by a rigidly policed labour market for African workers for more than a century, witnessed this oppressive system gradually collapsing before the end of apartheid (Sambureni 1997). By the 1970s the state control over African movement into the city was gradually weakening and, as a key indicator, the number of work-seekers 'endorsed out' (expelled from the city) declined. While very rarely making public or even private criticism of the regime of control, employers at the lower margin of the market increasingly took labour from the streets and then attempted to regularise employment if the attempt was made at all. Employers, as workers, sought relief from rigid control.

Undoubtedly the crucial factor in the break-up of the system was the strike movement of the early 1970s which involved tens of thousands of workers in the Durban region and the unions which grew in the period thereafter. This movement provided a coherent repudiation of the apparatus of control and exhibited the power to break up the old rigidities even before formal union recognition was conceded. The unions which emerged in Durban in the aftermath of the strikes combined with the Black Sash (a radical white women's anti-apartheid organisation) to contest the system of labour regulation. Although this was never given the character of an explicit campaign of opposition to the core element of the pass system, the launch of the Congress of South African Trade Unions (COSATU) in November 1985 propelled the tide of opposition among black workers to pass laws into a fundamental challenge to the pass system on a national basis. At the launch in Durban the recently elected President of COSATU, Elijah Barayi, demanded that the pass system be ended before 1 May 1986 or there would be a movement of national resistance to the passes. Although there was no organised follow-through of this demand, on precisely that date the regime announced that the enforcement of the pass laws would be ended. The momentous nature of the withdrawal of the pass system has to be brought to mind as the pass laws were demolished before the ANC was near to power.[5] The emphasis of control over African entry to the city and over contracts between employers and workers by the apartheid regime shifted after the collapse of the pass laws to an attempt to disperse or control the informal settlements springing up around the cities.

The promise of empowerment encouraged by political progress towards democracy and the possibilities of rapid expansion of employment prospects has been thwarted by the pressures of globalisation which threaten to nullify the comparative certainties in employment of the 1970s and 80s. In the field of the labour market the stagnation in employment and the segmentation of the local labour market remains, with poorly paid jobs being assigned to migrant workers and better paid jobs to the settled urban workers. The labour market is a study of change and continuity: in its fundamentals there has been broad continuity with many sectors still having an unbroken dependence on migrant labourers, with skilled work marked by enclaves of 'minorities' defensive of their position, and the unionised layer, which has a proud tradition in Durban, partly demobilised and equally defensive but confused about the possibility of resisting the encroachments on their job security and collective power.

Nowhere is the contrast more vivid than in the local textile industry led by the classical adversary of the labour movement from the 1970s, the Frame Group, which operated a ruthlessly anti-union policy in the huge plants of New Germany and the old mills of Jacobs. During the height of apartheid domination, the Group employed some 32 000 workers within southern Africa (although most were employed in Durban and Pinetown areas). The landmarks of the struggle for unionism, workers' rights and collective bargaining were the great strike of 1980 and the eventual recognition of the textile union in 1984. Tens of thousands of workers passed through the gates of its mills, many of the women militants are now in key positions in society, having been educated in trade unionism and resistance to the tyrannical authority of capital and state in the apartheid era. But the eventual victory of labour has been ambiguous and uncertain. The Frame Group now employs some 3 000 as mills have been closed and substantial retrenchments have cut numbers. Its imposing head office and blanket factory in the Jacobs industrial area in the south of Durban has been sold off as real estate. Under these conditions electoral victory and gains in labour law are somewhat hollow.

The New Period: 'The Patient, Largely Electoral Struggle of Reforms'

The post-apartheid period is marked by advances in some areas, ambiguity, and retreat in others. In comparison to the ringing denunciation of overtime and the prospect of Saturday work at the conferences of the old white-dominated labour movement, the present labour market is characterised by casual workers in the shops who are eager to work for longer hours during the weekends. Here are opportunities for women who have no other opportunities but at a price which few had envisaged in our recent past. The Department of Labour has projected a three-year plan of a whole range of activities; important legislation such as the amended Labour Relations Act and Basic Conditions of Employment have been passed into law. Everything appears changed, but the points of comparison with the old system remain in Durban: the rigid labour market segmentation of the past; training institutions which do not appear to mesh with the aspirations and possibilities of the unemployed; the continuation of migrant labour in mining and in other important low-wage sectors; and the restriction of women workers largely to the domestic and low-wage sectors.

The agency of reform has increasingly moved from the union to the union lawyer, the enlightened bureaucrat and the international labour market economist. This is the period defined by Jeremy Cronin, the leading theorist of the South African Communist Party, as a period of parliamentary action: the 'patient, largely electoral struggle of reforms' as the way forward for black workers (Cronin 1998). It is not clear in what way this increases workers' participation in these processes and brings greater control in their working lives – in fact the contrary seems the case. While there have indeed been significant reforms in law, the current period remains one of 'one step forward, two steps back'. With an economy characterised by a sharp decline in employment in mining and manufacturing, there has been in the trade unions a certain turn away from the goals of social equity and full employment and instead the complete engagement with the process of enrichment and participation in companies through investment rather than by co-determination through legislation (McKinley 1999). None of this seems linked to job creation. The whole question of thoroughgoing reforms in favour of the majority is contested and instead counter-reforms of a monetarist kind hang in the balance. There are significant legal changes which broadly improve the conditions of work and employment, but at another level there appears surprisingly little which substantially strengthens the position of workers in the labour market.

The political alliance which has brought about these revisions is increasingly tense. The African National Congress (ANC) in power has ruled over the biggest reduction in employment since the 1970s – a change which erodes the conception of reform. At the same time the trade unions are moving in a direction in which the battle for improved wages and working conditions is blunted by other preoccupations. The conception of 'strategic unionism' and 'social unionism' are the prescriptions for the unions acting as the motor of change in the labour market, but in reality there is the evolution of a dual practice of collective bargaining and investment strategies. The contradictions of this practice undoubtedly blunt the vigorous defence of workers' interests and clothe the strategic directives in ambiguity. This adds an entirely new dimension to the term 'business unionism' as practised in the United States which is unashamedly fixed on the goals of higher wages and benefits to the exclusion of wider socio-political goals. But the United States variant does not appear to be as openly committed to investment in companies in the industries they organise and as involved in such direct clashes of interest.

This is the context for local action workers' securing advances aimed at providing more possibility of employment, and extending the ambit of affirmative action. In this section of the chapter two initiatives will be examined which in a variety of ways are exploring the possibilities for change in the Durban labour market and meeting the need for new job opportunities. While reform initiatives have increasingly moved away from the city towards the national centre of power, the opposite trend now appears to be taking shape. These reform initiatives are limited and tentative, small scale and experimental, but they do raise crucial issues in terms of the substantive reform of the South African labour market.

The National Dock Labour Scheme

The position of stevedoring dock workers exposes, possibly more starkly than other sectors, the limits of legislative reform and state initiatives. The dock workers of Durban have had a history of confrontation with the labour repressive order from the early 1920s and have been a formidable presence within the most important economic activity of the city. In a highly contradictory development, the stevedoring workers' position at the inception of the ANC government in 1994 was, in a number of ways, more subject to casualisation and uncertainty than in previous decades. The process of deregulation, retrenchments and casualisation, particularly in the 1980s, had reduced the number of workers and worsened conditions (Hemson 1996). Although some representation had been made in the process of redrafting the Labour Relations Act, the new act of 1995 was limited to changing the framework of dock work solely in regard to a more precise definition of casual labour. Yet this had less impact on the negotiations to end casual labour conditions in the industry than a judgement in the Labour Court in Cape Town in 1996 which helped refine the definition of casual labour in the docks and challenged the existing practice of allowing 'permanent casuals'.[6] Although both these changes in the socio-legal framework brought about a certain change in attitude among employers, it was only through marches and strikes against casual labour conditions in the Durban docks that negotiations began in earnest to form a National Dock Labour Scheme (NDLS) nationally, starting with a pilot scheme in Durban.[7]

These negotiations, which led to the formation of the NDLS, help bring into focus the limits and possibilities for sectoral and local initiatives. The role of the stevedoring employers has been crucial; at a point late in 1996 a strategic change was evident as the very tentative discussions about a national initiative became possible. Although they had been advised by British dock employers to have nothing to do with any dock labour scheme,[8] negotiations began in earnest in 1997. Initially the Department of Labour appeared to have little to do with the initiative; but as negotiations proceeded they took a seat at the discussions without making any significant contribution. The role of the state in the evolution of the labour pool has been restricted and tentative even though the marches organised by the Dock Casual Workers' Organisation and later the Transport and General Workers' Union (TGWU) were directed at forcing the Department to take action. The union had hopes that the Department of Transport would take a pro-active role.

Historically, in other countries government has been critical in conducting reforms in dock labour schemes, usually under strong pressure from the labour movement. The role of the state in the South African initiative has been highly restricted, possibly reflecting the more recent trend internationally of counter-reform, of dock labour schemes being wound up and increasing casualisation being encouraged. Yet in the future, the state will have to shoulder responsibility for the increased stabilisation of employment within the scheme if it is to become a national system.

Despite a number of important concessions made by stevedoring employers in Cape Town following on the judgement of the Labour Court, negotiations for a national dock labour scheme have largely focused on Durban. These negotiations have centred on introducing a NDLS in two phases: firstly a pilot scheme to register the existing casual dock workers in a labour pool and to take casual workers solely from this pool; and secondly to provide a guaranteed minimum wage to workers on the dockers' register.

The first phase was anticipated to last six months and to provide the detailed information on demand for casual labour which would make a guaranteed minimum wage feasible. Critical to the opening of the second phase would be the role of the state: on the basis of the detailed knowledge of labour demand, the number of workers in the labour pool would be reduced through state support which would provide a severance payment for older workers who had been employed in the scheme for many years and who remain in employment mainly because they lack any pension. The 'pensioning' of older workers would then make a guaranteed number of days' pay feasible on the basis of reduced numbers who would be fairly continuously employed. The argument over the first step has focused on who was to implement the initial phase: at first the union was proposed, but in subsequent negotiations employers insisted on a 'reputable labour broker' who would take on the detailed task of maintaining the dock labour register, providing employers with labour and paying the workers a weekly wage. A tender was drawn up and the lowest bid was made by Mech-Elect, a company which has a contract to supply labour to the Simonstown naval docks.

The first phase of the NDLS was inaugurated in February 1998, without any public fanfare but with great enthusiasm from workers. The first task was to register casual workers who had been employed in the industry for a period. After several all-day Sunday meetings of dockers at Albert Park, some 1 500 workers were registered. On the first day of the scheme the scene was one of milling workers, long queues for registration, union marshals gathering the workers into groups for employment and company foremen anxiously scouting for labour. Despite anticipation of chaos for some weeks, the dock labour scheme worked reasonably well from its inception. There were some immediate hitches. Many who claimed to be fork-lift truck drivers and lashers were found to lack the appropriate skills. An attempt to engage taxis to take workers to the wharves broke down on the first day when the owners demanded payment equivalent to half a day's takings for a trip of about 5 km. Mech-Elect argued that these charges were exorbitant and hired its own truck. Generally employers made arrangements to provide their own transport.

The pilot NDLS has encountered a number of difficulties since its launch:

- There has been the absence of a number of employers from the Technical Sub-Committee which is debating and directing the pilot scheme.
- The membership of the Technical Sub-Committee itself has been contested by the TGWU which argues that the Scheme was a product of its planning and not that of the Dock Casual Workers' Organisation which entered the TGWU and then broke away eventually to form the Service Employees Industrial Union (SEIU).
- SEIU argues that a number of employers are not taking labour from the pool but are undermining the Scheme by continuing to use labour brokers.
- The overwhelming majority of workers claiming skills such as driving do not have certificates to prove their competence, and (when given the opportunity) many workers also demonstrated they did not have the job skills either.

- There have been complaints that workers do not arrive on time, and leave before completing their shift.
- Most problematically, workers complain that they have not been paid by the administrators of the pool, Mech-Elect, for their work on specific days and for overtime.

These complaints appear formidable, but significantly the pool has proved more resilient and durable than would be imagined from this list. The last issue listed above has potentially been one of the most destructive. Some weeks after the inception of the Scheme, dockers who claimed not to have been paid occupied the offices for a period and threatened to walk off the ships as soon as their basic hours had been completed. The difficulties were blamed on the employers not submitting the schedules of the workers employed daily to the Scheme so that accurate payslips could be drawn up. This was the reason for workers walking off shift early – these workers stated that they were completely disillusioned with the company and would no longer work overtime as they could no longer believe its promises to sort out the problems associated with overtime pay. Over the months these problems were gradually ironed out and a greater semblance of co-operation restored. The dispute raised the question of which agency actually employed the casuals, a question which was intrinsically difficult to resolve. The employers proposed a Disciplinary Code but this was received with a general lack of enthusiasm from the SEIU, which argued that since it was not clear who employed the workers, it would be difficult to frame an appropriate Disciplinary Code. The question was postponed until the second phase of the Scheme could come into operation.

The clash between the TGWU and SEIU has been one of the most difficult issues for the Technical Sub-Committee to address. At one point the Portnet Director argued that the issue should be 'ring-fenced': that the unions should sit down and arrive at a solution rather than allow the issue to destroy the Technical Sub-Committee. The other unions party to the Technical Sub-Committee, and particularly the Portnet unions, have voiced some concerns about the SEIU having exclusive channels of communication with Mech-Elect. All these concerns have been somewhat placed in perspective by hundreds of workers marching to the negotiations and demanding that the Scheme be speeded up and that the SEIU be regarded as their sole spokesperson. None of the other unions stated they had any significant membership among the dock casual workers although the TGWU claimed that the Scheme had resulted from its initiative.

The Scheme has to be judged primarily on the basis of whether it works or not. Although the record of daily employment has been kept since the inception of the Scheme, these figures have not been made publicly available and yet there has been a decline in complaints from employers over time. Employment of casuals has possibly been as erratic as in the previous period and Mech-Elect states that there has been a fairly consistent demand for workers in the upper range (500–1 000) although this has declined to just over 100 a day on certain occasions.[9] The difference with the previous period has been that the operation of the NDLS has smoothed out the periods of unemployment by limiting the size of the pool to the register. The labour brokers, who have been bitterly attacked by the workers for taking what is due to them in the form of a percentage, have been reduced to the periphery.

From the side of the workers, the NDLS pilot scheme appears a reasonable success: the opportunity for employment has increased (although there is not as yet a guaranteed weekly wage even though the six-month period of estimating demand has elapsed). The level of participation of workers in decisions about their destiny has significantly increased: the workers meet fairly regularly on Sundays and the shop stewards on Wednesdays to review progress of the Scheme and to iron out difficulties over conditions and organisation which arise.

Whether the Department of Labour will be prepared to provide the guarantees needed to fund the 'pensioning' of older workers is still an open question and because of a number of delays there has yet to be a fully representative group meeting with the ministry. The Department of Labour has a seat on the Technical Sub-Committee but generally does not participate in the debates or offer assistance, limiting its role to that of maintaining a 'watching brief' over the scheme. Such representation is indicative of uncetain support for the scheme. This approach raises the question of whether the Departments of Labour and Transport and the government as a whole are prepared to give the financial assistance needed to turn the pilot scheme into a national project guaranteeing a minimum weekly wage to South Africa's stevedores.

Despite a number of difficulties, the NDLS pilot project has now been placed on a reasonably strong footing and has won acceptance from its critics. Its achievements are not widely known. This project has gone unannounced in the press largely because of the uncertainty which attended its beginnings. Its hiring hall in Maydon Wharf at its inception was bleak and uninviting and remained little more than an open warehouse with few facilities for the workers beyond a limited number of showers and toilets. The vagaries of employment still remain. These truths are regarded by the workers as part of their obvious conditions of life as stevedoring casuals. But there is also a certain pride in its achievement: in the beginning the workers wore blue overalls with the initials NDLS embossed on the back in yellow, white helmets and safety boots. A number of workers have taken up accommodation in Cato Manor and can be seen taking the Francois Road route to work – a job and the prospects of family accommodation in the city for those who want it are no longer distant possibilities. The hated labour brokers are no longer seen on the waterfront, there are frequent possibilities for lengthy and exhaustive democratic discussion of all issues affecting the workers and better things are to come.

There is the possibility that the NDLS will fit into the much applauded model of the Gold Mining Summit which brought together industry leaders and worked out provisional plans to deal with vast retrenchments. If the Department is to favour sectoral and specific plans for reforming the labour market as the former Minister of Labour, Tito Mboweni, once suggested to the labour law conference, then the NDLS may receive greater recognition and support from government.[10]

JOB: Community Development and Local Employment

While the NDLS project has a distinct sectoral and national direction, there are other labour market initiatives which aim to link employment to community development and which are by definition local and community based. Possibly one of the most innovative labour market initiatives in the country which combines approaches towards community development, training, the provision of a labour bureau, and co-ordination with contractors to date in South Africa is JOB: the Job Opportunity Bureau.

JOB has resulted from two initiatives. After a leadership training programme conducted by the Social Policy Programme at the University of Durban-Westville, a database of participants was constructed in September 1997 to assist them in seeking jobs and preparing development projects by providing a curriculum vitae and verification of qualifications. At the same time the Cato Manor Development Association (CMDA) was reviewing its training programme and considering taking a new approach to contractors carrying out projects in Cato Manor to provide greater benefit to the community. In discussions the idea arose of negotiating tenders which would require contractors to take a certain proportion of their workers from the community. Although this was already happening to a limited extent, it was not clear on what basis this was taking place and whether the workers would receive adequate training. There were also sharp controversies as some areas within Cato Manor contended they had been shut out of the process and other areas regarded the projects as 'their own'. Altogether the labour question was proving a fruitful source of argument.[11] The idea arose that a database of work-seekers and their skills could serve as a resource from which the recruitment and training of workers from Cato Manor could be managed. These two initiatives combined and JOB was established to register work-seekers in Cato Manor, train them where necessary and negotiate with contractors for their employment. It was designed specifically not to select and employ work-seekers or take up labour matters on behalf of workers.

From the beginning of 1998 the CMDA has taken full responsibility for JOB which is housed on its premises. The single employee, the facilitator/co-ordinator, works through a network of relationships: with the training officer at the CMDA, with the Labour Committee which includes a representative from each Development Forum in Cato Manor, with training providers, and with the contractors. JOB involves registering work-seekers, checking certification, providing training, and undertaking the functions of a labour bureau in providing labour to community contractors. But these functions cannot be carried out independently from a range of community institutions – in such a poverty-stricken community there is a high level of conflict over job allocation.

Although JOB is active in encouraging the employment of local labour, employers have the final decision about which specific worker will be employed. When a contractor is appointed to undertake a project in Cato Manor, labour issues are now given particular attention. JOB liaises directly with the employer and gathers information on what kind of jobs will be required. The database and application forms are then consulted to build a list of what work-seekers are available from each area and what skills they possess. Since the job-seekers do not have phones, JOB and labour representatives drive around Cato Manor to speak to local labour representatives to find them when they are needed. These workers then report to the employer for assessment. Skilled people are put on probation for two weeks, attendance is checked and then a contract is signed. Some workers simply drop out before their probationary period is complete. Labour disputes have been reported but as a matter of policy JOB does not get involved.

The employment of local labour by contractors is a matter of much bitter contention in Cato Manor (as it is in Clermont and many other former townships) and has become a matter for patronage and threats to contractors (this is no idle matter as more than one contractor in

Cato Manor has been shot dead). As the leaflet put out by JOB explains: 'It is also due to the transitory nature and poverty of persons in these settlements that inevitable competitions of scarce resources, nepotism and power play in the allocation of job opportunities are evident.'[12] There have been many arguments and disputes over who gets what job, and particular areas feel that they were being unfairly excluded. The idea of JOB is to bring about some rational basis for the deployment of labour, to register the experience and credentials of work-seekers, and to ensure a proper mix of workers from the 11 areas of Cato Manor with the appropriate skills.

The launch of JOB in the early months of 1998 was met with great enthusiasm and initially the office was jammed with crowds pressing into the office. This created problems with other tenants of the offices where JOB is housed. The volume of registration also brought delays in building the database as attention had to be given to assist applicants in filling in the forms. Registration is a slow process: those registering are often illiterate and many are Sotho and Xhosa speakers, do not speak Zulu or English, and need someone to translate. The skill level of workers is also low and many cite their only employment experience as having assisted in a tuckshop.

Aside from these immediate practical questions, for additional reasons the registration of work-seekers was not an entirely straightforward process. The original database built by the Social Policy Programme was considerably modified with some 180 task listings appropriate to the building industry in carpentry, plumbing, painting and decorating, plastering and tiling, and bricklaying. These include tasks which considerably fragment existing trade definitions and are represented as 'excavation and timbering of trenches', 'install a shower', 'erect and dismantle scaffolding' etc. It would appear that this extensive documentation would bring reason to bear in the allocation of employment, but there have been additional complications. Although each of these jobs has an appropriate designation from the Building Industry Training Board (BITB), there is still controversy about the certification which would be accepted by the industry.

Some workers claim to have had work experience but possess no references, others have references but not the certificates requested by employers, and then finally there are workers with certificates which are not accredited by the industry. These complex distinctions are not readily appreciated by workers. A number of courses which the work-seekers have completed were provided as crash courses for the unemployed and have not been accredited by BITB which provides a specific registration number for the trainee confirming that the training has taken place.[13] Without the registration number, certificates have little standing. This in turn is only part of the problem. In addition, certification in training works at two levels: to provide documentation that a person has attended a course; and confirmation that certain performance criteria have been reached. An apparently simple trade such as bricklayer is certified at a number of levels: whether the worker has achieved both quality and productivity levels.

These complications have caused confusion for work-seekers who had imagined they were qualified in a particular task and incurred some resentment with the strategy of JOB to ask workers to undertake testing or further training to gain the requisite certificate. Although JOB has offered to provide selected work-seekers with training, they have been at times reported to be 'very stubborn', refusing to have their competencies tested and insisting that outsiders should not be given opportunities in the community. On the other hand, there are problems in offering training to work-seekers when often there is insufficient demand for the tasks in which they are being trained. The initial idea had been to train and place workers but there have been problems. As the facilitator has argued: 'It is meaningless to train a worker for the sake of training; rather there should be training to create jobs.' Training has also been complicated by the workers' attitude: at times there has been poor motivation among trainees.

In the short period in which JOB has been functioning, there have been distinct advances. The details of 436 individuals have been entered on the database and more than 300 work-seekers have been placed in jobs with contractors in the area. Cato Manor is desperately short of any forms of paid employment in the community and contracts which have been negotiated will bring to the community some R10 million in terms of wages paid. JOB has succeeded in bringing a number of jobs to the community and an increasing element of rationality into the allocation of jobs by contractors. There are often situations fraught with tension and potential violence, but there are also plans to meet the community's needs in a number of ways. The Labour Committee serves as the labour representatives from each area and there is now one labour representative being trained in Public Works policies and in tendering. JOB is careful not to promise too much through training because it is acutely aware of the possibility of generating an oversupply of specific skills; increasingly workers who have been trained are not employed directly but through sub-contractors who employ locals. Although this is not what was originally envisaged, JOB is now involved in the training of these contractors in how to run businesses and how to bring labour conditions in line with ILO standards.

The question of giving preference to local labour brings to the fore the complex interplay of advantage and disadvantage, of equity, cost and benefit, in contracting in development areas. While it seems reasonable to employ more local workers in developing a community, it is undoubtedly the case that this may be prejudicial to the existing employees of the contractor. Such contracting increases the job insecurity of workers in the construction industry which is already very insecure and which has been described in a recent official document as having 'an unstable and frequently insecure employment environment, jittery periods of financial assurance, an inbuilt bias towards urban centres of development, and an essentially erratic approach to integrating the construction industry with the vision and objectives of the RDP [Reconstruction and Development Programme]'.[14]

The jobs which have been achieved are in an industry in which contracts are short term. Some companies do not want to re-employ workers as they have full-timers available; everything is done on contract, but contracts can be renewed. One of the achievements of JOB is having secured greater job opportunities for women. Although contractors have stated they have no demand for women, JOB has argued for women to be employed in activities such as stone gathering and in other work which is not so physically demanding. The problem is compounded as women are not confident to work with men and need in-service training, but women's employment is rising.

Within the Cato Manor community some feel that JOB should do everything, others are not sure, and yet others are hostile. JOB's role remains controversial. Meetings of representatives of the Labour Committee and Development Committees have been called to explain the nature of contracts and the operation of JOB and a proposal has been put forward that at the beginning of each new contract there should be a full report to the Labour Committee and Development Committees to help overcome the disputes and controversies which still dog employment by contractors in the area.

Has a New Era Begun?

Durban, it is argued, has stood at the centre of currents and initiatives around the issue of labour which have had repercussions in broader political and social issues nationally. At crucial turning points pressures in the labour market have resulted in a series of shifts politically and socially which have moved the terrain of the local and, on occasion, national state onto different ground. In the period of segregation and apartheid, these pressures tended towards the reinforcement of state power in peculiar ways as the dialectic between class pressures and colonial employers initially and perversely added to the racial definition of that state. Central to all these developments has been the growth of Durban as the major port of South Africa and the expansion of a certain industrial base which has drawn together an initially heterogenous working class within which African workers have gained ascendancy.

The great advance made with the destruction of apartheid has carried a cruel contradiction. Simultaneous with the collapse of oppressive controls has come a long period of economic stagnation and decline which has undermined the hopes for greater employment and a more equitable labour market. In the aftermath of apartheid there has been a turn towards informal types of economic activity, towards an unproven tourist sector, and towards certain limited sectoral initiatives in labour market reform. As Durban's industries have shrunk under the pressure of a declining domestic market and under much reduced tariffs, the post-apartheid visions of sustained reconstruction and development have been replaced by the much more limited prospects of training and redeployment,. Perspectives for a revived local economy remain as promises. Durban's labour market appears in sharp contrast with that in Kerala State, India, where it is argued that unionisation and state intervention have 'fundamentally transformed the traditional character of labor relations' (Heller 1997: 71) through the unionisation of the unorganised sector and political articulation of social demands.

Much enthusiasm has been generated around the idea of the expansion of tourism as the key labour absorbing sector of the future to the extent that the political radical in a recent theatre production shouts the slogan: 'We must mobilise to make Durban a tourist destination.'[15] Energies are being focused on the development of employment in tourism, particularly after Durban has been proclaimed the convention centre of Africa by tour operators (Safm 16.05.01). Internationally it is argued that the period of industrial expansion is now being followed by services, especially in tourism. A recent study has shown that tourism is the world's largest industry providing 255 million jobs (one in nine workers globally) and 10.7 per cent of global wages in 1996. It is anticipated that the number of jobs will rise to about 385 million by 2006 due to the increase in tourism demand. Unlike other industries, it is argued that the expansion of tourism directly increases demand for labour. By the nature of personal service which is central to tourism there is little potential for labour to be replaced by technology and rising employment creation is guaranteed.

The potential jobs generated by tourism are estimated to be in the range of 10 per cent of the formal jobs of KwaZulu-Natal by the Natal Parks Board. At the most pessimistic it is calculated that 35 000 jobs would be created between 1995–2000 and at the most optimistic some 93 000. Most of these jobs would be centred in and around Durban (*New Vision* 1997: 7.12–7.13). It is generally acknowledged that these jobs are low-wage and often temporary, but they would meet some of the demand for employment in a region where there has been a job decline. This shift from higher to lower wage jobs reflects the trends internationally. Castells, for instance, argues that increased trade has resulted in unemployment internationally and that there has been a surge in wage inequality in the Organisation for Economic Cooperation and Development (OECD) area (1996: 238).

Globalisation has (at least) two sides: the penetration of forms of money-capital into all communities and nations, the commodification of human relations, and simultaneously the vastly expanded possibilities for human communication and thus for solidarity. The former appears dominant and is the stuff of newspaper headlines over exchange rates and similar matters; the latter is often confined to the conventional and unspectacular. While multinationals energetically prowl the limits of the inter-penetration of economies, political communication tends to flow along conventional paths, at times without a grasp of latent possibilities. A co-operation agreement, for instance, was signed at a special Metro Council meeting on 5 May 1997 between the Mayor of Rotterdam, Dr Bram Peper, and the Durban Metro Mayor, Obed Mlaba. In this accord, support was given, both financially and in transfer of skills in housing, tertiary education, the arts and social upliftment (*City Beat* newsletter 06.97). Unfortunately, no co-operation between labour was projected, more particularly between the workers of the two most important ports in their respective regions despite a willingness on the part of Rotterdam unions and the International Transport Federation to take such co-operation forward.[16] As has been argued by Castells (1996: 415) 'elites are cosmopolitan, people are local' and labour appears uncertain how to take up its global possibilities. Under these conditions globalisation appears a one-sided phenomenon undermining workers' conditions while its potential for human solidarity has yet to be explored. Increasingly in the new international division of labour, the less developed regions are developing as tourist rather than industrial zones. These trends are a challenge to the new thinking around local economic development, and pose acutely the question of planning and direction for a more rounded and integrated development of Durban.

NOTES

1. Labour Market Commission. June 1996. RP83/1996, paras 15 and 49.
2. Calculated from figures quoted in Freund (1995: 42).
3. By the late 1960s there were virtually no Indian workers employed as spinners, and only older male weavers, as younger workers sought better paid and less oppressive conditions than in the Frame textile factories.
4. Significantly there is no mention made at all in this study of white or Indian workers; the study is constructed as an ethnographic survey of African workers alone who happened to be employed at Dunlops. The strike, which was fundamental to African/management relationships, is not mentioned at all.
5. The leading theorist of the South African Communist Party, Joe Slovo, had argued with the author in December 1979 that the pass laws could never be withdrawn in South Africa and that after coming to power the African National Congress would be forced, as had Frelimo in Mozambique, to enforce rigorous controls over access to the cities or there would be chaos in these centres. The Mozambican authorities organised drives to force recent migrants back to the land in the early 1980s before the rising civil war forced that policy to be abandoned. Significantly also another neighbouring country, Zimbabwe, has also waged a war against the growth of informal settlements within its towns and cities with a ruthlessness which put the late apartheid state to shame.
6. William Kerfoot in the *Weekly Mail* 25–30.03.94.
7. Material in this section has been derived largely from notes made during participation in the Technical Sub-Committee and from being associated with the trade unions.
8. Interview with dock employers when the writer presented a proposal to the Technical Sub-Committee on the management of the labour pool.
9. Total employment is calculated over a 24-hour period which includes two main shifts of 12 hours or three of 8 hours.
10. Unfortunately the prospects are not very encouraging. Shortly before the Job Summit, Tito Mboweni, the Minister of Labour, downplayed the expectations of workers for initiative from government in relation to job creation. 'A day after the job summit it will not be raining jobs,' he told the 11th Annual Labour Law Conference. *Business Day* 02.07.98.
11. These controversies are by no means limited to Cato Manor. The preliminary conclusions from a study of local government in the Clermont area being conducted by the Social Policy Programme has brought to light evidence of heated argument over the employment of local labour for community projects.
12. JOB Opportuniity Bureau Presentation 1998.
13. The registration number allows independent verification of the certificate and serves as a back-up should the worker lose a certificate.
14. Foreword to the Green Paper (November 1997) by the Minister of Public Works.
15. The radical character in Angel Mama, Playhouse Theatre, June 1998.
16. Interview with Kees Maxey, International Transport Federation, July 1997.

REFERENCES

Burrows, J.R. 1959. *The Population and Labour Resources of Natal.* Pietermaritzburg: Natal Town and Regional Planning Commission.

Castells, M. 1996. *The Rise of the Network Society.* Oxford: Blackwell.

Chossudovsky, M. 1997. *The Globalisation of Poverty: Impacts of IMF and World Bank Reforms.* London: Zed Books.

COSATU. 'September Commission in 1997'. Report on the Future of the Unions.

Cronin, J. 1998. 'The Left is not Dead, It's Just Getting a Face-Lift'. *Mail and Guardian* 15.05.98.

Crush, J. 1984. 'Uneven Labour Migration in Southern Africa'. *South African Geographical Journal,* 66, 2.

Department of Public Works Green Paper. November 1997. 'Creating an Enabling Environment for Reconstruction, Growth and Development in the Construction Industry'.

Doeringer, P.B. and M.J. Piore. 1971. *Internal Labour Markets and Manpower Analysis.* Massachusetts: Heath Lexington Books.

Freund, B. 1995. *Insiders and Outsiders: The Indian Working Class of Durban, 1910–1990.* London: Heinemann and James Currey.

Heller, P. 1997. 'Social Capital as a Product of Class Mobilization and State Intervention: Industrial Workers in Kerala, India'. In P. Evans, *State-Society Synergy: Government and Social Capital in Development.* Berkeley: University of California Press.

Hemson, D. 1980. 'Class Consciousness and Migrant Workers'. Ph.D. thesis, University of Warwick.

——. 1996. 'Beyond the Frontier of Control? Trade Unionism and the Labour Market in the Durban Docks'. *Transformation,* 31, 83–114.

Stewart, B. Consultant on Training to CMDA, interviews, 04.12.97.

Mthembu, N. JOB Co-ordinator/facilitator, interviews, 10.06.98 and 02.07.98.

JOB Opportunity Bureau Presentation, 1998.

Katzen, M. 1961. 'Industry in Greater Durban, Part I: Its Growth and Structure'. Natal Town and Regional Planning Reports, No. 3. Pietermaritzburg: Natal Town and Regional Planning Commission.

Legassick, M. 1974. 'South Africa: Capital Accumulation and Violence'. *Economy and Society,* 3, 3.

Maylam, P. 1996. 'The Changing Political Economy of the Region *c.*1920–*c.*1950'. In R. Morrell (ed.). *Political Economy and Identities in KwaZulu Natal: Historical Perspectives.* Durban: Indicator Press.

McKinley, D. 1999. 'Union Investment Strategy: Socialist Unionism or "Social Capitalism"?'. *South African Labour Bulletin,* 23, 6.

Middleton, J., A. Ziderman and A. Van Adams. 1993. *Skills for Productivity.* Washington DC: Oxford University Press for the World Bank.

Mpanza, Z. and J. Nattrass. 1987. 'Poverty, Migration and Unemployment in Dumisa: A Rural Area of KwaZulu'. Working Paper No. 10. Rural Urban Studies Unit, University of Natal, Durban.

Mumford, L. 1961. *The City in History.* Harmondsworth: Penguin.

New Vision Strategy Consultants. 2 July 1997. 'Labour Trends Analysis: Towards a Strategy for Skills Development in KwaZulu-Natal'.

Padayachee, V. 1985. 'An Analysis of Some Aspects of Employment and Unemployment in the Durban Townships of Umlazi and Lamontville: A Preliminary

Investigation'. Occasional Paper No. 14. Institute of Social and Economic Research, University of Durban-Westville.

Pillay, P.N. 1973. 'A Poverty Datum Line Study Among Africans in Durban'. Occasional Paper No. 3. Department of Economics, University of Natal.

Report of the Commission to Investigate the Development of a Comprehensive Labour Market Policy. June 1996. Restructuring the South African Labour Market. RP83/1996.

Sambureni, N. 1997. 'A History of the Labouring Classes of Durban'. Ph.D. thesis, UNISA.

Sayer, A. and R. Walker. 1992. *The New Social Economy: Reworking the Division of Labor*. Cambridge MA: Blackwell.

Scharff, R.H. 1981. 'A Profile of the African Workforce in Durban'. Black/White Income Gap Project, Final Research Report No. 3. Department of Economics, University of Natal, Durban.

Schlemmer, L. 1977. 'The Situation of African Migrant Workers in Durban'. Centre for Applied Social Sciences, University of Natal, Durban.

Smith, R.H. 1950. *Labour Resources of Natal: A Summary of a Thesis.* Cape Town: Oxford University Press.

Standing, G., J. Sender and J. Weeks. 1996. *Restructuring the Labour Market: The South African Challenge*. Geneva: ILO.

Swanson, M. 1968. 'Urban Origins of Separate Development'. *Race*, 10.

Teeple, G. 1995. *Globalization and the Decline of Social Reform.* New Jersey and Toronto: Humanities and Garamond Press.

University of Natal, Department of Economics. 1950. *The African Factory Worker: A Sample Study of the Life and Labour of the Urban African Worker*. Cape Town: Oxford University Press.

Wolpe, H. 1972. 'Capitalism and Cheap Labour-Power: From Segregation to Apartheid'. *Economy and Society*, 1, 4.

CHAPTER EIGHT

Contesting the Urban Industrial Environment in South Durban in a Period of Democratisation and Globalisation

DAVID WILEY, CHRISTINE ROOT and SVEN (BOBBY) PEEK

In the 1930s, the Durban City Council and the local Chamber of Industries designed South Durban as an industrial centre with adjacent housing for the industrial work-force. Because of its proximity to Africa's largest harbour, the area's flat land was valuable for industry, though it required draining the largest wetlands on the east coast of the continent and canalising its rivers. Then in 1950, the Group Areas Act provided the legal underpinnings and financial resources to formalise the residential areas, to impose strict racial segregation and inequality, and to begin relocation of Coloured and Indian Durbanites to new segregated townships (Scott 1994). This plan subjected primarily black (but also a white) communities to the health risks and nuisances of living near this concentration of polluting industries, which include the nation's largest petroleum refinery, its second largest concentration of the petro-chemical industry, and a total of 180 smokestack industries.[1] South Durban's cauldron of pollution was created by an intertwining of the economic interests of industry, the security interests of the apartheid state, and the racial segregation interests of a major portion of the Durban white electorate. Interest in the health and well-being of South Durban's largely black communities was sacrificed.

With the arrival of democracy in the mid-1990s, in a wide variety of initiatives and forums, these communities have sought to influence the decisions which shape both the pollution in their communities and the future interplay of development and environment of South Durban. Reducing pollution from the existing industries is on the agenda of all the stakeholders to varying degrees. Simultaneously, however, government and corporations have considered plans to expand industry in the region, which brings prospects of *increasing* pollution if cleaner production is not implemented.

In order to understand the tangled web of communities and industry in South Durban and how they have addressed environmental issues there, it is necessary to analyse the interactions of corporations, the state, local and provincial authorities, non-governmental organisations (NGOs), and communities and their organisations. One must also consider the larger political context in which these interactions occur, particularly the national – and local – transitions to democracy, and the global economy into which South Africa is being integrated.

In this chapter we analyse the impacts of South Africa's transition to democracy and of globalisation on the social participation of South Durban communities in environmental issues. We begin by defining the nature and forms of social participation we studied in South Durban. Then we describe the democratisation, globalisation, and class and racial interests that have further shaped stakeholder participation in environmental issues there.[2]

Participation, Democracy, and Globalisation

From the vast literature on participation and social movements, we use the definition of participation developed by the research team of the United Nations Research Institute for Social Development (UNRISD). This concept was constructed by a group of scholars and practitioners who were studying community participation in a multi-country research effort in Latin America. They defined participation as 'the organized efforts to increase control over resources and regulative institutions in given social situations, on the part of groups and movements of those hitherto excluded from such control' (Stiefel and Wolfe 1994: 5).

Developed more than two decades ago, this definition has several enduring strengths and is particularly appropriate to post-apartheid South Africa. First, it highlights the empirical reality of the differences in political power within the society and the normative imperative for people who previously have been excluded from power to be involved in decisions affecting their lives.

Second, it does not limit the concept of participation by grassroots or community based organisations (CBOs) to 'reactive participation' in processes initiated by people from outside the community. In such reactive cases, previously excluded communities are 'target groups' who are being approached to concur in plans designed by others. Instead, the

UNRISD definition incorporates a variety of forms of participation that communities use to increase their control over decisions that affect them, ranging from co-operation in negotiations to disruption of initiatives sponsored by government or corporations. As a policy-oriented report on development pointed out, 'Dissent is at the heart of *participation*, for participation must imply the right to say to the establishment in all spheres – "yes" or "no" or "but" ' (South Commission 1990: 116, quoted in Stiefel and Wolfe).

What types of participation are possible and effective, however, is shaped both by the newly democratised political space of South Africa, by the interplay of race and class, and by the nation's accelerating reintegration into the global economy and polity, to which we turn now.

Impacts of the Transition to Democracy on South Durban

There are two elements of the transition to democracy in South Africa that have impacted on organising around environmental issues in South Durban. The first and obvious element is the universal franchise that has opened a new arena of political activity to the previously excluded majority. Black communities of South Durban have formal representation in city governance for the first time, including some councillors who are elected to represent wards.

At the national level, following the overwhelming electoral victory of the African National Congress (ANC) in April 1994, the party appointed ministers to head most of the departments of national government, thereby creating the possibility of greater responsiveness to the interests of the black majority. These appointments included Kader Asmal as Minister of Water Affairs and Forestry in 1994 and Pallo Jordan as Minister of Environmental Affairs and Tourism in 1996 after the National Party left the Government of National Unity (GNU). The bureaucracy in those departments changed little, however, because of the constitutional guarantee that civil servants would retain their positions for five years from 1994.

Second, South Africa's new democracy increased the political space for civil society. The White Paper on the Reconstruction and Development Programme (RDP) adopted by the GNU promised a new role for civil society:

> The empowerment of institutions of civil society is a fundamental aim of the government's approach to building national consensus. Through this process the Government aims to draw on the creative energy of communities. Structured consultation processes at all levels

> of government will be introduced to ensure participation in policy-making and planning, as well as project implementation (White Paper: Chapter 7).

During the long anti-apartheid struggle, the union movement, civic associations, and other mass democratic organisations alongside the ANC had claimed new political space for civil society. After the election, the ANC committed itself to participatory democracy in order to maintain political support from these constituencies that had played a crucial role in waging the struggle that brought it to power.

At the national level, the commitment to popular democracy was expressed in the formation of many consultative structures on various policy issues, including, most significantly, the National Economic Development and Labour Council (NEDLAC) as well as the Consultative National Environmental Policy Process (CONNEPP). With the election of President Mbeki in 1999, new ministers and deputy ministers were named to posts with responsibility for the environment, along with many other new staff appointments. Openness to input from civil society has been created over time, but has also been difficult to sustain.

In August 1994, the Durban City Council pro-actively committed itself to community participation in its environmental policy when it adopted Local Agenda 21, the programme for local governments developed by the United Nations Conference on the Environment and Development (UNCED) in Rio in 1992. The resolution pledged to institute 'a campaign . . . to develop a municipal environmental strategy and action plan which incorporates the principles of sustainable development, integrated environmental management and community participation'. Durban's Environmental Manager committed the city to 'a people-centered process that provides meaningful opportunities to develop partnerships for change at a local government level . . .' (ICLEI 1995).

Many consultative forums were established in South Durban, following the pattern of creating structures of consultation between government and civil society both at the national level and in the city of Durban.

Impacts of Globalisation on South Durban

First, we consider the impacts of globalisation – economic, political, and cultural – on South African environmental regulation and management and on community participation. Then we describe how these affect South Durban and the environmental struggles of communities there.[3]

The first impact of globalisation on South Africa results from its accelerating economic integration into the world economy. For several decades, broad, worldwide trends have seen international trade and direct foreign investment grow significantly. Distinctive in the more recent era is the centralisation of transnational finance and the vast expansion and new forms of cross-border operations of transnational corporations such as through leases, subcontracting, and joint ventures.

Economic globalisation in South Africa is not new. From the nineteenth century beginnings of mining on the Rand, South Africa's economy has been international, receiving both finance and technology from abroad. The Dutch Waal Straat of Cape Town and Wall Street in Manhattan symbolise the early capitalist incorporation of both societies. Since its beginnings in the nineteenth century, South Africa's petroleum refining has been integrated with the transnational petroleum industry. One of the refineries in South Durban was built in 1954 by Standard Vacuum Oil Company (later Mobil Oil) of the United States. The neighbouring Sapref refinery is jointly operated by BP Amoco (formerly British Petroleum) and the Anglo-Dutch based Shell Oil, and other petrochemical corporations are transnational.

For many governments, economic globalisation has meant implementing neoliberal economic policies that open their countries to foreign trade and investment. Two current nodes of these policies are the General Agreement on Tariffs and Trade (GATT) negotiations on international trade through the World Trade Organisation and the presently stalled negotiations on the Multinational Agreement on Investment that would severely limit the ability of states to regulate foreign investment. Also, a worldwide system of self-regulated corporate environmental management termed ISO 14000 has been negotiated through the International Organisation for Standardisation (ISO). (ISO 14000 does not create international emissions standards but rather calls for voluntary plans for which the only standards are the laws of the host country.)

Macro-economic policy is also markedly affected by globalisation. The government's Growth, Employment and Redistribution (GEAR) policy 'closely shadows the International Monetary Fund's (IMF) commandments' (Ryan 1996), involving liberalisation of finance, labour, and trade markets and reducing the government deficit (which requires cuts in social spending). Government officials presented these policies as the only realistic option and South African Director General of Finance Maria Ramos justifies GEAR as 'a very standard framework in other countries undergoing transition' (Wackernagel 1997). However, to many critics, including a host of NGOs that coalesced in the Campaign against Neoliberalism in South Africa, following the standard IMF formula is precisely the problem (Campaign against Neoliberalism in South Africa 1996). Criticism centres on the poor prospects of the GEAR policy for meeting the goals of the ANC Reconstruction and Development Programme in creating jobs and addressing basic needs of the impoverished.

Indeed, the number of jobs in manufacturing has declined despite an expansion of output under GEAR, including jobs in the petro-chemicals industry in South Durban. For example, Hoechst cut jobs when it redesigned and expanded its Wentworth facility, and Engen has eliminated 30 per cent of its maintenance positions. Citywide, Durban had 30–40 per cent unemployment and had lost about 23 per cent of its manufacturing jobs – 10 000 per year for four years – despite a vast injection of capital in the period 1993–98 (Canning 2001).

Globalisation has brought a shift in the industrialisation strategy of many countries from import substitution of the 1970s to the export promotion of the 1980s and 1990s. In South Africa, three policy initiatives are being implemented by the Department of Trade and Industry (DTI) to encourage both sales to the global market and investment by transnational corporations. First, in 1997–98, DTI proposed eight Spatial Development Initiatives (SDIs), regional corridors where incentives are designed to attract new investment, particularly from abroad. These incentives include accelerated depreciation and tax holidays, reduced national and municipal regulation, and municipal services provided at reduced costs. Second, some of these SDIs include Industrial Development Zones (IDZs) designed to 'crowd in' industrial development to make efficient use of infrastructure.[4] An IDZ has been proposed for South Durban in the area now used for railway marshalling yards. Liberalisation of the economy can also reduce foreign sales and income as was seen in Durban with the end of a mini-export boom after export subsidies were removed post-1995 (Valodia 1999: 86) and after ending of protective tariffs for South Africa's textile industry in KwaZulu-Natal.

Third, several industrial cluster investments are planned in which government and business leaders in a particular industry co-operate to develop a strategy to be internationally competitive. One such cluster is in the petro-chemicals industry. 'Project 2003', a joint venture between Sasol Polymer (formerly Polifin), a South African company, and a major foreign petro-chemicals company, would centre on a R7–8 billion ethylene cracker. It would increase production of ethylene to meet an impending shortage for downstream polymer plants in South Africa and for export. South Durban was one of the two possible locations for this investment, with feedstock scheduled to come from the Sapref refinery, which is planning a more than R1 billion expansion. South Durban's main advantage is its low transportation and labour costs and its proximity to the port. However, following the Asian economic crisis of the late 1990s, softened demand and a new plant in Malaysia reduced export demand for the proposed new South African plant, the ethylene cracker was deemed not viable until at least 2005.

Most globalisation theorists posit that the increased integration of the global economy has reduced the power of the state (Waters 1995: 98). Global production and exchange are increasingly conducted across borders and outside the control of nation states. The nature, scope, and capacity of the state have changed, and its regulatory ability has been reduced in some spheres (Held and McGrew 1994).

> Governments no longer possess the autonomy to pursue independent macroeconomic strategies effectively, even if they were to seek to do so (Garrett and Lange 1991: 543, quoted in Held and McGrew).

However, the state continues to have essential – and contradictory – functions: (1) to provide infrastructure and a stable regulatory environment for private corporations; and (2) to maintain some level of social welfare and natural environment that will support human habitation and economic production (Gould et al. 1996).

In the current period, the South African government reflects these contradictory roles. While it has increased the political space for civil society, it must also respond to pressures from the large South African based corporations that continue to dominate the economy (many of which are transnational in their own right) and from international financial institutions. The transition to democracy has given the state broader legitimacy for the first time, increasing its political authority nationally and internationally. But simultaneously, globalisation is decreasing the range of possible actions open to the state if its interests conflict with global interests. This trend is recognised by the progressive environmental movement in South Africa:

> The present government has not only inherited a colonial and apartheid past, it finds itself in a rapidly globalizing world in which its ability to act in the interests of the poor will increasingly come

into conflict with powerful international neoliberal economic forces whereby people and their environments become mere tradable commodities (Albertyn 1998).

The increased integration of the global economy with the dramatic development of electronic technologies has facilitated the rapid spread of information. The media organs of the powerful core nations disseminate norms of taste and style, material consumption, and economic organisation. The global information systems also afford opportunities for more and faster communication among people, including environmentalists who are organising against the messages and norms of powerful political and economic institutions. During the past two decades, a global environmental consciousness and movement has grown in many countries (Yearley 1996). It has been expressed in several different elements focusing on 'green' issues, global ecology, sustainable development, Local Agenda 21 community participation, and environmental justice issues.

A first element of global environmentalism focuses on global ecology, especially the issues of global warming, ozone depletion, and loss of biodiversity. This element includes problems that primarily have transborder effects and not those local issues that predominantly affect poor people such as contaminated fresh water or pollution from industries and waste sites located near human settlements. These global ecological issues are the focus of a number of international organisations including the World Bank.

A second element focuses on the green environment and wildlife conservation. This perspective has a long history in South Africa and is still reflected in the many 'green' organisations mobilised for wildlife preservation, parks, and recycling. This element is also found in the budget and policy priorities of the Department of Environmental Affairs and Tourism and provincial governments including KwaZulu-Natal, as well as in municipal greenspace programmes such as D'MOSS in Durban. Many of these are actively supported by major South African corporations. In South Durban, this concern is reflected in efforts to rehabilitate the Isipingo River estuary, in the Coastal Zone Management project, and in Keep Durban Beautiful programmes.

A third global environmental element centres on the concept of sustainable development, which attempts to define a way to mitigate the impacts of development and its attendant pollution on the environment while allowing for continued economic expansion. This perspective on global environmental problems was first popularised in

1987 in the Brundtland Report, 'Our Common Future', which posits a common human interest in the environment and downplays differences in class interests. A concomitant commitment to sustainable development was adopted by many governments and NGOs at the 1992 UNCED conference. Local Agenda 21 focuses on the role of local government and gives legitimacy to the participation of affected communities in addressing industrial development and pollution; however, the bias of Local Agenda 21 is for voluntaristic forums combining communities, corporations, and local governments, and this has been adopted by the Metro Councils of Cape Town and Johannesburg, as well as Durban.

A fourth global element focuses on environmental justice for human communities. This element concerns environmental issues that disproportionately affect the poor and people of colour, such as those who have been dispossessed from their natural heritage of land and those who live in an unhealthy environment despoiled by industrial pollution. It includes: (1) the movement against environmental racism in the United States; (2) organisations in South Africa such as the Environmental Justice Networking Forum (EJNF), EarthLife Africa, groundWork, and the Group for Environmental Monitoring; and (3) community based environmental mobilisations in South Durban, such as the South Durban Community Environmental Alliance (SDCEA). (Somewhat similar organisations have organised in other major South African cities.)

The South African government has been affected to varying degrees by all four of these elements of the emerging global culture of environmentalism. The Department of Environmental Affairs and Tourism (DEAT) has embraced the rhetoric of sustainable development, but this policy stance by the department responsible for environmental protection has had minimal influence over the government's industrial policy. As part of South Africa's priority to become more integrated into the global economy, the government has recently adopted some environmental regulations modelled after those in industrial countries. One example is in requiring mandatory environmental impact assessments (EIAs) under the National Environmental Management Act (NEMA) for new investments and for waste landfills.

The legal framework, budget resources, and culture of enforcement of environmental protection have changed very little, however. For example, little progress has been made on tightening industrial pollution standards or on enforcing them. Instead, the National Environmental Management Act, 107 of 1998, (<http://www.environment.gov.za/nema/index.html>) endorses corporate self-regulation. This bill also grants new opportunities to environmental CBOs and NGOs and to individuals by giving them standing to bring legal suit against polluting companies although its provisions for the public's right to information remains weak.

Recent Community Participation in South Durban Environmental Issues

These two trends toward greater democratisation and growing environmental consciousness are both reflected in recent environmental organising in South Durban. Community organisations in South Durban have a long history of addressing environmental issues – both pollution and green issues. These efforts included a legal suit mounted in the 1950s by the white community of the Bluff against the Standard Vacuum refinery; efforts in the early 1990s by the Merebank Residents' Association (MRA) to reduce noise, odours, and air pollution; and community campaigns to rehabilitate the Isipingo River and estuary in the 1980s.

Before the advent of democracy in the 1990s, these campaigns were largely unsuccessful. The secrecy and security systems of the apartheid state prevented civic organisations from gaining information about industries or from mounting successful pressure on industry to reduce their pollution.

In the mid-1990s, CBOs increased their mobilising to address the pent-up demands for redress of environmental ills in South Durban. New arenas for community participation were created, reflecting the democratic trend of creating development forums and other consultative structures. New multi-stakeholder forums created in South Durban beginning in 1994 included: (1) the Engen refinery's Community Awareness and Emergency Response (CAER) Committee; (2) the Sulphur Dioxide Management Steering Committee (which incorporated community representatives during this period); (3) the Waste-tech Monitoring Committee concerning the hazardous waste site in the African township of Umlazi; (4) the South Durban Steering Committee on Environmental Management; (5) the Coastal Zone Management Committee; (6) the Isipingo River Catchment Management Committee; (7) several environmental impact assessments (for example, for the expansion of the Hoechst chemical plant); and (8) community participation in a broad Strategic Environmental Assessment addressing the entire industrial zone of South Durban.[5]

However, community participation was not limited to partaking in these forums. The CBOs directed their efforts for mitigating pollution at various corporate and political leaders. First, community organisations sought direct improvements from corporate managers, such as in the MRA seeking clean-up of Engen's noxious holding ponds and

Envirowatch's pressure on Mondi to reduce their dumping ash in wetlands. Second, they sought action by municipal and national government officials to enforce regulations and respond to toxic releases, such as the dumping of waste into the Isipingo River by numerous companies and even the local authority and the toxic fumes emanating from the Umlazi IV waste site. Third, they attempted to influence government policy makers to seek an overhaul of national environmental policy through CONNEPP and a revision of the inadequate national policy on petroleum refinery emissions. Changes in national government policy such as these could potentially provide direct relief to communities by mandating changes by industry. Furthermore, improved government policy could increase the information and channels available to CBOs and NGOs, strengthening their ability to address pollution at the local as well as national levels. Examples of the latter type of policies could include legislation that granted local communities the right to know about toxic chemical emissions from nearby industries or the right to file legal suit against polluters.

As the UNRISD researchers found in their studies of local participation in many countries, CBOs in South Durban's communities utilised many different strategies in organising against pollution. In some cases, CBOs co-operated with more powerful stakeholders. For example, the CBOs provided advice to policy makers through the consultants for the Coastal Zone Management Committee and monitored the dumping of waste into the Isipingo River as a part of the management committee initiated by the national Department of Water Affairs and Forestry (DWAF). In other cases, the CBOs selected strategies that emphasized their differences with other stakeholders. For example, they held public protests against the Umlazi IV hazardous waste site and threatened to boycott forums in which Engen participated until the Engen management agreed to produce a plan to reduce emissions at its refinery. CBOs went to considerable effort in seeking information from companies and government officials for use in either negotiations or protests. Seeking media attention for egregious pollution problems was another tactic they used. News stories of health problems in South Durban and major industrial accidents have been particularly important in gaining the attention of national leaders and of reinvigorating local activism. CBOs also devoted time to educating and mobilising residents in their communities to build their base of political support. They built multiracial co-operation among organisations from different South Durban communities by creating the SDCEA with Coloured, Indian, African, and white communities, represented by 10 CBOs and two

NGOs, with churches participating as well. The SDCEA was arguably the first and longest-standing multiracial community based co-operation against environmental degradation. To facilitate their lobbying on environmental policy, they built working relationships with experts on pollution, as well as with NGOs such as EJNF and Earthlife Africa in Durban, Cape Town, and Johannesburg. They sought political support and expertise from environmentalists abroad including Communities for a Better Environment in San Francisco, the South African Exchange Program on Environmental Justice in Boston, and two Danish instututions. Some CBOs also engaged in electoral politics. For example, the MRA put forward a candidate for City Council who would raise their concerns about pollution with city government. Other CBOs lobbied candidates or officials directly.

Among the many environmental issues that community organisations addressed during this period, we have selected three cases: (1) closing the Umlazi IV hazardous waste site; (2) reducing sulphur dioxide (SO_2) pollution from the Engen refinery; and (3) a Strategic Environmental Assessment of South Durban to address environmental problems and industrial expansion and its impacts. We will consider the various strategies of participation that communities utilised in these cases and explore how democracy and globalisation have affected the communities' ability to achieve influence over these policies and problems.

Case 1: Closing the Umlazi Waste Landfill

The closing of the Umlazi IV hazardous waste landfill provides a case of a significant environmental improvement in which community organisations played a decisive role – closing a poorly constructed and ill-managed hazardous waste site that was polluting communities and a river. CBOs adopted a mix of strategies – some honed in the anti-apartheid struggles and others used newly available strategies available from the transition to democracy and the impacts of globalisation.

The hazardous waste landfill was built in 1986 to accommodate all but the most toxic of industrial waste from Durban and, indeed, most of the KwaZulu-Natal Province. When it was built, there was virtually no effective government regulation of hazardous waste sites. The two British firms that jointly operated the site through Waste-tech (Pty) Ltd claimed that they applied British environmental standards to the site, but both the design and management were poor by Western standards. (These British companies sold their interests in the company in the late 1980s as the international economic sanctions campaign grew.)

Almost from the time the site opened, there were complaints about the noxious stench from the site from nearby residents, particularly from pupils and teachers at the largely Indian Isipingo Secondary School and the nearby African Shumayela Secondary School in Umlazi. For several years, the principal, teachers, and parents at the school in Isipingo had complained repeatedly to the company, the Durban Medical Officer of Health, the Indian House of Delegates, provincial authorities, and DWAF to no avail. On some mornings, classes at the school were dismissed when the nauseating odours were particularly bad. Residents of Umlazi, represented by a prominent African physician who had spent years on Robben Island and a lawyer leader of the Black Lawyers Association, repeatedly called for remediation.

In addition to the noxious fumes, after only four years, leachate from the site contaminated the groundwater even beyond the boundaries of the landfill, ebbing towards the nearby Isipingo River. Also, arsenic and mercury – chemicals too toxic to be legally deposited in this landfill – were found in the leachate. Clearly, these highly hazardous wastes were being illegally disposed there by industry rather than in the waste sites explicitly created for the most toxic wastes. This is not surprising when only five per cent of the country's estimated five million cubic metres of toxic waste created each year 'turned up at hazardous waste disposal sites' (Ballance and King 1999).

In 1992, DWAF began drafting new 'Minimum Requirements for Waste Disposal by Landfill', based on models of regulations from Western industrial countries. The regulations specified that, before licensing, the interested and affected parties (I&APs) must be consulted about siting or expanding any landfill. In the early 1990s, environmental organisations in South Durban communities, led by the Isipingo Environmental Committee, concluded that requests for remediation had failed after dozens of complaints over the years and that the only solution was to close the site. In early 1995, when they learned through the mandated process of informing and consulting with I&APs that Waste-tech planned to enlarge the site and to extend its life for another decade, CBOs intensified their efforts to close the site. They were invited to sit on a monitoring committee to advise DWAF on whether to grant Waste-tech a licence to expand the site. This invitation posed a dilemma for organisations since they had already taken the position that the site should be closed.

CBOs alternately chose negotiations and protest politics according to changing circumstances. In mid-1995, approximately 1 000 Isipingo residents held a public demonstration to call for closing the landfill. This action drew the attention of DWAF to the poor management of the site. DWAF Minister Kader Asmal came to visit the site, where he was met by community activists who brought a group of international environmental impact assessment specialists meeting in Durban at the time. Soon thereafter, he issued a statement that, if possible, the site should be closed within six months.

The decision-making about the site took many twists and turns. After DWAF confirmed that it would not grant a licence for expanding the site and that its closure was certain (even if the date of closure was not), the CBOs agreed to participate in the Umlazi IV Landfill Closure and Rehabilitation Committee with a neutral facilitator hired by DWAF. DWAF regarded this committee as important, not only because of its role regarding this troubled site, but also because this was the first test of consulting I&APs under its new Minimum Requirements policy.

All the stakeholders agreed on a strikingly expansive mandate for this committee: to 'jointly decide, negotiate, monitor and evaluate matters relating to pre- and post-closure including the management of the landfill site'. Because it gave them clear authority in decisions about the waste site, this language was regarded as a model mandate by South Durban CBOs participating in a multi-stakeholder consultative body and by CBOs working on hazardous waste sites elsewhere in the country. In the end, however, the committee did not have the opportunity to fulfill this mandate.

In the committee, CBO representatives still had to fight to obtain information about site operations, company plans, and DWAF's policy. In frustration, CBOs organised more demonstrations calling for the site to be closed. Finally, they decided to hold a demonstration at the Waste-tech headquarters in Isipingo, where African Waste-tech employees, convinced by management that their jobs were at stake, threw rocks threatening the safety of the demonstrating Indian school children. In response to this heightened tension and without waiting for the committee to suggest a timetable for closure, Minister Asmal announced that the site definitely would be closed within six months. While some committee members objected to Asmal's unilateral action, CBO and environmental NGO leaders were pleased that their goal of closing the site finally was to be achieved.

The company – now named Enviroserv after merging with South Africa's other major waste company – was vulnerable to having its landfill closed for several reasons. Its poor management of the site, particularly the contamination of groundwater, made it very difficult for DWAF to support its plans for expansion. The original location of the landfill amidst residential communities during the apartheid era was also indefensible, and it violated the new Minimum Requirements regulations for separation from communities.

The Minimum Requirements, which reflected both the transition to democracy and the impact of global standards concerning environmental assessment, gave new leverage to CBOs. The CBOs sought to take advantage of this new tool of political participation but did not abandon protest politics, because the effectiveness of this new form of consultation was far from assured. This mix of negotiating and protest strategies allowed the CBOs to be heard by government authorities, who finally decided the case in their favour. CBOs' watchfulness and readiness to use multiple strategies continued to be needed even two years after the Minister's decision when CBOs learned that ash from the Mondi paper mill in Merebank that no longer could be deposited near their plant due to pressure from another CBO environmental organisation, Envirowatch, was now being trucked to the Umlazi waste site without consulting members of the monitoring committee.

Case 2: Demands that the Engen Refinery Reduce its Pollution

For years, the petroleum refinery, now operated by Engen, has been the largest single source of air pollution in South Durban and, after long campaigns by communities, a symbol of dirty industry in Durban. The company's response to the long years of community protests has been a story of the arrogance of corporate power and of the pro-industry bias of government. Surprisingly, in 1998, an agreement for reducing pollution was finally negotiated between the CBOs and Engen. Both South Africa's transition to democracy and its economic and political integration into the global system contributed to the gradually changing political context in which this agreement could occur.

The refinery is located directly across the street from two communities, Indian Merebank and Coloured Wentworth, and the prevailing winds often blow oil sprays, particulates, and smells northeastward to the white Bluff community as well. The facility was opened in 1954 by Standard Vacuum Oil Company of the United States, which later became Mobil Oil, as the first refinery in South Africa. Mobil decided to leave South Africa during the international sanctions campaign. In 1989, it rejected a more lucrative offer from a black consortium and sold the refinery to a white South African firm with Mobil's top manager as Chief Executive Officer. In 1996 when the company needed more working capital, Petronas, the state-owned petroleum company of Malaysia, bought a 30 per cent controlling interest in the company. By 2000, Petronas owned 80 per cent of the company, with the other 20 per cent held by Worldwide Africa Investment Holdings (Mbendi 2001).

The site also contains the works of Safor, a lubricating base oil refinery owned jointly by Engen, Caltex, and Total. The barbed and razor wire fence and imposing guard towers that surround this facility attest to its strategic importance during the apartheid era. The apartheid regime protected the oil industry, designating refineries as highly secret 'National Key Points'. Indeed, on 13 May 1984, an ANC unit carried out a grenade attack on this refinery as part of its sabotage campaign (Cowell 1984). The apartheid government's primary interest was in protecting its security and industrial capacity and decidedly not in safeguarding nearby residents or the natural environment from industrial pollution. For example, legislation governing air pollution, contained in the Atmospheric Pollution Prevention Act 45 of 1965, had woefully weak standards with trivial and ineffective sanctions for violations. The system of inspections and enforcement was then, and still is, inadequate, subjective, and lacking in transparency (Petrie 1992). Not only did the apartheid government afford no protection to people affected by pollution, but it restricted their capacity to seek redress. According to the refinery management, the Official Secrets Act 'prevented us from dealing at any level with the public about the business'.[6]

Despite the political constraints of working under the Nationalist government, CBOs mounted protracted protest against the refinery from the beginning of its construction in 1954. At that time, the Bluff Amenities Protection Association opposed the granting of the Manufacturer's Licence to the company and quickly complained to local councillors, members of parliament, and national government about its pollution. More than 1 000 people attended public meetings in the Bluff, and physicians there documented evidence of health complaints and dangers. People inside and outside Engen have commented that the Mobil management at the refinery was generally unresponsive to concerns of the community. As one corporate executive commented, 'It was a paternalistic American culture.' Indeed, in 2000, wives of former employees had lawsuits against the company for the death of their husbands from Engen-tolerated pollution (Paul Kirk, *Weekly Mail and Guardian*, 15–21.09.2000).

In 1989, when the refinery changed ownership, the MRA met with the new management and gained an agreement to clean up the noxious holding ponds and to build a wall to shield Merebank partially from a view of the facility. (The local authority and national DWAF had already pressed Engen to improve its management of the ponds.) In 2001, the ponds still occasioned complaints from residents. No progress was made, however, on the more serious issue of air pollution, which according to surveys many residents believed was causing health problems, including cancer (Wiley et al. 1996).

Soon after the April 1994 election, the refinery managers invited selected residents from Merebank, the Bluff, and Wentworth to join a Community Awareness and Emergency Response (CAER) Committee. The model for this committee came from the North American petrochemicals industry, where companies were concerned about their image in neighbouring communities after serious accidents in Bhopal (India) and West Virginia. Engen's forming of the CAER Committee – a voluntary, consultative structure between management and communities – fits the company's strategy at that time of publically identifying itself with change in South Africa. This was also evident in Engen's statements supporting the RDP and its advertising slogan, 'We're South African; We Care' and its many sponsorings of 'clean' sporting events.

At a CAER committee meeting a few months later, Engen explained that it wanted an agreement signed and a committee chairperson elected three months before President Mandela was to arrive to dedicate an expansion of the refinery that would enable Engen to enlarge its operations in Africa. The CBOs realised that Mandela's planned visit gave them a unique point of leverage. They presented a detailed new draft agreement to Engen that would require the company to commit to releasing information and to reducing emissions. Like Engen's CAER strategy, the CBOs used a model from abroad – developed by community groups at a refinery near Chicago, Illinois – for this proposed 'Good Neighbour Agreement'. Engen did not respond to the communities' proposal before Mandela's visit.

The CBOs turned President Mandela's visit to their advantage, organising a major demonstration at the refinery gate. As a result, Mandela stopped, met with their representatives that evening, and then called a larger second meeting, bringing together the CBOs, several cabinet ministers, and senior Engen executives. He urged them to work together to address the pollution problems, and the Engen CEO pledged that the company had the intent, the will, and the resources to address the problems.

Over the course of numerous meetings between Engen and the CBOs, in addition to several consultations facilitated by a DEAT official, the two sides were at a standstill. Engen intermittently rejected the legitimacy of designated CBO representatives and officers and selected other residents who they thought would be more compliant to attend their forums. Engen also continued to insist that its emissions were within the limits of their DEAT licence and that the view of many neighbouring residents that Engen's emissions were damaging to their health did not constitute proof, but only 'community perceptions'. Therefore, they persisted in their refusal to act unilaterally to invest in cleaner technology.

Instead, Engen demanded it would only take actions required by the Sulphur Dioxide Management Steering Committee of all the major SO_2 emitters in Durban. Founded in the 1980s, this committee consisted of corporations in South Durban with local and national government; then in 1995 the CBOs were added. That committee had designed a voluntary management system using a computer-generated 'Bluff Valley Model' (sometimes termed a 'Hawk model') whereby the major SO_2 emitters planned to burn low-sulphur fuel when atmospheric conditions inhibited dispersion of pollution, such as occurred often during winter inversions; however, no progress was made in this committee in actually reducing air pollution. After more than four years of discussing a management plan, committee members reached no agreement. During expected inversions of winter 1996, when some companies, including Sapref, agreed to respond to the committee's requests to burn cleaner fuel, Engen refused to comply.

Faced with this intransigence by Engen, the CBOs threatened to boycott any forum in which Engen participated. In addition, they threatened to take legal action against the company unless it agreed to develop a five-year plan to significantly reduce its SO_2 emissions. In late 1997, Engen told the CBOs that it was planning to adopt a multi-year SO_2 reduction plan as part of a broader environmental improvement plan. In March 1998, exactly three years after President Mandela had been greeted by protesters at Engen's gates, Engen and the CBOs reached an 'agreement in principle' on a plan which the CBOs believed would result in meaningful improvements. More than a year later, in May 1999, this agreement, the 'Engen Refinery Complex Environmental Improvement Programme', was approved by the DEAT, in what was reported as the first voluntary agreement between industry and civil society 'within the spirit of the National Environmental Management Act of 1998' (Challenor 1999). This voluntary agreement was signed into the permit, making it legally binding upon Engen, thus making Engen potentially liable to legal challenge from government if it did not meet the targets. The plan promises within five years a 65 per cent reduction in the SO_2 permit level (which represents the maximum daily emissions allowable) and also begins to address reductions in other pollutants.

What explains the long intransigence of the refinery management and then its decision to negotiate a pollution reduction plan with CBOs? Community organising against Mobil had almost no effect when the company was protected by the apartheid government, and the slowly growing international norms of environmental protection from industrial pollution held almost no sway in that government.

When the ANC came to power in 1994, the Engen management sought to establish close relations with the new government and at least to appear open to hearing concerns of the nearby communities. During the next two years, however, the company did not respond to the CBO concerns about pollution. Engen may have believed that it did not need to act because the government priority on the neoliberal macro-economic GEAR policy ran counter to investing in pollution control and imposing the costs of cleaner production on industry. The DEAT was not moving to tighten national air pollution policy. Thus, Engen was still shielded from community demands by simply asserting that it was complying with the letter of government policy.

Globalisation had ambiguous effects, however. Through global contacts, the CBOs gained useful information, allies, and resources. The CBOs were able to bring international standards into the debate, asserting that Engen's emissions were approximately 10 times what would be allowed in the US. Engen spent considerable money and time trying to undercut this argument by conducting research on the policies of nations which allowed higher pollution levels and more lax enforcement procedures than those in the US.

Over time, however, Engen perceived that reaching an agreement with the CBOs was in its interest. The national and local media covered the persistent protests by the South Durban CBOs concerning Engen's pollution, Engen's non-responsiveness to the communities, and the negative comparisons of Engen's emission with refineries abroad (see the major series in the *Natal Mercury* in September 2000). This eroded the corporate image which it was spending millions to create. The company was also increasingly isolated as other companies in the SO_2 Management Steering Committee developed pollution-reduction plans and voluntarily complied with the Bluff Valley Model, while Engen refused to do either. Also, CBOs concerned with refinery pollution in both South Durban, Cape Town, and Sasolburg had pressured the DEAT to consider setting tighter standards for refinery emissions, so there was a possibility of new pressures from government. (This process began to make serious progress only in 2001.) In addition, the petroleum industry had been told that, consonant with its new neoliberal agenda, government was planning to reduce regulation of their prices and imports. As a result, with rising demand for petroleum products, Engen could expect that its profits would increase, allowing it to accede to community demands and invest more easily in cleaner technology.

Case 3: Addressing Industrial Expansion in South Durban and its Environmental Impacts

While our two previous case studies concern the participation of South Durban's communities in mitigating pollution from existing industries, this third case focuses on their participation in a strategic assessment of the environmental impacts of industry and its proposed expansion in the years ahead. This case resulted from a long-awaited effort of the Durban Metro government to develop an assessment of the ecology of South Durban, its current social, economic, and environmental problems, and its plans for future development. Unlike the previous cases, this project was intended to bring all South Durban stakeholders – communities, industry, and government agencies – to the table for assessment and planning. It was made more urgent by a series of proposals for expanding South Durban industry (which would require individual environmental impact assessments) and mooted plans for an SDI or IDZ for Durban.[7] In a nation urgently needing to generate new investment and employment in response to the pent-up demand of the poor and the net job losses due to global competition, government put high priority on new industrial investment.

South Africa's integration into the global system has complex and ambiguous effects on processes of planning industrial development. On the one hand, economic globalisation requires expansion in an increasingly competitive world market, and economic planning to meet this challenge has become increasingly centralised. On the other hand, cultural globalisation, with access to massive new levels of information and international communication, brings a heightened consciousness about the environment, reinforces the legitimacy of local demands for environmental protection, and encourages community input into environmental assessment. These demands are consistent with the national trend toward democratisation, public consultation, and the requirements of the NEMA. At the same time, South African government and private institutions have been increasingly incorporated into the recent global cultures of environmental sustainability through the Local Agenda 21 and other programmes of development planning and impact assessment.

Three overlapping developments in South Durban reveal how the conflict in interests between economic growth and the environment of communities is being played out: (1) the Strategic Environmental Assessment (SEA) for the region and a number of recent EIAs of plans for corporate expansion; (2) plans by national government to promote industry in Durban through a Spatial Development Initiative (SDI); and (3) plans by national government for a petro-chemicals cluster which may be located in South Durban, all of which were addressed in the SEA in 1996 and released in final draft form in 1999. Now, such planned analysis and public participation is required under the NEMA.

In 1992, South Durban CBOs, initially the MRA, requested a strategic environmental assessment of the entire South Durban zone of industries and communities. Concerned about the growing toxic emissions in the basin, the MRA had demanded a moratorium on industrial expansions and new investments until this SEA was completed.

In 1996, having completed the Local Agenda 21 study which identified South Durban as a 'hotspot', the Durban Metro Council and South Central Local Council commissioned the SEA and contracted with CSIR and a team of independent consultants to conduct the assessment. The SEA study was originally conceptualised as dealing with the environmental concerns that the communities had been raising in the new democratic South Africa to improve their quality of life and to propose a strategy of sustainable development to minimise and manage the problems.[8]

But there was continuing difference of emphasis and expectation from the study managers and some of the stakeholders. While the communities continually pressed for careful assessments of pollution and health with higher standards than those inherited from the apartheid era and for financing of outside experts and community facilitation, the study team emphasized that, in spite of the different perceptions, 'the brief of the SEA . . . was a macro level study indicating likely constraints and opportunities for development in the Durban South Basin.'[9] Indeed, the Metro Council had said it wanted 'to resolve the conflict between industrial and local community needs'. This bifurcation of SEA goals reflected the division of power in South Durban – of a number of industries that together produce five per cent of the Gross National Product; of local government and other local institutions who have important alliances predominantly with industry while reporting to a local council elected by communities; and of communities that were relocated there against their will but who now have support from the Constitution, the party in power, and the elements of the wider global community for addressing pent-up community environmental needs.

The Metro allotted R2 million to this ambitious SEA project, which produced a large final report in 1999 supported by 50 other sub-reports, most by contracted consultants. This was the first time that the city had given serious attention to the full range of South Durban stakeholders and to the many social, economic, infrastructural, and pollution issues of the zone. In spite of the fact that the SEA commissioned no new basic research on the problems, the study did assemble much data and highlighted the large number of problems in the region, including the apparent saturation of air pollution (even allowing for the much higher amounts of SO_2 allowed by South African national standards than those of the World Health Organisation); the hazardous industrial traffic through neighborhoods by tankers with dangerous chemicals; the lack of industrial safety precautions for the communities; the faecal and industrial pollution of South Durban's Umbilo, Umlazi, and Isipingo Rivers; the decline of marine and riverine species and water quality; the high rates of unemployment and poverty in the communities (related to the rise of petro-chemicals and the decline of the textile industry); the problems of security and crime; and the high levels of hazardous and other solid waste produced in the basin. The SEA also included a large number of comments from I&APs.

In an appendix, the study provided a 36-page list of actions that could be taken to address many of the problems to increase services to industry and communities, reduce pollution, buffer industry and communities, and improve the quality of life and productivity. For each action needed, the metro agency responsible was listed along with the needed linkages with other metro, provincial, and national departments and agencies to address the issues.

The process of co-operation between the managers of the study and their consultants, on the one hand, and the communities on the other did not proceed well, and there were many differences of approach, understanding, and conclusion that separated the two at the end of the study. Because of these conflicts, tensions, and the difficulties of the SEA consultants in achieving participation they wanted from the communities, the SEA management team concluded that the current forms of participation should be altered. Instead of working with and through an environmental alliance of communities, the SEA report proposed to seek 'community involvement' instead of more powerful 'participation' in order to fast-track potential investors in Durban development projects. In the future, it is proposed, public participation will be institutionalised in 'a recognised structure of local government to prevent the haphazard and piecemeal methods' and to provide a 'One-

Stop-Shop' for developers and for planning and development assessments (CSIR 1999: 36).

What explains the tensions that resulted in this apparent separation, if not divorce, of the parties involved in the SEA, including what is probably South Africa's most advanced Metro government in dealing with the environment and the most capacitated, broadly focused, and well organised local multiracial environmental movement in the country?

First was the perception of many in local government and its allies that public participation was not productive with contentious communities and leaders. Although it was acknowledged that the communities had been moved to South Durban against their will and with bad city planning of housing and industry, the local communities were now often defined as 'the problem' and the limiters of development because of their objections to unhealthy emissions, rather than identifying excessive pollution by industry as the problem. The SEA report asserted:

> . . . (the) residents . . . were forced to suffer negative environmental impacts associated with the generation of wealth for the region. This has caused extreme dissatisfaction on the part of many residents with regard to current living conditions. As a result, community action has and will continue to place severe constraints on future industrial development in the Durban South Basin unless the situation is effectively resolved (CSIR 1999: v).

The communities and SDCEA proved to be independent and critical of the SEA processes. They criticised the SEA allotment of more than half of the total communication participation budget to consultants, rather than to the capacitation of the communities and the participation and facilitation expenses of the SDCEA, which had first raised the issues. And the SDCEA complained about the lack of transparency and of financial accountability.

There is a long tradition of Durban government using consultants for a wide variety of assessments and delivery of services. Many consultants and government officials believe that consultants are needed because government agencies do not have the staff to complete the work, especially for public participation, which they presume can become so protracted that it interferes with 'service delivery'. Even though many consultants are pleasant and even pro-community individuals, many CBOs have grown irritated with 'consultant-driven processes' in which they believe that information is collected from residents under lucrative contracts and delivered to government, leaving little benefit or capacitation for the communities. One CBO leader, who participated in the SEA and also in seven EIAs for individual investment projects, told us:

> We have a history with EIAs of well-paid consultants coming in and spending hours/days of valuable community leisure time extracting information and concerns and then watering these down in the final analysis to present to authority. The community then spends its time contesting these findings.

In the face of limited resources from the city, the SDCEA obtained support from the Danish Nature Foundation and Danish Cooperation on Environment and Development, with which the communities made 10 formal written submissions to the SEA on various issues, a product that few environmental movements around the world could muster.

The communities also voiced many substantive differences with the SEA study (SDCEA 1999). They criticised using only weak South African air pollution standards rather than more widely accepted international standards; about limiting pollution comments primarily to SO_2 and excluding volatile organic compounds (VOCs) and heavy metals; and excluding African Umlazi, Clairwood, and Lamontville, as well as the Island View petroleum complex and harbour which are of great concern to residents of the Bluff. The communities also perceived a favouritism toward industry of the CSIR and the SEA team and an inattention to enforcement and penalties for polluters. They especially saw that favouritism when the SDCEA's written proposal for a mixed-used option for South Durban (of additional housing and light industry) was dismissed in favour of a purely industrial option. Perhaps most acutely opposed was the suggestion that sustainability for South Durban could be achieve only by choosing a petro-chemical or harbour future for the basin (achievable only by voluntary, or perhaps forced, movement of residents), without any analysis of the economic and employment benefits, the human, social, cultural, and economic costs of relocating the communities, or the issues of environmental justice involved. Finally, there were complaints that there was insufficient reportback to communities.

The communities were very frustrated with the study's conclusions on air pollution – an issue they had focused on for years. The SEA's air quality assessment admitted that '. . . there exists no formalised and systematic reduction strategy' for South Durban air pollution. In addition, the SEA had no measurements of the many pollution particulates, of carcinogenous benzene (recently found in an air sample near Merebank's Settlers Primary School taken by the 'Bucket Brigade' organised with assistance from Communities for a Better Environment from San Francisco), and of other suspected VOCs (Carnie 2000a). During the study, the communities knew that there was evidence that SO_2 average loads exceeded World Health Organisation (WHO) guidelines by a factor of two to four, that SO_2 emissions had long been misreported by SAPREF (which SAPREF admitted soon after the SEA was completed), and that the concentrations often peak at very high levels (Cooper 2000). Furthermore, the communities, black and white, had a strong conviction that lung dysfunction, asthma, and cancer have resulted from a wide variety of pollutants in Bluff, Merebank, and Wentworth. Based on a six-week informal research project sponsored by the *Natal Mercury* and *Business Report*, Dr Duane Blauw, a public health specialist at the University of Natal Medical School, estimated that leukaemia (blood cancer) in young children was 24 times higher than elsewhere in South Africa. (Carnie 2000b) Yet without health or epidemiological research in hand, the SEA report concludes on the 'Living Environment Sector' that

> . . . the impacts on the Durban South Basin are complex and cumulative. This results in a composite of sometimes relatively minor impacts which, when added together, detract significantly from the quality for life of residents . . . Research has shown that, for the most part, this risk [to safety and health from hazardous industrial installations] has been well managed by major industrialists . . .

Mutual dissatisfaction between the local authority and the community representatives over participatory processes had grown to such an extent that co-operation became extremely difficult at this critical juncture when the future of South Durban was being considered. Several local authority officials complained that the CBO representatives were demanding, contentious, and placed needless barriers in the way of development. The feelings were accentuated by the racial cleavage between largely white, upper middle class study teams, managers, and consultants who are assessing and analysing largely poorer black communities. One long-time environmental leader observed:

> The more fundamental problem is that we are all so very polarised that even reasonable suggestions from communities are disregarded. We really need to spend much energy coming to a better understanding of different perspectives.

The substantive components of the SEA, like many other recent studies of South Durban, were desktop assessments because there was no funding to collect new data on pollution in the basin. As one CBO activist said of the SEA study: 'There is a tendency to restate the obvious with no new insights being gained. True ground-breaking research does not occur.'

By the time the SEA began, five years after the MRA's request, it may have been overtaken by plans of national and municipal government to attract investment to South Durban as part of an SDI and possibly a petro-chemical industry cluster. The attention to strategic environmental assessments, however, has also grown as the DEAT found the SEA useful as 'a process of integrating the concept of sustainability into strategic decision-making'[10] and built community participation into the new NEMA.

But the power in this SEA study lay with the goals of industry and the belief of the leadership that this might produce at least some new jobs, even though petro-chemical industries require fewer workers than many industries. South Durban residents, even with foreign funding and thousands of residents' hours of input, were severely challenged to counterbalance the demand for increased industry – regardless of its environmental and employment impacts – as the country seeks to survive in the storm of global competition.

The decision-making about the futures of the South Durban communities is not finished, and many of these decisions will be made in the political arena, not on the desktop. Other international and national voices may be heard in the debate as well. The crucial importance of leadership and vision was shown in May 2001, when the DEAT Minister Valli Moosa announced that the DEAT, which had been known for lax or no enforcement of air pollution and/or permit regulations in the 1990s, was 'moving headfast in dealing with air pollution in both Durban South and the entire country'(Ministry of Environmental Affairs and Tourism 2001). Moosa and DTI Minister Alec Erwin jointly announced intentions to mount: (1) a health risk analysis and epidemiological study to assess air pollution impacts on human health; (2) phasing out burning of coal and heavy fuel oil; (3) improved measurement of fugitive emissions of tank farms; (4) moving toward adopting the WHO standards on SO_2; (5) improved monitoring of SO_2, NO_x, and VOCs; and (6) strengthening enforcement capabilities. National political leadership, as also shown in President Mandela's 1995 visit, had the capability to cut through the complex conundrums of local affected parties to redefine the priorities.

Conclusion

The CBO campaigns that took place in South Durban in the second half of the 1990s showed that democratisation enlarged the political space for community participation. At last, black communities had become the constituents of all government structures, and their concerns gained a new legitimacy. The new Constitution even gives them – and all South Africans – the right 'not to be injured by their environment', and litigation against environmental nuisances and damages has a new validity under the NEMA, even though penalties remain astonishingly weak.

After the 1994 election, the government strongly encouraged consultation with civil society, and we have witnessed the resultant explosion in the number of consultative structures in South Durban. However, this participation was not undergirded by strong right-to-know legislation. (The Open Democracy Bill, which would give effect to Section 32(1)(b) of the Constitution, has not yet been passed.)

In this more democratic era, the state no longer protects corporations from public inspection. The companies know they *may* incur government attention if their environmental problems are extreme, even though national environmental regulations and budget for pollution monitoring and enforcement are still completely inadequate.[11] Mandatory EIAs have the potential to provide meaningful community input, but often companies and government view this process simply as a bothersome delay rather than a serious investigation of potentially negative environmental impacts of their investment plans, and communities often see the EIAs as rubber stamping development proposals.

Globalisation has heightened the attention to the environment on the part of government, corporations, NGOs, and communities. Government has adopted a number of environmental programmes from abroad and has sought advice on environmental issues from other industrial countries. Some corporations that operate in the global market-place seek the imprimatur of certification for complying with voluntary international environmental standards. CBOs have benefited from new information on pollution problems and standards from abroad, and they have been supported with foreign expertise and occasional funding. However, communities are rejecting new corporate programmes.[12]

Democratisation and globalisation have had many and sometimes contradictory influences on community participation in the three cases we studied. In the case of the Umlazi hazardous waste landfill, new mandates for consultation with I&APs – consistent with both democratisation and the global environmental culture – provided CBOs with important information about the plans of both the company and government, enabling them to make better-informed choices about their strategies. Joining the monitoring committee enhanced their legitimacy as representatives of communities with a long history of grievances. But it was public protest by CBOs that was most important in influencing DWAF's decision to close the hazardous waste landfill. While such protests may have alienated some government and corporate officials from CBOs, such actions demonstrated the seriousness of the CBOs' concerns, and they are a form of political expression that is protected by government.

The companies usually preferred to avoid what they term the 'culture of protest' from black communities that came from the mobilisations of the mass democratic movement in the 1980s. 'It is time for a culture of consultation, not of confrontation,' said one consultant, because confrontation alienates, interferes with, and retards 'delivery of these very services and development that the communities need'. Organisations in the black communities, however, often perceived that, even in the new South Africa, they are faced with powerful corporations, weak national regulation, bureaucrats who often continue their historical alliance and common culture with the companies, little information on complex pollution issues, limited financial resources to command legal or technical expertise, and, therefore, little power to achieve their interests. In such a situation, communities have needed to retain the option to boycott or disrupt consultative processes that they believe empower the already powerful and leave the less powerful weak.

Globalisation had ambiguous impacts on Engen. Its interests in expanding both exports and petroleum exploration throughout Africa and in demonstrating to national government that it was concerned about the environment finally led it to adopt an environmental improvement plan negotiated with the community and signed into the permit by government. In an era when the global culture of environmentalism is growing, Engen's continuing refusal to reduce its emissions damaged its corporate image, made it appear increasingly isolated among major South Durban companies, and increased the likelihood of pressure from national government. The CBOs' access to knowledge, expertise, and solidarity from both within South Africa and abroad also strengthened their campaign against Engen. Of decisive importance was the CBOs' perseverance in exerting pressure on Engen and in publicising its pollution, along with their willingness to continue to negotiate for more than three years.

Research with environmental activists in California and Louisiana,[13] as in South Durban, suggests that communities are more likely to succeed in campaigns focused on particular companies which have unusually bad pollution, extremely poor management, or accidents (for example, the Umlazi IV waste site and Engen Refinery). To succeed, CBOs must be open to a range of types of participation and must make tactical choices during each campaign, assessing the opportunities and constraints that they face at each particular juncture.

Success in campaigns to oppose new investments in heavily polluting industries (such as the plans for expansion of the petro-chemical industry in South Durban) are much more difficult to achieve. The interests of powerful economic actors – whose strategies are shaped by pressures from an increasingly competitive global economy – threaten to eclipse the interests of community residents seeking a cleaner environment.

In South Durban, CBOs became frustrated, sometimes exhausted, with the huge amount of unremunerated and after-hours work required for participating in environmental forums, EIAs, and the SEA which usually gave them little influence over major decisions about their environment. As CBOs observed that their agendas were not being addressed in many of these forums, they became less willing to co-operate. In addition, the repeated use of consultants by the local authority to organise participation by communities is seen increasingly by the CBOs as paternalistic, non-democratic, and accruing to the economic benefit of those professionals rather than these poorer and usually black, under-resourced communities. These dynamics have led to an atmosphere of growing distrust and suspicion between CBOs and the consultants, local authorities, and companies, which make it increasingly difficult for consultative processes to succeed.

Government policy at any particular time reflects the relative strength of contending political forces seeking to further their interests (Stifle and Wolfe 1994). In South Durban, the companies are seeking to expand in concert with the government economic strategy and have considerably greater influence than the communities affected by their pollution even when organised by experienced movements such as the SDCEA. Despite the political constraints of globalised economic policy, well-conceived participation by mobilised communities in some cases can tilt government in their favour. Even if those victories are unpredictable, sometimes only marginal, and almost always long in coming, they motivate CBOs to continue to demand their right to democratic participation and to work to improve the environment of the entire South Durban Basin. The challenge to this newly democratic government and its local authorities, as they seek to design a globally competitive city, is to bring these communities to the table to co-manage South Durban's development and environment in a way that rebalances the power between industry and the communities and insists on cleaner technology and good practice to make co-habitation possible – locally and internationally – in the global community.

NOTES

1. We use the racial categories adopted by the apartheid government because they have historical meaning and because the legacy of apartheid means that racial identify still significantly affects the residential and economic patterns of the country today. We use the term 'black' to refer to all African, Coloured and Indian people.
2. Research for this paper began in October 1994 in Durban with a 10-month period of intensive fieldwork as a portion of the case studies completed at the Institute for Social and Economic Research at the University of Durban-Westville for the Local Agenda 21 Project of the City of Durban (see note 4 below). Research has continued since that time in 1995–98 through a number of interviews of company executives, government officials, and community leaders by David Wiley and Sven Peek, as well as through correspondence and reviews of primary documents. Funding for this research 1994–95 was provided by a Michigan State University All University Research Initiation Grant, the Fulbright-Hays Faculty Research Awards Program of the US Department of Education, and contract funding from the city of Durban to the University of Durban-Westville Institute for Social and Economic Research. Research 1995–2000 was funded by the African Studies Center, International Studies and Programs, and Department of Sociology at Michigan State University.
3. A fuller discussion of the aspects of globalisation and their impacts on government, corporations, and community organisations in South Africa appears in Root et al. (1999) and in Root et al. (2000).
4. The IDZ programme has been created by DTI's Enterprise Organisation to encourage international competitiveness by offering world class infrastructure, linked to an international port or airport, with human resource development, compliance with environmental standards, facilitating customs clearance, duty-free import of raw materials, zero rate on VAT for supplies in South Africa, and other government facilitation (DTI 2001).
5. We have written more extensively about these environmental forums in South Durban in Wiley et al. (1996).
6. Personal correspondence from an Engen manager, 1996.
7. In May 1997, the Department of Trade and Industry (DTI) convened a workshop to discuss proposals for the Durban SDI, to which no community representatives or public media were invited. At the last minute, the organisers allowed two CBO representatives to attend and hastily organised a press conference. During the following year there was no public input on the SDI. Instead, the DTI stated that it would announce its plans after consulting with other state agencies that operate the harbour and railway yards. Other SDI and IDZ initiatives, however, had overridden questions of environment, though the DEAT now promises to be more proactive on all such development plans.

8. 'The need for the study was motivated by local communities in the Durban South Basin who, since the advent of democracy have been mobilising around environmental issues' (CSIR 1999: ii). 'The overall objective of conducting a SEA would . . . be to improve the quality of life of all residents in Durban South Basin and proposing a sustainable development strategy that would allow these problems to be minimised and managed' (Physical Environment Service Unit, Urban Development Department, Durban Metropolitan Council, 1996, quoted in CSIR 1999: 3).
9. Quoting Sean O'Beirne of the 10-member SEA Study Team in 'Minutes (Summary), SEA Workshop 31 March 1999', *Strategic Environmental Assessment in South Africa: Guideline Document.* CSIR with Department of Environmental Affairs and Tourism (DEAT), 2000, Appendix 3.
10. In this guideline document framing the policy, the DEAT uses Strategic Environmental Assessment in three ways: to indicate a process to ensure sustainability; a 'structured, proactive process to strengthen the role of environmental issues in strategic decision making' (Tonk and Verheem 1998); and 'a process to assess the environmental implications of a proposed strategic decision, policy, plan, programme, piece of legislation or major plan'. (See DEAT, White Paper on Environmental Management Policy for South Africa, 1998.)
11. The DEAT's 2000–01 budget for 'Environmental Quality and Protection' was cut by 23 per cent to only five per cent of the total DEAT budget, which is less than 15 per cent of the budget the DEAT allots to the 'green issues' of Biodiversity, Marine, and Coastal issues.
12. See the criticisms of the assumptions and methods of bilateral voluntary agreements for managing industrial pollution with Environmental Management Co-operation Agreements by Albertyn and Hall (2000) and the argued need for government regulation of the environment.
13. 'Research on Community Organization Negotiations with Industry', a research project by David Wiley and Christine Root supported by the Spivack Program in Applied Social Research and Social Policy of the American Sociological Association.

REFERENCES

Albertyn, C. 1998. 'Sustaining the Democratic Process: Towards an Enabling Environment for Popular Participation in Environmental Governance'. Unpublished. 25.05.98.

Albertyn, C. and J. Hall. 2000. 'Environmental Management Co-operation Agreements: A Soft Tool at the Cutting Edge of Pollution Control in South Africa'. Unpublished paper. A report to groundWork on aspects and possible implications of a government-industry initiative that is designing and promoting bilateral voluntary agreements as a contribution to managing industrial pollution. 08.2000.

Ballance, A. and N. King (compilers). 1999. 'State of the Environment South Africa 1999: An Overview'. Report on the internet on the national state of the environment for South Africa. <http://www.ngo.grida.no/soesa/> (accessed on 08.11.2000).

Bishop, C. 1997. 'Row over Developing the Wild Coast'. *Weekly Mail and Guardian*, 17.10.97.

Campaign against Neoliberalism in South Africa. 1996. 'On the South African Visit by IMF Managing Director Michel Camdessus'. <http://aidc.org.za/archives/stm16101996_cansa.html> (accessed on 16.10.96).

Canning, D. 2001. 'Durban on the Brink of Economic Crisis'. Independent Online, originally published in the *Natal Mercury*, 24.01.2001.

Carnie, T. 2000a. 'New Gadget Joins Fight Against Dirty Air'. *Natal Mercury*, 11.12.2000.

——. 2000b. 'Suffer Little Children: Cancer and Air Pollution in Durban South: Fact or Fiction?' The Poison in our Air Series, *Natal Mercury* and *Business Report*, 11.09.2000.

Challenor, M. 1999. 'Historic Durban Environmental Deal Reached'. *Daily News*, 07.12.99.

Cooper, A. 2000. 'Sapref Congratulated for Honesty'. *Daily News*, 01.02.2000.

Cowell, A. 1984. 'Rebels Attack South African Refinery and are Slain'. *New York Times*, 15.05.84.

Crompton, R. 1995. 'An Industrial Strategy for the Commodity Plastics Sector'. Industrial Strategy Project, University of Cape Town.

CSIR/Environmentek. 1999. 'Durban South Basic Strategic Environmental Assessment, Final Integrated Report'. CSIR Project No. JX01J prepared for Durban Metropolitan Council Environment Branch, August.

Department of Environmental Affairs and Tourism. 1998. *White Paper on Environmental Management Policy for South Africa*. Pretoria: DEAT. <http://www.environment.gov.za/docs/> (accessed on 18.11.99).

——. 2000. *Strategic Environmental Assessment in South Africa: Guideline Document*. Pretoria: DEAT and CSIR. <http://www.environment.gov.za/docs/> (accessed on 06.06.2000).

Department of Trade and Industry, the Enterprise Organisation. 2001. 'Industrial Development Zone Programme'. <http://www.dti.gov.za> pp. 10–117 (accessed on 22.10.2001).

'Durban Metro State of the Environment and Development: 1999 – The Economy'. 1999. <http://www.ceroi.net/reports/durban/drivers/economy1/pressure.htm> (accessed on 10.10.99).

Garrett, G. and P. Lange. 1991. 'Political Responses to Interdependence: What's Left for the Left?' *International Organizations*, 45, 4.

Gould, K., A. Schnaiberg and A. Weiberg. 1996. *Local Environmental Struggles: Citizen Activism in the Treadmill of Production*. New York: Cambridge University Press.

Hatch, G.P. n.d. (*c*.1997). 'Petrochemical Options for South Durban: South Durban Strategic Environmental Assessment Option Document 1'. CSIR.

Held, D. and A. McGrew. 1994. 'Globalization and the Liberal Democratic State'. In Y. Sakamoto (ed.). *Global Transformation: Challenges to the State System*. Tokyo: United Nations University.

ICLEI (International Council for Local Environmental Initiatives), 1995. 'Case Studies on the Local Agenda 21 Process: Municipal Durban, KwaZulu-Natal Province, Republic of South Africa'. <http://www.iclei.org/> (accessed on 05.06.2001).

Mbendi Profile: Engen Petroleum Ltd. Online. Internet. <http://www.mbendi.co.za/coen.htm> (accessed on 06.06.2001).

Ministry of Environmental Affairs and Tourism. 2001. 'Progress Report and Media Statements: Moosa Reports Back on Durban South Industrial Basin'. 15.05.2001.

Petrie, J.G., Y.M. Bruns and W. Bray. 1992. 'Air Pollution'. In R.F. Fuggle and M.A. Rabie (eds). *Environmental Management in South Africa*. Cape Town: Juta.

Root, C. and D. Wiley, with S. Peek. 1999. 'Globalization, Democratization, and the Environment in the New South Africa: Social Movements, Corporations, and the State in South Durban'. In W.L. Goldfrank, D. Goodman and A. Szasz (eds). *Ecology and the World-System*. Westport, CT: Greenwood Press.

——. 2000. 'The Impacts of Globalization on Environmental Struggles in a South African City'. In P.S. Aulakh and G.M. Schechter (eds). *Rethinking Globalization(s): From Corporate Transnationalism to Local Interventions*. London and New York: Macmillan Press and St Martin's Press.

Ryan, C. 1996. 'COSATU Can't Make up its Mind about Malaysia'. WOZA, Inc., 25.11.96.

Scott, D. 1994. 'Communal Space Construction: The Rise and Fall of Clairwood and District'. Ph.D. thesis, University of Natal, Durban.

South Commission. 1990. *The Challenge to the South: The Report of the South Commission*. New York: Oxford University Press.

South Durban Community Environmental Alliance. 1999. 'The South Durban Strategic Environmental Assessment: A Response by the Residents of South Durban with Annexures'. Submission to the Durban Metro, 04.11.99.

Stiefel, M. and M. Wolfe. 1994. *A Voice for the Excluded: Popular Participation in Development: Utopia or Necessity?* Geneva: United Nations Research Institute for Social Development.

Tennille, N.F. and T.P.G. LeQuesne. 1997. Proposed IDZ and Harbour at Coega: The Issues. <http://www.ru.ac.za/departments/law/SAenviro/cntry/coega/proveccid.html> (accessed on 05.12.97).

Tonk, J. and R. Verheem. 1998. 'Integrating the Environment in Strategic Decision-Making: One Concept, Multiple Forms'. Paper presented at the 18th annual meeting of the International Association of Impact Assessment, Christchurch, New Zealand. (Quoted in DEAT 2000, Glosssary, p. 9)

Valodia, I. 1999. 'Trade Policy and Industrial Development in Durban'. *Transformation*, 39.

Wackernagel, M. 1997. 'Gear is not Magic, But It's Working'. *Weekly Mail and Guardian*, 27.06.97.

Waters, M. 1995. *Globalization*. London and New York: Routledge.

White Paper on Reconstruction and Development Process. Quoted in Nene, B. 1997. *Building an Understanding on Community-Based Development Fora*. Urban Strategy Department, Durban Metro Council. January.

Wiley, D., with C. Root, S. Peek and S. Ramurath. 1996. *Negotiating Environment and Development in South Durban: Communities, Industries, and Authorities*. A Research Report for the City of Durban developed at the Institute for Social and Economic Research, University of Durban-Westville.

Yearley, S. 1996. *Sociology, Environmentalism, Globalization: Reinventing the Globe*. London: Sage.

Part Four

Basic Needs

The City of Durban Conference which took place at the University of Natal in July 1998 and around which this collection is based, was an exciting and stimulating event but it certainly contained embedded tension between the macro and micro, those promoting development and those promoting democracy.

This final part contains this tension we see through examining Durban from below, taking the perspective of the mass of Durbanites who live at or not much above the bread line. How does the city work for them and how does meeting their needs change the city? The following chapters focus on the question of provision of basic needs for the majority of the Durban population. They look at fresh produce, energy and medicine. By using the post-modern construction of 'D(urban)', Nesvåg forces us to confront the aliennesss and potency of the city for many of its newer inhabitants. This part's authors focus on how deracialisation coupled with globalisation impacts particularly on the needs of the more precariously placed. Witt shows the gradual shift in provision of fresh produce from the marketing arrangements of small-scale Indian gardeners to the corporate structured world characteristic of mid-twentieth century South African capitalism and then to new forms as the so-called informal sector begins to recover from the oppression to which it was subjected. In the last 20 years, the distribution networks have changed enormously in character as has the spatial specificity of these networks, but the power relations have been much slower to change. Annecke reveals remarkable detail in demonstrating the gap between international 'best practice', the means through which development agencies, official and unofficial, propose and establish policy ground rules and how things really look in lived experience. She provides a sense of how poor women actually meet their energy needs in a specific situation with a specific history. Nesvåg also looks at gender relations and the informal sector and provides a rich political case study of the slow and uncomfortable approach of the local state to a sector that often seems uncontrollable to those in authority. These chapters shed light on the extent to which poor develop their own autonomous perspectives that resist to some degree any form of state structuration.

A striking feature of them all is that, despite the harshness of the conditions of the existence of the poor, including the street hawkers, survival is rarely to be understood in terms of the war of all against all, of the battling individual. Instead, the establishment of social networks, affinity groups, structured organisations, knits people together. Does research such as this actually highlight new unregulated forms of accumulation from below that the state cannot channel, discipline or benefit? Work suggesting such patterns in other African countries is rich and suggestive but in Africa's deep south the 'informal sector' remains largely derivative in character, surviving on the interstices of a capitalism very much under the sway of the big players who have marked out their territory under the old regime. Annecke, for instance, suggests that successful accumulation depends on the ability to mobilise familial or other networks and is relatively uncommon – and social in character.

Apart from the connections made possible through the transformation of the local state, one would perhaps have to find a way into the world of crime and drugs or sectors such as moneylending in order to identify substantial newcomers who might challenge the established Durban elite. Yet the way in which the poorer parts of the population are able to integrate themselves into the urban fabric, the extent to which they cease to be excluded, and the effective management of basic needs (housing and transport are amongst the obvious subjects of analysis that require more attention) will be critical to the kind of life that Durban makes for its population in the century to come.

The tensions this part reveals are not the sign of an insuperable divide, although they certainly point to the imperfection of any solution. Nor do they suggest the irrelevance of effective governance. Policies could be more creative: Witt proposes far more encouragement, for instance, of urban agriculture as part of a politics of helping the poor to survive in Durban. As with Wiley et al. in the previous part, Annecke's critique of policy in energy suggests the real possibilities of better policy in a democratic dispensation. Nesvåg, in particular, implies that the forces that operate in Durban today, if unable to satisfy pressures and demands from all directions, are also not impervious to voices from below and that progress in creating a city that will work for the majority of people is indeed possible, if difficult, to achieve.

CHAPTER NINE

The Apartheid of Basic Facility Provision in the City of Durban with a Focus on Energy

WENDY ANNECKE

This chapter exposes the hardships in the lives of people, and particularly women, living at 'the bottom of the pile' in a city divided by race and class and wracked by violence between two political parties (the African National Congress and Inkatha), as well as the violence of the state which threatened them with forced removal and the destruction of their homes. It does this through examining the experiences of a group of people who arrived as refugees from political violence in 1990 at a site they called Canaan. Canaan was 10 km from the city centre and surrounded by wealthy neighbours but lacked all basic facilities such as water provision, sanitation and energy services. The chapter describes the construction and reconstruction of identities and dwelling places and how women made provision for their households in the context of a multitude of simultaneous demands. It focuses on the contribution of energy to fulfilling everyday tasks and describes the energy services used. It analyses the quality, quantities and cost of daily and monthly consumption, the variety of social and small-scale economic activities that developed on site and resulted in the re-acquisition of appliances and accumulation of skills and profits, and the development of a set of social dynamics within the community.

Finally the chapter considers the expressed need for electricity and the contribution which this quintessential modern energy carrier could make to such settlements. In a postscript the success of the accelerated national electrification programme post-1990 is noted and the impact of global trends both to liberalise and privatise parastatals such as the electricity utility, Eskom, and to curtail their emissions are highlighted.

Different Perspectives

One afternoon in 1991, the committee from Canaan was invited to a meeting with the mayor of Pinetown at the Pinetown municipal offices. The mayor sat at the head of the board room table in the ornately carved mayoral chair, flanked on his right by men in suits. The shack dwellers sat down the left side of the table in clothes newly washed in water from the storm-water drain at the bottom of the land on which they had settled. They accepted the offer of tea and sat, with their nervously twisting hands discreetly under the table, waiting. The group as a whole looked quiet, composed, and ready for business. The mayor was in a genial mood. The Canaan settlement was being threatened with forced removal[1] and the mayor's purpose was to offer land in the Mariannridge area. He opened the meeting with every intention of making the Canaan Committee feel welcome in the plush Pinetown parlours. He smiled affably and, speaking slowly and deliberately, said: 'I have an aeroplane. I fly over you and your families in the bush at Canaan at least once a week on my way to Lanseria Airport. I come in low over the hill and can see where you live so I understand the conditions that you live in . . .'

It became evident that whatever the mayor did understand through his view from the clouds, it did not include the politics of squatting. The Canaan people knew that if they accepted the mayor's offer and moved onto land to which many others had prior claim, they would face more violence and they had no wish to become embroiled in another conflict. Their historical and immediate experiences had taught them to resist the offer of a better life so persuasively made. They had lived the ground rules, they knew that promises made in the upper strata of society had little correlation with their everyday lives. The global imperatives which have compelled the liberalisation and privatisation of the electricity utility are somewhat akin to the mayor's perspective: pervasive without being penetrating, homogenising rather than insightful. Five years later the Canaan people could have warned the government that in their experience, the lure of foreign investment in exchange for restructuring parastatals and utilities, would provide only cold comfort for the people on the ground. Of course they were not asked. The committee members could, and did, decline this offer of what was best for them, but the poor are not, even in the new democracy, able to influence larger decisions made on their behalf, and while global markets pressure the restructuring of water and, in particular for this study, the electricity utility, many poor people simply endure the consequences.

The meeting in the mayor's parlour reached a stalemate, then disintegrated. The Canaan Committee trailed out into the parking lot where they watched the mayor, somewhat less affable, jump into a sports car and race off to his next appointment. The shack dwellers hailed taxis to take them home, and while they waited, bemoaned the fact that they had missed prime tipping time at the dump and would have to buy food and paraffin at the spaza shop which they could ill afford. They debated whether it was worth being on the committee for the hot tea with milk and sugar and being able to use the toilets at the mayor's parlour, and how they would be criticised for bringing no good news. As daylight faded, the taxis dropped them back into their twilight world, where women carrying water were just visible through the acrid smoke which rose from the wood fires and mingled with the smell of paraffin burning and people peeing in the path. The Canaan Committee wondered aloud whether the authorities would ever understand their living conditions, and whether there would ever be any recognition of rights to services such as water, housing and electricity.

The Energy Sector and Domestic Energy Use During the Apartheid Years

Domestic energy use, and in particular low-income households' energy use was not a priority of the apartheid state. In reaction to international sanctions, the government was preoccupied with self-sufficiency and fuel security (Eberhard and Van Horen 1995: 36). Accordingly, the National Energy Council, the research arm of the Department of Mineral and Energy Affairs, focused on technical and strategic issues, and despite the rest of the world's forays into energy for development and services for the poor (Cecelski et al. 1979; Goldemberg et al. 1987), little domestic or energy poverty research was commissioned in South Africa. Some quantitative and technical studies of fuels used by the poor, biomass (wood, crop waste, dung) and renewables (solar water heating) had been done (Gandar1984; Bembridge and Tarlton 1990; Viljoen 1990) but the prevalence of paraffin use by the majority of women in South Africa had escaped researchers' notice. Annecke's study (1992) was the first to document paraffin use and to place women, as the primary users, at the centre of the analysis. Thereafter a study by Ross (1993), further work by Annecke (1994) and a three-year national investigation led by White et al. (1996), funded by the Department of Mineral and Energy Affairs (1995–98), ensured a better understanding of the most commonly used household fuel. In 1995 Davis and Ward (1995: 5) were able to quantify paraffin use: they estimated 82 per cent of all low-income households in South Africa used paraffin every day, and by then considerably more was known about how it was bought, sold, bartered and burned.

The study described here seeks not only to situate low-income households' energy needs within the context of other basic needs, but also to capture the conditions in which the people lived, particularly the women of Canaan. Fuel-use patterns are embedded in other practices which are more easily foregrounded. Although unnoticed most of the time, domestic life cannot be conducted without energy which constitutes one of the continual and essential elements of productive and reproductive lives, making the connection between people and their activities. Since women are the primary users and managers of domestic energy, the study of the different carriers provides insights into a number of aspects of women's lives. Data is drawn largely from a general survey of the area requested by the Canaan Committee and conducted by Ardington in 1991 and two in-depth domestic energy studies conducted by Annecke as part of a wider contribution to the settlement.

Women are not a homogenous group and do not share the same experiences of domesticity. Some of the differences in experience are most obvious in the practicalities of providing cooked food and hot water for members of the household on a day-to-day basis. This is not an issue in the lives of middle-class women in the city of Durban whose access to electricity permits a seamless range of activities. At the flick of a switch, there is electric lighting, hot water in the geyser, a meal cooked in a microwave, a computer turned off in favour of a television programme. A few finger movements and a car starts or a friend answers a phone. Any other energy needed, be it avgas for private aeroplanes, petrol for cars, candles for ambience, gas or charcoal for braai-ing, is as readily available as electricity, through an efficient system of suppliers and distributors.

This, however, was not the case for those living in the numerous informal houses within the greater Durban region who have been bypassed by the electricity grid for over a century. Durban was the sixth city in South Africa to install an electricity reticulation system in 1897[2] (Eskom 1995) and over the years commerce, industry, white suburbs and some formal Coloured, Indian and black townships, including parts of KwaMashu and Umlazi, were connected to the grid. The state's low-cost housing programme ended in the mid-1970s, after which time informal settlements proliferated, but because few were recognised as legal and permanent, homes were not electrified. Almost 100 years after the first electric lights had been turned on in Durban, half the population still did not have electricity[3] and shared this condition with 65 per cent of urban and rural people throughout South Africa (National Electricity

Regulator 1995). Just a decade from the new millennium some 18 million South Africans used biomass or hydrocarbon fuels (coal, gas or paraffin) for cooking, heating and lighting every day.

In urban areas where woodfuel is limited, hydrocarbon use is common. Paraffin was introduced into the country before the turn of the century and is used primarily for cooking, while wax candles are used for lighting (Annecke 1992). On the highveld, coal is also widely used for space heating and cooking but Durban's hot, humid climate makes it impractical, so that despite the relative proximity of coal mines (Newcastle and Dundee), very little coal is used in Durban. At the time of the study Liquid Petroleum Gas (LPGas) had not been marketed for large-scale domestic use in low-income households with the result that it is considered dangerous and expensive and not widely used. Although an ANC election slogan had been 'Electricity for All', the White Paper on energy policy published in 1998, advocated the notion of 'energy' (rather than electricity) for all, and as part of this plan, LPGas has been combined with solar home systems in what is known as an 'energisation package', and installed in several rural areas. The demand and distribution networks for the most commonly used urban fuels, wood, paraffin and candles, function somewhat differently to power lines, grid and electricity connections, or the public-private partnerships used to deliver the energisation packages, and are described here as they functioned in Canaan in the early 1990s.

Canaan: The Land of Milk and Honey?

The Canaan study was undertaken between 1989 and 1992 at a time when the struggle between the state and political groupings was bloody and fierce. Thousands of people from the townships around Durban fled their homes (Aitchison 1990). Although the clashes hardly touched the people living in suburbia, the impact on the economy was felt in terms of the increased housing shortages, lost jobs and salaries, disrupted networks and dislocated families. At the level of household welfare, this translated into destitution as households who had lost everything struggled to find ways to meet their basic needs including food and fuel. They became refugees in Durban and had to reconstruct their lives.

Some of these displaced people found their way to the heavily treed, steep slopes of a hill above the Umgeni River, adjacent to the N2 highway and just 10 km from the city centre. Here, where just Johnny Lantern[4] and a few itinerant associates had lived for two years, the newcomers took shelter among the trees and began to carve out small spaces for themselves. Beatrice Memela's experience was typical:

> I have five children. I arrived here on 6 April 1990. I am from Siyanda. They burned our houses and then we ran away. We can never go back there. They burned everything, all my belongings (Annecke 1992: 12).

The new arrivals had to procure, for themselves and their children, the means to build a shelter, water to drink, food to eat, fuel to cook with and ways to make a living. These concomitant needs defy the linear chronicling given here. Excerpts of the people of Canaan's narratives are offered in an attempt to convey the human dimension, the difficulties and dilemmas of a few of the thousands of people who had been poor but settled, and found themselves in the midst of violent political upheaval, stripped of their meagre possessions and having to start again. Busisiwe Dlamini recalled her disorientation:

> I came because I saw there were already three families. The people told me: 'We are also staying here. We are just hiding ourselves.' I didn't even have five cents in my pocket. My first day I slept at someone's house. The second day I tried to build with cardboard from the dump and I slept in my paper house. I felt helpless (Annecke 1992: 3).

In April 1990, Dlamini's was the fourth house to be built, by the end of August that year there were some 250 shacks, and by May 1991 there were 429 dwellings and some 1 500 people living at Canaan (Ardington 1992: 3). The settlement owed its name to a young priest who, having fled a burning house, thought the place a haven compared to the war-torn township. For the first few months it may have been, but a year later the settlement was far from heavenly. There was no fresh water supply, no waste disposal, no drainage and no schools or clinics for the now substantial population (Black Sash 1990). The site was shale and considered unsuitable for upgrading by the Department of Roads who owned it, but there was nowhere else to go, the townships were still in flames, and by then other people seeking to live close to town had joined the settlement.

The materials for Busisiwe Dlamini's flimsy house came from the municipal dump some 20 minutes' walk from Canaan, across the N2 highway. The dump became central to the lives of most of the people at Canaan. Not only did it supply building materials for shelters, but as will be seen, it also supplied food, fuel, furniture, furnishings, clothes and an income for some. It was used by a variety of supermarkets and small construction companies, as well as the residents of the affluent parts of Overport and the Berea, and constituted a link in time and space between the affluent throwaway society and the displaced people.

Over time each household arriving at Canaan built a structure which usually consisted of a single room with a floor space of about nine square metres. A variety of materials salvaged from the dump were incorporated into the construction, making each shelter unique. Bricks, iron and plastic, different types of wood and hardboard were put to use. An old masonite menu from a roadhouse (Eggs and Fries 2/6; Toasted Sandwiches 2/-), estate agents' FOR SALE signs and a Toyota crate became panels in walls, while the wire-meshed windscreen of a Putco bus (intended to protect the driver from stone-throwing) served as a burglar-proofed window. Inside the imperfections of the uneven walls were papered over with sheets of plasticised, rain-resistant fruit juice, milk and iJuba cartons which had been discarded by printers and salvaged from the dump.

Despite their poverty, women went to considerable lengths to make their houses cosy and attractive and re-create the homes they had fled. They covered broken furniture with cloth found at the dump, washed in the storm-water drain and pressed with irons heated on paraffin stoves. Fresh and artificial flowers found on the dump, pictures and crocheted anti-macassars adorned homes. Outside appearances were less important, nonetheless some exterior walls were painted, some flowers and vegetables were planted and a broken umbrella in a wooden electric cable reel served as garden furniture for several houses. It was largely the women who took responsibility for making their shacks look attractive. Since most women headed their own households and, in keeping with Todes and Walker's finding (1991: 8), placed great importance on the fact that each owned her own shack, this homeliness was being created for themselves and their children.

A safe water supply was more difficult to find than building materials.

> When I first came to Canaan I was helpless. I didn't even have water to drink. I got water, the very unhealthy water from the pipe, and it made me sick (Annecke 1992: 39).

Initially new and desperate residents used the storm-water drain which ran at the bottom of the hill alongside the highway for drinking and washing. But several people complained of being ill after drinking it or getting sores after washing in it. Although some women said they knew about boiling water to clean it, they did not have the pots or the fuel to do so. Clean water was sought from the neighbours, and for almost a year some of the more affluent and hospitable Indian households neighbouring the settlement allowed Canaan people to take water from their garden taps.[5] But as the settlement grew and became more permanent, petty thieving began and the neighbours' generosity dwindled. Thereafter Canaan people depended more heavily on the nearby cafe owners who began to sell water, or they walked across the highway to the fire hydrant which had been fitted with a tap to serve the needs of a group of people at Kennedy Road who lived adjacent to the dump. Not surprisingly, animosity developed between the relatively small group of people who were used to having the choice pickings of the dump and their own water supply, and the growing number of residents of Canaan who swarmed to the dump and formed queues at the fire hydrant. Several threats, quarrels, and a stabbing ensued. Canaan women became reluctant to fetch water. At a community meeting towards the end of 1990, a man chided those outsiders who were ostensibly assisting Canaan but were not dealing with the real issue:

> We've got no water. How can we live without water? The birds in the sky, the animals, even the snakes, all must drink water. But we as humans have not got water and we are suffering. We hear about a post box and we are grateful. We hear about a telephone and we are grateful. But we hear nothing of water. We cannot live without water (Annecke 1992: 39).

After further conflict with the Kennedy Road residents, 16 deaths on the highway (primarily of women and children carrying water), numerous requests to the authorities, and 18 months after the first people arrived, a tap was fitted to a fire hydrant close to the Canaan settlement in September 1991 (Annecke 1992: 48).

A shelter and water were necessities but so was food. When asked 'where do you shop?' over half the respondents replied: 'At the dump' (Ardington 1992: 30). Just past the fire hydrant at Kennedy Road, the dump was relatively conveniently situated for obtaining supplies. Women were especially conscientious shoppers, many going to the dump twice a day at what were known as the rush hours – at about nine o'clock in the morning and three in the afternoon. Men on the other hand seldom went to the dump unless it was in response to a message to help carry home a large item such as roofing or a wardrobe. Those women who tried to make a living from the dump spent all day raking through the rubbish, chopping crates and packing cases and wood into manageable pieces, gathering cardboard, sail sheeting, milk and fruit carton wrappers, cloth and clothes. Plastic was much sought after as were bits of metal and anything which would serve as furniture or ornaments. There was an established network of dump-pickers and waste buyers of which the Canaan women soon became part, and began to sell their pickings in return for small sums of money.

Food was also salvaged from the dump. Expired frozen and tinned food and no-longer-fresh fruit and vegetables which had been discarded by supermarkets were collected. The experience of scarcity was not new but, for many, scavenging brought new lows to their lives and this distress was articulated at a community meeting in 1991:

> A lot of people here are unemployed. Most of the food we eat and the material we build with we get from the dump. That's something we're living out of. There's some nurses that promised to help us but they haven't helped us yet. They say the food we're eating from the dump is unhealthy and can make us sick. There is no help for that because they are not coming here to help us and we're living from the dump. Most of the people whose belongings were burnt out are based on the dump. That's our biggest problem here. So this means whatever sickness we get over here we get from there on the dump because the food we're eating is very unhealthy because it's food that's already been thrown away. It's stuff that's expired already. Sometimes we have nothing to cook it with. That's our biggest problem (Annecke 1992: 57).

It was despite such obstacles that people began to re-establish themselves. During the first year of its existence the settlement expanded rapidly. Predictably it housed young people; 60 per cent of the population were between 15 and 40 years old, and there were slightly more women than men, a ratio of 52:48 (Ardington 1992: 9). There were relatively few old age pensioners and adolescents. Many children who should have been living with their parents had been sent away for safety. This meant that many households were incomplete, and were further disrupted as women stretched their meagre financial and emotional resources, going in search of, or to visit various members of their separated families. Incomplete households may have accounted for the relatively small household size, which was on average three to four people (Ardington 1992: 3).

Men were more likely than women to have full-time paid jobs (Ardington 1992: 15) so, having built somewhere to live, women were noticeably active in finding ways to support their households. Regular employment, with inflexible hours and employers, however financially desirable, was seen to inhibit women's movement between their family members and create further dilemmas and stress, so that several women said they were trying to do 'something' until their families were settled, whereupon they would look for a regular job. Informal income generating activities included carrying water for others, selling fruit and vegetables, building shacks for newcomers, scavenging, hairdressing, candle and soap making, healing, knitting, dagga selling, making clothes, gathering wood to sell at Canaan and running shebeens. For the most part these provided small and unpredictable incomes for precarious existences, necessitating for the most part day-to-day living and expenditure patterns familiar to researchers working in marginalised communities (De Kock 1986; May and Stavrou 1989; Sutcliffe 1989).

The people of Canaan were poor but not uniformly so. Recorded personal monthly incomes ranged from R10 to R1 735 and averaged R495 (Ardington 1992: 21). One of the highest recorded incomes was that of the spaza owner and is discussed later. Household per capita incomes were calculated by dividing household income by the number of persons resident in the house, without allowance for age or sex. These incomes ranged from R2 to R1 500 and averaged R177 per capita (Ardington 1992: 21). The medians in both cases were well below the mean and indicate a concentration of households at the lower income levels. Those above included most of the people who had moved to Canaan to be closer to their work or town and had stable incomes. Almost half, however, had household incomes below R400 per month and per capita incomes of below R125 per month. Although the highest household per capita income was R1 500, 90 per cent were below R400 and 60 per cent below R150 per month. This meant that 57 per cent of households had incomes below the Household Subsistence Level[6] (Ardington 1992: 21). Water, food, fuel and transport were categories of primary expenditure, although in the beginning there was no money even for food. Gretta Ndukwana said:

> When I came to Canaan it was very difficult and things were really bad. My possessions had all been burnt down. Busisiwe advised me to go to the dump. In the beginning I found it very difficult to go there. But we had nothing to eat. There I would find an old cabbage and peel off the outside. I would find a small good part inside and come back to Canaan and cook it so the children could eat (Annecke 1992: 52).

Food and Fuel

Ndukwana cooked the cabbage in a rusty pot from the dump over a fire made from wood collected from the bush nearby. There was, of course, no electricity and those who had fled violence had not brought their wick or pump paraffin stoves with them so they had to find other ways of heating and cooking until they could buy new ones. For the first couple of months most people did as Ndukwana, and used wood gathered from the open bush adjacent to Canaan, although 20 per cent of respondents reported obtaining firewood from the dump (Ardington 1992: 27). By the end of the first year a small proportion said they bought wood from 'sellers' who had brought it in from rural areas and found their way to Canaan. The movement of firewood around South Africa remains largely undocumented. It would appear that there is a significant trade in wood from rural to urban areas but very little is known about the areas of origin, quantities sold or information networks which led to sellers finding their way to ready markets such as Canaan. When the Working for Water campaign swung into action in the mid-1990s and alien vegetation was cleared, it increased urban access to woodfuel considerably, but the long-term consequences of this still have to be evaluated.

Paraffin and candles have their disadvantages but they are preferable to wood, so that as soon as people could afford to buy candles and buy or borrow stoves they substituted these for wood. Relatively efficient informal distribution channels, which have evolved without planning or regulation, exist for paraffin.[7] The Canaan people could buy it in bulk from garages and supermarket chains for approximately R25 for 20 litres, but few people had the means to transport a 20 litre drum back to Canaan, so they bought small quantities from the local café and paid accordingly. Three months after the first wave of houses was built, a spaza shop opened at Canaan, others soon followed. This meant paraffin and candles were now available on site. Paraffin was sold for about R1.60 for 750 ml with small differences from one spaza to another. By the end of 1991 only four per cent of respondents did not report some expenditure on paraffin, and half of the paraffin consumed was obtained from spaza shops within Canaan. Most of the balance was bought from the local café which also sold water. The amounts spent per week ranged from R2 to R25 and averaged R6 (Ardington 1992: 27).

At the same time 91 per cent of households reported some expenditure on candles. The average expenditure was R3 a week with a range of R1 to R16 (Ardington 1992: 27). Candles were bought singly or in packets of six from the local spaza. Each house used from a half to two a night, at a cost of about 50 cents per candle. Thus the newly opened spazas at Canaan were making a small but regular income from domestic energy sales which contributed to the owners' financial stability. The very presence of the spazas contributed to a growing sense of identity and stability of Canaan even though the community was already being threatened with removal by the authorities.

Ardington's general survey in 1991 was followed by a more thorough investigation of fuel use in 40 households. Acquiring some form of stove was a priority and by the end of 1991 all 40 households had achieved this. There were 26 paraffin stoves, 14 paraffin primuses and two gas stoves. The next appliances to be bought were irons, and within a year 39 households had paraffin-heated irons. In addition six had paraffin lanterns and one had a gas light. Twenty-three had battery-operated radios, two had hi-fis powered by car batteries and one a television. The gas refrigerator referred to later was bought after this survey (Annecke 1994: 43). Increased appliance ownership may be an indicator of an improved standard of living (Davis 1995: 12), but in this case households were gradually replacing appliances they had lost rather than accumulating new ones so that appliance acquisition was understood to be a necessity, a step towards regaining the lifestyles to which they had been accustomed rather than a sign of upward mobility.

At the end of 1992, when the households were monitored again, wood was still being used by 32 of the 40 women as a supplement to paraffin, primarily for heating water (for washing), and half the women still used wood for cooking on a regular basis. Eighteen of the women collected wood freely from nearby bush, three collected it from the dump and eleven bought it from 'sellers' at R2 a bundle. Households used about 10 kg of wood a week. Brewing beer in the traditional manner accounted for half of this.

Expenditure on paraffin monitored in the same households over the year from 1991–92 showed an increase in weekly fuel expenditure in the lower categories. Average minimum expenditure increased from R6 to R9.50 a week although the top of the range remained around R25 a week. Only two respondents did not report any paraffin use. One was a full-time student who used gas, the other an older, very poor woman who used only wood. On average, households consumed just over a litre of paraffin a day but expenditure depended not only on how much was used but also on where it was bought. The lowest price paid for paraffin was 60 cents for 750 ml, the highest R1.80 and the average R1.37. Most households simply bought from the spaza closest to them and paid accordingly. There was an element of group identity growing and it was thought that supporting local spazas rather than buying outside Canaan was the right thing to do (Annecke 1992: 103). The households surveyed used paraffin for daily cooking and heating water. Six of the 40 used paraffin for lighting and one, the full-time student, used a gas lamp. LPGas was used in additional to paraffin for cooking by only two households, it was bought from a shop in KwaMashu at R20.95 for a 15 kg cylinder.

Expenditure on candles had remained much the same over the year. Thirty-nine of the 40 households used candles for lighting. On the whole each household still used one candle a night. Thirty-one of the women bought candles from a spaza, either singly, in which case they cost 40–50 cents each, or in packets of six, some of which worked out cheaper, between R2.29 and R3.50 per packet.

By 1992, 25 of the 40 households had bought radios operated on dry batteries; three had car batteries for larger appliances. The majority of batteries were PM9s bought from spazas, and contributed significantly to energy costs although women did not include them in their estimation of how much they spent on energy each month.

Altogether monthly expenditure on energy services consumed between eight per cent and 14 per cent of the monthly household income. This is a substantially larger proportion than the three to five per cent of income spent by most middle class households on electricity (Eberhard and Van Horen 1995: 65) and reveals the cost of inefficient fuels, fuel-switching and buying in small quantities. Total monthly expenditure on energy by these households ranged from R40 and R220 per month and averaged R70 (Annecke 1994: 45). These inclusive amounts were an indication of the relatively improved conditions of households which had been settled for up to two years in Canaan.

Women were continually conscious of the need to be frugal:

> If I buy only one bottle of paraffin and one candle every day I use only that amount, so I am disciplining myself. Also if I only have some few cents I must buy food, some paraffin, one candle and what about the bus fare? (Annecke 1992: 78).

They complained that men and children did not share their concerns. Childrens' excesses – but not men's – could be curbed if the woman was at home to oversee paraffin used for making tea and ironing, but not men's. One woman, trying to save money by buying candles in packets rather than one at a time said:

> I tried by all means to buy a packet of six and not let my husband

> know. Otherwise he will sit up all night using all the candles (Annecke 1992: 81).

This comment offers an insight into domestic arrangements and raises questions around household resource management, authority and power. While women are responsible for fuel selection and purchase, they may not have control over use. Because of their precarious situations and the uncertainty created by irregular incomes, the women considered it prudent to spread their daily disbursements over a number of small purchases rather than paying for any one large item. Being able to buy paraffin in small quantities on a daily basis makes it an ideal fuel for households in precarious positions, whereas gas and electricity require more substantial outlays. Saving from an irregular income, putting aside an amount to buy a packet of candles, an appliance or pay a bill is difficult for those who derive their incomes from irregular informal activities and requires different management procedures to those anticipating a regular income. But there were factors in addition to cost which determined food and fuel choice.

'I had no money so I cooked bread today,' said Thembakazi Mnisi. Bread is made with flour, salt, a raising agent such as sour milk, beer or yeast and water. The ingredients are mixed together thoroughly, the dough is placed in waterproof plastic packets and boiled in water over a paraffin flame for over an hour. The combined cost of the paraffin to cook on and the ingredients make it twice as expensive to bake as to buy – even at an inflated price at the spaza. When asked about this, a woman said:

> The bread we make is so nice. It is so nice if a woman makes bread and it's not too much work. First you mix the dough, then you have to wait a l-o-n-g time for it to rise if you use yeast. Then you have to find one or two packets that don't have holes. You put the well-risen dough inside and tie it up securely so it doesn't get wet and it gets crusty. Then you boil it on the stove for an hour and it smells good. Then when it's ready, it's all hot and steamy and smells good and the children will say: 'Ooh, Ma, you've made bread,' and eat the whole lot and go to sleep without asking for more (Annecke 1993: 52).

In this case the process, the product and the outcome outweigh the monetary value. The ability to satisfy notions of good mothering and housekeeping has greater meaning than the price tag. The expense and inconvenience of paraffin and the extended cooking time pale into insignificance in the face of approval from children, and the woman feeling she had fulfilled her role of provider of food and care, satisfactorily.

Another instance of immediate cost not being significant was the occasion of an unexpected windfall. Such unanticipated cash might be spent entirely on a 'feast' for the evening meal. This would include meat cooked on a fire outside and phutu (maize meal) and gravy cooked indoors on a paraffin stove. Energy use on these occasions was lavish: as much wood as was needed to keep the fire blazing through the meal and as much paraffin as was necessary to cook large quantities of the staple. In contrast with the extreme care usually exercised, this extravagance may seem incongruous but under the circumstances the two philosophies of frugality and a 'live for today' splurge, were not incompatible. The thrift evident in the rational approach of day-to-day budgeting and minimal expenditure ensured the household's physical survival, while the relatively extravagant meal served as a morale booster, providing the rare satisfaction of full stomachs, relief from otherwise relentless hardship, and an element of hope otherwise often missing.

Energy Intensive Income Generation

It is worth taking a closer look at two of the income generating activities at Canaan which were energy intensive. Both were concerned with the provision of food and drink, but the ways in which this was managed were quite different and determined to some extent by the structure of the households concerned. Ms Mnisi made food for hostel dwellers.

> Ms Mnisi is a 34-year-old woman. She is originally from the Transkei. Before she came to Canaan she was at Lindelani where the violence was. She had been there for some five years. Now she is here at Canaan, she stays in a one-roomed shack all alone. Her two sons are in the Transkei, looked after by her mother and father.
>
> She is not formally employed; her day starts at 2.00am when she starts her cooking. She uses her paraffin stove to cook different types of food. She sells to people who are working at Maydon Wharf, men who stay in hostels and therefore bring no lunch boxes with them. Sometimes she cooks things like phutu and chicken curry or samp and beans or beef curry. When this is cooked she dishes into disposable containers and charges R2.50 per bowl. Selling food like this she is able to earn up to R100 a week.
>
> Every day she has got to leave her shack at 6.00 in the morning. By 11.00 in the morning she is back. Some of her customers take food on credit and pay her on Fridays when they get paid. That way

> she has learned to keep books in a basic manner. She is able to save up to about R500 a year with the help of joining a stokvel with her friends in Durban North. At home her duties consist of washing dishes and pots, cleaning up her shack, cooking a light supper which is mostly amazi with bread or phutu, or tea and bread with an egg. She has an early night because she wakes up as early as 2.00am to cook so to sell fresh food to her customers again. For all her food, be it for her own use or for selling, she uses paraffin only. For light she uses candles (Mkhize in Annecke 1994: 34).

In this way, by getting up at 2 am, cooking, catching a bus to the hostels in Jacobs, selling the lunch packs and catching the bus back to Canaan, Ms Mnisi was able to earn R80–R100 a week, and to save R44 a month in addition to the money she sent her parents each month to take care of her two sons. Although she did not calculate the production costs on a regular basis, Ms Mnisi knew the likely cost of the ingredients, kept records of what she took in daily sales and what her customers owed her, and was able to make an informed estimate of her profits. She excluded herself from many of the Canaan community activities because she did not want to get caught up in any more conflict; her concern was her children and providing the means to raise them well. In order to do this she had to send them away, being without them enabled her to keep the extraordinary hours necessary to conduct her business.

On the other hand, a large household was one of the reasons that the Memela's spaza thrived. It was the first spaza to be opened at Canaan, and headed by a dominant woman, it went from strength to strength. Mrs Memela[8] was head of an extended family of ten, three daughters, two sons, the girlfriend of one son, three granddaughters, and a grandson. For the first few months all members of the household picked the dump every afternoon. Not only were they able to collect more cardboard than other pickers but they soon learned to exaggerate the weight by wetting the inside layers with water, and since the bundles were sold by weight they profited. Soon they were able to build an extra room, buy stock and start a spaza. At this stage, three of the adults stopped picking the dump: two found formal employment, one became a vegetable seller, and the others worked in the spaza. Regular wages from the formally employed assisted the development of the business. By the end of 1992 there was not only a shop but also a well-patronised shebeen that offered its customers entertainment through a car battery-powered music and television system, cold beer and cold drinks from an LPGas refrigerator, and deep fried hot 'bits' and chips. The former were chicken feet and heads, also known as walkie-talkies. Owning a refrigerator meant that chicken could be bought in bulk and stored. Sizakele Mkhize (in Annecke 1994: 30), recorded the household's daily activities:

> They've got a five-roomed shack and what I've noticed here is that everybody here at home fully participates in household chores except for Nanti's last born son [a baby]. It's a matter of you work for your plate of food, and everybody is under a very strong supervision from Mrs Memela. It is Mrs Memela's rule that every one of her children must play a major role towards earning money or bringing food, whether from the dump or from KwaKathi – who is a shop owner and he always needs people to collect plastics and cardboard. At the end of each day those who do this kind of job for him, he gives them vegetables, bread, polony, cheese – things that are about to be thrown away for the day. This is given to the one who worked hardest or, so to say, gets the most cardboard. So Mrs Memela's children, when there is nothing to be done at home, go to either the dump or to KwaKathi. Whosoever goes to Mrs Memela's house notices that there is always enough of everything every day.
>
> Their day starts at 5.00 am, feeding the chickens and preparing breakfast by one of the women or Musa, Mrs Memela's last born son, who also fully partakes in daily chores just as much as his sisters, though he is only eleven years old. What I noticed is that Mrs Memela doesn't do much around the house except to supervise the smooth running of the things. For breakfast they made boiled eggs on paraffin stove with bread and margarine and tea with milk. For the whole family to be satisfied they bought three loaves of brown bread. It took thirty minutes to prepare and feed everybody breakfast.
>
> On another day, when there was little time pressure, cooking was done outside on a fire, and everyone shared the tasks. For their next meal which was going to be lunch, they made a fire outside and cooked samp and beans in a three-legged pot which takes two to three hours to be cooked depending on the weather. If it's not windy it's cooked quickly because the fire is fine, but when it is windy it takes a little bit longer. During this time I see the children are always at the fireside because they've got to be constantly putting wood on the fire and to blow when the flame dies down. They also have to pour water so that the samp doesn't get burnt.
>
> At about eleven, Mrs Memela asks for tea from her children or even before that when somebody comes in she orders for tea for the person who has just come in. Her joint is a favourite because one

> always finds very cold drink or beers there. What's more notable is all her children are not at school because they couldn't find one. Also notable is that she's got more money than most of the people in the community; they always come to borrow from her. At night they have what they are cooking for the shebeen – meat or bits cooked on the gas and some phutu with greens cooked on the paraffin stove.

In this case a large family was not a burden but an advantage, and each contributed in valuable ways to maintaining the household. A dominant senior woman directed the course of events, and made most of the important domestic decisions. Overall she managed the household, the spaza and the shebeen. A blurring of the traditional expectations and gender roles worked to the economic advantage of the household. Contrary to usual custom, the son's girl friend was accepted into the house before marriage, men and women assisted with the domestic responsibilities, one woman had formal employment and all, including the children and the boy-child, contributed in some way to their upkeep. The reason given for the children's not attending school (that there was no school that would accept them) may have been valid, but it was also true that the children were needed at home. Without the children to attend to the cooking fire and gather the wood and cardboard and food that they did every day, there would have been a little less, and a little less still if school uniforms had to be bought and school fees had to be paid. The household was stable and hard-working and was willing and able to help others, for example by extending credit to households within Canaan.

The Memela household's financial stability, regular income plus business interests meant that they had a wider range of choices than many other households, and this was actively exercised in their daily fuel-use. When they first settled at Canaan they used wood, then paraffin and candles were used as well as wood, later a gas stove and refrigerator were added for efficient cooking and cooling for the shebeen respectively, then a car battery was bought for the television and music centre. Unlike some other households, the transition to higher order hydrocarbons and the appliances necessary to use these did not occur to the exclusion of wood. The children supplied the labour necessary to collect firewood and tended the fire for the cooking of phutu and samp.

Fuel consumption was heavy and expenditure on energy was R220 during the month of the study, but it could hardly have been used more judiciously. LPGas for quick cooking and refrigeration is probably the best value for money, the regular use of wood (free but for the children's opportunity costs) kept the cooking expenses down, and only the television and music may have been more efficiently operated by mains than a battery. No monitoring of costs or sales in the spaza or shebeen was done on any consistent basis, so profit was difficult to calculate. However, increasing sums of money were available to the household and Mrs Memela's estimate of an income of R1 500 in 1991 increasing to R2 000 per month in 1992 was probably accurate.

The elaborate domestic arrangements of the two income generating projects were in part due to the nature of the enterprises, but would they have been assisted by access to electricity? It is clear in the case of Ms Mnisi that electric lighting would have made her tasks of preparation and cooking at 2 am in the morning easier, although LPGas rather than paraffin or electricity offers the more efficient method of cooking. In the Memela household, electric lighting and a connection for the entertainment centre would have been of immediate benefit, but overall the advantages of electricity were not obvious because the energy choices had been made so shrewdly. There appeared to be little benefit in replacing wood and the children's time and labour with electricity unless there was a school nearby that was prepared to enrol them, and unless prospects for the future, such as employment, outweighed the immediate benefits of child labour and free fuel. Needless to say this upwardly mobile household was as keen as any other to have access to electricity, and was willing to pay for it. However, when asked to rank a range of services in the order of willingness to pay, most women ranked electricity lower on the list than water, houses, education and clinics suggesting that the provision of electricity should be integrated into the delivery of basic services rather than supplied in isolation.

Reflection

The study attempted to make visible the ways in which energy use is embedded in domestic activities and small-scale enterprises that are conducted from the home base. For those households without electricity, the time, effort and expense of multiple fuel use has been described. Wood has to be collected whereafter the fire and food have to be carefully tended; paraffin has to be bought daily and stored carefully because it is poisonous and a fire hazard (Annecke 1992; Ross 1993; Mehlwana and Qase 1996). Candles burn out quickly and are also a fire hazard, gas is heavy and has to be transported from inconvenient depots. The lack of electricity was felt not only with regard to lighting and cooking but also as a psychological barrier to improvement. A connection to the grid has symbolic as well as practical value, but access to electricity is constrained by systems and structures beyond the control of households such as those at Canaan and others who do not have tenure. Durban has been at the forefront of innovative and extensive delivery systems, delivering lifeline water supplies and transforming the electricity department into the Energy Department. Aware of the limits to electrification the latter has been considering alternative forms of energy, and piloting the implementation of energisation packages. The area of the new Unicity (2000/01) was increased by 68 per cent to include rural areas under traditional authorities (Oelofse and Goff 2001). The growing numbers of poor and needy, as well as the politics of supply, will continue to present major challenges to the municipal departments responsible for the provision of basic services.

Postscript

The provision of electricity to all South African households is a political issue. Historically South Africa had the capacity to supply all its citizens, but when it failed to do so, access to electricity became one of the indicators of difference between black and white, rich and poor, suburb and township, urban and rural. By the 1990s, the South African electricity industry had been operating profitably for almost 100 years, albeit serving commerce and industry and only 30 per cent of the population. Post-Second World War the national electricity utility, Eskom, established itself as one of the largest utilities in the world responsible for generating, transmitting and distributing exceptionally cheap electricity. It was able to do this by building power stations designed to use the abundant low-grade coal produced in South Africa with little thought given to include environmental or social costs in the tariff. This huge and profitable monopoly was well suited to the task of rolling out the grid to those previously bypassed. In 1991 only 30 per cent of the households in South Africa were electrified, but by the turn of the century over 2.5 million additional domestic connections had been made, bringing the number of electrified households to about 67 per cent (Marquard and Eberhard 2000: 5). Financially robust and non-tax paying, Eskom was able to supply heavily subsidised connections at a nominal cost to the new consumers and to cross-subsidise low-consumption customers from high consumption ones (Davis 1997: 100).

Until the end of 1997 it looked as if the ANC's election promise of 'electricity for all' might be kept, but a number of contradictory demands on the utility have begun to take their toll. The new dispensation required that the highly secretive and self-sufficient energy sector open itself to scrutiny, including international examination. This required attention to simultaneous demands, including those for transparency, restructuring, and the inclusion of environmental costs in the electricity tariff. Pressure for the liberalisation of the electricity supply industry and the introduction of competition began to mount at the same time as the climate change negotiations and green house gas mitigation became international concerns. These different global considerations have produced new sets of challenges and tensions. On the one hand, pressures to restructure have threatened the capacity to deliver and subsidise new household connections (Barbeton 1998). On the other hand, global concerns with carbon dioxide emissions indicate that the current inadequate environmental safeguards will have to be addressed, in all likelihood through a tariff hike. In both cases the poor suffer the consequences.

At the local level the changes have translated into a slowing down of the electrification programme, uncertainty about jobs and demonstrations against the privatisation (or corporatisation) of Eskom. The 1998 White Paper on Energy Policy promised *energy* rather than *electricity* for all, marking a major shift in the government's position. The financial viability of continuing the electrification programme has been questioned, but not answered with any certainty. One of the questions arose out of an incorrect assumption about uptake. Eskom anticipated an average consumption rate of 300 kWh per month, whereas the actual uptake for new consumers has been about 80 kWh which fails to deliver a sustainable rate of return (Davis 1997: 100). Potential new consumers could have predicted their consumption patterns more accurately than the engineers and computer models: when questioned closely about what they thought they could afford or would be prepared to pay for electricity, most of the women at Canaan said they were willing to pay between R20 and R30 per month which is approximately half what planners anticipated (NER 1996) and an accurate reflection of uptake among the poor. Had the planners consulted more widely on this issue, the electrification programme might have been designed quite differently to accommodate low levels of recovery.

On the other hand, over the years Eskom has become more proficient at its task. An unanticipated consequence of experience, skills-enhancement, regional competition and technological advances, has been that instead of the cost per connection rising as it was assumed would be the case when more remote areas were reached (Davis 1997: 100), Eskom stabilised its connection costs at around R4 000 per household. Just as it achieved this remarkable feat, the utility finds itself in the throes of restructuring and handing over major responsibility for the continuation of the electrification process to the new Regional Electricity Distributors (REDs). The details of the REDs, including how electrification will be funded, are yet to be made known, but they will have neither the financial muscle nor the human resources that Eskom had. In a baffling move the government has switched its support from electrification to the installation of energisation packages (solar home systems and LPGas cylinders). These cost more than grid electricity connections and are considered inferior by most recipients (Annecke 2002). Many poor women will probably not be surprised that just when it was about to be their turn to receive facilities, the rules changed but they may be angry.

NOTES

1. Eviction notices were served on the settlement on 7 August 1990.
2. After Kimberley (1891), Johannesburg (1891), Cape Town and Pretoria (1894), and Pietermaritzburg (1896).
3. By the end of 1997, 50 per cent of all South Africans households were electrified.
4. A figure well known in informal settlement lore and whose story has been recorded by Lynn Robertson-Hotz, but remains unpublished.
5. Ardington notes that in August 1990 about eight per cent of the people of Canaan still fetched water from their neighbours.
6. This Housing Subsistence Level was derived from the Institute for Planning Research at the University of Port Elizabeth's household subsistence data, and adjusted for the smaller households at Canaan.
7. The price of paraffin is regulated but is not policed beyond bulk distributors.
8. Mrs Memela's life's journey is recorded in Ndukwane, G., T. Memela, D Phakati and T. Qqwabe. 1992. *No Space to Plant and Other Stories by the Women of Canaan*. New Readers Project, Centre for Adult Education, University of Natal, Durban.

REFERENCES

Aitcheson, J. 1990. 'Interpreting Violence: The Struggle to Understand the Natal Conflict'. Centre for Adult Education, University of Natal, Pietermaritzburg.

Annecke, W.J. 1992. 'We Are So Poor: An Investigation into the Lives of Ten Women Living in an Informal Area in the Durban Functional Region with Particular Reference to the Role of Domestic Fuel'. M.A. thesis, University of Natal, Durban.

——. 1993. 'Fuel for Thought'. *Journal of Energy in Southern Africa*, 4, 2.

——. 1994. 'An Investigation of Fuel Use by Urban Women'. Report to the Department of Mineral and Energy Affairs, Pretoria.

——. 2002. 'The Rich Get Richer and the Poor Get Renewables'. Forthcoming in AGENDA July/August.

Ardington, E. 1992. 'Buckpassing in Canaan: An Example of Authorities' Failure to Address the Needs of Informal Urban Dwellers'. Working Paper No. 24. CSDS, University of Natal, Durban.

Barbeton, C. 1998. 'Restructuring the Electricity Distribution Industry: An Analysis of the Proposed Ownership and Governance Structures of Regional Electricity Distributors'. *Development Southern Africa*, 15, 3.

Bembridge, T.J. and J.E. Tarlton. 1990. 'Woodfuel in the Ciskei: A Headload Study'. *South African Forestry Journal*, 154.

Black Sash. 1990. 'Black Sash Advice Office Report'. Natal Coastal Region, Durban.

Cecelski, E., J. Dunkerley and W. Ramsey. 1979. *Household Energy and the Poor in the Third World*. Washington DC: Resources for the FutureWashington.

Davis, M. 1997. 'Financial Analysis of the Electrification Programme'. *Development Southern Africa*, 14, 1, pp. 97–120.

Davis, M. and S. Ward. 1995. 'Household Energy-Use Patterns in Rural Areas: The Effects of Access to Electricity'. Energy and Development Research Centre, University of Cape Town.

De Kok, R. 1986. 'Garbage Picking as a Strategy for Survival'. M.A. thesis, University of Natal, Durban.

Department of Mineral and Energy Affairs. 1998. *White Paper on the Energy Policy of South Africa*.

Eberhard, A. and C. Van Horen. 1995. *Poverty and Power: Energy and the South African State*. London: Pluto.

Eberhard, A. and A. Williams (eds). 1988. *Renewable Energy Resources and Technology Development in Southern Africa*. Cape Town: Elan.

Eskom Statistical Yearbook. 1995.

Gandar, M. 1984. 'The Poor Man's Energy Crisis: Domestic Energy in KwaZulu. Second Carnegie Inquiry into Poverty and Development in Southern Africa'. Conference Paper No.156. University of Cape Town.

Goldemberg J., T. Johansson, A. Reddy and R. Williams. 1987. *Energy for Development*. Washington DC: World Resources Institute.

Makgetla, N. 2001. 'Privatisation by Any Other Name'. *Mail and Guardian*, 26.04–03.05.2001.

Marquard, M. and A. Eberhard. 2000. 'Towards Energy Equity, Efficiency and Environmental Sustainability in South Africa: Policy Challenges'. *Energy for Sustainable Development*, IV, 4. Special Issue on South Africa, pp. 3–7.

May, J. and S. Stavrou. 1989. 'The Informal Sector: Socio-Economic Dynamics and Growth in the Greater Durban Metropolitan Region'. Rural Urban Studies Working Paper No.18. Rural Urban Studies Unit, University of Natal, Durban.

Mehlwana, A. and N. Qase. 1996. 'Social Determinants of Energy Use in Low-Income Metropolitan Households in the Western Cape (Phase 1)'. Department of Minerals and Energy Report No. EO9420.

National Electricity Regulator (NER). Annual Report. Johannesburg.

Oelofse, C. and J. Goff. 2001. 'Evaluating the Suitability of the City of Durban in Terms of the Implementation of the Models for Sustainable Development Project'. School of Life and Environmental Sciences, University of Natal, Durban.

Ross, F. 1993. 'Transforming Transition: Exploring Transition Theories in the Light of Fuel Use in a Squatter Settlement'. *Journal of Energy in Southern Africa*, 4, 2, May.

Sutcliffe, M. 1989. 'Informal Settlements in Natal-KwaZulu: A Research Register'. Sponsored by the Urban Foundation. University of Natal, Durban.
Todes, A. and N. Walker. 1991. 'Women and Housing Policy: Analysing the Past, Debating the Future'. Paper presented at the conference on Women and Gender in Southern Africa at the University of Natal, Durban, 30 January – 2 February.
Viljoen, R. 1990. 'Energy Use in Low-Income Dwellings in the Winter Rainfall Area'. Report No. GEN 138. Energy Research Institute, University of Cape Town.
White, C., O. Crankshaw, T. Mafokoane and H.Meintjes. 1996. 'Social Determinants of Energy Use in Low-Income Metropolitan Households'. Department of Minerals and Energy Report number EO9423.

CHAPTER TEN

The Development of Mass Street Trading in Durban

The Case of Muthi *Trading*

STEIN INGE NESVÅG

The development of mass street trading is one of the most important developments in the political economy of Durban since the 1970s. By creating employment and income opportunities for thousands, and by providing cheap and symbolically important goods and services to the urban marginals, street trading has drastically changed the lives of Durban's poor, and has forced forward a redefinition of (D)urban life, space and culture. As the majority of the street traders today are women, the emergence of mass street trading is also the history of active and defiant women creating a productive sphere for themselves in an oppressive environment. I therefore argue that the tendency to focus entirely on the problems and challenges facing marginal women in the informal sector should be complemented with an approach which views women as actively *conquering* a bustling street market economy.

This chapter will describe some of the historical factors that led to mass street trading in the late twentieth century, and will focus on the trade in so-called 'African traditional medicine', or *muthi*.[1] By *muthi* trading I mean the trade in *muthi* products and healing services which involves gatherers, traders (mostly on the streets and in the *muthi* markets, but also operating from shops), *inyangas* (traditional doctors, specialists in medical healing) and *sangomas* (diviners, spiritual healers). By creating 14 000 jobs and with an estimated total value of R170 million, the *muthi* trade is one of the largest and most important sectors of Durban's street trade economy (INR 1997; FAO 1998). Studies have shown that Durban is the most important centre for the *muthi* trade in the southern African region, with an unprecedented scale, sophistication and intensity (Cunningham 1992).

Early Street Trading in Durban

Historical research shows that street trading is a long-established element of the urban informal sector (La Hausse 1984; Maylam and Edwards 1996; Rogerson 1983, 1985, 1989). Before the early 1980s street traders in Durban were subject to a well-entrenched tradition of repression, harassment and prosecution (Maylam 1982, 1985; Rogerson and Hart 1989; Maylam and Edwards 1996). Yet the first three decades of the twentieth century, street trading flourished, as it was allowed to operate with relatively few restrictions (Maylam 1982; La Hausse 1996). La Hausse has shown how, in the early 1900s, African traders from rural areas entered Durban on five-day passes to hawk (La Hausse 1984). In part, this early African informal sector was a part-time rural-urban and male-dominated phenomenon.

In response to Durban capital's particular needs for labour, and despite influx control and segregation, the African population in Durban engaged in various types of formal and informal labour. In the formal colonial economy, the most important employment sectors for Africans in the beginning of the twentieth century was as *togt* labourers, mainly comprising dock workers, washermen, domestic servants,[2] rickshaw pullers,[3] Native policemen, and as assistants in shops and offices. Around these employment opportunities serving white capital's needs grew a thriving informal economic sector. Street traders started to establish themselves around key transport nodes and outside the various sites of economic and social activity, such as the hostels for *togt* labourers, around the many eating-places and illegal liquor houses (*shebeens*), and both inside and outside formal and informal market places that emerged.

The Warwick Avenue Triangle and Grey Street areas, which today form the largest informal street market area in Durban, have a long history of hawking. Initially, most of the non-white enterprises in nineteenth-century Durban were run by Indians. These Indian businesses came to dominate quite a large portion of the western parts of the Central Business District from the end of the nineteenth century. Adjacent to this thriving Indian commercial area around Grey Street, grew the prime site for African trade: the Native Market in Victoria Street and the nearby market system in Warwick Avenue. By the turn of the century, both Indian and African trading areas were consolidated as 'non-white' economic zones with a bustling trade. The Indian trade in the Grey Street area had then, as it has now, a more formal 'shop-like' character with a larger turnover, as opposed to the smaller and more stall and pavement operation styles typical of African merchants. The most important goods and services in the street market economy around the turn of the century were vegetables, fruits, meat, second-hand clothes, prostitution, transport services, domestic services (clothes washing), African beer (*utshwala*), and *muthi* products and healing services.

The Muthi Trade

Since its establishment in Durban around the turn of the century, the *muthi* trade has been an important part of Durban's street trade economy. The trade expanded with the increasing urban demand for *muthi*. This demand for *muthi* products and traditional healing services stems from the widely held belief amongst Africans that good health and success, or disease and misfortune, are not chance occurrences, but are due to the will or actions of sensate agents (individuals, ancestral spirits, or a deity). *Muthi* and traditional healing is believed to be able to influence all aspects of life, as it has the power to intervene and mediate between these different influences. The *muthi* trade thus has a strong backing of religious and cultural ideas, which makes it a profitable, and highly interesting economic activity. It is believed that 80–85 per cent of the African population use *muthi*, most often in conjunction with biomedicine (FAO 1998). *Muthi* entails a complex classification system of herbal and animal medicines according to their traits, properties, gathering method, uses, preparation and administration.

Muthi traders, *inyangas* and *sangomas* started to sell their *muthi* and healing services from the various social and economic junctions for Africans that emerged in the early 1900s. At this stage, *muthi* trading was predominantly a male activity. This can be attributed to the fact that African urbanisation throughout the segregation and apartheid eras was predominantly male. 'Native policy' focused on regulating the influx of *productive* African males, while women who were perceived as having no economic value to the colonial town were discarded. Women were instead assigned a purely *reproductive* role; a role which was to be served in the rural areas. The presence of African women (and children) in urban areas represented family life, which again was seen as symbolising the increasingly intolerable permanency of Africans in the town.

The early (D)urban *muthi* trade was also highly specialised and centralised in the sense that relatively few men controlled the trade, giving it a form of a condensed trading sector centred around a few highly accumulative units. At this time, *muthi* trading was one of the few options open for men who wished to enter the capitalist economy independently from the missionaries (Beall and Preston Whyte 1985). These early *muthi* traders were not merely targeted for their burgeoning illegal street trade. Antagonistic official responses to the *muthi* trade since the late 1800s introduced the beginning of a long and comprehensive struggle for medical rights and the control of health. The first official legislation pertaining to the *muthi* trade came in the 1890s with chapter 14 in the Code of Native Law (Law 19) of 1891, and the Zululand Proclamation (No. VII) of 1895. Natal was the only government in South Africa that legalised the trade, but through elaborate and strict laws. The Zululand Proclamation laid down the conditions under which *inyangas, sangomas* and herbalists were allowed to practice for gain; the procedure to obtain a license, the maximum fees they were allowed to charge, patient rights, and which treatments and medicines were prohibited. *Muthi* traders were perceived as dealing with 'witchcraft' and 'mumbo-jumbo' medicines and practices, and were accused of trading on the 'Native's innocence'. Despite these early official paternalistic concerns for African medical consumer rights, the *muthi* trade expanded during these first three decades until it reached a scale where the Natal Pharmaceutical Society began to feel the competition. Traders had expanded their range of goods to include patent drugs, and some of the more successful traders even opened up *muthi* shops and post-order businesses. In 1928, the Medical, Dental and Pharmacy Act (No. 13 of 1928) sparked a long and intense struggle between *muthi* traders (through the Natal Native Medical Association) and the Natal Pharmaceutical Society and various levels of government. Act No. 13 together with the Witchcraft Suppression Act (No. 3 of 1957), and later strict nature conservation laws slowly but effectively drove the *muthi* trade underground or out to the emerging townships outside Durban. Indians gradually took over most of the urban supply function by opening up *muthi* shops in the Indian business district around Grey Street, and it was only with the revival of street trading in the 1980s, that the *muthi* trade re-established itself on the streets of Durban again.

Most of the other street trading niches experienced the same fate as the *muthi* trade. Legislation became too harsh for a viable street trade, and from the late 1930s and 40s Durban's street traders were slowly driven out into the peri-urban areas, while a few, mainly Indians, were 'formalised' into the municipal market system. Between the late 1940s and the late 70s, there was only a minuscule and transitory street trade in Durban. Only very few and desperate people, mainly African women, and a few Indians trading outside shops in the Grey Street area braved the law.

Anti-Street Trade Legislation in Durban

Street trading in Durban has been viewed in the same way as the notorious 'birds in the cornfield' – to borrow an analogy from Stadler's (1979) study on squatter movements in Johannesburg. In the view of the dominant discourse, street traders symbolised the manifestation of 'non-whiteness', disorder, and the primitive, and their 'de-urbanising' activities were perceived as sponging off the urban capitalist project. Street trading and other informal sector activities also posed a serious threat to the labour intensive industry, and undermined the entire logic of the migrant labour system. The development of repressive legal and regulatory systems made it almost impossible to trade from the 1940s up to the early 1980s. Legislation pertaining to street trading was as elaborate and strict in Durban as in other cities in South Africa, and there were a number of acts, ordinances and bylaws at the various levels of government that restricted street trading.

In general, the most important official instrument for controlling and regulating street trading has been the concession or withholding of trading licenses (Rogerson 1989). In addition to Act No. 18 of 1897 relating to licenses for wholesale and retail dealers mentioned earlier, the Black (Urban Areas) Consolidation Act No. 25 of 1945 and the 1950 Group Areas Act were the most significant pieces of legislation which contained clauses that restricted street traders (Rogerson 1989). Both acts debarred African street traders and small businesses from trading in the city. The Natal Ordinance 11/1973 further restricted street trading. This provincial legislation restricted hawking of goods within 100 m of a fixed formal business, and prevented hawkers from taking up fixed stands by allowing them to occupy a spot for only 15 minutes, after which they were to move at least 25 m away. Furthermore, the Ordinance stipulated that all traders required a suitable license to hawk or trade. But it was the Durban city street trading bylaws of 1962 (section J6) that were the most comprehensive and specific, and which totally outlawed street trading. The effect of the above restrictions was to define street traders as illegal intruders into the city, making them eligible for prosecution by the Durban City Police. Therefore, the experience of street traders in Durban was, up until the mid-1980s, marked by regular harassment by city officials in the form of arrests, confiscations and fines. However, despite the harsh legal and regulatory environment, there was defiance and resistance, mainly led by African women. To these women, who had no other means of survival, the constant threat of prosecution was regarded as less of a burden than the threat of starvation.

Deregulation of Street Trading in the 1980s

In the early 1980s, the Durban local authorities started to reconceptualise street trading. This was partly due to changing sentiments at a national level, where focus started to shift towards acceptance, encouragement and upgrading, resulting in the formation of the Small Business Development Corporation and Urban Foundation. But more importantly, as a result of the growing mass defiance by street traders, the city accrued increasing costs for policing the small enclaves of street trade that had begun emerging in the Warwick Avenue area. The liberal regime of Progressive Federal Party city councillors and a new generation of progressive city planners were slowly coming to the realisation that law enforcement was increasingly impossible, and they started to concede the economic immorality and dysfunctionality of existing legislation. The combined effects of massive urbanisation due to the collapse of apartheid influx control measures in 1986, escalating urban unemployment, organised mass resistance and strong international pressure, as well as the general international move towards economic liberalisation and increasing international focus on the informal sector and its potential contribution to solving problems of unemployment and poverty, all led the process towards deregulation and formalisation of street trading.

These developments resulted in the launch of two official studies into street trading in Durban: the Market Survey in 1983 and the Hawker Report in 1984 (City Engineer's Department 1983, 1984). These reports, which studied the street market system, its extent, location, and policy options, marked a watershed in official policy towards street trading in Durban and later, in other South African cities. The reports concluded that the illegal status of the street trader had to be re-evaluated. The content and recommendations of the reports were perceived as radical at that time. The initial plan was to move all informal sector activities out of the Central Business District in a typical apartheid 'separate development' fashion, so that the highways and freeways could continue to dominate the Warwick Avenue area. But the Market Survey (1983) pointed out the fact that this market area was important precisely because of its location and the flow of pedestrians that the nearby communication termini facilities created. It stressed the need for the market system to exist in the area. The Hawker Report (1984) investigated the role of street trading in Durban's economy and argued for a more flexible approach towards the regulation of street trading. It recommended a simpler licensing procedure, but more importantly, it introduced the idea of a number of 'immune zones' in the Central Business District where hawkers could operate on a 'free for all' or 'first-come' basis. The Hawker Report considered that an element of control was essential to any functioning street trade economy, but emphasized that control measures should be fair to those within the system. The two documents were relatively well received and the necessity for this form of trade was later recognised in principle by the City Council. In 1985, a sub-committee was established to find practical ways of implementing more favourable policies towards street traders. In addition to the institution of designated trading areas, a more lenient policing approach was adopted. Another outcome of the report was the introduction of a new vending license to replace the archaic hawker license. This move created a simpler and more appropriate set of licensing requirements.

The policy approach adopted in Durban differed from other South African cities in that it attempted a more loosely regulated control system (Rogerson 1989). Three years after Durban's reconceptualisation of street trading, came the 1987 White Paper on Privatisation and Deregulation. This central state policy document saw the imperative for encouraging entrepreneurship and stressed that the approach to regulation should emphasize the promotion of economic activity and be less directed towards its control. Although Durban's approach towards street trading in principle was in line with this deregulation move, officials in Durban were still struggling to find practical ways of putting these principles into action.

The policy of non-prosecution towards the end of the 1980s contributed to a dramatic increase in street trading in Durban, which had the positive effect of creating much needed employment, but also gave rise to a number of problems. The deregulation process resulted in problems of co-operation between traders and the authorities as street traders were uncertain of their rights. It also meant that city officials were unable to respond to problems and complaints – which again resulted in public perceptions of lack of interest or initiative on the part of the City Council. An increasing number of complaints came from the media and commuters, ratepayers and residents' associations about the growing 'problem of street trading'. Ironically, this relative lack of official regulation and control also brought in new problems for the street traders. New sorts of informal control mechanisms came to fill the void, including arbitrary 'take-overs' of trading areas with extortion of 'rent', informal supply cartels with their own means of controlling prices, and protection rackets and mafias. This mainly affected female traders and those with the least resources and weakest networks. The opening up of informal trading also introduced new conflicts between traders, often based on race (Indian versus African versus white), or stemming from newcomers who had no respect for, or knowledge of, the existing 'informal' rules governing the organisation of street trade.

There were several developments in the Warwick Avenue market system during the second half of the 1980s. When the Hawker Report was written in 1984, there were approximately 200 traders in the entire Central Business District (City Engineer's Department 1984). Counts done in September 1988 revealed that there were approximately 600 traders in the Warwick Avenue area alone, which had increased to approximately 700 in February 1989, and 800 in June 1990 (City Engineer's Department 1989, 1990). At the same time, there was an increase in the number of African traders operating in the area and a decrease in the number of Indians. In 1984, an average of 71 per cent of the traders were African, rising to 98 per cent in 1990 (City Engineer's Department 1990). The male percentage changed slightly as more men entered the street trade sector: from 33 per cent in 1984 to 40 per cent in 1990 (City Engineer's Department 1990). This figure suggests that women paved the way for men, who only started joining the street trading sector when it became relatively safe. Official documents also report that the scale of operations had grown substantially with the range of goods and services offered becoming more diverse and complex. The most popular items for sale in 1990 were fruit, vegetables and *muthi* products, and the tendency was for traders selling similar goods to group spatially, forming informal street markets (City Engineer's Department 1990). There were also reports of higher incidences of 'litter and disorganisation' in the area. Despite these developments, the City Engineer's Department noted that the implementation of the philosophy of 'reasonableness' towards street trading had been 'fairly successful', and that street trading was now 'firmly entrenched in the Central Business District's economic structure' (City Engineer's Department 1990: 71–2).

The Street Trading Boom in the 1990s

The 1990s saw a boom in street trading in Durban, with the numbers of street traders reaching a formidable 19 800 in 1997 (Markewicz Report 1997 in the *Daily News* 21.08.97). The lenient policies formulated in the mid-1980s were seen as one of the reasons for this growth. Other important factors were natural disasters (two floods and a severe drought) and the widespread political violence that dominated the province in the 1980s and 1990s, which drove people from their rural homes and into Durban. Not only did these developments result in an explosive change in the volume of street trade, but they also led to an important shift in the form and structure of street trading. The burgeoning informal street trading sector in Durban is today a predominantly female-driven economic sector. Estimated mean for all sectors and trading areas of

Durban's street trade economy show a 60:40 per cent split between female and male traders (Economic Development Department 1998). In the case of the *muthi* trade, which is one of the largest and most profitable sectors, approximately 80 per cent of the traders are women (INR 1996). Instead of focusing entirely on the problems facing marginal women *placed* in the informal sector, one should not exclude the possibility that these defiant and determined women may have *conquered* the streets. In a situation of growing formal unemployment due to global recession in the late 1990s, the informal sector, and especially street trading, has proven a successful route to accumulation. Although at times minimal and often highly fluctuant, this new income has already altered the position of women in the household and in society in general (Moser 1989; Tripp 1997).

In 1991, the Business Act (No. 71 of 1991) regarding the licensing and conducting of businesses was passed by central government. The act introduced a new dispensation for street trading, restricting the powers to pass regulations or bylaws that prohibited street vending. Durban local authorities were dissatisfied with certain definitions and provisions of the act, as they wanted greater control of street trading. For example, the act did not authorise Durban's 'immune zones'. During the following years, Durban officials worked hard to amend sections of the Business Act, as it took away their legislative means to regulate street trading. A unique situation occurred where a degree of anarchy in Durban's streets prevailed for three years (between 1993 and 1996), which also saw a massive increase in street trading. The informal management problems faced by street traders in the late 1980s were intensified.

The early 1990s were dominated by the lack of state legitimacy and an unstable political climate due to the negotiations leading up to the democratic elections in 1994. With international attention focused on South Africa, white administrators were increasingly bound by an emerging 'political correctness' that focused on human rights and democracy and which made it practically impossible to attempt to clamp down on informal trading. These factors, combined with the Business Act's deregulation policy, forced the Durban authorities to sit down and formulate new street trading bylaws, and this turned out to be a slow and complex process. The Informal Trading and Small Business Opportunities Department (Informal Trade Department) was established in 1993 to help address the growing problem of street trading and the lack of functional legislation, as well as to negotiate with street traders who by now had organised themselves into various bodies, all claiming representation in the process. Not all of these organisations were taken seriously, as some of their leaders operated more in self-interest. There were, however, a few exceptions from this trend. Most important of these, was the formation of the Self-Employed Women's Union (SEWU) in 1994, which by using a labour union type of organisation has evolved into a powerful voice for female street traders and other self-employed women around the country.

After amendments to the Business Act in 1993, which conceded some powers back to local authorities, new street trading bylaws were finalised in September 1995 and implemented in January 1996. Street trading now became restricted to demarcated sites within two main areas: the Central Business District core and the beachfront. Traders were now restricted to operate between 6 am and midnight only; overnight sleeping at the place of trade was forbidden; the erection of any structures prohibited; and certain health and hygiene provisions were laid out (Municipal Notice 96 of 1995). The new street trading bylaws were met with strong opposition from street trader organisations. SEWU and other organisations complained that they were not consulted in the drawing up of the new bylaws. They forcefully argued that the new laws automatically criminalised street traders. They claimed that the prohibition of traders sleeping overnight at their places of trade was unreasonable, as there had been a long-standing demand for the provision of overnight accommodation. In addition, the bylaws ascribing comprehensive cleaning responsibilities to street traders unfairly shifted a public responsibility onto marginal street traders. They argued instead that the city had a responsibility for the workplace of the traders (SEWU memorandum 30.11.95). Despite these and other objections, city officials immediately initiated various 'clean-up operations' to clear the streets of illegal trade.

The year 1996 was marked by this tough stance against street trading, with pre-dawn blitzes on street markets. I was present at one of these raids (at 4 am on 30 September 1996) when over 40 heavily armed policemen, together with several rubbish disposal trucks, moved into the Warwick Avenue area, and removed illegal shelters that were erected by *muthi* traders in Russell Street and Leopold Street. Traders put up the shelters because they were tired of waiting for a new market and because the *muthi* (and the traders themselves) needed protection from the weather. According to a senior police official, street traders supported the move to clear up the area as it posed a serious health hazard ('*I have never seen so many cockroaches or such big rats. These traders have no ablutions and they live, sleep, trade and defecate in the same place . . .*), and the structures were hindering both traffic and pedestrian flow ('*It was only a matter of time before a bus had an accident or a blow out, and drove into the shacks and killed dozens of people*') (quotes from *The Saturday Paper* 05.10.96).

The street traders' version was different. The branch leader for SEWU in Russell Street handed a memorandum to the City Police condemning the police action. The statement said: 'We find it unacceptable that police are sent in to harass us without the responsible authorities being able to provide us with any alternatives' (*Daily News* 30.09.96). She was quoted in the newspaper as saying that the Informal Trade Department had been promising them a new market for the last two years, and called on the department to allow the traders to trade as they did until a new and more suitable place was found for them. A new *muthi* market was finally erected in October 1998, after constant and efficient pressure from the Russell Street *muthi* traders.

Throughout 1997 and 1998, Durban officials continued their drive to gain control over the growth of street trading. In an attempt to regulate the trade, and to 'inculcate a culture of payment', a monthly trading site rental fee was introduced in January 1998 (R10 for those without shelter; R35 for those with). The generated revenue was to go towards a special fund, which in the words of a councillor would 'bring us some money, and will pay for the control measures, such as security for street traders' (*Daily News* 24.09.97). The new policy in this regard had worrying similarities with the oppressive and notorious 'Durban system' initiated some 80 years earlier. That system had used compulsory city beerhall revenues to pay for the minimal services provided for the African population (Maylam and Edwards 1996). Perhaps not surprisingly, the response was similarly recognisable, taking a typically anti-apartheid form of non-compliance and defiance, which to a certain degree rendered these measures unsuccessful. Towards the end of 1997, city councillors moved to enforce street trading legislation and were once again forced to apply for an amendment or the repealing of the National Business Act.

Deregulation and the Muthi Trade: The Russell Street Muthi Market

Aside from being one of the largest and most visible sectors of the street market economy in Durban today, the *muthi* trade also has a high proportion of women. According to a report from the Food and Agriculture Organization of the United Nations (FAO 1998), the *muthi* trade generates some 14 000 jobs in Durban. Furthermore, the report estimates that 1 500 tonnes of plant material are traded annually, with a value of R21 million (the raw unprocessed products). These products have added value when prescribed by healers, and the FAO report has worked out that in Durban alone some 4 million products are dispensed annually, adding R152 million to the R21 million traded in raw products.

Within the Warwick Avenue market system, *muthi* traders operate from the newly erected *muthi* market on two unfinished viaducts over the Berea Station, and from the upgraded facilities on Russell Street bridge. Shops, consultancy offices, and now traditional hospitals, have also been opened up at other places to meet the increasing demand for *muthi* and traditional healing services. The Russell Street market is the largest *muthi* market in southern Africa, and is regarded as one of the main centres of the regional trade in traditional medicine (Cunningham 1992; FAO 1998; INR 1988).

Throughout the repressive apartheid years, a small group of defiant *muthi* traders erected stands on a temporary basis on the pavements under the Eilat viaduct and between the Berea Station and the Old Market site (now the Victoria Market), servicing the increasing flow of African pedestrians and commuters. These traders were constantly harassed and threatened by the Durban City Police and had to anticipate, and indeed account for, regular confiscations of their wares in their daily enterprising. More and more traders joined them throughout the 1980s, and in 1990, the *muthi* market mushroomed, gradually expanding up the broad pavement on the Russell Street bridge and around the corner down Leopold Street towards Market Street. Within weeks, all available trading spaces were occupied as the rumour spread about the illegal and spontaneous invasion of these prime trading sites. These developments coincided with other mass defiant invasions of urban space (i.e. the resettlement of Cato Manor from 1990). As mentioned above, the authorities could do little to stop this process because of the peculiar conditions that the political transformation created.

A study by the Institute of Natural Resources (INR) from 1996 showed that there were approximately 400 retail stores in the *muthi* market, with an estimated 200–300 traders active at any one time (INR 1996). Approximately 80 per cent of the traders were women, and their incomes ranged from less than R200 to more than R2 000 a month, with a mean of R440 (INR 1996). The report claimed that the impact on job creation was significant, and estimated that the Russell Street market alone generated between 600 and 1 000 jobs including the actual traders, their assistants and gatherers. The total incomes earned (including operating costs) was estimated to be between R1.06 and R1.58 million per annum. This last figure, the INR report notes, may in fact be an underestimate. Interviews and informal conversations I have had with traders have revealed higher incomes and unveiled a strategic marginalisation discourse in the public and official sphere, especially expressed towards surveys like these (Nesvåg 1999). My rough estimates would easily double those of the INR report.

In October 1998, a refurbished *muthi* market opened with proper shelters, electricity and water. The new *muthi* market in Russell Street was the result of a long-standing demand from the *muthi* traders who were promised new facilities in 1994. After organising themselves under the SEWU, these women managed to survive seemingly endless negotiations with the Informal Trade Department and other official bodies, police raids, and an internal power struggle between SEWU and a male-dominated street committee. The *muthi* traders now have the finest street market in Durban which promises increased trade and improved working conditions, and they are awaiting the final construction of an accommodation complex with a child-care centre. This 'urban development project' is evidence of active strategic actors, who with great persistence, have managed to improve their quality of life.

The Politics of Street Trading in Post-Apartheid Durban

The deregulation process in Durban since the 1980s has, as shown above, been dominated by confusion and conflict due to the absence of a clearly articulated management policy. Even after the implementation of the new comprehensive bylaws, street trading is still largely uncontrolled and unregulated. But the period has also been marked by official passiveness, or incompetence in dealing with the street trader problem. In spite of substantial funds allocated from central government via the Reconstruction and Development Programme, and a wealthy municipal economy, it was only towards the end of the 1990s that the Durban local authorities started to improve conditions for street traders. One reason for this delay is that the Durban post-apartheid development drive has been an 'anti-politics machine', to borrow a concept from Ferguson (1990); a *depoliticised* development process, whereby politics has been seen as hindering development by creating unnecessary power struggles which has entailed an official refusal to face popular politics. City officials have expressed this quite openly by blaming 'development' delays on the chaotic state of street trader politics. This has created much conflict, as street trader organisations have constantly complained about a lack of representation and consultation in the process. Secondly, as in most development projects, a technical and quantitative assessment of 'the problem' has been regarded as imperative. But it has proven difficult to determine the precise extent and location of street trading, due to its intrinsically complex, spontaneous and fluctuating character. This technical and reductionist approach often creates various 'infrapolitical' strategies of resistance and manipulation, which are also seen as further obstructing and delaying 'development'. During the development project of building the new *muthi* market close to the Russell Street bridge, planners counted only a dozen *inyangas* amongst the 400 traders in Russell Street. In their plans, they therefore made provisions for consultancy rooms for these *inyangas*. But after the plans were presented to the traders, many more claimed to be *inyangas*. Some entrepreneurs earned money from this by offering three-week evening courses to *muthi* traders and then awarding them *inyanga* 'certificates'. 'Traditionally', it takes up to 10–12 years to train an *inyanga*.

The politics of street trading has not undergone the changes one could expect from the introduction of democracy, and the city bureaucracy has constantly blamed local politicians for their lack of engagement. The political transformation has created an increasingly powerful but conservative African middle class which has brought lots of hope but little practical results for the urban poor. Street trading is still perceived as a major problem, and an eye-sore in the urban landscape one wishes to present to the booming tourist industry. Street traders are thus still seen as 'birds in the cornfield' by both politicians and other powerful urban interest groups, and *efficient* policy to meet the demand for control and regulation has been forced into the mould of apartheid ideology and practice. Ambivalently or paradoxically, this has been seen as the only effective solution, but at the same time impossible to implement in post-apartheid South Africa.

There also seems to have been a lack of collaboration within street trader organisations, who have been competing for members and representation. For example, SEWU, by virtue of their exclusive statutes, pitched themselves against the other, male-dominated organisations in the name of 'female empowerment' in order to attract members. The various local government departments involved in the issue (Informal Trade Department, City Police, City Health Department, Architecture, Parks and Recreation, Economic Development) were not sufficiently co-ordinated in addressing the problem. The relationship between the Informal Trade Department, and the various street trader organisations was always tense. One of the problems noted by SEWU officials and members was that the Informal Trade Department was still filled with the same people who harassed street traders under the previous dispensation.

As alluded earlier, one can gain interesting insights into the informal economy by focusing on the benefits of 'informality'. Contrary to theories of female marginalisation, I believe it is appropriate to say that women *conquered* the streets of Durban rather than just being *forced* there. Most studies of the informal sector focus on the problems and challenges facing street traders, while few mention the advantages of operating 'informally'. It is indeed true that women face serious problems in the form of sexual violence, crime, intimidation from male traders, and conflict between child-rearing duties (as mothers) and trading functions (as traders). Much of the resistance to anti-street trade legislation is based on the fact that all attempts at controlling and regulating the industry ('formalisation') are seen as threats to their comparative advantages: no tax, no records, no rent (although this varies a lot) and no regulations. Traders will, therefore, resist reforms whatever the benefits may be and use a strategic marginalisation discourse to morally justify it. Post-apartheid developers and planners know how powerful this resistance discourse is, and people on the ground know how valuable it is.

According to a report from 1997, Durban's 20 000 street traders earned between R200 and R1 000 per month, totalling a monthly earning power of over R3.8 million (Markewicz, English and Associates 1997, in *Daily News* 21.08.97). Amongst the most important goods offered by street traders today are: fresh produce, prepared foods, traditional medicine products, meat, alcohol, second-hand clothing, household goods, arts and crafts, newspapers and magazines, and flowers. The most prevalent services include: minibus-taxi transport, hair salons, shoe repairs, traditional healing, telephone kiosks, prostitution, car/taxi mechanics, and rickshaw transport. Hawking is primarily located in public spheres where there is a high concentration of pedestrian movement and activity. In general, there are large clusters of traders around the major nodes or key installations such as transport terminals, or along routes (streets, roads, bridges) which link either different transport terminals and/or transport terminals with other important nodes of social and economic activity. Despite the new bylaws and licensing system, the degree of control has only been limited, as most of the traders operate outside these restricted areas and without licenses. In the demarcated trading areas, more people tend to have licenses due to frequent controls, but even here 'illegal' trade dominates. One reason for this is that people do not wish to comply to the new regime which they still deem unfair. It is an indication of a fundamental disjuncture in society-state relations over who makes the rules of the game and what they should be. The fact that there still exists an illegal horde of informal traders suggests that people, through their non-compliance, wish to change the present dispensation.

NOTES

1. Zulu term used as a synonym for medicine. Literally, *umuthi* means 'tree' or 'shrub'.
2. La Hausse (1984) estimates the African servant population between 1902–09 at approximately 2 000 (in Friedman 1987: 163).
3. In 1899, some 11 445 men were registered as pullers, and about 740 rickshaws were in daily use. By 1902, which appears to have been a boom year, an astonishing 2 170 rickshaws thronged the streets and in all, 24 020 men were registered as pullers (Posel 1997: 202).

REFERENCES

Beall, J. and E. Preston-Whyte. 1985. 'How Does the Present Inform the Past? Historical and Anthropological Perspectives on Informal Sector Activity in Early Twentieth Century Natal'. Paper presented to the Conference on the History of Natal and Zululand, University of Natal, Durban.

City Engineer's Department. 1983. 'The Market Survey: An Analysis of the Warwick Avenue Market System'. City of Durban.

——. 1984. 'The Hawker Report: A Geography of Street Trading in Durban'. City of Durban.

——. 1989. 'Street Trading: A Policy Approach for the Warwick Avenue Area'. City of Durban.

——. 1990. 'Street Trading in the CBD: A Monitor Survey of the Warwick Avenue Area and the Beachfront'. City of Durban.

Cunningham, A.B. 1992. 'Imithi IsiZulu: The Traditional Medicine Trade in Natal/ KwaZulu'. M.A. thesis, University of Natal, Durban.

Economic Development Department. 1998. 'Draft Street Trading Statistical Report (July 1998)'. Discussion Document. Durban Metropolitan Council.

Ferguson, J. 1990. *The Anti-Politics Machine: 'Development', Depolitization and Bureaucratic State Power in Lesotho*. Cambridge: Cambridge University Press.

Food and Agricultural Organisation. 1998. *Marketing of Indigenous Medicinal Plants in South Africa: A Case Study in KwaZulu-Natal*. Rome: Food and Agriculture Organization of the United Nations.

Institute of Natural Resources. 1988. 'An Investigation of the Herbal Medicine Trade in Natal/KwaZulu'. Institute of Natural Resources Investigational Report No. 29. University of Natal, Pietermaritzburg.

——. 1996. 'The Russell Street and Ezimbuzini Muthi Markets: A Situation Analysis'. Institute of Natural Resources Investigational Report No. 143. University of Natal, Pietermaritzburg.

——. 1997. 'The Marketing of Indigenous Medicinal Plants in South Africa: A Case Study in KwaZulu-Natal'. Institute of Natural Resources Investigational Report No. 164. University of Natal, Pietermaritzburg.

La Hausse, P. 1984. 'The Struggle for the City: Alcohol, the Ematsheni and Popular Culture in Durban, 1902–1936'. M.A. thesis, University of Cape Town.

Maylam, P. 1982. 'Shackled by the Contradictions: The Municipal Response to African Urbanisation in Durban, 1920–1950'. *African Urban Studies*, 14.

——. 1985. 'Aspects of African Urbanisation in the Durban Area before 1940'. In R. Haines and G. Buijs (eds). *The Struggle for Social and Economic Space: Urbanisation in Twentieth Century South Africa.* Durban: University of Durban-Westville.

Maylam, P. and I. Edwards (eds). 1996. *The People's City: African Life in Twentieth-Century Durban.* Pietermaritzburg: University of Natal Press.

Moser, C. 1989. 'Gender Planning in the Third World: Meeting Practical and Strategic Gender Needs in World Development', *World Development* 17, 11.

Nesvåg, S.I. 1999. 'D'Urbanised Tradition: The Restructuring and Development of the Muthi Trade in Durban'. M.Soc.Sci. thesis, Economic History Department, University of Natal, Durban.

Rogerson, C.M. 1983. 'The Casual Poor of Johannesburg, South Africa: The Rise and Fall of Coffee Cart Trading'. Ph.D. dissertation, Queens University, Kingston, Ontario.

——. 1985. 'Feeding the Common People of Johannesburg, 1930–1962'. *Journal of Historical Geography*, 12.

Rogerson, C.M. and D.M. Hart. 1989. 'The Struggle for the Streets: Deregulation and Hawking in South Africa's Major Urban Areas'. *Social Dynamics*, 15, 1.

Stadler, A. 1979. 'Birds in the Cornfield: Squatter Movements in Johannesburg, 1944–1947'. *Journal of Southern African Studies*, 6.

Tripp, A.M. 1997. *Changing the Rules: The Politics of Liberalisation and the Urban Informal Economy in Tanzania.* Berkeley: University of California Press.

CHAPTER ELEVEN

Fresh Produce Distribution Networks in the Durban Metropolitan Area

HARALD WITT

The question of urban survival, and urban food security specifically, in African countries has given rise to a significant body of literature over the last few decades. Much of the original stimuli to this particular issue came in the 1970s when various concerns such as rapid urbanisation, the inability of countries to meet the basic needs of their own populations, the woodfuel crisis and a growing reliance on imported foodstuffs for urban populations became the main focus of attention. An additional stimulus to the question of food security in Africa has been the investigation into the impact of structural adjustment programmes and trade liberalisation on society in general and on the agricultural sector in particular.

The 1970s also witnessed the 'discovery' of the 'informal sector' as an important arena within which urban populations were able to generate livelihoods for themselves. As the distribution of food is an important component within this sector it comes as no surprise that the more recent questions that seek to understand urban food security and food distribution systems have also been intrinsically connected to the analysis and promotion of this sector. In addition to the acknowledgement of an 'informal' sector there has also been a growing recognition of the importance of food production in many African cities. It is now commonly acknowledged that urban agriculture, particularly the production of vegetables, is an important activity in many of these cities. Despite suppression by local governments and a general lack of official recognition in many parts of the continent the 'informal sector' and urban agriculture have contributed significantly towards urban food security. Not only have these two 'sectors' provided numerous employment opportunities for urban dwellers but they have also ensured that reasonably priced food was made available to urban populations.[1]

This chapter examines an urban food distribution system in a city in South Africa, the Durban Metropolitan Area (DMA), giving due consideration to the role of urban agriculture and the 'informal sector'. The way in which food systems are organised and structured is an important aspect of urban survival. In South Africa the question of urban survival is also shaped by the history of apartheid and legislation which restricted movements to, and settlement in, urban areas in the country. In the sprawling metropolis of Durban, the legacy of this past means that the vast majority of its black residents live in townships or shacklands on the periphery of the city and are poor. As these communities continue to struggle under conditions of increasing economic hardship, the manner in which these residents are integrated into local food distribution systems, either as consumers or as active participants, becomes a matter of great importance.

Most approaches to food systems in Africa have tended to concentrate primarily on the distribution of staple foods, especially cereals (Guyer 1987). This is due to the dependency of many African countries on imported cereals to satisfy domestic demand and therefore ensure food security. As South Africa is generally considered to be self-sufficient in the production of domestic cereals, the liberalisation of trade has had a less dramatic impact on the availability of staples.[2] Instead, this chapter focuses on the distribution of fresh produce, tracing the distribution of such produce from its source to its final sale to consumers, highlighting differences among the economic participants and the opportunities for income generation and accumulation. A key reason for choosing fresh produce is that it is the major commodity traded by the 'informal sector' in the DMA, while fruit and vegetables are also those agricultural crops that have the most potential for cultivation in an urban environment.

Fresh Produce Production in the DMA: Self-Sufficiency to 'Self-Insufficiency'

Although South Africa is self-sufficient in fresh produce, the DMA specifically, is not. Despite the recent expansion of the municipal boundaries of the DMA to include several rural based communities, agriculture continues to be a minor contributor to the local economy. This is not to say that pockets of commercial and subsistence forms of agriculture do not exist within the sub-region. However, despite a commitment by local government towards a more multifaceted and sustainable development path, existing agricultural activities in the DMA are poorly supported and are often threatened by urban and industrial expansion. Where the availability of land may be conducive to urban and peri-urban forms of agriculture, such potential is often left unexplored because of the lack of political will, poor urban planning and availability of resources. The ability to ensure higher levels of attaining food security in the DMA is therefore undermined.

Durban has not always been 'self-insufficient' in terms of food production. In its very early history, the city of Durban produced much of the fruit, vegetables, dairy products and meat required by its inhabitants (Hurwitz 1957). The historical advantages that producers in and around the city had enjoyed in terms of market proximity were, however, rapidly undermined by a variety of factors. A key factor was the growth in population numbers leading to higher levels of urbanisation and industrialisation and thus exerting pressure on land available for cultivation. In addition, the development of a state-supported agricultural sector in the interior led to a more competitive environment in the marketing of fresh produce. Farmers in the interior were increasingly able to produce more efficiently and cost-effectively than localised producers due to the more favourable climatological factors and lower land prices that facilitated large-scale production. This was especially true for fruit, and for bulk vegetables such as potatoes, tomatoes and onions. The growing importance of farmers in the interior was directly linked to the establishment of a more sophisticated transport infrastructure that allowed for the distant sourcing of fresh produce. The rapid shift from a degree of food self-sufficiency to 'self-insufficiency' had major implications for the manner in which the city related to the hinterland. It also had major implications for the manner in which food was sourced and distributed in the Durban area.[3]

The marginalisation of localised fruit and bulk vegetable production did not, however, signal the total demise of agricultural activities in the Durban area. Many individuals and households still maintain a foothold in some form of agricultural activity, thus maintaining a well-established tradition in the Durban area. Before examining these various activities and the manner in which they are integrated into the existing distribution systems, a brief overview of the historical practices of urban and peri-urban agriculture will be given. Not only is this important in understanding the changing dynamics between an industrialising city and its relationship to a more productive hinterland but it also provides evidence of the potential that may exist in the promotion of urban agriculture as an alternative employment strategy for urban populations.

Self-sufficiency of the original settlement in Durban was based on the ability of white settlers to produce 'most descriptions of vegetables' as well as a variety of other food crops (Hurwitz 1957). These products were augmented by the agricultural surpluses, primarily maize, generated by an emerging African peasantry. In the early 1870s, a number of previously indentured Indian labourers began to turn to market gardening beyond the immediate boundaries of the Borough of Durban. Within a decade or so these market gardeners began to dominate the local production of a variety of agricultural crops, including the production of fruit and vegetables (Halliday 1942). It is an analysis of this particular sector that may provide a model for contemporary urban and peri-urban agricultural programmes.

These early agricultural activities, especially those of the market gardeners, played an important role in the process of primitive accumulation for many households, facilitating the upward mobility of future generations. The dominance of market gardening as an occupation and the rise of market gardeners as a sub-class probably reached its zenith in the 1930s. In subsequent years, the enlargement of the municipal boundary to facilitate the growing demand for industrial and residential land and an inability to compete in a modernising sector contributed to the declining importance of this sub-class of producers in the Durban area (Freund 1995). But the declining importance of this sector should also be located within an environment that witnessed the growing imposition of racially motivated interventions by the state. Indian market gardeners often outcompeted white farmers; and although this was of economic benefit to the residents of Durban, it also gave rise to growing racial tensions with white producers. These tensions ultimately contributed to the introduction of a legislative environment that sought to protect the economic, political and social interests of the expanding white population.

Small-scale farming on the margins of Durban was, however, not the exclusive domain of Indian market gardeners. Many blacks on Durban's periphery retained an agricultural base either to supplement other sources of income or for home consumption. Black farmers had done much to sustain white settlements in the nineteenth century, but their contribution to the food economy slowly waned in the twentieth century as access to land and commercial markets declined. Black farmers on mission lands or in areas like Inanda continued farming relatively successfully until the 1960s. In general, however, the densely populated shacklands, freehold settlements and municipal locations that housed Durban's black population left little land available for productive agricultural activities (Swanson 1996), even of a subsistence nature, although remnants of an agricultural base were, and continue to be, retained.

Urban Agriculture in the DMA

As with most African cities, the DMA has retained an agricultural component in its overall mix of economic activities. This has not been confined exclusively to the peri-urban margins of the DMA where land is more accessible. Indian market gardeners can still be found in numerous cells scattered throughout the sub-region. There are also a substantial number of white farmers involved in various types of small-scale agriculture where conditions are suitable (Interview, Garesh Naidoo, 02.07.96).[4] Numerous agricultural activities are also found in the predominantly black townships. Much of this production is primarily for subsistence purposes while Indian market gardeners and white farmers generally produce for commercial purposes. This is not to say that no black owned commercial farming takes place within the DMA, as the farmers in the Inanda and Ndwedwe areas will confirm, yet at present most commercial farming in the DMA is undertaken by Indian and white producers.

These small-scale farmers produce a rich variety of vegetables, although low value bulk vegetables such as cabbages, onions and potatoes are generally not produced and fruit production, where it does occur, is often a coincidental by-product. The emphasis is on high value perishable products such as various lettuces, peppers, Swiss chard and other 'greens' or highly specialised products such as 'Indian herbs'. Distinctive is the production of 'jam tomatoes'; a vegetable that is rarely found on the major municipal markets yet is an essential component of Indian cuisine in the DMA. In fact the continuing survival of many small-scale farmers in the DMA is probably highly reliant on their ability to service the specific and specialised needs of the local Indian community. It is interesting to note that supermarkets have identified the potential advantages that can be gained by cornering this particular niche market. This has had direct implications for the manner in which the relationship between the surviving Indian market gardeners and big capital in the distribution chain has evolved.

Since the 1980s there has been a resurgence in the promotion of urban and peri-urban agriculture in the DMA. It is difficult to determine the source of this interest yet it appears to have originated from two specific interest groups. Firstly, many of the newly graduated town planners employed by various planning departments during this period had been exposed to the growing international literature on urban agriculture. The concept was, however, not immediately adopted or integrated into urban planning despite the proven success of small-scale agriculture within the DMA, both historically and at present. Secondly, there were growing political concerns of urban administrators over the levels of urbanisation as rural-urban migration continued to increase rapidly in the 1980s, often motivated by political instability and violence. As many of the newly urbanised were retrenched farm workers, authorities considered urban agriculture an appropriate tool for absorbing at least some of the urban unemployed.

The recognition of urban agriculture as an urban development strategy did not, however, translate into a coherent programme or plan of action. Although public institutions such as the Department of Agriculture and the Department of Health provided some guidance and assistance, this was primarily on an ad hoc basis. Instead it was mainly due to the effort of various non-governmental organisations (NGOs) and welfare organisations that some form of agricultural base was regenerated in the predominantly black residential areas in the DMA. Due to these efforts, numerous community gardens and individually owned plots have been successfully established in the DMA, providing many households with direct access to fresh produce. Such efforts were, however, neither co-ordinated nor were they located within a broader development initiative. As a result, the success of urban agriculture as a development tool has been difficult to assess. Nonetheless, it would appear that urban agriculture has the potential of fulfilling many of the stated development objectives being articulated by government at all levels and should thus be pursued with greater vigour.[5]

Distribution of Fresh Produce in the DMA

Much of the international discussion on food distribution systems refers to two contrasting distribution or supply systems referred to as being either 'informal' or 'formal'. It is however, as Drakakis-Smith (1990) has noted, not sufficient to merely identify these, or even an intermediate sector, as these terms imply some exclusivity, and do not reflect the existing realities of the real nature of interrelatedness between different 'sectors'. This is especially true of the production and distribution links within the fresh produce sector in the DMA. Here the so-called 'informal' activities often dovetail and inter-change with what are more conventionally understood as 'formal' activities as a particular product moves along its own unique distribution chain. It is therefore argued that there is a need to see the economy as a continuum 'with a more formal end and a less formal end' (Witt 2000; Skinner and Lund 2000).

In addition to this academic divide, there is also the more conventional separation of a commodity distribution chain into either wholesaling or retailing operations. Although specific definitions of these sectors do exist, there appears to be a general acknowledgement that if more than half the sales of a particular institution are sold for resale then that particular operation is considered a wholesaling operation. Alternatively, if more than half the sales of an institution are sold directly to consumers, then such an institution is considered to be a retailing operation (Marx 1991). To further complicate the issue there are two additional channels of distribution recognised within the fresh produce industry itself. One of these is referred to as an 'official' channel, while the other is referred to as a 'direct' channel. The former refers to recorded sales that take place within the legally constituted municipal markets, and more specifically the bulk Municipal Fresh Produce Markets (MFPMs). The latter refers to the proportion of national fresh produce sales that circumvent these official channels and are as a result often unrecorded.

Although these descriptive or definitional terms appear to be fairly innocuous, they bring with them a series of prejudices, tensions and strategic alignments, not only within the industry as a whole but also in terms of policy-making and regulation. This is perhaps best epitomised by the 'formal' versus 'informal' debate. The academic separation of 'informal' economic activities from 'formal' economic activities has done much to undermine the status and the establishment of a facilitating environment for the 'informal sector' within the broader economy. Definitions of the 'informal sector' that have not fully grasped the complexities of the 'informal' economy may give rise to inappropriate or ineffective policy measures. Further evidence of the political significance attached to these definitions can be found in the tensions that have arisen between the administrators of 'official' markets and the proponents of 'direct' channels. As 'official' sales at MFPMs are considered to be the key price-setting institutions for the fresh produce sector, 'direct' sales are often seen to be undermining this particular process, thus giving rise to feelings of mistrust and antagonism within the industry as a whole.

As most fresh produce distributed within the DMA would originate from the Durban Municipal Fresh Produce Market (DMFPM), data on the origins of produce marketed through this channel should be able to give some indication of where fresh produce is sourced.[6] According to market officials only 20 per cent of the vegetables (volume) marketed through official channels originates either in the DMA or the province as a whole (Interview, Pieter Wilke, 25.04.96).[7] Due to direct sales, it is possible that this underestimates the contribution of local farmers to the local consumption of fresh produce.[8] Nonetheless, most of the fresh produce consumed within the DMA would therefore be sourced from the remainder of the country. In other words, the fresh produce distribution system in the DMA is not merely a localised or provincial system but is one that is thoroughly integrated into national distribution channels and structures.

Once sourced, such fresh produce then has to be distributed throughout the sub-region to ensure that even the most remote corners of the consumer market are satisfied. In the DMA the DMFPM is the central cog in the sourcing and distribution network. But due to the actual size of the sub-region, the large population, the variety of cultures, variable income distribution and so forth, an array of wholesaling and retailing institutions have emerged over time. These vary in size, the degree of capitalisation, and the manner of organisation. They are also associated with different returns and earnings potential, ranging from the purely survivalist through to multi-million rand enterprises.

Many of the opportunities within these distribution networks were clearly defined by the opportunities and constraints that evolved under the segregationist and apartheid policies of the past. The different echelons within the distribution hierarchy were and largely still are occupied by specific race groups. This racial segmentation within the distribution network has meant that opportunities for black participants were often limited to the lowest and least rewarding echelons in the hierarchy. Recent political changes have done very little to alter the racial composition of this segmentation while the deregulatatory measures that have accompanied the ushering in of democracy have merely re-emphasized the entrenched racial hierarchy with blacks dominating opportunities in the previously prohibited street trading sector. This resurgence of street trading or the 'informal' distribution of fresh produce is one of the most prominent changes in the distribution network in recent years and will be explored further below.

Deregulation, however, has not only impacted upon the nature of distribution networks. The past 30 years have also witnessed the growing deregulation in the actual marketing of fresh produce. Since the time of Union, the growing concern of the state over the marketing of fresh produce had given rise to the promulgation of a variety of legislative and other controlling measures to streamline the industry. By 1971, the whole of South Africa was considered a 'controlled area' and no one could 'operate a fresh produce market without approval of the Minister of Agriculture' (Marx 1991). In reality the imposition of an all-embracing regulatory regime was impossible and in subsequent years many of the regulatory mechanisms have either become obsolete or have been withdrawn. Much of the recent debate within the fresh produce industry revolves around the privatisation of the MFPMs; a radical departure from the discourse several decades earlier.

Municipal Fresh Produce Markets in the DMA

The food distribution networks in Durban have changed significantly over the last 150 years or so. This has been primarily in response to the changing demographics of the city while racially biased legislation and the changing socio-economic conditions of its populace have also influenced the manner in which food has been distributed and consumed within the greater Durban area. As mentioned earlier, the DMFPM could be considered as the central cog in the sourcing and distribution of fresh produce in the DMA. The origins of this market can be traced back to the establishment of a market square in the mid-nineteenth century in what is currently the centre of the Central Business District (CBD) of the city. In subsequent years the market was relocated several times, each time moving further and further from the CBD and closer and closer to the outer margins of the city.

In some ways the physical relocation of the market is synonymous with the modernisation, racialisation and expansion of the city of Durban. The central location of the first market could, for example, be seen to be indicative of the social and economic importance of food (agriculture) and the trading of food to the resident population. Furthermore, although evidence is hard to come by, it would appear that this early market did not distinguish buyers or sellers in terms of race but rather as suppliers or consumers. It is uncertain whether the later construction of a closed market, a slight distance away from the original market square, brought with it the growing racial exclusivity that had begun to permeate settler society and which had begun to characterise the commercial way of life in Durban. But by 1940, when the main market, now referred to as the City Market, had been relocated once more, this time to the Warwick Triangle area, racial divisions had already become deeply entrenched in the manner in which fresh produce was marketed and distributed within the Durban area. In symbolic terms, the physical relocation could also be seen to indicate a shift in the primary concern of Durban's white residents. With the successful expansion of a capitalist agricultural sector and a sophisticated transport infrastructure, the Durban area had achieved a more secure access to food and it became the turn of commercial and other business interests to dominate the landscape of the central Durban area.[9]

In close proximity to the new location of the City Market were several other municipally owned markets that had been established in the early twentieth century. These were often referred to as the Indian Market Properties and included the Early Morning Market ('Squatters Market'),[10] the Indian Market (Victoria Street Curio and Spice Bazaar) and the Native Meat Market.[11] By 1940, the physical infrastructure for the distribution and marketing of many essential foodstuffs, and specifically fresh produce, in the Durban area had clustered itself on the western periphery of the city.

Although the bustling crowds prevalent within the broader market area would have given the appearance of a racially mixed trading environment, this was not entirely accurate. The segregationist policies of the state, fully endorsed and often refined by municipal authorities, ensured that commercial interests in the various markets were entirely defined by race.[12] This was made possible by the introduction and enforcement of regulations and controls through a municipal licensing system and the associated municipal bylaws. In general, black traders were fully excluded from participating in the municipal fresh produce markets. Trading in the City Market was the exclusive domain of whites, while Indians traded from the Indian Market and the Early Morning Market. Although certain licenses issued to Indian traders in the Indian Market specified that they were only allowed to sell to 'non-Europeans', no such restrictions applied to traders in the fresh produce markets. The concentration of the fresh produce markets and the strict regulating of hawking activities ensured that a high degree of control had been imposed on fresh produce distribution channels in Durban by the 1940s – a system of control which also generated additional revenue for the municipal coffers.[13]

In the 1970s, several factors contributed towards the demise of many of the existing marketing structures and facilities in the Warwick Avenue-Victoria Street area. The rapid expansion of Durban's commercial and industrial sectors had contributed much to a significant increase in road and rail traffic. This was exacerbated by the need for an efficient transportation system that would bring black workers from the periphery of Durban to their place of work. As the Warwick Triangle area had become the central locus for both road and rail commuters, the existing transportation infrastructure had become inadequate. In addition, the growing tendency for fresh produce to be transported by road rather than rail led to increased traffic congestion at the City Market. Any expansion of market facilities would have resulted in a decline in customer parking space for an increasingly mobile population. Furthermore, city authorities were reluctant to invest continually in these marketing facilities as their maintenance costs increased.

The rise of these infrastructural shortcomings coincided with the growing concern of the state over the physical condition of the various municipal fresh produce markets throughout the country. Although the Union Market Advisory Board had obtained a certain amount of supervision over fresh produce markets in 1956, this was considered to be insufficient. In 1965 the state therefore established the Slater Commission to investigate the declining popularity of municipal markets, as well as the sales methods, the reasons for considerable price fluctuations and so forth at these markets (Marx 1991). The state also claimed that municipal markets did not have the broader interests of the country at heart, concentrating only on satisfying local needs. These concerns, together with the reluctance of municipalities to invest in their markets and the subsequent deterioration of such markets, provided the state with the perfect opportunity to gain greater control over fresh produce markets nationally (Marx 1991).

The final recommendations of the Slater Commission were translated into a legislative act when in 1970 the state passed the Commission for Fresh Produce Markets Act (Act 72 of 1970). This signalled an attempt at greater state intervention in the marketing of fresh produce in South Africa. The act envisaged a new state-driven initiative to introduce more rigour to the manner in which municipal markets in the major urban centres in South Africa were being managed. The Act also recommended the establishment of a Commission for Fresh Produce. In 1971, this Commission was appointed to co-ordinate the activities of the fresh produce industry and assist in the improvement of existing markets. A system for greater co-ordination between municipal markets was also introduced (Marx 1991). The Act also made provision for markets to be declared National Fresh Produce Markets (NFPMs) and provided some assistance to local authorities for the establishment of new, or the improvement of old, markets.

In 1972 there were approximately 100 municipal markets, yet only 15 would ultimately be recognised as NFPMs by the state.[14] One of these would be the present bulk market located on Flower Road in Clairwood, which replaced the City Market in February 1975. Until the late 1980s there was little, if any, change or modification to this particular distribution channel. Yet as the national role of marketing boards and other regulatory institutions increasingly came into question, the NFPMs themselves became the subject of investigation once more. As the traditional marketing boards reconstituted themselves into privatised producer organisations, placing greater emphasis on controlling quality and disseminating information, similar issues were being raised within the discussions on the future of the NFPMs. In 1989, the Commission for Fresh Produce Markets, acting on the calls from various stakeholders in the fresh produce industry, called for a new investigation into the status of NFPMs. The relevant research was facilitated by the Human Sciences Research Council of South Africa which published their findings in a series of reports in 1991.

One of the more important recommendations to emerge from the main report on NFPMs was that ownership of NFPMs be privatised. It was also recommended that the Commission for Fresh Produce Markets Act be repealed (Marx 1991). The momentum generated by the report has led to the growing deregulation of fresh produce distribution networks. In 1993, legislation that determined state control of the NFPMs was repealed. The management and control of these markets was referred back entirely to local municipal authorities. This triggered off a series of debates on how municipal markets could best be managed, a discourse dominated by various privatisation models. The debate is complex, pitting various interest groups against one another. There is the question of efficiency while there is also uncertainty as to whether a privatised bulk market would continue to be motivated by the principle of providing the broad population with quality fresh produce at affordable prices. As yet, this particular issue has not been resolved.

It is difficult to determine what impact the growing deregulation of the fresh produce industry has had on the actual value and volumes of trade that move through official channels. Firstly, other than potatoes there were no other marketing boards for the remaining vegetables, so it is unrealistic to assume that deregulation would have resulted in the breakdown of institutionalised channels.[15] This may, of course, be less true for fruit, although marketing boards in these industries were often established to facilitate and co-ordinate exports.[16]

Secondly, there have always been direct sales, yet whether these have increased is difficult to determine as most farmers would normally utilise a variety of distribution channels depending on market prices, convenience, the nature of the product, personal bias and so forth. Although the increasing number of farmers' markets and the growth in supermarkets may suggest that a growing proportion of fresh produce is being sold direct, this is difficult to determine as such sales are not recorded. Instead, it is suggested that due to the determined effort by, for example, supermarket fresh produce distribution centres (DCs) to access high quality produce, the quality of fresh produce marketed through official channels may deteriorate (Interview, Pieter Wilke, 30.07.96).[17] This may, in turn, impact on the price levels of fresh produce and as the 16 bulk MFPMs are the key price-setting mechanisms for the industry as a whole, it is argued that farmers nationally will in future suffer from deteriorating prices (Interviews, Pieter Wilke, 30.07.96; Kobus Rademeyer, 24.05.96).

A group of farmers who appear to have shifted most substantially from official marketing channels are the market gardeners in the DMA. In recent years the fresh produce DCs of the various supermarket chains have increasingly sought to capture the localised production of vegetables and more specifically the so-called production of 'Indian herbs'. As a result many Indian farmers in the DMA have entered into exclusive marketing 'agreements' with the supermarket fresh produce DCs. In addition to the supermarket chains, farmers have also resorted to semi-formal markets such as the 'Bangladesh' market located in Chatsworth. These shifts to direct marketing channels, together with the declining number of farmers in the DMA as a whole, would suggest a fall in the participation of local farmers in official markets.

The Early Morning Market

The market most affected by the declining participation of farmers has been the Early Morning Market located in the Warwick Triangle area. This is one of the several markets referred to earlier as the 'Indian Market Properties' and together with the Farmer's Retail Market located at the DMFPM and the Verulam Fresh Produce Market are the only other surviving municipal or official distribution channels located in the DMA. The Early Morning Market was established in 1934. The original aim of this market was to act as a retail market for the numerous small-scale Indian farmers involved in agriculture in the DMA.[18]

Until the 1970s, the Early Morning Market was recognised as the primary fresh produce retail outlet in the city and although the volumes of trade have continued to expand, the trading dynamics have changed substantially. The original success of the Early Morning Market was primarily due to its convenient location and the fact that it was the main outlet for the remaining Indian market gardeners and small-scale farmers in the DMA. It also prospered due to the close proximity of the City Market. Since the 1940s, stallholders in the Early Morning Market had been conveniently located to source fresh produce both from local farmers and from the bulk City Market where produce was sourced nationally.[19] The successful exploitation of this particular relationship, combined with a degree of business acumen, often laid the economic foundations for the success of many of the current key role-players in the fresh produce industry.

A typical example would be the Maharaj family who control a substantial proportion of the trade in the fresh produce distribution industry. Although the dominance of this family in the industry is associated with the names of the three brothers, H.L., P.L. and Lalla Maharaj, the foundations to the success of these bothers were laid somewhat earlier. According to one of P.L. Maharaj's sons, Ronnie Maharaj, his grandfather began the family's involvement in the business in the 1920s by selling from a simple wheelbarrow in the Warwick Triangle. Together with his three sons (H.L., P.L. and Lalla) the grandfather soon expanded the operations of the family both within the market and outside the market. By the 1960s the family controlled twelve stalls at the Early Morning Market, while one of the sons had set up P.L. Maharaj, as a wholesaling company. A retailing agency by another of the sons, H.L. Maharaj, was also established. Both enterprises have subsequently become synonymous with the fresh produce industry in Durban (Interview, Ronnie Maharaj, 21.05.96).[20]

Although such examples illustrate the potential for capital accumulation within the sector, these are generally the exceptions rather than the rule. The vast majority of traders and farmers that still utilise the Early Morning Market generate very modest incomes. These varying experiences however, do raise interesting questions about capital accumulation, upward mobility, entrepreneurship, risk taking and so forth. In other words, how do certain individuals with apparently very similar resources to other individuals, manage to accumulate capital and become upwardly mobile? What are the constraints that prevent others from achieving similar success? Examining the specific features of these individual success stories falls beyond the scope of this chapter.

The very same factors, such as congestion and neglect, that led to the relocation of the City Market had obviously also impacted upon other markets in the Warwick Triangle area, including the Early Morning Market. In addition, the growing dominance of supermarkets located in shopping centres in the suburbs, bringing with it the convenience of 'one-stop' shopping, would have affected the patronage of its white and Indian clientele. This decline was partially compensated by the escalation in black commuters who congregated in the Warwick Triangle and utilised the market to purchase their fresh produce requirements. Already by the early 1980s more than half the customers were black (Interview, Khumen Naidoo, 22.08.96).

In 1986, the Influx Control Act was repealed and although street trading was still considered an illegal activity, more and more traders began to join the few already existing traders on the streets surrounding the Early Morning Market. A few years later the trickle of street traders had turned into a flood pre-empting the deregulation of street trading in 1994. This explosion in street trading has had the most dramatic impact on the Early Morning Market. Instead of being a predominantly retailing outlet, it now serves primarily as a wholesale market to the flourishing 'informal sector'.

The change in trading dynamics, together with the shift in the client base, all located within a framework of broader political change has resulted in numerous tensions within and outside the market. Invariably, as the overwhelming majority of stallholders in the market are Indian and street traders are almost exclusively black, the issue of race rather than class often underlies many of these tensions. Indian stallholders feel increasingly 'squeezed' on the one side by city authorities, whose political brief it is to support the predominantly black street traders, and by street traders, on the other side, who are accused of hijacking trading opportunities from the stallholders. As evidence, stallholders point to the high number of outstanding rentals, which they feel is indicative of declining profits, and a shortage of parking facilities, neglect of services, and the general social decline of the area, all of which discourage customers. Street traders, they maintain, have 'free' use of facilities while the conversion of potential customer parking into taxi ranks has been to the benefit of street traders rather than Market stallholders.[21]

Simply collapsing these tensions into a racial paradigm would appear to reflect reality, yet would also be simplistic. At one level, stallholders experience some form of economic marginalisation and would certainly feel a degree of political disempowerment. This is possibly best illustrated by the fact that although the overwhelming majority of stallholders remain Indian many of the market staff who in the past were also Indian, have now been replaced with black administrators. Yet at a more fundamental level it has much to do with the insecurities and fears that come from change and the inability to adapt to rapid change. The changes in the market, which started gradually, gained momentum by the late 1980s. By the 1990s, the market had changed in terms of its internal organisation, its clientele, and immediate trading environment, while the racial composition of market stallholders had remained the same. In other words, within a short space of time only a handful of farmers still continued to utilise the market, the majority of the clientele were now black with a significant proportion being street traders, while a sea of black street traders now surrounded the actual market. Much of the uncertainty generated by these rapid changes is articulated by stallholders in the market as a threat to their livelihoods as they can no longer compete, and profits have slumped due to the unequal playing fields.

Determining whether the profit levels of stallholders have declined is difficult to gauge. However, and as is described below, most street traders would source their produce from within the Early Morning Market. Although the nature of the transactions has changed within the market, we would expect volumes of trade not to be affected. Market officials who monitor and control the movement of fresh produce into the market substantiated this. As approximately 80 per cent of the produce sold at the market comes from the DMFPM, such officials would certainly have noticed any decline in sales from within the Early Morning Market (Interviews, Pieter Wilke, 25.04.96; Sam George, 19.07.96).[22] Ironically, the current shift from being a predominantly retailing operation to a predominantly wholesaling operation is in fact a continuation of earlier practises where the majority of hawkers and peddlers in the city sourced their fresh produce from the Early Morning Market (Burrows 1961). Due to the stricter regulatory environment of the 1950s and 1960s, most of these particular activities had gone into decline in the post-war period. The more recent deregulation of street trading, however, has once again opened up opportunities for such activities.

Despite numerous problems the market does, it is argued, have a future as it is the 'poor man's market', it does not have 'fancy prices', and you are guaranteed fresh produce (Interview, Sam George, 19.07.96). The key role of the market in the provision of fresh produce to street traders and to commuters in general should ensure the economic viability of the market in the future. However, as the state, and therefore local government, is committed to extending greater economic opportunities to its key political constituency, it is unlikely that the overwhelming dominance of Indian stallholders in the Early Morning Market will continue indefinitely. To ensure broader public access to stalls in the market, city officials have already changed the manner in which vacant stalls are made available. In the past, vacant stalls were simply auctioned off; now a tendering process has been introduced to attract a wider audience and to level the playing fields (Interview, Thulani Nzama, 19.04.2000).

Wholesaling

In addition to the wholesaling operations conducted by the various municipal markets in the DMA, there are also a variety of privately owned wholesaling enterprises. There are essentially two different types of wholesalers in the fresh produce distribution network, although one of these can be further subdivided giving a total of three distinctive types of institutions. These operations are primarily distinguished by their physical relationship to the DMFPM, their clientele, their relationship to big capital and their vertical integration in the fresh produce distribution network. The first of these would be the corporately owned distribution centres (DCs) of the various supermarkets that operate in the DMA. These DCs would source their produce from all available sources, including direct sales from farmers and, of course, the DMFPM. These institutions would generally only service their respective retail outlets, leading to some form of vertical integration within the sector. Although these wholesaling operations have contributed substantially to the manner in which the dynamics in the fresh produce sector have changed over the last few decades, they will not be discussed at any great length. This is primarily because opportunities for individual accumulation of capital within these structures are severely limited.

The two other wholesaling operations are more typical of this genre. The distinction between these two is primarily one of location, which in turn impacts on the manner in which such wholesalers source their product. The first of these wholesaling enterprises operates as an independent, privately owned business physically located outside the perimeter of the DMFPM. Such an enterprise would source fresh produce from a variety of sources including direct sales from farmers. These products would then be resold to other wholesalers or retailers, with a smaller proportion possibly going to consumers directly. In the DMA such wholesalers do not constitute a significant number, with participants waxing and waning over time. As sales are not recorded officially, it is difficult to determine the volumes of fresh produce that pass through these wholesalers. One of the more dominant of these wholesaling operations, however, claimed to have an annual turnover of more than R60 million (Confidential interview (A), 21.05.96). Although unsubstantiated, it was not implausible. More importantly, it gives an indication of the capital that can be generated within certain sub-sectors of the industry.

The second category of wholesalers are the wholesaling operations located on the premises of the DMFPM, often referred to as secondary traders. The granting of trading licenses to these wholesalers coincides with the growing deregulation of markets and marketing referred to above. The formal motive for the co-option of these traders was to 'legalise' the ongoing wholesaling operations that were already taking place outside the DMFPM walls. Such co-option would also curtail the real and potential haemorrhaging of official fresh produce sales, although some secondary traders have maintained a presence outside the DMFPM. In other words, it was an attempt by market officials to retain control over the marketing of fresh produce in the DMA. It is therefore not surprising that these traders are prevented from sourcing their fresh produce directly from farmers. In fact, according to municipal bylaws these wholesalers are forbidden to do so. Instead, these enterprises are only permitted to source their produce from the trading floors of the DMFPM.

The location and sourcing limitations imposed upon these wholesalers has also given rise to a certain peculiarity that has raised the ire of farmers who market their fresh produce through the DMFPM. The point of contention originates from the fact that a secondary trader, who purchases on the DMFPM floor, immediately adds a percentage to the selling price, having moved the product literally only the width of the DMFPM wall. Farmers obviously contend that the prices demanded for their product by secondary traders reflect a 'market' price, which the farmers are entitled to. The counter argument to this position is that secondary traders offer an actual service to customers. It is argued that they operate longer hours (the DMFPM floor closes at 10 am), often repackage the commodity, make up specific bulk orders, extend credit, and as they take actual ownership of the produce they also take on the associated risk (Interview, Pieter Wilke, 25.04.96). This service and the degree of risk are therefore reflected in the added cost.

There are currently 49 secondary traders located on the premises of the DMFPM. Most of these traders have a long association with the distribution of fresh produce in the DMA and all are Indian. Together with the buyers from the dominant supermarkets, these secondary traders are the key buyers from the DMFPM. The operational scale of these traders varies immensely although it is commonly acknowledged that buying is dominated by between five and six key wholesalers, but this does include one or two of the independent wholesalers mentioned above. According to informed sources, it is not uncommon for members of this select group to make weekly purchases that exceed R1 million (Confidential interview (B), 25.04.96). Much of this is made possible by the fact that the DMFPM extends a seven-day credit to the major buyers. These key wholesalers, as with most wholesalers in the fresh produce industry, in turn extend credit to their clients. As one source at the DMFPM pointed out, ultimately the dominant wholesalers are 'nothing more than money lenders' (Confidential interview (B), 25.04.96).

The extension of credit is a crucial component of the fresh produce distribution chain, which together with the high perishability of the products being traded introduces a high degree of risk and instability into the sector. It is this factor, however, that also allows for relatively spectacular rises and equally spectacular falls within the industry. The recent extension of the distribution chain to include the burgeoning street trading sector has further intensified the overall risk factor. Wholesalers are ultimately caught in a vicious cycle where buyers who are unable to pay their debts have to have their debt repeatedly rolled over in the hope that they will eventually be able to repay their existing debt. Wholesalers cannot afford to cut off indebted buyers as the opportunity of recouping the outstanding debt is lost. As a result wholesalers have been 'pushed to the limit' by buyers (Confidential interview (B), 25.04.96). Under such conditions it could be assumed that the DMFPM would consider itself to be at risk, yet this does not seem to be the case. This is probably due to the fact that credit channels within the DMFPM are formally constituted and defaulting would result in prompt and far-reaching legal action. Farmers marketing through the DMFPM are obviously least at risk as payment for sales off the market floor are legally guaranteed.

The need for wholesalers to move large volumes and to move them as rapidly as possible in order to maximise their earning potential has occasionally given rise to speculation as to how some wholesalers conduct their business. The dominance of the above-mentioned major wholesalers, for example, has led to speculation that through their combined buying power these traders have the ability to manipulate prices and extend buying monopolies over certain products. Exerting monopoly control over prices in a sector as diverse as the fresh produce sector is, however, extremely difficult, especially in an environment where farmers tend to exploit a variety of distribution channels. Unless exclusive marketing arrangements can be established with farmers, the domination of a particular echelon within the fresh produce industry would be more about the ability to manage and direct large volumes of trade, rather than an ability to manipulate market prices to suit a particular enterprise.

In a 'static' market such as the main bulk market (DMFPM), there is a greater possibility for buyers who control vast amounts of capital, and therefore buying power, to manipulate prices or to monopolise a degree of control over a particular product on a given day. This monopoly control would, however, require the collusion of marketing agents who are predominantly white. It is therefore not surprising that questions on 'irregular activities' often take on a particular racial slant. Given that a specific echelon in the distribution network is dominated almost exclusively by Indians, while the dominant servicing institution within the DMFPM, namely the market agents, are exclusively white owned, it is not surprising that economic tensions that characterise all industries should manifest themselves as racial conflicts or tension.

Speculators

There is another echelon that is worthy of mention in the fresh produce distribution network. This is the group of speculators or 'tarmac farmers'[23] who provide a vital, yet much maligned, function in the distribution network. Broadly speaking, the term 'speculator', in the fresh produce industry, refers to a non-producing, independent individual who will purchase, transport and then either sell or distribute, fresh produce. Although a 'speculator' may spontaneously purchase some or other fruit or vegetable, and then hope to sell it at an inflated price, such speculative transactions are generally not common. This is primarily due to the perishable nature of fresh produce that makes it difficult to hoard for any length of time. Profits are therefore realised more by prices changing spatially rather than over time. In other words, the price differential between that obtained at the farm and a particular market or between different markets. These prices also tend to be more predictable and less speculative.

This particular echelon in the distribution network is again dominated by the presence of mainly Indian operators although several small-scale black operators have also begun to penetrate this particular niche at the lower levels.[24] The scale of operation and the capital outlay of the various players in this sector varies tremendously. It is also a sub-sector that has given rise to great mythological figures whose prominence and influence have taken on gigantic proportions in the world of fresh produce distribution. There are 'chilli kings', 'madumbi kings' and 'kings of greens'. Notably there are no 'queens'! Although it is difficult to measure the exact volumes that are traded by the members of this self-proclaimed 'royal family' they are certainly not insubstantial.

The most visible of these 'speculators' would be the 'mielie' traders who have a long history of trading from a specified area located at the back of the Early Morning Market. The recent growth of the 'informal sector' and the return to favour of the cooked 'mielie' on the streets of Durban has contributed to a mini explosion of 'mielie speculators'.[25]

The modus operandi of these traders is similar to the numerous other small- to medium-scale 'speculators' that operate in the DMA. Most would source their products from a 300 km radius from Durban. They would pay cash for their product, would buy in bulk, there would be no packaging involved and often speculators would even do the actual harvesting (Interviews with 'speculators' congregated on the disused offramp Durban, 11.04.2000).

Opportunities for the accumulation of capital within this particular niche vary tremendously. Several large-scale 'speculators' have, for example, managed to accumulate substantial amounts of capital over a very short period of time. This has enabled them not only to invest heavily in their own transportation but, in one particular case, has even led to the direct control of several farming operations in the Northern Province (Interview, Mustafa Haneef, 19.07.96). This also illustrates the fact that many of the more large-scale speculators would travel vast distances to source their produce. To fully utilise the economies of scale in terms of transport costs such 'speculators' would also have invested in super-length trailer trucks. As with most 'speculators', these large-scale operators will have some direct or indirect relationship with the Early Morning Market, although of course they may also service the main municipal market, other wholesalers or even supermarkets. It was estimated that at certain times of the year the 10 most dominant speculators servicing the Early Morning Market would be responsible for more than 70 per cent of the tomato trade (Interview, Khumen Naidoo, 22.08.96). To streamline the distribution costs many of these 'speculators' would 'control' stalls within the Early Morning Market with one such 'speculator' claiming to control 40 stalls (Interview 'Baby' Ramaan, 11.04.2000). The 'ownership' of a significant number of stalls in the market enables such 'speculators' to move large volumes directly into the 'informal' or street trading sector.

According to market officials the number of small-scale 'speculators' has increased since the late 1980s (Interview, Khumen Naidoo, 22.08.96). Small-scale here would refer to single operators working from their own vehicles, generally bakkies, which very often had been purchased from retrenchment packages (Interview, Moses Chili and Sam Mandlevu, 19.07.96). Although this coincides with the deregulation of street trading and marketing in general, it is difficult to determine whether there is a direct relationship between the two features. What is more interesting about this growth, however, is that an increasing number of black operators have begun to penetrate this particular sector at the lower echelons (Interview, Thulani Nzama, 19.04.2000). This would seem to indicate that, as with the 'informal sector', entry is relatively easy, providing of course that sufficient start-up capital can be sourced. Yet if the state is seeking to broaden the participation of economically marginalised individuals, then such endeavours in the fresh produce sector should be supported and affordable capital be made available.

Retailing

The municipal markets described above are key components in the distribution of fresh produce throughout the DMA. The numerous wholesalers and speculators that exist provide further conduits for the flow of fresh produce. At another level in the distribution pyramid are the various supermarkets followed at a lower level by smaller shops, greengrocers, general dealers, cafes and so forth that are then followed by spaza shops and finally street traders. The latter two options constituting the basis of the so-called 'informal sector' which is the most visible, yet also most diverse, segment of fresh produce distribution. As noted above, however, when seen within the context of a fresh distribution system hierarchy, it is far more helpful to see such activities as a less formal end of a broader economic field of activity. This is especially important when policy considerations are being evaluated, as any intervention at any particular level in the distribution network will in all likelihood impact on another, regardless of whether such activities are considered 'formal' or 'informal'. As the current policy thrust of officials within the DMA towards the promotion of economic opportunities within the 'informal sector' is geared primarily at street trading, it is this activity that will now be examined in more detail.

The term street trading, when referring to a specific activity within the 'informal' economy is accurate only in that it describes the physical presence of traders operating from a street. What is does not do is elaborate on the intricate and diverse economic interests and 'employment relationships' within any particular sub-sector on the street. The fruit and vegetable sub-sector is no exception. In general, fresh produce retailing on the streets consists of three major players; the suppliers of produce, the 'owners' of the trading site, and the individuals selling produce from those sites. In many instances of course, all three aspects of trading (that is if sourcing could substitute for supplying) can be collapsed into one individual. On the whole, and despite the elaborate networks that occur within the supply side of the fresh produce sector, most street traders in the DMA are responsible for sourcing their own products, controlling their own sites and selling from that site. Yet this does not preclude the existence of more complex partnerships that also characterise the sector, nor the degree of differentiation that may occur among suppliers, site-owners and sellers (Witt 2000).

Street trading in Durban has a long and contorted history – a history which is intrinsically tied into the emergence of a socially and, later, racially stratified urban population. It is a phenomenon which also links into the history of eating-houses, beerhalls, shantytowns, market gardening, townships, proletarianisation, markets and urban survival. So, although the movement of fresh produce through unstructured or less formal distribution channels is not a new phenomenon in Durban, the sudden proliferation of hundreds of street traders certainly is. This has come about due to the easing of trading restrictions, and attempts by national and local authorities to stimulate self-employment initiatives. Until recently a barrage of municipal bylaws and national state policy, often influenced by segregationist and apartheid ideals, had sought to control the participation of traders in the distribution of food in Durban. The key element in this control had always been a licensing system.

As a result, blacks were not allowed to trade as peddlers or hawkers outside their residential areas. Despite these restrictions, the use of the streets of Durban, however, remained contested and authorities never succeeded in totally eliminating 'illegal' trading.[26] As the political will of authorities to continue imposing the impossible began to wane in the 1980s, so the marginalised and unemployed began to recapture the streets, bringing with it a need for a new urban order. In many ways the 1984 Hawker Report[27] by the City Engineer's Department can be seen as a watershed in the changing attitudes of local authorities in Durban although a softening of attitudes can be traced back to the 1970s. Street trading was officially deregulated in April 1994.

Most 'informal' traders in the DMA are concentrated in the Durban CBD where the number of 'informal' traders has increased rapidly in recent years. Although reliable figures on the number of 'informal' traders operating in the CBD are hard to come by they would certainly number in the thousands.[28] Estimates for 'informal' traders in the remaining DMA are not even worth considering due to the magnitude and diversity of the sector. Due to this dearth in reliable statistics, it is equally difficult to determine the number of traders involved in the trading of fresh produce.[29] The proportion would, however, be significant although also dependent on the seasonal and actual availability of specialised products. Many traders choose food, and fresh produce in particular, because of very low entry barriers and because it is associated with lower risks than other goods. Perishable, leftover produce can also be consumed thereby reducing the risks to subsistence.

It is estimated that approximately 40 per cent of the fresh produce retailed in the DMA is distributed through the 'informal sector'

(Interview, Kobus Rademeyer, 24.05.96). 'Informal' traders in this sector procure their fresh produce from a variety of 'formal', 'semi-formal' and 'informal' sources although the Early Morning Market is probably the fulcrum around which much of the CBD's, and the DMA's, 'informal' trade revolves. Officials, for example, estimate that between 85 and 90 per cent of the fruit sold by the 'informal sector' in the DMA originates from the DMFPM through its 'extension' the Early Morning Market (Interview, Kobus Rademeyer, 24.05.96).[30] So, even though it is difficult to attach a value to the 'informal sector', a crude deduction from official sales at the DMFPM would provide some indication. The average annual turnover at the market is around R370 million. Of this it is estimated that sales worth some R130 to R140 million will ultimately be sold through the 'informal' economy, equating with an annual street value of approximately R160 to R170 million (Interview, Kobus Rademeyer, 18.04.2000). Added to this would have to be the direct sales and here, for example, a prominent wholesaler claimed that the approximate turnover of the 'informal' market in the company's 'distribution zone', which did extend beyond the DMA, was close to R1 million a week (Confidential interview (A), 21.05.96). These are, however, extremely crude estimates and a much more sophisticated analysis of the sector is required to gain a more accurate picture of the turnover in this sector.

In terms of food security, street trading is often seen to play a crucial role in the reproduction of the household. Not only does the sector provide income-earning opportunities for those individuals excluded from the formal labour market, but simultaneously, as the lowest yet most penetrative stage of food retailing, it will make food accessible to virtually most households. Yet there is little doubt that the vast majority of street traders, trading in fresh produce, are generally what could be referred to as survivalist. This does not preclude street traders from earning a reasonable income despite the precarious nature of street trading and the risks involved. Street interviews revealed a vast array of incomes, with some traders admitting to a daily turnover of R1 500 (Street interview conducted by Thulani Mkize, Durban, 14.04.2000).

So the question needs to be asked – are all street traders survivalists or do street traders gradually move up the economic ladder? In other words, is there a growing differentiation within the sector? Are there any particular success stories in the 'informal' economy? Undoubtedly there must be and most city officials involved with the 'informal' economy will be able to relate some or other anecdotal story to illustrate the success of an individual who has made it 'big', Fanie Gaza of Fanie's Food Market being a case in point. One of the more spectacular success stories is that of N.S. Sekhokhone who had graduated from being a peach-seller on the streets of Durban prior to deregulation, to the ranks of 'shop-owner', multiple taxi-operator and 'informal' fresh produce wholesaler (Interview, N.S. Sekhokhone, 19.07.96).

Yet as was pointed out by city officials, 'success stories' also need to be contextualised within an analysis of the household.[31] Often individuals would state that earnings off the street were sufficient to purchase a home or were sufficient to send a child to university. That such possibilities exist is not disputed, yet often the earnings from street trading would contribute to a wider household income from which the related opportunities may arise. In other words, earnings from street trading, together with the earnings from economic activities of other household members and social benefits or grants, may provide for a larger capital base from which a proportion of income may in turn be used to purchase a home or to send someone to university. Earnings from the 'informal' economy may also be utilised by other household members to broaden the economic base of the household. Household members now have access to an income that may cover transport costs. This allows them to become more pro-active in the labour market. Alternatively, such earnings could also be used as start-up capital for other income-generating opportunities for household members.

Opportunities for accumulation and economic success at the 'informal' end of the broader economy are certainly possible, yet should not be overestimated. As with any other echelon in the distribution network, there is also a large degree of differentiation within the 'informal sector', although the vast proportion of participants appear to be permanently trapped at a survivalist level with very little scope or opportunity for upward mobility. The factors that inhibit or constrain this mobility of individuals at this level are complex. It is therefore important that the development of policies that seek to encourage a greater degree of participation in the 'formal' economy, by facilitating access at the 'informal' end of the economic spectrum, do so from a well-informed position. If such policies are to be successful, it is also highly likely that some degree of state intervention would be required, as market forces alone would not provide the necessary support for entrants seeking to move up the economic ladder.

Conclusion

As a large metropole the DMA is not self-sufficient in the production of food. Although this has some implications for achieving food security within the DMA, it also provides the city with an opportunity of promoting urban agriculture as a development strategy for the urban poor. Not only will this enhance the levels of potential employment, but it will also lead to greater self-sufficiency in the production of food for the city and higher levels of food security for its inhabitants. Notwithstanding this potential however, the DMA will still be heavily dependent on sourcing food, including fresh produce, outside its immediate boundaries or even the provincial boundaries.

The manner in which this food is sourced and distributed within the DMA is therefore of crucial importance to the local population. It is often the inadequacies of these distribution systems in other African countries that have given rise to great concern to politicians, academics and development practitioners. This particular chapter has therefore sought to investigate the efficiency of local food distribution by focusing on a particular distribution system, mainly the distribution of fresh produce. In the DMA, this particular distribution system appears to be well established with a distinctive hierarchical structure. The structure is dominated by the Municipal Fresh Produce Market which is the primary sourcing and distribution agent in the hierarchy. Although numerous other distribution agents may source fresh produce directly from farmers, the greater proportion of fruit and vegetables consumed in the DMA would have passed through this particular market. The dominance and efficiency of this market which, through the well-developed road infrastructure, is well integrated into agricultural production countrywide and is therefore the key to ensuring that the DMA enjoys a level of food security, in fresh produce at least.

Although there are several other municipal markets in the DMA that may act as an outlet for farmers or speculators, the greater proportion of the combined volume of fresh produce sales passing through these markets would also have passed through the main municipal market. The remaining fresh produce consumed in the DMA is sourced and distributed through a multitude of other possible channels. The institutions or participants that constitute these channels form a typical hierarchy where each echelon is characterised by certain features. In the lowest rung would be street traders, followed by a variety of other retailers and then wholesalers, before culminating in the main municipal market. Entry into the lowest echelon is relatively easy, as the large number of participants in the sector indicate. Exiting this particular echelon is however, equally easy while the factors that contribute towards upward mobility are extremely complex and have not been elaborated upon in this chapter.

It would suffice to say, however, that the physical and institutional framework for a sound distribution network for fresh produce exists in the DMA. The deregulation of street trading has further enhanced the actual distributing mechanisms, while simultaneously providing numerous employment opportunities for many of the sub-region's poor. Yet despite the soundness of the distribution system, the legacy of apartheid is still deeply entrenched within the actual power structures of the network and there is a specific racial divide between the various echelons of the distribution system. Although these are being slowly eroded, change is hardly discernible. In addition, as the vast majority of the city's poor live on the outer reaches of the distribution network, they would ultimately pay the highest prices for fresh produce due to the greater transportation costs incurred by distributors.

Locating the physical structures or physical locations that constitute a food supply system is a necessary, yet not a sufficient, condition for understanding the relationship between poor people and food markets. The focus of this chapter has concentrated primarily on the distribution of fresh produce – motivated by the fact that the distribution of such produce takes place through highly visible market mechanisms. In addition, it is also the primary food product sold by traders in the 'informal sector'. Yet, to fully understand or to fully appreciate how poor people are integrated into this particular food supply system further questions need to be asked. These would, for example, include an analysis of family food expenditure, investigating what proportion of such expenditure is spent on products sourced within these specific food supply systems.

NOTES

1. The importance of these 'sectors' has subsequently been recognised by a variety of development institutions such as the World Bank, the International Labour Organisation (ILO), the Food and Agricultural Organisation (FAO) and so forth. These institutions have encouraged governments and non-governmental organisations to support the expansion of the 'informal sector' and of urban agriculture as livelihood strategies. Such programmes would enhance food security, a primary goal of most development initiatives, while simultaneously also fulfilling some of the goals of a sustainable development path.
2. This statement needs to be qualified to some extent. Self-sufficiency is often determined by climatological factors. In addition, the deregulation of agriculture and the lowering of protective tariffs have put increasing pressure on local cereals such as wheat that can now be imported at a lower cost.
3. It is difficult to determine at what particular point in time the DMA shifted from being self-sufficient to self-insufficient in the production of food. Much would

depend on the particular product under consideration, the seasonal nature of agricultural production, and the fact that accurate data is difficult to access. It could be argued that a combination of developments would have contributed to firstly the DMA and secondly the province becoming increasing self-insufficient in the production of food. Many varieties of fruit and vegetables were and continue to be successfully propagated in the DMA or province but very many of these were unable to compete with other regions once urban markets became integrated into the national production grid.

4. Such cells can be found in Wyebank, in the Gillitts-Stockville area, at Durban's International airport and at Peacevale-Cliffdale. There is also some small-scale farming in the Drummond-Bothas Hill area, in the Canelands area and most un- or under-utilised land on the margins of Chatsworth, Verulam, Phoenix and so forth.
5. To realise the potential of urban agriculture would, however, require greater commitment from local and regional authorities and should be integrated into urban renewal and urban development programmes as a whole. The city has recently launched a new initiative that seeks to explore the potential of urban agriculture. Not only will urban agriculture involve the cultivation of food crops, but cash crops such as medicinal herbs and ncema grass are also being considered.
6. According to market officials about 64 per cent of traceable vegetables pass through the Durban Fresh Produce Market (Interview, Pieter Wilke, 25.04.96).
7. In terms of production only between five and seven per cent of South Africa's total potato production takes place in the province. In terms of other vegetables such as cabbage, cauliflower, green beans and so on, KwaZulu-Natal can be considered to be self-sufficient. The issue of self-sufficiency does, however, need to be qualified as the production of certain vegetables is often a seasonal activity. In other words, the total volume harvested in KwaZulu-Natal may equate with total consumption yet during peak production periods a surplus may have to be exported from the province, while at other times the particular product may have to be sourced from other parts of the country.
8. According to Koos Swart from the Model Agency at the DMFPM there are approximately 640 vegetable farmers in the province who utilise the DMFPM from time to time. The majority of these are white, with approximately five per cent Indian. Another estimate claims that approximately 200 Natal farmers use the market on a consistent basis of which between 30 and 40 per cent is Indian. Wim Jacobs, from Botha and Roodt, another agency at the DMFPM, claims that only some 30 KwaZulu-Natal farmers use the market of which half are Indian and half are white. Another agency put this figure at between 20–25, although this excluded maize and sugar farmers who temporarily move over to vegetables to stimulate their cash flow (Interviews, Koos Swart, 22.08.96; Wim Jacobs, 14.06.96; Gerhardt Kruger and Mario Allers, 14.06.96).
9. It is interesting to note that the growing physical peripheralisation of the bulk market went hand in hand with a process that witnessed the squeezing out of agricultural activities in the greater Durban area.
10. The term 'Squatters Market' comes from the fact that prior to the construction of the Early Morning Market vendors either sat on boxes or squatted cross-legged next to their fruit and vegetables stands in the streets around the Victoria Street Market (Burrows 1961).

11. These markets have a rich and vibrant history but the racial, cultural, ethnic and religious factors that often contributed to and characterised much of the early history of these institutions will not be elaborated upon in this chapter (see for example Vahed 1999).
12. The increasing racialisation of market activities is probably best reflected by an article in a local newspaper published in 1950, which reported that 'Apartheid Now Comes to Vegetables' as the market had apparently begun to even label products based on the race of the growers. There were now, according to the report, 'Indian or non-European cabbages and carrots and other vegetables, as distinct from the varieties grown by the European, with African and Indian labour'. Previously, the article claimed, certain buying areas on the market floor were allocated according to race, yet never had there been a distinction as to who produced vegetables (*The Leader*, Saturday 21.10.50).
13. This excluded the City Market, which was managed separately.
14. Recently another municipal market, namely the bulk fresh produce market in Nelspruit, has been included in the realm of 'national' markets.
15. The marketing of fresh vegetables in South Africa has never been controlled by, or subjugated to any statutory marketing arrangements. The exception being the potato industry which until recently was controlled by a Potato Board. This lack of state intervention is probably due to the variable nature of vegetable production, marketing and distribution. Also the multitude of producers, the rich variety of products and the high degree of perishability of most vegetable products have made it almost impossible to regulate or to exert some form of control over this dynamic sector.
16. Although the existence of a Banana Board, a Citrus Board, a Deciduous Fruit Board and the Potato Board ensured some conformity to a state regulated system within the industry, the vast majority of products sold through FPMs were not controlled by a marketing board, nor were the FPM's themselves controlled by any specific legislation other than municipal bylaws.
17. It was suggested that the volumes of fresh produce passing through the DMFPM have not necessarily declined as a result. Instead, many farmers now utilised the market as a 'dumping ground' to move fresh produce that could not be sold through direct channels. Market officials were, however, quick to point out that many farmers eventually returned to the market once the relationship with institutions such as supermarkets deteriorated.
18. The Farmer's Retail Market was established in 1977 in response to the partial destruction of facilities in the Victoria Street Market and Early Morning Market, while the original Verulam Market dates back to the late nineteenth century although the construction of the current facilities were only completed in 1984.
19. The City Market would have been used to source bulkier low value vegetables such as potatoes, cabbages, squashes, pumpkins and onions, as well as fruit. More perishable crops such as leafy vegetables, 'greens', Indian herbs and so forth would have been sourced from local farmers.
20. The H.L. Maharaj operations have reconstituted themselves into what are now known as 'Housewives' Markets' while the P.L. Maharaj operations have diversified into property development and other food related operations such as 'Meat World'.
21. A general consensus gained from interviews conducted at the Early Morning Market in 1996, 1998 and 2000.
22. The remaining 20 per cent is sourced from wholesalers, farmers and 'speculators'.

23. A term utlised by T. Pillay, Manager, Verulam Market, 27.07.96.
24. The number of white 'speculators' in the DMA is negligible.
25. It is estimated that in peak season some 28 tons of cooked 'mielies' are sold per working day, generating a weekly turnover of some R1 million (Durban Metropolitan Council 2000).
26. This is best epitomised by the long history of street traders such as N.S. Sekhokhone, Chair of the Brook Street Traders Association and Derek Shange, a street trader.
27. Nesvåg discusses this report in more detail in Chapter 10.
28. The number of street traders in the CBD for example varies between 5 000 and 13 000, although not all traders may be trading at any one time.
29. Estimates of street traders specialising in the selling of fresh produce vary from 75 per cent (Interview, Khumen Naidoo, 22.08.96) to either five or four out of ten street traders (various sources quoted in Posel 2001).
30. See also Pentz (1992: 95).
31. This point was raised during discussions with Sue Wilkinson and Richard Dobson, Warwick Junction Renewal Project, Durban, 18.04.2000.

REFERENCES

Baker, J. and P. Pedersen (eds). 1992. *The Rural-Urban Interface in Africa*. Uppsala: Nordiska Afrikainstitutet.

Burrows, H.R. (ed.). 1961. *Studies of Indian Employment in Natal.* Natal Regional Survey, Volume 11. Cape Town: Oxford University Press.

Drakakis-Smith, D. (ed.). 1990. *Economic Growth and Urbanization in Developing Areas.* London: Routledge.

Drakakis-Smith, D., T. Bowyer-Bower and D. Tevera. 1995. 'Urban Poverty and Urban Agriculture: An Overview of the Linkages in Harare'. *Habitat International*, 19, 2.

Durban Metropolitan Council (DMC). 2000. 'Durban's Informal Economy Policy'. Economic Development Department, Durban.

Freund, B. 1991. 'The Rise and Decline of an Indian Peasantry in Natal'. *The Journal of Peasant Studies*, 18, 2.

Guyer, J. (ed.). 1987. *Feeding African Cities: Studies in Regional Social History.* Bloomington: Indiana University Press.

Hurwitz, N. 1957. *Agriculture in Natal: 1860–1950.* Natal Regional Survey, Volume 12. Cape Town: Oxford University Press.

Langley, D.S., B. Maloa and J. Van Zyl. 1993. 'Agricultural Marketing: Vegetables'. Occasional Paper, LAPC, World Bank Rural Restructuring Programme for South Africa, Braamfontein.

Leader, The. Saturday 21.10.50.

Marx, S. 1991. *Fresh Produce in South Africa. Main Report: Marketing of Fresh Produce in the Republic of South Africa.* Pretoria: HSRC.

Maylam, P. and I. Edwards (eds). 1996. *The People's City: African Life in Twentieth Century Durban.* Pietermaritzburg: University of Natal Press.

Nyanteng, U. 1998. 'Food Supply and Distribution to Accra and its Metropolis'. Proceedings AMA-FAO Workshop, Accra, Ghana.

Pentz, D.C. 1992. 'Informal Street Trading: A Case Study of Warwick Avenue', M.TRP., University of Natal, Durban.

Posel, D. 2001. 'A Motivation and Guide for Strategic Action in the Informal Sector'. Report submitted to the Economic Development Department, Durban Metropolitan Council, Durban.

Rakodi, C. (ed.). 1997. *The Urban Challenge in Africa.* Tokyo: United Nations University Press.

Skinner, C. and F. Lund. 2000. 'Interim Report of the Technical Task Team to Develop an Effective and Inclusive Policy on the Informal Economy for the North and South Central Local Councils', Durban.

Vahed, G.H. 1999. 'A "Public Nuisance": The Victoria Street Early Morning Squatters Market, 1910–1934'. *South African Historical Journal,* 40.

Van Deventer, J.G. 1991. *Die Distribusie van Vars Groente en Vars Vrugte in die Republiek van Suid Afrika.* D.Com, University of Pretoria, Pretoria.

Wilhelm, L. 1997. 'Food Supply and Distribution to Francophone African Cities'. Summary of Papers and Discussions at the FAO-ISRA Sub-regional Seminar, Dakar.

Witt, H. 2000. 'Formal and Informal Economy Linkages in the Fruit and Vegetable Sector'. Study 2.3. Research Report for Technical Tasks Team for the Informal Economy, Durban.

Interviews

Moses Chili and Sam Mandlevu, small-scale 'speculators', Early Morning Market, 19.07.96.

Confidential interview (A), 21.05.86.

Confidential interview (B), DMFPM, 25.04.96.

Sam George, 'Gatekeeper', Early Morning Market, 19.07.96.

Mustafa Haneef, large-scale 'speculator', Early Morning Market, 19.07.96.

Wim Jacobs, Botha and Roodt Agency, 14.06.96.

Gerhardt Kruger and Mario Allers, Duiker Agency, 14.06.96.

Ronnie Maharaj, Director of P.L. Maharaj Wholesalers, 21.05.96 (interview conducted together with Henry Bernstein).

Garesh Naidoo, Extension Officer, Department of Agriculture, 02.07.96.

Khumen Naidoo, Supervisor, Early Morning Market, 22.08.96.

Thulani Nzama, Manager, Early Morning Market, 19.04.2000.

Kobus Rademeyer, Director, Markets and Informal Sector, Durban, 24.05.96; Executive Director, Markets and Informal Sector, Durban, 18.04.2000.

'Baby' Ramaan, large-scale 'speculator', Early Morning Market, 11.04.2000.

N.S. Sekhokhone, Chair of the Brook Street Traders Association, 19.07.96.

Koos Swart, Model Agency, 22.08.96.

Pieter Wilke, Management, DMFPM, 25.04.96; 30.07.96.

Index